QUALITY IMPROVEMENT
IN EMPLOYMENT
AND OTHER HUMAN SERVICES

QUALITY IMPROVEMENT IN EMPLOYMENT AND OTHER HUMAN SERVICES

MANAGING FOR QUALITY THROUGH CHANGE

by

JOYCE M. ALBIN, M.Ed.

Senior Research Assistant
Specialized Training Program
Center on Human Development
University of Oregon
Eugene, Oregon

·P A U L·H·
BROOKES
PUBLISHING C°

Baltimore • London • Toronto • Sydney

Paul H. Brookes Publishing Co.
P.O. Box 10624
Baltimore, Maryland 21285-0624

Typeset by Brushwood Graphics, Inc., Baltimore, Maryland.
Manufactured in the United States of America by
Victor Graphics, Inc., Baltimore, Maryland.

Library of Congress Cataloging-in-Publication Data
Albin, Joyce M. (Joyce Monteau), 1949–
    Quality improvement in employment and other human services : managing
    for quality through change / by Joyce M. Albin.
        p.   cm.
    Includes bibliographical references and index.
    ISBN 1-55766-092-1
    1. Handicapped—Employment—United States.   2. Handicapped—Services
for—United States—Quality control.   I. Title.
HD7256.U5A682   1992
331.5'9–dc20
                                                                91-45115
                                                                     CIP

(British Library Cataloguing-in-Publication data are available from the British
Library.)

CONTENTS

FOREWORD

One evening this winter I left work at City Hall with a co-worker. We rode down the elevator talking about how nice it would be when spring came and it would no longer be dark when we left at 5 o'clock. We said our usual, "Have a good evening!" and headed our separate ways. I walked the 3 minutes to the parking ramp, got in my car, paid my fee, and headed home. Fifteen minutes later, a little longer than usual because of falling snow and slick roads, I was home.

My co-worker went out the automatic door, took a harrowing ride down an ice-slicked ramp, and waited for a bus with a wheelchair lift . . . and she waited, and she waited. Two hours later she was delivered to her apartment half frozen from sitting in the blowing snow in the dark of a Wisconsin winter night.

When I happened to hear about the situation several days later, I went to talk to the transit operations people to find out why and how often this happened. What I learned reinforces what I have come to believe is endemic to many bureaucratic institutions. The people who ran the transit system were as frustrated as the people they served. Although the transit workers tried very hard to do their jobs well, as I observed them in their work environment, what I saw overrode any illusions of efficient operation. Telephones were ringing, nerves were frazzled, and staff members were threatening to quit. The director told me ridership demand had increased over 40%, while the budget for staffing and equipment had remained the same.

It was obvious that the old quick fix of finding fault and pointing fingers would not help. In fact, complaining bitterly to them about my co-worker's experience would be both inappropriate and unproductive. These people were not trying to make it difficult for individuals with disabilities to have transportation. They were doing their best within a system incapable of producing quality service.

Hundreds of other stories like this are played out everyday, not just for persons with disabilities, but for anyone requesting and expecting quality service: whether it's getting your cat licensed, catching a bus, getting your child into a special reading class, or waiting for the right signature so you can proceed with a much needed procedure change. Karl Albrecht in his book, *Service America* (1985), calls these "Moments of Truth." How these moments are managed determines your perception of the organization and its values. But more important, these moments of truth shape how we feel about and treat one another. The customer who sits waiting in the snow for 2 hours becomes more resentful about the system and its inept staff. The staff members in turn become defensive and hide from their customers—customers who *could* provide them insight into how the system could be changed to work more efficiently and to serve them better. This is a vicious cycle created by the systems in which we all work. And it is played out in how we all increasingly blame others and attribute negative motives to them but ultimately create very little change in the system.

Yogi Berra, the legendary Yankee catcher, once said, "You can see a lot by observing." What I have observed—whether it is looking into why my co-worker had to wait in the snow for 2 hours or studying the transit system with the help of the people who run it—is a lot of dedicated, talented people who are fundamentally powerless to change the system.

Dr. W. Edwards Deming, the American most heralded for his contribution to post–World War II Japan's economic success, developed a simple rule of thumb he calls the 85%–15% rule. The 85%–15% rule says that 85% of the problems in organizations are systems problems beyond the control of the front line service providers. Only 15% are problems that the front line persons, in fact, can change by themselves to improve the quality of service delivery. For example, how is a mechanic working on repairing city vehicles supposed to provide timely service when it takes 24 mostly bureaucratic steps to get a new part? How can we keep a fleet of buses on the road when there are over 50 steps and 4 months of processing time involved in hiring a new bus driver? How can we expect new saplings to grow in gravel along newly constructed roadways when we do not have open communications systems to tell the engineers to design a strip of top soil along the road in which the forestry department can plant the new trees? The victims of these scenarios are not just the customers who receive poor service, but also the vehicle mechanics, bus drivers, foresters, and employment specialists who are blamed for systems that need serious overhaul.

Streamlining our service delivery systems to meet customer expectations will require a radical shift in the way we currently do business. First, it will require driving out fear so front-line people who see opportunities for improving services can make these improvements or easily gain access to people who can. Second, it will require leadership willing to clear the barriers so employees, management, and the customer can collaborate to redesign the service delivery system.

As Dr. Deming continually reminds us, we are entering a new economic era in which there is no natural imperative that dictates that organizations that do good work should or will survive. He emphasizes the point that hard work and good intentions are not enough. Organizational survival in a world where quality of service will be paramount will require profound knowledge. That profound knowledge comes through everyone working together, understanding who our customers are, identifying their needs, and working to meet those needs. It means going beyond meeting minimum standards or assuming that more money thrown at a situation, in fact, will result in an empowered customer.

The profound knowledge Dr. Deming talks about is the knowledge that every employment support specialist and person with a disability has access to everyday: what they feel and observe. What makes this knowledge profound is having the skills and tools to collect it, analyze it, and utilize it to improve everything we do. These can be learned. Unfortunately, in too many organizations they will not be learned because those in power are fearful of losing control. These organizations will not survive in the new economic era.

Those who are exploring ways of adapting Continuous Quality Improvement to their organizations understand the long-term nature of the journey. They also know it will take persistence and courage. Old methods of management that were adapted to the public sector during the heyday of smokestack industry will die hard. Management by control, the definition of quotas and numerical goals without the input of service delivery persons, and reliance on inspection and monitoring as the means of assuring quality all are vestiges of this paradigm.

In 1986, when we began introducing Continuous Quality Improvement to government for the first time the reaction was predictable: "It's fine for widget factories like Ford and Xerox but it has no place in the public sector." Today hundreds of public sector organizations are exploring ways of adapting Continuous Quality Improvement principles and practices to their organizations.

Joyce Albin and the people who have contributed to the development of this book have made a pioneering contribution to the field of rehabilitation. I encourage you to make use of it. Talk about it with your fellow professionals, experiment with it, but most of all improve on it. The universals expressed here are the grist for great stories of improvement.

There is no lack of good intentions or hard work in the field of rehabilitation. The level of dedication is unsurpassed. Now let us add the profound knowledge that will put your organizations in the forefront of quality service delivery. Continuous Quality Improvement gives us the opportunity to fix the systems that left my co-worker to sit in the cold for 2 hours and the bus operators feeling powerless to change the system to better meet her needs. Hats off to Joyce Albin and all the others who have the courage to break through the old paradigm to a new era of quality service.

Thomas J. Mosgaller, M.S.
Madison, Wisconsin

REFERENCE

Albrecht, K., & Zemke, R. (1985). *Service America! Doing business in the new economy*. Homewood, IL: Dow Jones-Irwin.

FOREWORD

In 1987, I celebrated my birthday in the Esquire Club, a nightclub in Osaka, Japan. Our Japanese host brought us there to show us presentations on what the Japanese call Total Quality Control (referred to in the body of this book as Continuous Quality Improvement). We were a group of Americans on a pilgrimage to Japan to discover Total Quality Control (TQC) from the font of all TQC. We attended the Deming Prize ceremony and visited several Deming Prize–winning companies (including Komatsu Toyota and Suntory Brewery). They used fairly predictable applications showing dramatic improvement in the products and services and the work processes that bring them about. (Did you know that Toyota averages 100 suggestions per year per employee, and only those suggestions that were successfully implemented are counted?) But it was the presentation in the nightclub that was the greatest shock to me. I left the Esquire Club convinced that if they could do TQC, everybody could do TQC!

I believe we are long past the point when any American business manager or agency director can legitimately say, "It does not apply to me." Total Quality has leaped from manufacturing to service industries, from the private, for-profit sector to public and nonprofit organizations. TQC has infiltrated schools, hospitals, state revenue departments, police departments; the list goes on and on. Those who say that it does not apply to them are hanging on to an old paradigm and an approach to management that are disappearing.

In this book Joyce Albin brings TQC into another frontier: the world of rehabilitation and employment services for people with severe disabilities. It is a welcome addition to the literature of the quality movement. This work is a judicious blend of expertise in rehabilitation, community-based employment, and other human services, with some practical approaches to introducing the principles and methods of Total Quality.

Total Quality demands three basic disciplines of us. First, we must be committed to our customers and clients and obsessed with providing the customers with services of such quality that we delight them. Call this dynamic, Quality. Second, we must use the hard-nosed, data-based statistical applications combined with the logic of improvement and careful systems-minded planning. Call this dynamic, the Scientific Approach. Finally, there is the discipline of teamwork: We are all in this together, on the same side, pulling in the same direction, helping each other; if not, we will fail and our customers will suffer. Call this dynamic, All One Team. (We also refer to these dynamics as the Joiner Triangle™.) The three dynamics are woven throughout this book. We owe our thanks to Joyce Albin for creating a well-integrated approach to Total Quality for community-based employment services.

Peter R. Scholtes, M.Ed.
Joiner Associates
Madison, Wisconsin

PREFACE

ORGANIZATION OF THE BOOK

This book is divided into four major sections. Part I describes the context of change in employ-ment services for people with severe disabilities, as well as the theoretical basis for the book. Tracing the development and current status of employment services, including supported em-ployment, Chapter 1 provides a historical perspective for current efforts to improve services. Chapter 2 presents the basic principles of Continuous Quality Improvement and begins to provide direction on how to apply those principles in service organizations. Chapter 3 goes further into Continuous Quality Improvement with an in-depth discussion of "customer," offering lessons learned in business and industry for achieving a customer focus.

Part II focuses on changeover from facility-based services to integrated community-based employment supports, using changeover as a context for introducing direct applications of a few basic quality improvement strategies. This part is based on work with Kristen Magis-Agosta in developing the manual *Self-Assessment for Changeover to Supported Employment: A Troubleshooting Approach* (1989), which was developed with the support of the Oregon Mental Health and Developmental Disability Services Division. The material presented here incorpo-rates feedback received on that manual, as well as other changes.

Chapter 4 opens Part II with a discussion of the nature of changeover from facility-based to community-based employment services from the perspective of organizational change and development. Chapter 5 presents *troubleshooting*, one of the fundamental strategies of Contin-uous Quality Improvement. Troubleshooting offers a systematic approach for locating the most significant cause for organizational performance issues. Chapter 6 takes troubleshooting to another level and offers a strategy called the *Performance Engineering Matrix* for analyzing performance problems attributed to individual staff members. The methods presented in both of these chapters are introduced to assist readers in understanding the theoretical framework of the *Self-Assessment Guide for Changeover to Supported Employment* in Chapter 7. The *Guide* is a tool specifically designed to assist programs in applying quality improvement methods to troubleshoot performance during changeover to supported employment. The chapter in-cludes a description of how the *Guide* should be used by employment providers or others interested in pursuing improvements in the outcomes of community-based employment services.

Part III of this book moves to presenting a set of valuable concepts and techniques for systematically addressing quality improvement in organizations, with examples drawn pri-marily from employment services. Chapter 8 describes *performance templates* as a tool that may be used for planning, evaluating, and improving performance outcomes. Chapter 9 continues the focus on systematic methods by offering, in simplified terms, some of the fundamental concepts and processes of quality improvement. Thus, Chapter 9 explains complexity, varia-tion, and stability in processes and defines a seven-step method for quality improvement. Chapter 10 contains information on a set of specific techniques or tools that may be used within that seven-step method. Tools presented include methods useful for describing and analyzing processes; for brainstorming; and for collecting, displaying, and analyzing data and may be applied to support data-driven decisions to improve the processes and outcomes of any organization.

Part IV turns to addressing more global, organization-wide issues in pursuing a quality transformation. It focuses on strategies for initiating and maintaining a quality improvement program. Because an organization consists of its personnel, Chapter 11 concentrates on strat-egies for supporting employees to work to achieve the mission. This chapter includes guide-lines for staff recruitment, development, and evaluation. Chapter 12 presents suggestions for devising an initial blueprint for guiding organizational change. Chapter 13 offers the story of a rehabilitation agency that began to incorporate the philosophy and strategies of Continuous

Quality Improvement to assist it in achieving changeover from facility-based to integrated community employment services.

Chapter 14, the last chapter, offers some final advice about potential barriers to successfully implementing organizational change, whether it be change to community-based employment or to Continuous Quality Improvement. This chapter also discusses some of the specific challenges to implementing quality improvement that are faced by organizations providing community-based employment services for individuals with severe disabilities. The chapter concludes with some guidance for individual readers, whether they be front-line staff or the organization leaders, who want to pursue quality improvement.

THE KEY TO QUALITY IMPROVEMENT

Together, these chapters present both a theoretical approach and practical applications that, hopefully, will be used to improve the quality of organizational performance in achieving individual outcomes in community-based services. This text has taken a simplified view of some difficult concepts. If it succeeds in its purpose, however, it will raise many questions seeking deeper explanations and further knowledge. The key to quality improvement is in living it. Continuous Quality Improvement cannot be an academic exercise, increasing one's knowledge of concepts and techniques. Read as much about Continuous Quality Improvement and Total Quality Management as you can find. Pursue the questions that are raised. However, the only way truly to understand quality improvement is to live the new philosophy and use its methods every day.

> "And the point is, to live everything. *Live* the questions now. Perhaps then, someday far in the future, you will gradually, without even noticing it, live your way into the answer." (Rilke, 1984, pp. 34–35)

REFERENCES

Albin, J.M., & Magis-Agosta, K. (1989). *Self-assessment for changeover to supported employment: A troubleshooting approach.* Eugene: University of Oregon, Technical Assistance Brokerage.
Rilke, R.M. (1984). *Letters to a young poet* (S. Mitchell, Trans.). New York: Random House.

ACKNOWLEDGMENTS

The first work on this book began as the result of a technical assistance request from the Multnomah County Employment Council (Portland, Oregon) to the Technical Assistance Brokerage at the University of Oregon in Eugene. The Council asked for an instrument that would allow facility-based rehabilitation programs and work activity centers to do self-assessments to identify training and technical assistance needs during changeover to supported employment. Based on that request, Brokerage staff proceeded to define the desirable features of such an instrument and to research available tools that could meet the needs of service providers in Multnomah County or elsewhere. Unfortunately, we could find none that met all of the features that we believed were necessary to guide service provider organizations effectively through the rapidly shifting demands of changeover to supported employment. Therefore, Brokerage staff developed a manual to meet that need.

That manual, entitled *Self-Assessment for Changeover to Supported Employment: A Troubleshooting Approach*, provided a basis for the material included in Chapters 4 through 7 of this book. I co-authored that manual with Kristen Magis-Agosta, who at that time was with the Oregon Technical Assistance Corporation. Our work on the self-assessment manual was funded through an intergovernmental service agreement between the State of Oregon's Mental Health and Developmental Disability Services Division (MHDDSD) and the University of Oregon's Specialized Training Program to establish the Technical Assistance Brokerage. The Brokerage served as the technical assistance and training component of the 5-year state systems change project, the Oregon Supported Employment Initiative (OSEI), which was funded from 1986 to 1991 through the federal Office of Special Education and Rehabilitative Services, Rehabilitation Services Administration. I thank James Toews, Assistant Administrator of MHDDSD, Office of Developmental Disability Services, and Barbara Brent, OSEI Project Director, for their support for the initial work on this project and their willingness to allow me to include a revision of the self-assessment manual in this book.

As Project Coordinator for the Technical Assistance Brokerage, I had the opportunity to work with a variety of communities and rehabilitation programs throughout Oregon, as well as in other states, to help them plan for and implement local systems change to supported employment. The lessons learned from that work were invaluable in helping me to clarify my ideas regarding the possible applications of the philosophy and strategies of Continuous Quality Improvement to the process of managing change in employment services for persons with severe disabilities. However, I owe special thanks to two organizations who permitted me to work with them in testing the approach: Polk Enterprises, in Independence, Oregon, and ICON Employment Services, in northern Virginia.

Karen Ross, Polk's Executive Director during the period described in this book, basically provided me a laboratory for developing applications of quality improvement technology to changeover of a facility-based program to community-based employment services. Karen's personal openness, encouragement, and insight regarding the transformation process in her organization have been central to my ability to complete this book. I value her ongoing support for this project more than I can express. Polk's management staff participated throughout the planning for organizational change that is presented in Chapter 13, and shaped that change through their knowledge, experience, and questions. In addition to management staff, the members of the first quality improvement team at Polk—self-named Alpha Star—taught me many lessons about installing quality improvement techniques in an organization. Therefore, my thanks go to them for their patience during my early work in providing support to a quality improvement team involved in supported employment.

ICON Employment Services, located in Alexandria, Virginia, is an organization that was initially developed to provide technical assistance and training to the five-county northern Virginia region and has since become a supported employment direct service provider as well. Harriet Yaffe, Executive Director, has given me repeated opportunities to work with her and her staff to design and test quality improvement applications. I thank her and her staff for their support.

The Technical Assistance Brokerage also provided me the opportunity to work on an ongoing basis with a group of service providers undergoing changeover to more integrated employment services. Through a series of forums on changeover, I learned some of the strategies for pursuing and managing changeover that are included in this book. While all members of the forum series deserve thanks, I owe special thanks for this series to the initial planning committee: Karen Ross, Dan Guevara, Tim Rocak, and Rob Tarver.

The Employment Projects at the Specialized Training Program, University of Oregon, has provided a unique environment for my work. I have been consistently challenged and regularly introduced to new concepts by my colleagues, while being given the freedom to pursue personal development in accomplishing required project tasks. The Employment Projects staff also have contributed immeasurably to the work that resulted in this book. In particular, Dennis Sandow and Larry Rhodes introduced me to the concepts of Continuous Quality Improvement and taught me ways to apply them to employment services. Their writings provided a wealth of information, as well as a mental challenge. I am indebted to them.

For editing, commenting on, and assisting with the text, I thank David Mank, Bill Lynch, and Judy McCartney of the Employment Projects, and Carole Monteau, Chevron Corporation. Vincent Ercolano and Natalie Tyler at Paul H. Brookes Publishing Company provided invaluable editorial assistance throughout the development and publication of this book. In addition, I thank my friends for their patience in surviving many months of lack of attention from me, for enduring my obsessive conversations about "the book," and for their encouragement for completing this work.

Finally, it is important that I thank Thomas J. Mosgaller, Quality and Productivity Administrator for the City of Madison, Wisconsin. With his perspective as a former community organizer and his experience with Continuous Quality Improvement in the public sector, he has stretched the depth of my understanding of the philosophy of improvement far beyond the strategies and tools that it includes. It is for this reason that I feel honored by his contribution to the completion of this book.

The development of this book, in itself, has been an example of continuous improvement. Based on growing experience with applying the philosophy of quality improvement as the months of writing continued, the material included in the book improved. Indeed, as I pass this to the publisher, it is in the midst of a continuous stream of improvement. As time passes, so long as we continue to take on the struggle, our collective ability to apply the philosophy of Continuous Quality Improvement to human services or to the public sector will improve far beyond what is presented in this text. If this manual assists by helping some of us to take a few more small steps along that path, it will have succeeded in fulfilling its purpose.

INTRODUCTION

This book is about a new approach to improving quality in services. The approach appears deceptively simple, but to adopt it fully requires a significant shift in the basic philosophy of service management, as well as in day-to-day operations. This new approach, known by a variety of names such as "Total Quality Management," "Quality Improvement," and "Total Quality Control," is referred to here as "Continuous Quality Improvement." Although it was first explored in industrial and business settings, Continuous Quality Improvement offers strategies to personnel in human services, the public sector, and elsewhere for improving personal and organizational performance while managing organizations in an environment of continuous change.

VALUES AND ASSUMPTIONS UNDERLYING THIS BOOK

The development of this book was guided by the following set of assumptions that reflect the author's underlying values for providing employment services to individuals with severe disabilities:

- Employment in integrated settings offers improved quality of life to many individuals previously considered incapable of working at all, or incapable of working outside sheltered settings. Nationally, individuals with severe disabilities are being given more and more opportunities to work in regular settings with ongoing support. Outcomes achieved (e.g., increased earnings, fringe benefits, physical integration, social integration, relationships formed with nondisabled coworkers, and meaningful contribution to the culture of the workplace and to productivity) point to the benefits that could accrue if more people with disabilities had the opportunity to work in integrated settings with support.
- Integrated community-based employment, whether or not it meets current federal and state definitions of supported employment, is valuable. The approaches presented in this book do not assume that the employment options to which they are applied must meet the formal definitions of "supported employment." However, these methods may be used by programs wishing to improve their outcomes to meet those definitions.
- Conversion, or "changeover," from facility-based services to community-based employment with support is a shift in service delivery methodology that is desirable from the perspective of enhancing the quality and diversity of options available to individuals with disabilities, as well as from the perspective of enriching community environments. In communities throughout the country, individuals who previously had opportunities to work only in sheltered settings now are successfully joining the regular workforce. Organizations that have undertaken changeover have discovered greatly enhanced outcomes with the switch to more integrated employment services.
- Changeover to community-based employment services does not have to be addressed as an "all or nothing" effort. Because of local conditions, structures, needs, or values, an organization may choose to change only a portion of its facility-based services to integrated employment opportunities. While this book has been written with a clear bias toward integrated community jobs for service recipients with severe disabilities, the methods presented in this book do not assume that an organization is providing solely these employment services, nor do these methods assume that an organization is in the process of changing over 100% of its facility-based services to supported employment. However, it is assumed that changeover to any degree does require restructuring some part of the basic resources of an organization.
- Organizational change requires prioritization. Changeover of a part or all of an organization's services from facility-based to community-based employment support is a complex, demanding task that requires extraordinary effort and commitment from the board, managers, staff, and others involved with the organization. Because of this, changeover requires that participants, who are faced with a large array of issues needing attention, prioritize their efforts to ensure that those issues presenting the greatest opportunities for improving performance are addressed first.

- Integrated, community-based supported employment represents a potentially limitless range of possible organizational designs, types of work, and support methods. It certainly is not limited to a few specific "models." Instead, it is defined by the wide variety of creative efforts that are required to match the specific interests and support needs of individuals with disabilities with the interests and abilities of available community employers. These efforts reflect the capacity of organizations to work with companies to design and deliver support that meets the unique needs of specific individuals with severe disabilities.
- Each service provider organization, with its varied relationships with the surrounding economic, social, and political environments, is unique and must operate in an environment that is constantly changing. The needs and strengths of an organization continually change as a result of both internal and external pressures. Therefore, whether or not an organization is undergoing a formal changeover in the nature of the services it provides, the organization is—and always will be—in a constant state of change. To be successful, to achieve valued outcomes, even to stay in business, organizations must be prepared to respond to these constant changes.
- The staffs and boards of directors of rehabilitation organizations and other service providers are committed to providing high quality services to people with disabilities. Likewise, the personnel in other public sector agencies or private service organizations are committed to quality, as well. Thus, the ideas and approaches in this book are offered as tools for helping to *improve* quality, whatever its current status, rather than as complaints about the nature of existing services.
- Service providers are responsible for many of the performance improvements actually experienced by individuals with disabilities. As service technologies have improved and the collective vision of the potential of people with severe disabilities has changed, service providers have consistently played the critical role in transforming good ideas into actual outcomes for people with disabilities. At this writing, one of the most recent examples of this has been found in supported employment. Employment service providers, including rehabilitation agencies that previously offered only facility-based services, are embracing the emergence of supported employment as one strategy to improve employment outcomes for people with severe disabilities.
- People with severe disabilities deserve to be respected and valued for their real and potential contributions to enriching our communities and our lives. As service providers, government agencies, and others in the community, we have a collective responsibility continuously to improve our ability to assist service recipients to participate in and contribute to their communities. Simply maintaining the status quo, or the current best efforts, is never enough. However, continuous improvement may be achieved in the quality of the services we provide through an ongoing self-assessment and feedback process.

WHO SHOULD READ THIS BOOK?

The information in this book will be helpful to personnel in many different fields who have a role in providing services. Continuous Quality Improvement is a philosophy of management, and, therefore, it may be adopted in any organization by the personnel who have an ongoing commitment to improving the quality of what they do.

Personnel in Rehabilitation and Community-Based Employment Organizations

This book is directed primarily toward the staffs and boards of directors of organizations that provide employment services for people with severe disabilities, including facility-based rehabilitation organizations, community-based supported employment providers, and those organizations that are changing at least a portion of their facility-based services to more integrated employment opportunities. The book will be useful to organizations providing integrated community-based employment services, as well as to those that are only beginning to plan for developing such services. Because these groups make up the primary target audience, most of the examples presented reflect their perspective.

Government Agency Personnel Involved with Employment Services

Although directed primarily to service providers, the information presented in this book also offers direct guidance to those government agencies responsible for providing, purchasing, and/or assuring the quality of employment services. It presents a new way of defining the relationship between service purchasers and service providers that should eliminate adversarial relationships that often grow between these groups. In addition, by providing a management strategy that is embedded within service provider organizations and is focused on ongoing service improvement, this book offers an alternative to externally based quality assurance. Thus, personnel in government funding agencies should read this book to become familiar with another method for assuring service quality.

Beyond offering a strategy for assuring quality of purchased services, the principles and methods of Continuous Quality Improvement may be applied directly by public sector agencies responsible for purchasing or monitoring employment services, such as state offices of vocational rehabilitation, mental health, or developmental disabilities. Federal, regional, county, other local offices, or even individual counselors or case managers in offices may adopt these principles and methods to improve individual or group performance, even when other levels or divisions of the bureaucracy have not embraced them.

Other Public Sector Personnel

Because this book offers a new approach to management in service provision to persons with severe disabilities it should be useful to those in other public sector agencies, as well. Public sector personnel may directly apply the philosophy and methods in their own jobs, offices, or departments. Indeed, Continuous Quality Improvement has been found to be applicable in improving the performance in widely differing public sector settings, from a city government (Box, Joiner, Rohan, & Sensenbrenner, 1991) and police department (Couper, 1990), to the federal Food Stamp Program (Affholter & Kramer, 1987) and Department of Defense (Carr & Littman, 1990).

Personnel in Organizations Offering Other Types of Services

While the examples included in this book are drawn primarily from employment services for people with mental disabilities, the principles and methods presented are universal. They may be applied to employment services for other groups, such as individuals with chronic mental illness, traumatic brain injury, or physical disabilities. Furthermore, the information contained in the book may be applied to other types of services, as well. For example, the performance of residential service providers, school programs, or case management services can be improved through the principles and strategies presented here.

Consultants Who Offer Technical
Assistance and Training in Management of Services

The principles and techniques provided here also can be used by technical assistance and training groups providing assistance to service providers, government agencies, or others. These personnel may apply the self-assessment instrument in Chapter 7 directly to identifying and prioritizing training and technical assistance needs of their clients involved in changeover to supported employment. Furthermore, consulting and training personnel may wish to apply the management methods presented here in their own organizations and use them in working with service recipients and others to improve individual or organizational performance.

Faculty and Students in Human Services Fields

Because this book presents difficult concepts and methods in simplified ways, the book may be used as a text in introductory courses addressing quality improvement issues in management of human services organizations. Its inclusion of both theoretical and practical information offers a useful blend for classroom texts.

REFERENCES

Affholter, D.P., & Kramer, F.D. (Eds.). (1987). *Rethinking quality control: A new system for the Food Stamp Program*. Washington, DC: National Academy Press.

Box, G.E.P., Joiner, L.W., Rohan, S., & Sensenbrenner, F.J. (1991). Quality in the community: One city's experience. *Quality Progress, 24*(5), 57–63.

Carr, D., & Littman, I. (1990). Quality in the federal government. *Quality Progress, 23*(9), 49–52.

Couper, D.C. (1990). Police department learns 10 hard quality lessons. *Quality Progress, 23*(10), 37–40.

*This book is dedicated to all who have taken on
the never-ending struggle and discipline required by the
continuous pursuit of quality.*

QUALITY IMPROVEMENT
IN EMPLOYMENT
AND OTHER HUMAN SERVICES

PART I

THEORETICAL AND HISTORICAL PERSPECTIVES

This book revolves around three central themes: supported, community-based employment, change, and Continuous Quality Improvement. Each chapter, while focusing on one or another of the themes, also addresses the interaction among them. Continuous Quality Improvement is itself a management philosophy for both managing and pursuing change. Thus, the approach is well-suited to issues arising in changeover to supported employment, as well as the ongoing changes experienced by rehabilitation services. Throughout the text, therefore, explanations of the principles and methods of Continuous Quality Improvement describe applications to changeover to supported employment and to rehabilitation.

Part I provides the historical and theoretical framework for the remainder of the book. Chapter 1 traces the history of change in employment services for individuals with severe disabilities. Change in employment services since the 1970s has resulted in significantly improved outcomes for many individuals who previously had been relegated to the back wards of society. The apparent ongoing nature of change in service approaches, as presented in Chapter 1, begins to build the case for the need for a management approach in human services that supports change.

Chapter 2 responds to that need by introducing five fundamental principles of Continuous Quality Improvement and their relationship to managing change. Continuous Quality Improvement offers both a management philosophy and a set of methods that were first applied in Japanese industrial settings in the early 1950s and have since grown in acceptance in American industry. Quality improvement incorporates scientific methods, an obsession with quality, and an understanding of the need for releasing the full potential of employees. The final chapter in Part I presents quality improvement's overriding emphasis on customers, offering strategies to assist in making an organization's various customer groups into partners in its success. Using examples from community-based employment and rehabilitation, Chapters 2 and 3 provide the theoretical background for the remainder of the text.

Chapter 1

The Changing Face of Employment Services

Since 1984, when the term "supported employment" was first defined by the United States Office of Special Education and Rehabilitative Services (OSERS) (Office of Special Education and Rehabilitative Services, 1984; 34 CFR, Part 373), the field of rehabilitation has faced drastic and rapid changes. These changes, however, reflect only the most current evolutionary phase in the development of employment services for adults with severe disabilities. Since the first development of organized community services, change has been constant.

THE EARLY YEARS

Often organized by parents and charities, the first community programs for adults who were considered to have severe disabilities were designed to offer parental respite, day care, recreation, training in self-help skills, and activity therapy (Bellamy, Rhodes, Bourbeau, & Mank, 1986). In fact, the federal government defined a "work activity center" as a program for "handicapped workers whose physical or mental impairment is so severe as to make their productive capacity inconsequential" (29 CFR, Part 525). Federal labor regulations included protection for people in the activity centers from being mixed with others who had less severe disabilities and were participating in the more work-oriented sheltered workshop programs (29 CFR, Part 525). Some states even specifically prohibited activity center programs from doing real work, largely due to the regulations attached to the federal Title XIX funds that supported certain programs serving people considered to have severe disabilities (Bellamy, Rhodes, Mank, & Albin, 1988).

By the 1970s, a system of adult services had developed in which placement into real community job opportunities was expected to emerge as the long-term result of movement through a series of "readiness" training programs in prevocational and vocational training agencies. The actual result of the growth of the service system, however, was that people with more severe disabilities were given little, if any, access to paid work or to the other benefits that accrue from employment in regular, integrated work settings.

Work that was available to sheltered workshops was usually used as a means of preparing individuals for competitive employment and, therefore, was most often reserved for persons with less severe disabilities. Indeed, in 1979 the Department of

> "We need to conceptualize our systems as complex, dynamic, nonlinear, and not entirely predictable, and to apply the best tools available to their analysis, their understanding, and ultimately to their management." (Boggs, 1990, p. xii)

Labor reported that the average earnings of people with mental retardation in work activity centers were approximately $29 per month, as compared to $131 for those in the more work-oriented, regular program workshops (U.S. Department of Labor, 1979). So, unfortunately, while this "flow-through model" was somewhat effective in serving individuals who required shorter-term training and work adjustment which would lead to unsupported competitive employment, it did little to assist citizens with more significant disabilities. It did not help those who appeared to be unable to work without special support to gain access to regular work settings. Indeed, based on the average length of time spent at each level of the service continuum, one study (Bellamy et al., 1986) reported that a person with mental retardation in an adult day program could expect to take an average of between 47 and 58 years to move through the levels of the system into competitive employment. Thus, those individuals entering the lowest level of the system at age 21 could not expect to be ready to move into unsupported competitive employment until they were between 68 and 79 years old.

Our friends, neighbors, and relatives with more severe disabilities were caught in a system that demanded that they acquire certain knowledge and skills, that they meet the criteria for each program level before moving on to the next, and, eventually—if the system functioned as planned—that they move on to employment in integrated settings *without* support. The logic of the system was believed to be flawless. However, the data indicated that, for the most part, people with severe disabilities remained in nonvocationally- and prevocationally-oriented activity centers (Bellamy et al., 1986). Between 1968 and 1976, there was at least a fivefold increase in the number of individuals with mental retardation served in sheltered workshops and activity centers, largely as a result of the number of people stalled in the system (Bellamy et al., 1986; Bellamy, Sheehan, Horner, & Boles, 1980).

CHANGING VISION

During the 1970s, the vision of what was possible began to change. In the 2 prior decades, early researchers had demonstrated that people who had severe disabilities could learn to perform work tasks (e.g., Crosson, 1966; Loos & Tizard, 1955). In the 1970s, the research confirmed that people with severe disabilities—including those with profound mental retardation and multiple disabilities—not only could learn to perform work tasks, but could master complex vocational tasks and perform them productively, with the appropriate use of task analysis and behavioral training principles (e.g., Bellamy, Horner, & Inman, 1979; Bellamy, O'Connor, & Karan, 1979; Bellamy, Peterson, & Close, 1975; Gold, 1972, 1973, 1976; Rusch & Mithaug, 1980). One of the leaders in the field during this time was Marc Gold, at the University of Illinois, who developed effective training techniques that have since been taught to thousands of people who provide educational or employment-related services. However, despite the development of an effective instructional technology with which to teach vocational skills to people who were previously considered incapable of learning complex tasks, the typical experience of an adult with severe disabilities did not change.

The work completed by Marc Gold and others led to further interest in demonstrating the productive capacity of persons with severe disabilities. Tom Bellamy, Rob Horner, and their colleagues at the University of Oregon (e.g., Bellamy et al., 1988; Paine, Bellamy, & Wilcox, 1984); Lou Brown's work group at the University of Wisconsin at Madison (e.g., Brown, 1973; Brown et al., 1984); and Paul Wehman and his staff at Virginia Commonwealth University's (VCU) Rehabilitation Research and Training Center (RRTC) (e.g., Wehman, 1981), to name a few, established demonstration projects that addressed the nature of school and adult services for persons with severe disabilities. In the first few years of the 1980s, dissemination of new models for providing structured—as opposed to sheltered—employment began. A few of the new employment-oriented approaches to day services that emerged during this period included: the Specialized Training Program's Mobile Crew, Supported Jobs, and Enclave Models (e.g., Mank, Rhodes, & Bellamy, 1986; Rhodes & Valenta, 1985) and VCU's Supported Competitive Employment Model (e.g., Wehman & Kregel, 1985).

One significant contribution made by these models was their demonstration that people who had previously been considered incapable of working outside of segregated settings could be trained to work productively alongside their non-disabled peers. Just as important, however, was their effect in unfreezing the then-prevalent approach to serving people with severe disabilities, that is, using large, segregated, facility-based sheltered workshops, work activity centers, and developmental programs. Although the average program size nationally was about 50 people with disabilities (Bellamy et al., 1986), many programs in urban environments had grown to serve hundreds of people with disabilities in a single location.

The federally funded demonstration projects provided a catalyst for change. Occasionally, battles raged among academicians and others regarding the relative merits of paid versus voluntary work experiences, entrepreneurial versus personnel support models, and individual versus group placements. However, despite these differences, a consensus emerged regarding both the feasibility and the validity of a more integrated approach to providing support to people with severe disabilities (e.g., Bellamy et al., 1984; Brown et al., 1984).

Also in the mid-1970s, Congress passed legislation that dramatically changed school services for children with disabilities. Public Law 94-142, the Education for All Handicapped Children Act, 1975—amended in 1990 to become the Individuals with Disabilities Education Act (IDEA)—required that public schools provide a "free appropriate public education" for all children, including those with significant disabilities. As the 1970s passed, students and their parents in more and more communities came to expect and demand services, in particular, services provided in more integrated settings. Faced with growing pressure from the parents of the first generation of students with severe disabilities aging out of school, which was coupled with the mounting evidence from the demonstration projects of the feasibility of employment in more integrated settings given appropriate support, and with other factors, the federal government announced the development of the National Supported Employment Initiative in 1984 (Office of Special Education and Rehabilitative Services, 1984).

DEVELOPMENT OF SUPPORTED EMPLOYMENT

Sponsored by the Rehabilitation Services Administration (RSA) of the federal Office of Special Education and Rehabilitative Services (OSERS), the National Supported Employment Initiative began to award systems change demonstration grants first to 10, then, by 1985, to a total of 27 states around the country. Supported employment was initially defined broadly as paid work in integrated settings with ongoing support (e.g., *Federal Register,* 1984; President's Commission on Employment for Individuals with Disabilities, 1988). But it soon was regulated by more stringent guidelines, including a requirement for a minimum of 20 hours per week of paid work. Definitions of previously broad terms became narrower. For example, "integrated settings" was redefined as regular work settings in which no more than eight persons with disabilities are working together, and "ongoing support" was redefined to mean at least two support-oriented visits per month to the worksite (*Federal Register,* 1987). Some states further restricted the definition of supported employment, for example, by accepting only individual jobs in regular work settings as instances of supported employment.

Despite the additional rules and narrower definitions, or perhaps because of them, community after community developed supported employment programs, by establishing new programs, by adding components to existing rehabilitation agencies, or by pursuing conversion or changeover from facility-based services to supported employment programs (e.g., National Association of Rehabilitation Facilities, 1990; Rehabilitation Research and Training Center, 1990). The growth of supported employment was phenomenal. Between 1986 and 1988 alone, 1,423 providers of supported employment services were established (Rehabilitation Research and Training Center, 1990).

Since 1984, local examples of supported employment services have proliferated, and the approaches to designing organizational structures and support systems have become more diverse. Suddenly, it became difficult to identify a specific program as a mobile work crew or an enclave, an individual job or a cluster placement, a dispersed enclave or a stationary crew. Reflecting the skills and creativity of local service developers; using lessons gained from the early model development efforts; attending to the local constraints, needs, and resources for program development; and designed to meet the interests and support needs of the individuals it is meant to serve, supported employment now comprises a practically limitless range of service design possibilities. Defined by service outcomes—particularly paid work and integration—supported employment offers a flexibility in service design that permits service developers to match individuals and support methods with the business economy of the local community.

CURRENT ISSUES IN SUPPORTED EMPLOYMENT

In 40 short years from the 1950s to the 1990s, the nature of employment services for individuals with severe disabilities has totally changed. Replacing the predominance of segregated, activity-oriented day care programs are rapidly emerging services designed to assist even our citizens with the most severe disabilities to assume their place in society in the regular work force. Some states are reporting that as much as one third of their service systems for adults with severe disabilities have now been changed to more integrated, community-based jobs with ongoing support (Office of Developmental Disability Services, 1991). More change can be expected, as well. In 1990, Congress passed Public Law 101-336, the Americans with Disabilities Act (ADA). The impact of ADA on employment opportunities for individuals with severe disabilities is yet to be known. Triumphs notwithstanding, many questions remain about the future of supported employment.

Economics of Change

Rehabilitation agencies have played a vital role in the expansion of supported employment. Recognizing that reorganizing their resources is a viable means to extending supported employment services, many facility-based sheltered workshops and work activity centers have begun restructuring to do just that (Rehabilitation Research and Training Center, 1990). Because these programs receive the greatest share of the funds available through federal and state agencies for services for individuals with severe disabilities, restructuring their existing service approaches is critical to further expansion of supported employment. However, many programs fear the impact of the extra costs of establishing a new service program, while maintaining the old one, that are incurred during the period of changeover to supported employment. In addition, the economic recession apparent at the beginning of the 1990s has raised questions about the feasibility of continued rapid expansion of supported employment.

Uneven Results

Despite the evidence of the real benefits to those individuals lucky enough to have access to supported employment opportunities, the results of supported employment remain uneven. The list of concerns is lengthy. Lack of access to supported employment for individuals with more severe disabilities, inadequate job retention rates, the uncertain level of true integration offered by some approaches to supported employment, the potential isolation of individuals with disabilities within less-than-accepting communities, and difficulties of achieving the 20-hour-per-week minimum with all participants have continued to be concerns as supported employment becomes a cornerstone of the service system for adults with severe disabilities (e.g., Nisbet & Callahan, 1987; Rhodes, Mank, Sandow, Buckley, & Albin, 1990; Wehman, Kregel, & Shafer, 1989). Moreover, these issues do not reflect isolated instances; rather, they are repeated in community after community across the country (e.g., DiLeo & Hagner, 1990; Rehabilitation Research and Training Center, 1990). For example, job retention success varies widely from report to report. Lyon, Domaricki, and Alexy (1988) indicated a 48% statewide retention rate in Pennsylvania, while Lagomarcino and Rusch (1988) reported retention of approximately 70% in a 3-year project with 53 model programs in Illinois.

The vision for supported employment holds the promise of dramatically improved employment outcomes, including full community participation. However, the efforts to implement supported employment on a widespread basis have lagged behind this vision. Improved management methods, continued technological development, and effective dissemination strategies are needed to help service providers fulfill the vision for supported employment in communities throughout the country (Buckley, Mank, & Sandow, 1990; Storey, Sandow, & Rhodes, 1990).

Quality Assurance

In the first years of supported employment, most state, county, and local agencies responsible for purchasing and assuring the quality of services waived or ignored many regulations and monitoring procedures, originally designed for use with facility-based services, in order to provide the flexibility required to develop innovative services in integrated settings (Rhodes et al., 1990). However, as supported employment has become a significant piece of the service system in many states, and concerns over uneven results have continued, both funders and organizations providing supported employment have been seeking methods to improve the outcomes of existing services; to ensure the quality of the services provided; and to protect the health, safety, and rights of supported employment participants (Rhodes et al., 1990; Specialized Training Program, 1989).

These rapidly changing service systems need a whole new way to think about how to assure—and how to enhance—quality in diverse and dispersed locations. The philosophy of Continuous Quality Improvement offers an approach to addressing this need. Continuous Quality Improvement will not replace the need for technological development and dissemination related to community-based employment. However, it offers a management strategy that matches many of the current needs of rehabilitation service providers who are implementing supported employment. The following chapters discuss the basic principles of that approach, and provide several specific applications of those principles that have been used in supported employment programs or in facility-based programs undergoing changeover of at least a part of their services to supported employment.

REFERENCES

Bellamy, G.T., Horner, R.H., & Inman, D. (1979). *Vocational habilitation of severely retarded adults: A direct service technology.* Baltimore: University Park Press.

Bellamy, G.T., Rhodes, L.E., Bourbeau, P.E., & Mank, D.M. (1986). Mental retardation services in sheltered workshops and day activity programs: Consumer benefits and policy alternatives. In F.R. Rusch (Ed.), *Competitive employment issues and strategies* (pp. 257–271). Baltimore: Paul H. Brookes Publishing Co.

Bellamy, G.T., Rhodes, L.E., Mank, D.M., & Albin, J.M. (1988). *Supported employment: A community implementation guide.* Baltimore: Paul H. Brookes Publishing Co.

Bellamy, G.T., Rhodes, L.E., Wilcox, B., Albin, J.M., Mank, D.M., Boles, S.M., Horner, R.H., Collins, M., & Turner, J. (1984). Quality and equality in employment services for adults with severe disabilities. *Journal of The Association for Persons with Severe Handicaps, 9*(4), 270–277.

Bellamy, T., O'Connor, G., & Karan, O. (Eds.). (1979). *Vocational rehabilitation of severely handicapped persons: Contemporary service strategies.* Baltimore: University Park Press.

Bellamy, T., Peterson, L., & Close, D. (1975). Habilitation of the severely and profoundly retarded: Illustrations of competence. *Education and Training of the Mentally Retarded, 10*(3), 174–186.

Bellamy, G.T., Sheehan, M.R., Horner, R.H., & Boles, S.M. (1980). Community programs for severely handicapped adults: An analysis of vocational opportunities. *Journal of The Association for the Severely Handicapped, 5*(4), 307–324.

Boggs, E.M. (1990). Foreword. In V.J. Bradley & H.A. Bersani (Eds.), *Quality assurance for individuals with developmental disabilities: It's everybody's business* (pp. ix–xiii). Baltimore: Paul H. Brookes Publishing Co.

Brown, L. (1973). Instructional programs for trainable-level retarded students. In L. Mann & L. Sabatino (Eds.), *The first review of special education* (Vol. 2, pp. 84–96). Philadelphia: Journal of Special Education Press.

Brown, L., Shiraga, B., York, J., Kessler, K., Strohm, B., Rogan, P., Sweet, M., Zanella, K.,

VanDeventer, P., & Loomis, R. (1984). Integrated work opportunities for adults with severe handicaps: The extended training option. *Journal of The Association for Persons with Severe Handicaps, 9*(4), 262–269.

Buckley, J., Mank, D., & Sandow, D. (1990). Developing and implementing support strategies. In F.R. Rusch (Ed.), *Supported employment: Models, methods, and issues* (pp. 131–144). Sycamore, IL: Sycamore Publishing.

Crosson, J. (1966). The experimental analysis of vocational behavior in severely retarded males (Doctoral dissertation, University of Oregon). *Dissertation Abstracts International, 27,* 3304.

DiLeo, D., & Hagner, D. (1990). *Conversion to supported employment: Initiatives and strategies.* Concord: New Hampshire Developmental Disabilities Council.

Federal Register. (1984, September 25). Developmental Disabilities Act of 1984. Report 98-1074, Section 102 (11)(F).

Federal Register. (1987, August 14). Final regulations. Vol. 52(157), 30546–30552.

Gold, M. (1972). Stimulus factors in skill training of the retarded on a complex assembly task: Acquisition, transfer and retention. *American Journal of Mental Deficiency, 76*(5), 517–526.

Gold, M. (1973). Research on the vocational habilitation of the retarded: The present, the future. In N. Ellis (Ed.), *International review of research in mental retardation* (Vol. 6, pp. 97–147). New York: Academic Press.

Gold, M. (1976). Task analysis of a complex assembly task by the retarded blind. *Exceptional Children, 43*(20), 78–84.

Lagomarcino, T.R., & Rusch, F.R. (1988). A descriptive analysis of reasons why supported employees separate from their jobs. In C. Hanley-Maxwell & D. Harley (Eds.), *Proceedings from the 1988 Annual Meeting of The President's Committee on Employment of People with Disabilities* (pp. 45–49). Carbondale: Southern Illinois University.

Loos, F., & Tizard, J. (1955). The employment of adult imbeciles in a hospital workshop. *American Journal of Mental Deficiency, 59*(3), 395–403.

Lyon, S.R., Domaricki, J.W., & Alexy, S.L. (1988). *A study of job retention in the Pennsylvania supported employment program.* Pittsburgh: University of Pittsburgh, Program in Severe Disabilities.

Mank, D.M., Rhodes, L.E., & Bellamy, G.T. (1986). Four supported employment alternatives. In W.E. Kiernan & J.A. Stark (Eds.), *Pathways to employment for adults with developmental disabilities* (pp. 139–153). Baltimore: Paul H. Brookes Publishing Co.

National Association of Rehabilitation Facilities. (1990). *Conversion: Restructuring for integrated community placement.* Washington, DC: Author.

Nisbet, J., & Callahan, M. (1987). Achieving success in integrated workplaces: Critical elements in assisting persons with severe disabilities. In S.J. Taylor, D. Biklen, & J. Knoll (Eds.), *Community integration for people with severe disabilities* (pp. 184–201). New York: Teachers College Press.

Office of Developmental Disability Services. (1991). *Report of the vocational outcomes system.* Salem: Oregon Mental Health and Developmental Disabilities Services Division.

Office of Special Education and Rehabilitative Services. (1984). *Supported employment for adults with severe disabilities: An OSERS program initiative.* Washington, DC: Author.

Paine, S.C., Bellamy, G.T., & Wilcox, B. (Eds.). (1984). *Human services that work: From innovation to standard practice.* Baltimore: Paul H. Brookes Publishing Co.

President's Commission on Employment for Individuals with Disabilities. (1988). *Fact sheet on supported employment.* Washington, DC: Author.

Rehabilitation Research and Training Center. (1990, Winter). *Growth of supported employment.* Richmond: Virginia Commonwealth University.

Rhodes, L.E., Mank, D., Sandow, D., Buckley, J., & Albin, J. (1990). Supported employment implementation: Shifting from program monitoring to quality improvement. *Journal of Disability Policy Studies, 1*(2), 1–18.

Rhodes, L.E., & Valenta, L. (1985). Industry-based supported employment: An enclave approach. *Journal of The Association for Persons with Severe Handicaps, 10*(1), 12–20.

Rusch, F., & Mithaug, D. (1980). *Vocational training for mentally retarded adults: A behavior analytic approach.* Champaign, IL: Research Press.

Specialized Training Program. (1989). *A quality improvement project for supported employment.* (Proposal submitted to the Office of Special Education and Rehabilitative Services, National Institute on Disability and Rehabilitation Research, Field Initiated Research [84.1336]). Eugene: University of Oregon.

Storey, K., Sandow, D., & Rhodes, L. (1990). Service delivery issues in supported employ-
    ment. *Education and Training in Mental Retardation, 25*(4), 325–332.
U.S. Department of Labor. (1979). *Study of handicapped clients in sheltered workshops* (Vol. II).
    Washington, DC: Author.
Wehman, P. (1981). *Competitive employment: New horizons for severely disabled individuals.* Balti-
    more: Paul H. Brookes Publishing Co.
Wehman, P., & Kregel, J. (1985). A supported work approach to competitive employment of
    individuals with moderate and severe handicaps. *Journal of The Association for Persons with
    Severe Handicaps, 10*(1), 3–11.
Wehman, P., Kregel, J., & Shafer, M.S. (Eds.). (1989). *Emerging trends in the national supported
    employment initiative: A preliminary analysis of twenty-seven states.* Richmond: Virginia Com-
    monwealth University, Rehabilitation Research and Training Center.

Chapter 2

A New Way of Thinking About Quality in Services

The Philosophy of Continuous Quality Improvement

It is important to remember how rapidly change has occurred in services for people with severe disabilities. We no longer live in a time when communities simply want a place that will provide families with respite during the day and where people can be protected from harm, provided with activities to fill their days, and taught personal management and prevocational skills. Now, more and more communities are demanding that rehabilitation and other service agencies provide the support that will allow individuals with severe disabilities to work, live, and play in natural, integrated settings. Along with this change in vision, service providers and public sector funding agencies are faced with mounting pressures from a variety of sources, such as inadequate funding levels, ongoing deinstitutionalization efforts, expanding needs for services, demands for improved service quality, and the revolution in the technology of providing services. Organizations are struggling to keep pace.

Based on the history of change in services for people with severe disabilities since the 1950s, one wonders whether a period of stability can be expected in the next 30 years. It is doubtful. Already, participants in supported employment, their parents, advocates, and concerned professionals are seeking approaches for improvement. For example, methods are being developed to assist co-workers and employers to plan for and provide the support needed by individuals with disabilities working in their companies (e.g., Mank, Oorthuys, Rhodes, Sandow, & Weyer, 1992; Rhodes, Sandow, Mank, Buckley, & Albin, 1991). Changes in the objectives for services, as well as changes in the strategies used to meet those objectives, can be expected to continue.

Service purchasers and service providers will continue to need ways to manage employment services that help them to keep pace with the ongoing changes in the collective knowledge, skills, and vision of quality. Supported employment is not the ultimate answer to the employment service needs of people with significant disabilities. Just as better ideas and technology have superseded previous approaches to service delivery problems, supported employment is being replaced by better approaches to meeting the needs of individuals with disabilities.

Service providers and others need an approach to service delivery that constantly reevaluates quality, that seeks to *improve the vision of quality* as well as seeking to achieve that vision. We need a way to challenge ourselves continuously in what we do in order to improve the quality of the services provided to people with severe disabilities—and to improve the outcomes of services. Furthermore, we need a method of identifying the changing expectations for quality, in keeping up with the ongoing revolution in service technology, and in managing organizations to meet those changing demands.

FUNDAMENTAL PRINCIPLES OF CONTINUOUS QUALITY IMPROVEMENT

The parallels between the historical development of the need for a system that addresses quality improvement in employment services and the development of the same need in business settings are striking. Since the 1950s, American manufacturing industries have faced a variety of challenges. With rapidly expanding quantity and complexity in goods and services, with rising national and foreign competition, with increasing demands for improved quality at a lower cost, and with sweeping changes in manufacturing technology, from the late 1970s more and more companies have embraced a new method to increase competitiveness, to improve quality, and to achieve excellence (Juran, 1989; Rubenstein, 1991; Scholtes, 1988). This new method has required a radical change in their approach to managing their businesses (Deming, 1986).

Variations of the new approach have been given different labels, including *Total Quality* (Holpp, 1989; Linkow, 1989); *Quality Leadership* (Scholtes, 1988); *Total Quality Control* (Feigenbaum, 1983; Mizuno, 1988); *Total Quality Management* (Coate, 1990); and *Managing for Quality* (Juran, 1989); among others. However, the general method is often referred to as Continuous Quality Improvement, a name that captures its ongoing attention to improving the processes, products, and services of an organization. The approach was first applied on a widespread basis in Japan in the early 1950s, based on the advice and teaching of an American statistician, W. Edwards Deming (Mizuno, 1988; Walton, 1986). The applicability of this approach to enhancing quality in employment services, in other service industries, or in the public sector is clear. Indeed, as time goes on, the literature on quality improvement is including more and more examples drawn from service (e.g., Boothe, 1990; Holpp, 1990; Smith, 1990); educational (e.g., Barrows, Melvin, Ashmore, & Romstad, 1991; Coate, 1990); and public sector settings (e.g., Box, Joiner, Rohan, & Sensenbrenner, 1991; Carr & Littman, 1990; Couper, 1990).

The developers and champions of Continuous Quality Improvement— business leaders and statisticians such as W. Edwards Deming, Joseph M. Juran, Arnold Feigenbaum, William G. Hunter, and Philip Crosby—have used different approaches to defining the basic principles of quality improvement and quality leadership. Dr. Deming, who has been called the "Father of the New Industrial Age" and the "Founder of the New Economic Era" uses 14 points to describe the strategies that businesses must adopt to be competitive and to survive (Scholtes, 1988). Revised occasionally and reprinted frequently over the years, these 14 points have formed the foundation for the new philosophy of quality management (Deming, 1982, 1986; Walton, 1986). They are written in a way that most clearly applies to manufacturing settings, so their meaning for rehabilitation services and public sector agencies may not be immediately evident. However, they are provided here without comment simply to introduce Dr. Deming and his words to human services workers.

DR. DEMING'S 14 POINTS ON QUALITY TRANSFORMATION

"1. Create constancy of purpose toward improvement of product and service, with the aim to become competitive and to stay in business, and to provide jobs.

2. Adopt the new philosophy. We are in a new economic age. Western management must awaken to the challenge, must learn their responsibilities, and take on leadership for change.

3. Cease dependence on inspection to achieve quality. Eliminate the need for inspection on a mass basis by building quality into the product in the first place.

4. End the practice of awarding business on the basis of price tag. Instead, minimize total cost. Move toward a single supplier for any one item, on a long-term relationship of loyalty and trust.

5. Improve constantly and forever the system of production and service, to improve quality and productivity, and thus constantly decrease costs.

6. Institute training on the job.

7. Institute leadership. The aim of supervision should be to help people and machines and gadgets to do a better job. Supervision of management is in need of overhaul, as well as supervision of production workers.

8. Drive out fear, so that everyone may work effectively for the company.

9. Break down barriers between departments. People in research, design, sales, and production must work as a team, to foresee problems of production and in use that may be encountered with the product or service.

10. Eliminate slogans, exhortations, and targets for the work force asking for zero defects and new levels of productivity. Such exhortations only create adversarial relationships, as the bulk of the causes of low quality and low productivity belong to the system and thus lie beyond the power of the work force.

11. a. Eliminate work standards (quotas) on the factory floor. Substitute leadership.
    b. Eliminate management by objective. Eliminate management by numbers, numerical goals. Substitute leadership.

12. a. Remove barriers that rob the hourly worker of his right to pride of workmanship. The responsibility of supervisors must be changed from sheer numbers to quality.
    b. Remove barriers that rob people in management and in engineering of their right to pride of workmanship. This means, *inter alia*, abolishment of the annual or merit rating and of management by objective.

13. Institute a vigorous program of education and self-improvement.

14. Put everybody in the company to work to accomplish the transformation. The transformation is everybody's job." (Deming, 1986, pp. 23–24)

Although each of the quality improvement experts uses different words, and somewhat different lists of basic concepts, the words they use reflect similar principles. These experts insist that an obsession with quality outcomes—as defined by the customer—must become the mission of the entire organization. They believe that to be successful, an organization must use new methods for empowering employees to work to achieve that mission. These methods include training in how to use systematic, data-based approaches for making decisions related to improving the existing processes in the organization.

The purpose of this chapter is to translate Dr. Deming's 14 points, and the messages of other quality experts, into a few fundamental principles that can be applied to management in community-based employment, rehabilitation, and other service settings. Because of the importance of the concept of customers to Continuous Quality Improvement, Chapter 3, "Customers and Quality Improvement: Lessons for Rehabilitation and Supported Employment," focuses on the definition of customer and customer roles in quality improvement. Applications of these principles to rehabilitation, changeover, and community-based employment are expanded in later chapters.

Principle #1: Establish a Mission To Lead Quality Improvement

Whatever your business happens to be, your mission must be able to lead quality improvement efforts. Establishing such a mission provides the context to support efforts toward quality. In rehabilitation services, including supported employment, the mission must guide continuous improvement of the quality of services. To do that, an organization's mission must be defined in a way that will assist its members in recognizing quality, in determining how well the organization is achieving that quality, and in taking any steps needed to improve its performance. Unfortunately, most mission statements in rehabilitation agencies do little to guide personnel actions.

Mission statements too often are written as one or more paragraphs that vaguely describe the kinds of services provided by an organization and the ultimate cultural objective of its activities. Organizations have believed that a mission statement should be written in a way that is broad enough that it is unlikely to change over the course of several years, and that is flexible enough to allow new strategies. The unfortunate result of such broad statements is that they may be so vague that they give little direction to the organization and its members, beyond defining the general field or geographic area in which the organization provides services. Such a mission statement permits the organization and its members to do practically anything, providing little direction for prioritizing goals, strategies, and activities.

As a mission statement grows longer, it becomes more complex, less understandable, and certainly not memorable. When asked, staff members are usually able to provide only a general description, if any, of the mission of the organization. Unclear about the core of the organization's mission, staff members move through

---

FUNDAMENTAL PRINCIPLES OF CONTINUOUS QUALITY IMPROVEMENT

1. Establish a mission to lead quality improvement.
2. Develop an obsession with quality.
3. Create a unity of purpose.
4. Empower employees to work to achieve the mission.
5. Use a systematic approach to find opportunities and to improve performance.

**TYPICAL RESPONSES OF STAFF MEMBERS TO THE QUESTION,
"WHAT IS YOUR ORGANIZATION'S MISSION?"**

- "I think I read it during my orientation, but I couldn't tell you what it says now."
- "I've never seen it."
- "It has something to do with serving people with disabilities."
- "I don't know."
- "Ask my supervisor; she'll know."
- "I'm only a job coach. I didn't know that I should know about that."
- "I don't think we have one."

---

their jobs based on their personal perceptions of quality, rather than on a unified vision of the future. As mission statements grow more complex, they become less useful for helping board members and employees to understand their roles in the organization.

To initiate the change to a quality orientation, a rehabilitation or community employment organization must take a new approach to defining its mission. The mission statement must help the members of the organization to maintain a clear focus on quality, giving direction to their activities by defining desired products or outcomes. Furthermore, a mission statement that is short and simple—that requires only a few words, rather than a few paragraphs—will help all members of the organization to understand and embrace it.

> A mission for leading a quality transformation:
> "Job Success and Satisfaction"

The mission of an organization is important in successfully leading a movement to imbed quality in every aspect. Whether the organization's business happens to be providing work evaluation, job development, food stamps, or supported employment, the mission must keep the organization oriented to improving quality. Chapter 8 on performance templates provides a useful tool—the ACORNS Test—for evaluating organizational mission statements.

HOW *NOT* TO WRITE A MISSION STATEMENT

Smith Rehabilitation Agency is an organization whose mission is to provide rehabilitation services support to assist individuals requiring our services to achieve the highest possible quality of life. Smith Rehabilitation Agency is committed to providing high quality services to meet the needs of the community of Smith and surrounding areas. This mission includes a focus on the importance of cooperation, respect for the individual, individual service planning, and open communication. Using the best available service strategies, Smith strives to meet the educational, recreational, and vocational needs of its clients.

A RECOMMENDED FORMAT FOR MISSION STATEMENTS

Uncomfortable with limiting your mission statement to just a few words? Accustomed to mission statements that contain a great deal of information, including defining target populations, geographic areas, organizational values, and principal strategies? Here is a format to solve your dilemma:

Create a short and simple mission statement, such as: "Job Success and Satisfaction," "Integration through Employment," or "Employment Partnerships." Select a statement that captures the ultimate outcome that the organization is seeking to achieve. Below that, list the significant values, target populations, or other information that you feel is important to further define your organization. Use these statements as further explanations to assist in interpreting the mission to staff members and others, or as operating guidelines to lead decision-making. However, use the shorter mission statement, highlighted at the top of the page, as the words to be remembered by all members of the organization, to guide their performance. Here is an example:

FGH EMPLOYMENT SERVICES MISSION STATEMENT

Job Success and Satisfaction

FGH Employment Services is organized to promote long-term job success and satisfaction for individuals with severe intellectual disabilities who previously have not been given opportunities to participate in the community of work. Focused in the Greater Metropolitan Area, FGH uses the following principles and values to guide our work:

- Individuals with severe intellectual disabilities deserve the opportunity to participate fully in natural, community employment settings along with their nondisabled peers. Thus, FGH services may extend beyond the time and place of work if needed to assist in developing full community participation.
- The services provided by FGH are designed to be least intrusive to natural settings, while using the most effective technologies currently available.
- FGH defines and evaluates quality services through actively and frequently recruiting feedback from its most significant customers: the individuals receiving services, their employers, the county and state agencies funding the services, and the staff members of FGH. Furthermore, the input of FGH's secondary customers is valued as an additional source of information for improving services. Thus, FGH solicits feedback from residential providers, families, and advocates for individuals receiving services, and other employment service providers, as well. FGH believes that building long-term partnerships with these customers based on respect and open communication will support our mutual success.
- The employees of FGH are the key to achieving our desired objectives. Therefore, FGH believes that it is important to support employees' personal and professional growth and to offer enjoyable, meaningful jobs that promote long-term commitment to the organization. The organizational structure, policies, procedures, and management methods, therefore, must be designed and implemented to support employees in achieving FGH's mission.

PRINCIPLE #1: ESTABLISH A MISSION TO LEAD QUALITY IMPROVEMENT

MISSION STATEMENTS SHOULD:

- Define the overall desired outcome for the organization.
- Be clear and concise.
- Lead quality improvement efforts.
- Provide a context to support quality.
- Assist in recognizing quality.
- Assist in evaluating the organization's performance.
- Help staff members to understand their roles in the organization.
- Provide direction for prioritizing goals, strategies, and activities.

Principle #2: Develop an Obsession with Quality

> "The hallmark of successful quality programs is not any particular technique, but a process of 'living' quality day in and day out." (Peters & Austin, 1985, p. 526)

In a manufacturing firm that has embraced Continuous Quality Improvement, quality is not simply the domain of the quality assurance department, quality inspectors, or management. On the contrary, quality improvement experts understand that quality cannot be achieved if it is viewed as the sole domain of the quality assurance department, nor can it be achieved profitably through post hoc inspection. Instead, quality must be built into the product at every step, eliminating unnecessary inspections and rework that add costs—but add no value—to the product or service (Deming, 1986; Juran, 1989). Quality, therefore, is viewed as being the responsibility of the employees who order materials, who receive materials, who assemble parts, who transport parts, who ship orders, who provide customer service in the field, who answer the telephone, who sweep the floors, and so forth. All employees are trained to have pride in the company, to look for quality, to inspect the parts with which they come into contact, and to do something about improving quality if they discover a problem. Each individual employee assumes responsibility for quality.

The best organizations, therefore, have developed a pervasive obsession with quality. These organizations develop a culture that is based on quality; the company's style, attitudes, stories, language, and beliefs, from top executives to line employees, support the effort for quality. These organizations also understand that all members contribute to the quality of the product or service and have a role in ensuring that performance meets or exceeds quality expectations. Imai uses the Japanese term *kaizen* to reflect the concept of ongoing improvement of quality involving *everyone*, including top management, middle managers, and workers (Imai, 1986). With *kaizen*, employees take pride not only in the quality of their product or service, but also in the company in which they work, performing tasks that might be outside their formal job descriptions if the tasks will improve the quality or appearance of the company or its product or service. Thus, a top executive can be seen emptying an ashtray in the lobby, or an assembler notifying engineering of malfunctioning equipment. Quality improvement relies upon a constant attentiveness by all employees to look for the small and large ways in which they can improve what they do. Quality improvement is not only the result of extensive, team-based, quality improvement projects, as discussed in later chapters. It is also the result of a stream of modest ideas and innovations produced every day by employees in all parts of an organization (Imai, 1986). With Continuous Quality Improvement, employees are encouraged and rewarded for bringing improvement ideas, no matter how small, to work.

> "We don't seek to be one thousand percent better at any one thing. We seek to be one percent better at one thousand things." (SAS Group President Jan Carlzon, cited in Peters & Austin, 1985, p. 68)

Quality improvement experts understand that embedding an obsession with quality in an organization cannot be achieved overnight. They assert that adopting the principles and methods of Continuous Quality Improvement cannot be treated as another short-term program—the latest in a long line of management fads. To succeed in a quality transformation, as it is sometimes called (e.g., Deming, 1986; Scholtes & Hacquebord, 1987), Continuous Quality Improvement must reach into the basic philosophy of the organization, as well as into its operations and that of its suppliers. Achieving such a fundamental and enduring change in the way an organization does business can be expected to require at least several years to implement, and ongoing vigilance after that.

Because the picture of quality is constantly changing (as seen in Chapter 1), the job of achieving quality is never done. Therefore, an organization needs an ongoing process to identify its current definition of quality and to support change and innovation to move the organization and its products or services toward that definition. Implicit within the principle, "Develop an Obsession with Quality," promoted by quality experts, therefore, is that this obsession must also become a lifelong commitment that drives both organizational and individual behavior.

Organizations providing rehabilitation, supported employment, or other human services can also benefit from developing a similar, pervasive obsession with quality. Indeed, supported employment organizations, with their dispersed loca-

PRINCIPLE #2: DEVELOP AN OBSESSION WITH QUALITY

- Establish a culture that views quality as the responsibility of *all* employees.
- Look for ways to improve quality everyday in small ways.
- Recognize employees who make even modest improvements in quality.
- Make a long-term commitment to quality that includes ongoing vigilance for improvement.
- Use quality improvement processes to identify changing definitions of quality and to support changes in the organization to meet the new definitions.
- Replace post hoc and external inspection systems by building in quality at every step.
- Live quality. Top managers should demonstrate an obsession with quality through their own actions and improvement activities.

tions for service provision, must rely upon staff members taking responsibility for quality. Each staff person must be alert to how quality can be maintained and improved within the unique setting in which he or she is working. Quality may even be defined differently in different settings. For example, appearance may be part of how a restaurant defines quality, but not how a warehouse does. Therefore, staff members must also be alert to differences in quality expectations and to changes in those expectations, as well as being prepared to adjust to meet those different demands.

The change to the philosophy and methods of Continuous Quality Improvement, however, must extend beyond service providers to service purchasers. For many years, funders have believed that, in order to achieve quality in services, they could write regulations and standards, and then monitor service providers for compliance with quality standards. In the ever-changing world of community-based supported employment, however, most states have found their existing quality assurance strategies to be inadequate. This would not be surprising to quality improvement experts, who would view such monitoring for compliance to standards as an external inspection strategy, inappropriate to the purpose of improving the quality of the service outcomes provided to service recipients. Instead, they would recommend replacing most standards with developing an obsession with quality that pervades the service provider organization, so that all employees are clear about what quality is and take ownership of achieving quality outcomes.

Principle #3: Create a Unity of Purpose

For an organization to be most effective in achieving its mission, all members of the company must understand the mission and their roles in achieving that mission. In fact, the mission must drive each individual's priorities and activities. Such a unity of purpose throughout an organization ensures that all employees work together with the same vision toward achieving the same outcomes.

In changeover to supported employment, staff members may feel confused about what the organization is doing. For years, it may have provided rehabilitation services through a sheltered workshop setting. During changeover, priorities, resources, and staff time begin to shift to new ways of providing services. Some staff members may continue to work to strengthen the facility-based program, while others are pressing for change. Such differences lead not only to conflict, but also to lost resources. Developing a unity of purpose among the staff members ensures that all employees understand the new direction and work in concert toward it.

Several strategies may be helpful in creating a unity of purpose. A mission statement that is short, simple, understandable, and easy to remember is a start. Staff orientation programs that teach new staff members about the history, values, traditions, and future of the organization are very useful in bringing new members into the team (Stratton, 1991). In addition, a common language and other symbols that reflect the organization's mission can be helpful. Thus, selecting a mission and symbols that value change, providing a strong orientation program for new staff, and using a language that reflects a business image and demonstrates respect for the individuals receiving services from the organization are strategies that may help many rehabilitation organizations to rally staff around a common purpose. Such strategies are particularly useful for organizations that are undergoing a major change in direction, such as that required in changeover from facility-based services

One rehabilitation organization, in the process of total changeover to supported employment, has selected a theme to help keep everyone focused: QISS—"Quality Is Success and Satisfaction." The executive director uses it during staff meetings as a format for eliciting staff input and as a route for delivering rewards for staff performance.

to supported employment. Probably most critical, however, is the demonstrated commitment and vision of the organization's leader (Mizuno, 1988).

Creating a unity of purpose and a shared vision is a critical role of the organization's leader. Leaders must have the fortitude to carry forth the purpose through daily conflicting priorities, communicating a clear vision of the organization's ideals and objectives. Joseph Juran insists that top managers must personally become leaders in managing for quality, taking on active roles in the process of quality improvement (Juran, 1989). An organization's leaders must demonstrate quality improvement through their own actions, which will reinforce the vision and direction of the organization. In adopting the philosophy of Continuous Quality Improvement, and in moving to community-based employment services, the vision communicated by the top manager of an organization is crucial to success.

Chapter 4, in discussing the cultural issues related to changeover to supported employment, presents additional information on change strategies for achieving a shared vision—a unity of purpose—to support the cultural shifts typically required to accomplish substantial organizational transformations such as changeover to supported employment.

Principle #4: Empower Employees To Work To Achieve the Mission

Effecting a quality transformation within an organization requires that all employees be actively engaged in working toward achieving the mission. Implementing this principle results in making the most of the energies of all staff members. For most organizations, however, this will require a significant shift in how they manage their staffs.

PRINCIPLE #3: CREATE A UNITY OF PURPOSE

- Make the mission permeate the organization. Be clear about how all jobs, activities, policies, procedures—all facets of the organization—tie into achieving the mission.
- Communicate a clear vision. Top managers are responsible for conveying a vision of the organization's future to all staff members. Creating a shared vision is a critical role of the organization's leader.
- Help all staff members work together toward achieving the same vision.
- Use staff orientation, a common "language," and symbols to reflect the mission and vision of the future.

"A spirit of teamwork must pervade the organization, a spirit strong and pervasive enough to supersede the attachments that people normally form in relation to other common bonds such as profession, function or rank."(Scholtes & Hacquebord, 1987, p. 3)

Underlying the philosophy of Continuous Quality Improvement is the belief that employees *want* to do a good job. Thus, managers must believe that staff members, as a whole, not only want to do a good job, but given the right tools, resources, and information, likely will do so. Rather than protect turf, power, and knowledge, managers must take on the job of moving knowledge and power throughout the organization.

Competitiveness among staff members must be replaced by open communication, teamwork, and collaboration. The staff must recognize that the only struggle should be the constant struggle to achieve desired levels of quality, and not a struggle for power within the organization. Frequent two-way communication between staff members, as well as between staff and managers, is needed to improve effectiveness, along with frequent feedback on performance that is not burdened with blame.

During a quality transformation, it may be that the existing organizational structure needs to be replaced with another: one that helps staff members interact with each other, and with others outside the organization, instead of placing barriers between them or encouraging hierarchical relationships among them. Rehabilitation professionals involved with facility-based services are only too familiar with age-old conflicts between "Production" and "Rehab." These conflicts are largely based on the formal division that exists in the structure between those departments in most rehabilitation organizations. With often widely differing experience and training, operating within environments characterized by dissimilar demands and constraints, and given limited opportunities to communicate with each other, it should not be surprising that rehabilitation specialists and production supervisors often clash. Developing a spirit of teamwork and cooperation that cuts across such departmental and professional barriers is an important strategy in improving performance.

Often, the causes of chronic problems within organizations originate in different departments (Deming, 1986). An unacceptably high rate of job loss in supported employment, for example, could be related to the manner in which the jobs are initially developed; to the analysis of the job, the job setting, and job supports used prior to actual job placement; to the lack of identification and encouragement of the use of supports naturally available in the work place; to the orientation and training provided to the worker and his or her co-workers; to the relationship with the individual's home provider; and so forth. In some supported employment organizations, functions in some of these areas may be served by different individuals or even by individuals in separate departments, for example, marketing, job training, and rehabilitation services. If so, then bringing these individuals together for discussion is the only way to discover the root causes of the job loss problem and design effective corrective actions.

The experience of one organization that restructured in order to implement quality improvement principles is presented in Chapter 13. That organization created a set of Work Teams and Project Teams to build an organizational structure that brought together individuals who previously had been in separate departments. The new structure also communicated a clear message that the organization was shifting from a traditional, hierarchical structure to one in which rank or position had less influence than team membership. This message was important to help direct service staff persons, traditionally pictured at the bottom of organizational hierarchies, to take a new perspective on their roles.

Restructuring may also reflect a new attitude about who makes decisions. Moving the responsibility for decision-making to those directly involved with the issue should not only save time, but also result in better decisions. Employees who work directly with the problem at hand have deeper knowledge of the issue and, because they will have to live with the result, care that a good decision is made. Given appropriate guidelines for making good decisions, trained and coached by manager-experts in decision-making processes and tools, and provided with training and support in needed content areas, work teams can effectively make decisions that will move the organization more rapidly toward accomplishing its mission. Some companies have implemented "self-directed work teams." In these teams, a group of employees assumes responsibility for a whole product or process, including functions typically performed by supervisors and managers, such as planning

---

PRINCIPLE #4: EMPOWER EMPLOYEES TO WORK TO ACHIEVE THE MISSION

- Promote teamwork.
- Break down barriers to communication both inside the organization and between members of the organization and its customers.
- Restructure to reduce or eliminate hierarchical boundaries and formal channels of communication.
- Form work groups that cut across boundaries of departments, professional status, function, and rank.
- Encourage communication flow that is directed *from* employees *to* the managers.
- Treat communication of all types as positive rather than threatening.
- Give work teams authority to make decisions: Decisions should be made by the people who are closest to the problems.
- Permit employees to assume ownership of ideas and accomplishments related to achieving organizational goals, and to participate in planning processes.
- Provide decision-making guidelines for work teams as they assume authority.
- Drive out fear in employees by eliminating unreasonable objectives, inappropriate performance reviews, threats, punishment, and second-guessing.
- Provide employees with ongoing access to a vigorous program of education and training to provide them with the philosophy and tools needed to perform their jobs well.
- Stop relying on isolated experts. Change their jobs to focus on moving their knowledge throughout the organization.
- Provide frequent encouragement and recognition for efforts, accomplishments, and ingenuity.
- Treat all employees as customers.
- Believe that employees *want* to do a good job.

schedules, budgeting, hiring and firing personnel, and problem-solving (Harper & Harper, 1990). Quality organizations, therefore, in order to empower staff must maintain a vigorous program of education and training to ensure that staff members have the knowledge and skills they need, when they need them, to perform well. Increasing the knowledge and skills of individual employees, of course, also has the benefit of increasing their value to the organization.

Employees also need opportunities to assume ownership of ideas and accomplishments related to achieving organizational goals. Being part of a self-directed work team, participating in planning goals and strategies, contributing ideas for performance improvement, and being recognized for the contributions that they make to the organization's performance are important to giving employees ownership of what they do. A sense of ownership helps staff members feel they are important to the organization and encourages them to care about what the organization accomplishes.

Dr. Deming and other quality improvement experts believe that empowering staff members can only be accomplished if their fear can be reduced or eliminated (e.g., Deming, 1986; Lowe & McBean, 1989). Fear is a tremendous barrier to quality improvement. Fear of repercussions causes staff members to try to make things look better than they are, to be reluctant to disclose problems or errors, and to hesitate to make decisions. Yet, quality improvements can only be made when the picture that is drawn by a staff member is accurate, so that problems and errors are uncovered and investigated (Deming, 1986). Traditional management approaches instill fear in staff by using a top-down approach to communication, in which staff members are expected to listen to managers and seldom are given an opportunity to speak openly to them. Management by objectives and employee evaluations in which employees are held accountable for reaching numerical quotas that are beyond their control to reach build employee fear as well (Deming, 1986). Staff members whose decisions are frequently changed or questioned by managers who are not involved with the situation at hand become fearful of assuming responsibility for making decisions.

Instead, managers must reward employees for uncovering problems and discussing errors. Mistakes offer valuable information for improving performance and must be treated in this regard. Employees who have a history of being punished when they make a mistake must learn that punishment will not occur in the future. Instead, the organization must treat the issue as a piece of information to be understood, not as an error with blame attached. In industry, quality improvement experts such as Joseph Juran recognize that at least 85% of problems can be corrected only with changes in the systems in which people work (which are largely determined by management), and less than 15% are really under the control of individual employees (Scholtes, 1988). W. Edwards Deming (1986) estimates that as much as 94% require changes to the system. This view, therefore, sees the greatest performance improvement opportunities as being related to fixing the system and processes in which employees work, rather than by placing blame on employees for problems or errors they could not control. The performance of an organization is not as simple as the statement, "It just takes good people." Instead, managers must recognize their roles in creating and improving the systems that are largely responsible for staff performance. Empowering all employees to improve these systems will make the organization even more effective in achieving its mission.

Empowering employees also means that managers must develop the habit of encouraging employees, that is, providing support for their work and for their motivation to work toward fulfilling the mission. Acknowledging efforts, providing recognition for significant accomplishments, encouraging ingenuity, and providing time to participate in quality improvement efforts are some of the strategies that managers should use on a daily basis throughout their organizations. For example, a vocational rehabilitation agency might ask the counselor who has achieved the highest number of supported employment closures to provide training to other counselors, or an employment specialist who has made a special effort to help develop a culture that supports changeover might be given an opportunity to attend a conference on supported employment. Even recognition in small ways—a pat on the back, or an announcement at a staff meeting—can help to support employee motivation to work.

Managers must learn to treat the organization's staff members with the same respect that they regularly offer to external customers. Soliciting staff input and responding to staff feedback are two basic strategies. Top managers must come to understand that the staff, who are in daily contact with employers and individuals receiving support, are the most important members of the organization. They know most intimately the organization's most critical processes, that is, the processes that are directly encountered by customers. They are the ones who, according to Dr. Deming, possess "profound knowledge" of their jobs. Managers must learn to listen often and carefully to what staff members say, for it is the staff who best understand the inner workings of the organization.

Principle #5: Use a Systematic Approach
To Find Opportunities and To Improve Performance

In this last principle, Continuous Quality Improvement offers a strategy for improving performance based on a systematic analysis of accomplishments and problems. Quality improvement methods offer a variety of tools, such as flowcharting, graphing, and brainstorming, to improve performance, many of which are presented in later chapters. Some of the concepts underlying these tools are discussed here.

PRINCIPLE #5: USE A SYSTEMATIC APPROACH TO FIND OPPORTUNITIES AND TO IMPROVE PERFORMANCE

- Compare performance against the customers' definition of quality.
- Use data as a basis for making decisions, and only collect data when they will result in an action being taken.
- Select for attention the area or accomplishment that offers the greatest opportunity for improved performance.
- Recognize the structure in work; that is, identify the processes in what appears to be haphazard.
- Analyze the processes and the variables that affect the processes.
- Plan, implement, evaluate, adjust, and standardize the intervention used to improve performance.
- Teach everyone in the organization to use systematic methods for decision-making.
- Emphasize preventing rather than correcting problems.

Using a systematic approach means that everyone in an organization must learn to use data to make decisions. Too often, organizations make important decisions based only on the opinions or perceptions of one or a few particularly vocal staff members or managers. While opinions and perceptions may also be useful, when real data are made available, data rather than emotions should drive decisions. Managers have a responsibility to teach all employees how and when to collect, organize, and analyze data. Data can be a powerful tool to help employees improve performance, from targeting the improvement opportunity and analyzing the factors that affect performance, to selecting the most appropriate solution. Questions that might be raised about an organization's performance include:

- Why are the people in job sites losing their jobs? What should we do about it?
- Why are 65% of the people who are working in the community working less than 20 hours per week? Is it the way we are developing jobs? Is it due to needing to keep earnings below the levels allowed by the various Social Security programs? Is it because of constraints required by the available transportation? What action can we take to have the greatest impact on improving this outcome?
- Why is our staff turnover rate so high? How can we reduce it?

Such questions can be answered accurately only through analysis of data available on job loss, work hours, and employee turnover. Without a commitment to data-based decisions, organizations may choose an intervention that is not directed at the true cause of the problem, thereby wasting valuable resources.

Staff members in rehabilitation organizations often resist collecting data because they lack an understanding of its importance, or have seen that too often data only fill folders and are forgotten. With a Continuous Quality Improvement focus, however, the only reason to collect data is to take action. Data are needed only for making decisions, and unless data will be used, they need not be collected. With training on collecting and using data for making decisions, staff members are able to support the decisions they make when questioned by managers. "Is that your opinion or do you have data to support it?", should become a common question in an organization implementing quality improvement principles.

Using a systematic approach to improve performance also helps staff members to recognize the structure in work, that is, to recognize that what appears to be haphazard actually encompasses basic processes, and to identify them. This is easy to see in a manufacturing environment, where components and subassemblies are prepared in separate departments and then go to other areas for final assembly and shipping. In supported employment and rehabilitation, however, the processes being undertaken may appear less obvious. Yet, identifying the process that is, or should be, in place is one of the first steps to improving outcomes.

If the activity of orienting workers to their new job sites is viewed as a process, the process may be standardized, with information available for how each step along the way is to be performed and for the outcomes that are expected from it. Staff members can be trained to carry out each step and to troubleshoot a step when it does not work as planned. Looking at work in terms of processes can bring organization to what otherwise feels like chaos. Processes such as job development, employer support, job analysis, self-management, individual planning, and so forth are more easily studied and improved when their components are understood and the factors—both internal and external—that affect the processes can be identified.

Understanding and standardizing a process that is known to work well will both

"An essential step in quality planning for service processes is . . . making the actual process highly visible. . . . A process that is not highly visible hides quality problems. When the actual process is highly visible, it is easy to trace the origins of poor quality." (Kacker, 1988, pp. 39–42)

improve performance outcomes related to that process and save time by preventing problems and mistakes. Therefore, in an organization that is committed to Continuous Quality Improvement, there is an emphasis on preventing rather than correcting problems, and there is an understanding that long-term quality improvements require substantial investment. Sending in a job coach in response to an employer complaint (e.g., to fix the filing errors of a supported employee or to rewash the dishes that were not washed clean) does nothing to improve the underlying sources of quality problems. Unfortunately, however, many rehabilitation and supported employment organizations concentrate their efforts more on fixing mistakes than on preventing them, never being able to catch up with the original problem.

Using a systematic approach to improving performance also provides guidance for taking action. Once the performance opportunity has been selected, the processes related to the performance outcome identified, and the root of the problem discovered, using a systematic approach leads organizations to plan interventions to improve performance and to evaluate the effects of those interventions. Based on the resulting data, the intervention can be adjusted to improve performance further or to become standardized so that others in the organization using the same process can also use the strategy. This approach is sometimes referred to as the Shewhart Cycle (e.g., Deming, 1986); the Japanese refer to it as the Deming Cycle (e.g., Imai, 1986).

In the Shewhart Cycle (Figure 2.1), also called Plan-Do-Check-Act or P-D-C-A, the goal is to implement changes smoothly and effectively. Based on data that led to a decision to make a change, the Shewhart Cycle is used to **Plan** the major steps of the change that will be made, who will be involved in carrying out each step, what training will be needed, what products or outcomes are expected, how the action will be evaluated, how problems will be handled, and so forth. In the **Do** portion of the

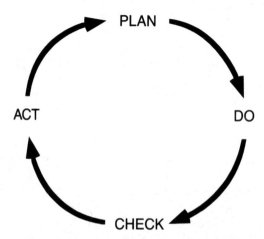

Figure 2.1.   The Shewhart cycle. (Based on Shewhart, W.A. [1939]. *Statistical method from the viewpoint of quality control.* Washington, DC: U.S. Department of Agriculture, p. 45.)

cycle, a pilot or test of the planned change is implemented. Next, one must **Check** the impact of the change by closely monitoring the pilot study, its progress, and its effectiveness based on the plan. **Act**, the last step of the Shewhart Cycle, involves looking for ways to refine the change and for the lessons that have been learned in making the change. From these, one determines what will be required to standardize the process improvements and to extend them to other places in the organization. The Shewhart Cycle provides a powerful tool for an organization to use to systematize its approach to improving performance, and to document the effects of the changes it implements. The Shewhart Cycle is the fundamental strategy applied in the philosophy of Continuous Quality Improvement.

MANAGERS AND QUALITY IMPROVEMENT

Implementing the philosophy of Continuous Quality Improvement requires that everyone in an organization, but particularly managers, take on a new way of thinking about customers, organizations, employees, and decision-making. Managers must take on a new role, letting go of previous roles that involved making the decisions and overseeing their subordinates. Instead, managers must take on a role of mentor and provide an example of adopting the new methods. By incorporating the principles in their own jobs, managers present a powerful model for other staff members to imitate. By teaching and encouraging their staff to use data for decision-making, to take a systematic approach to performance improvement, and to let go of their fears related to performance, managers can extend the power of Continuous Quality Improvement throughout the organization.

Implementing this philosophy requires that managers believe in teamwork and problem-solving. They must trust that, given the necessary tools, their staff *want* to do a good job. And, they must commit to having data, rather than emotions, drive the decisions that are made in their organizations. It means eliminating power as the basis for staff relationships. It means that managers must excel at planning, organizing, facilitating, and encouraging employees in order to implement quality improvement procedures in every part of the company, in addition to helping others achieve their quality improvement goals. Managers must begin to lead their companies to excellence with an unwavering commitment to quality improvement. For some managers, this shift in roles will be exceedingly difficult.

Continuous Quality Improvement requires full commitment, and, while any organization may begin to employ the tools of quality improvement today, fully embracing the approach will require strong leadership and an ongoing emphasis long into the future. The remainder of this book presents specific strategies and tools that may be employed to apply these principles, and examples drawn from agencies that are in the process of changeover from facility-based to community-based employment services.

REFERENCES

Barrows, L.K., Melvin, C.A., Ashmore, S.M., & Romstad, D. (1991, April). *Interdistrict collaboration for school-focused quality improvement.* Paper presented at the Fourth Annual Hunter Conference on Quality, Madison, WI.

Boothe, R. (1990). Who defines quality in service industries? *Quality Progress, 23*(2), 65–67.

Box, G.E.P., Joiner, L.W., Rohan, S., & Sensenbrenner, F.J. (1991). Quality in the community: One city's experience. *Quality Progress, 24*(5), 57–63.

Carr, D., & Littman, I. (1990). Quality in the federal government. *Quality Progress, 23*(9), 49–52.

Coate, L.E. (1990). *Implementing total quality management in a university setting.* Corvallis: Oregon State University.

Couper, D.C. (1990). Police department learns 10 hard quality lessons. *Quality Progress, 23*(10), 37–40.

Deming, W.E. (1982). *Quality, productivity, and competitive position.* Cambridge: Massachusetts Institute of Technology, Center for Advanced Engineering Study.

Deming, W.E. (1986). *Out of the crisis.* Cambridge: Massachusetts Institute of Technology, Center for Advanced Engineering Study.

Feigenbaum, A.V. (1983). *Total quality control* (3rd ed.). New York: McGraw-Hill.

Harper, B., & Harper, A. (1990). *Succeeding as a self-directed work team.* Croton-on-Hudson, NY: MW Corporation.

Holpp, L. (1989). 10 reasons why total quality is less than total. *Training, 26*(10), 93–103.

Holpp, L. (1990, March). Ten steps to total quality service. *Journal for Quality and Participation,* 92–96.

Imai, M. (1986). *Kaizen: The key to Japan's competitive success.* New York: McGraw-Hill.

Juran, J.M. (1986). A universal approach to managing for quality: The quality trilogy. *Quality Progress, 19*(8), 19–24.

Juran, J.M. (1989). *Juran on leadership for quality.* New York: The Free Press.

Kacker, R.N. (1988). Quality planning for service industries. *Quality Progress, 21*(8), 39–42.

Linkow, P. (1989). Is your culture ready for Total Quality? *Quality Progress, 22*(11), 69–71.

Lowe, T.A., & McBean, G.M. (1990). Honesty without fear. *Quality Progress, 22*(11), 30–34.

Mank, D.M., Oorthuys, J., Rhodes, L., Sandow, D., & Weyer, T. (1992). Accommodating workers with mental disabilities. *Training and Development Journal, 46*(1), 49–52.

Mizuno, S. (1988). *Company-wide total quality control.* Tokyo: Asian Productivity Organization.

Peters, T., & Austin, N. (1985). *A passion for excellence: The leadership of difference.* New York: Warner Books.

Rhodes, L., Sandow, D., Mank, D., Buckley, J., & Albin, J.M. (1991). Expanding the role of employers in supported employment. *Journal of The Association for Persons with Severe Handicaps, 16*(4), 213–217.

Rubenstein, S.P. (1991). The evolution of U.S. quality systems. *Quality Progress, 24*(5), 46–49.

Scholtes, P.R. (1988). *The team handbook: How to use teams to improve quality.* Madison: Joiner Associates, Inc.

Scholtes, P.R., & Hacquebord, H. (1987). *A practical approach to quality.* Madison: Joiner Associates, Inc.

Shewhart, W.A. (1939). *Statistical method from the viewpoint of quality control.* Washington, DC: U.S. Department of Agriculture.

Smith, F.W. (1990). Our human side of quality. *Quality Progress, 23*(10), 19–21.

Stratton, B. (1991). How Disneyland works. *Quality Progress, 24*(7), 17–30.

Walton, M. (1986). *The Deming management method.* New York: Dodd, Mead.

ADDITIONAL READINGS

Blanchard, K., & Johnson, S. (1982). *The one-minute manager.* New York: William Morrow & Co.

Carlzon, J. (1987). *Moments of truth.* Cambridge, MA: Ballinger Publishing.

Crosby, P. (1979). *Quality is free: The art of making quality certain.* New York: McGraw-Hill.

Deming, W.E. (1938). *Statistical adjustment of data.* New York: Dover.

Deming, W.E. (1975). On statistical aids toward economic production. *Interfaces, 5*(4), 1–15.

Gilbert, T.F. (1978). *Human competence: Engineering worthy performance.* New York: McGraw-Hill.

Hoernschemeyer, D. (1989). The four cornerstones of excellence. *Quality Progress, 22*(8), 37–39.

Ishikawa, K. (1976). *Guide to quality control.* Tokyo: Asian Productivity Organization.

Ishikawa, K. (1985). *What is total quality control? The Japanese way.* Englewood Cliffs, NJ: Prentice-Hall.

Joiner, B.L., & Scholtes, P.R. (1985). *Total quality leadership vs. management by control.* Madison : Joiner Associates.

Juran, J.M. (1988). *Juran on planning for quality.* New York: The Free Press.

Peters, T. (1987). *Thriving on chaos: Handbook for a management revolution.* New York: Harper & Row.

Peters, T.J., & Waterman, R.H. (1982). *In search of excellence: Lessons from America's best-run companies.* New York: Harper & Row.

Rhodes, L.E., Mank, D., Sandow, D., Buckley, J., & Albin, J. (1990). Supported employment implementation: Shifting from program monitoring to quality improvement. *Journal of Disability Policy Studies, 1*(2), 1–18.

Tribus, M. (1986). *Deming's redefinition of management.* Cambridge: Massachusetts Institute of Technology, Center for Advanced Engineering Study.

Zeleny, M. (1987). Management support systems: Towards integrated knowledge management. *Human Systems Management, 7*(2), 59–70.

Zemke, R. (1989). Employee orientation: A process, not a program. *Training, 26*(8), 33–38.

Chapter 3

Customers and Quality Improvement

Lessons for Rehabilitation and Supported Employment

Companies implementing Continuous Quality Improvement are obsessed with staying close to their customers. Through this obsession, companies strive to develop long-term partnerships with customers to promote business success. This customer obsession creates a customer-focused attitude that permeates the organization and underlies several components: 1) a knowledge of who the organization's current and potential customers are, 2) an emphasis on active listening to customers and pursuing their input, and 3) a responsiveness to customer needs. W. Edwards Deming (1986) insists that customers are the most important part of the production line. In organizations exploring quality improvement, the entire culture supports meeting the needs of the customer. These companies may be referred to as customer-driven.

This chapter highlights the concept of customer from the perspectives of industry and Continuous Quality Improvement, examines barriers that exist in rehabilitation and supported employment agencies to achieving an obsession with customers, and presents strategies—used successfully by companies implementing quality principles—that may be adopted by rehabilitation organizations to increase their customer focus.

WHO ARE THE CUSTOMERS?

Becoming customer-driven implies that an organization is clear about who its customers are. With a knowledge of its customers, a company may directly seek their input; respond to their needs; and even, perhaps, be able to anticipate their future wants. One complicating factor in developing a customer orientation in rehabilitation and supported employment, however, is that a clear picture of the customer is much more difficult to draw in human services than in private industry.

Customer as Defined by Industry and Quality Improvement

From an industry perspective a customer is, very simply, someone who purchases products or services. However, the resources that rehabilitation and supported employment service providers need to deliver services are often received from third-party funding agencies, which act as service purchasers. Yet, few service providers would identify third-party funding agencies as their primary customers. Instead, organizations usually consider service recipients, that is, the individuals receiving agency support to find and maintain jobs, as their primary customers.

> Industry's definition of a customer:
> A customer is someone who
> purchases products or services.

Employment service provider organizations often identify a second group of primary customers: employers and businesses providing work and jobs for the people receiving support services. Employers provide a clearer example of a customer in rehabilitation because employers may provide resources, such as financial compensation and work to be performed, to service provider organizations, as well as using their services to help locate and support employees with disabilities. This customer relationship is most clear in cases where the employer contracts with the rehabilitation organization to perform an agreed-upon amount of work. Facility-based rehabilitation programs have long understood the importance of satisfying the needs of this group of customers in order to stay in business.

Yet, even the role of employers as customers is somewhat muddled in supported employment. This is particularly true when individuals with disabilities are hired directly by the company and the rehabilitation organization's role is only to provide services to help the company successfully employ them. In such cases, the labor of the individuals with disabilities is purchased by the employer, in a direct employer-employee relationship. However, the services these employees receive from a supported employment organization are most often purchased by a third-party funder, such as the state vocational rehabilitation, mental health, or developmental disability agency, or some alternative source. From the standard industry standpoint, that third-party funder must be viewed as the customer, for that source is purchasing the support service, rather than the employer. Few instances currently exist of employers directly paying service provider organizations to support their efforts to employ individuals with severe disabilities. Yet, such a relationship would parallel that between a company and its "employee assistance program"—typically a contracted service to provide counseling, drug and alcohol programs, and other support services to its regular work force.

Continuous Quality Improvement offers a very different perspective on the definition of customer: A customer is whoever is "next in line" in a process to receive a product or service. This definition requires that the label of customer shift, based upon the immediate relationship between two parties. For example, a manufacturing firm's suppliers would be viewed as customers when the firm is giving them specifications for the firm's next order for parts. Once those parts are to be delivered, however, the manufacturing firm becomes the customer. Likewise, in the rehabilitation industry, a county funding agency would be the customer when it received a required report (a product) from a service provider agency, and the service provider would be the customer of the funding agency when it received a memorandum (another product) from that agency containing information on how to present that report.

> Continuous Quality Improvement's definition of a customer: A customer is whoever is next in line in a process.

This definition of customer also directs an organization that is undergoing a quality transformation to look within itself, for its employees must be viewed as customers as well. Employees are customers in that they are the recipients of an organization's policies, procedures, resources, and systems. Indeed, individual employees are customers of each other as they move through the work day providing or receiving products or services from other employees. This concept is most clear when applied to a manufacturing assembly line. In an assembly line, workers rely upon the assemblers before them to perform accurately and completely the assemblies assigned to their work stations. Thus, the second assembler in the line is a customer of the first, the third of the second, and so forth: Each is a customer who is next in line to receive the partially assembled product. Each is a customer who must receive a product that meets quality expectations in order to do his or her own job well. The same concept of customer as the person who is next in line may be applied equally well to rehabilitation and supported employment. The job coach who is receiving training (a service) from her supervisor is the supervisor's customer; the manager receiving the monthly income-expense statement (a product) is the bookkeeper's customer.

Understanding that employees are customers suggests improving individual relationships within organizations as a strategy to support accomplishment of the mission. With Continuous Quality Improvement's perspective that a customer is whoever is next in line, many employee interactions become customer interactions. When an executive director gives the draft of a report to an administrative assistant to be finalized for an upcoming board meeting, the manager must recognize that both the administrative assistant and the board members are the manager's customers. The notion of board members as customers of that report is easily understood: Any director wanting to keep his or her job will make sure the report includes the types of information that the report's customers—the board members—have requested, and in a format that will please them as well. A wise director requests and responds to feedback from the board as customers of the report. However, to increase effective performance, the director also should be asking the administrative assistant as a customer, "How can I make your job of putting together this report go more smoothly?", and be prepared to respond to that input.

The notion of employee-as-customer goes to the heart of quality improvement, defining a culture that is as supportive of its own employees as it is of its external customers. This concept is closely related to the fundamental principle, "Empower Employees To Work To Achieve the Mission," and will be revisited several times throughout this text. Taking on a "staff are customers, too" philosophy will help an organization make great strides toward empowering its staff to accomplish the mission. Treat-

> "Workers who feel relatively good about their jobs, their colleagues at work, and the company at large are more likely to join a never-ending pursuit of total quality." (Scholtes & Hacquebord, 1987, p. 21)

ing employees as customers is likely to have at least one important effect: Employees are likely to treat customers in ways similar to the way they themselves are treated.

Suppliers as Customers

Companies embracing Continuous Quality Improvement understand that developing strong relationships with their suppliers, as well as with their customers, will improve business. Indeed, these companies know that to be most effective they must extend the methods of the total quality approach to their supplier network. These companies select suppliers based on their ability to deliver quality products and services on time, rather than basing that decision on which supplier offers the lowest purchase price. As they implement their own quality transformations, the best companies work with fewer suppliers, developing long-term relationships in which a concern for mutual success is the overriding factor. These companies find that it is good business to work with suppliers who themselves are committed to quality improvement and, in many cases, help them to do so.

In quality improvement parlance, a supplier is someone who is "next *in front* in line." If a process is to work smoothly, the supplier (in front) must pass on to its customer (next in line) a product or service that meets the customer's quality needs and expectations. Thus, not only do many interactions between individuals or organizations involve customer interactions, they involve a supplier as well. And, as was discussed for the role of customer, the role of supplier also shifts based on the nature of the immediate interaction between the two. Thus, in manufacturing firms or in rehabilitation services, groups and individuals with whom an organization works may at one time be functioning as the organization's suppliers, and at another as its customers. In any case, the same objectives and strategies apply: Staying close to their suppliers will promote business success, just as staying close to their customers will. Thus, companies strive to develop long-term partnerships with customers and with suppliers. To do so with suppliers—just as with customers—they must understand who the organization's current and potential suppliers are and pursue their input. Open communication and feedback between a company and its suppliers, focused on improving the quality of their interaction, will make mutual success more likely.

Given the similarities between strategies for working with customers and strategies for working with suppliers, as well as the way in which the labels constantly shift based on the nature of the immediate interaction, it is not necessary continually to be concerned about separating the roles of customer and supplier. As is evident in Figure 3.1, suppliers to rehabilitation service providers *do* also fill the role of customer at one time or another. For the purposes of this text, therefore, suppliers will be viewed as simply a type of customer and will be referred to as suppliers only when the distinction is important.

Defining Customers in Rehabilitation and Supported Employment

Based on the perspectives of industry and Continuous Quality Improvement, therefore, customers in rehabilitation may come from several different groups. For most rehabilitation and supported employment service provider organizations, primary customers probably come from four major groups:

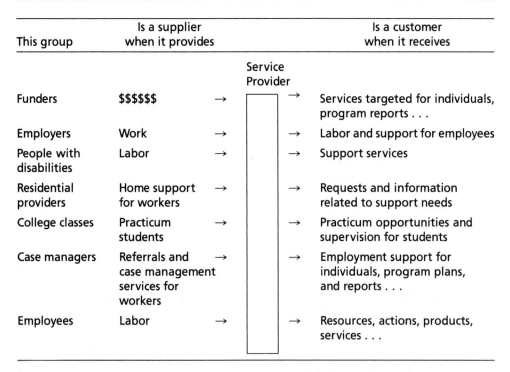

This group	Is a supplier when it provides			Is a customer when it receives
			Service Provider	
Funders	$$$$$$	→	→	Services targeted for individuals, program reports . . .
Employers	Work	→	→	Labor and support for employees
People with disabilities	Labor	→	→	Support services
Residential providers	Home support for workers	→	→	Requests and information related to support needs
College classes	Practicum students	→	→	Practicum opportunities and supervision for students
Case managers	Referrals and case management services for workers	→	→	Employment support for individuals, program plans, and reports . . .
Employees	Labor	→	→	Resources, actions, products, services . . .

Figure 3.1. Sample supplier and customer roles related to rehabilitation service providers.

1. The individuals with disabilities who are receiving support services
2. The public and private sector firms providing jobs or contracts
3. The government agencies funding and regulating services
4. The staff members of the organization itself

These are the groups most directly involved in purchasing or receiving the greatest part of the products or services of the organization.

Other customers also may be identified, however, and may be referred to as secondary customers if their relationship is not related as directly to the majority of the organization's products and services. For example, individuals and organizations that are providing residential services to the supported employees, or the family members and advocates for the individuals receiving employment services, may be viewed as customers—or suppliers (earlier, rather than later in line)—in their respective relationships with the organization. Look at residential providers as an example. Employment providers clearly rely upon residential providers for services that assist in supporting employment success. Residential providers may have an effect on the worker's appearance, work attendance, travel to and from work, participation in a full social life outside work, and so forth. Indeed, residential providers are the recipients of many requests from employment providers to help with issues such as appearance, attendance, and transportation. Interacting with residential providers as customers or suppliers brings a new perspective to what often are problematic relations.

This rough definition of secondary customer may be applied to other individuals or organizations: 1) the United Way may provide a small percentage of the operating capital based on completion of a proposal (a product) and other requirements,

POSSIBLE CUSTOMERS OF AN EMPLOYMENT SERVICE PROVIDER

Primary customers

- Individuals with disabilities receiving support services
- Funding agencies and their staffs
- Businesses (including the employer and employees) providing work or jobs
- Employees of the employment service provider

Secondary customers

- Residential support providers of the individuals receiving services
- Family members and advocates of the individuals receiving services
- Alternative funding sources, such as United Way
- College classes providing practicum students
- Organizations providing volunteers

and thus be viewed as a secondary customer (or supplier); or 2) a local college may provide practicum students used by the agency, based on supervisory support and practicum opportunities provided by the agency (a service).

Different types of rehabilitation and supported employment organizations, offering different types of services and products, would have different sets of customer groups. Facility-based service providers likely would define their customer groups somewhat differently than would organizations that provide only supported employment services. Indeed, because the role of customer is based on the actual relationship with an organization, each organization should define its own *specific* customer list.

State funding and regulatory agencies involved in rehabilitation and supported employment services—such as vocational rehabilitation, mental health, or developmental disability agencies—would have a different set of primary and secondary customers than would service provider agencies. For example, they might define as their customers the higher-level, umbrella agency (e.g., the state's department of human resources); specific committees of the state legislature; their service provider vendors; relevant federal funding and regulatory agencies; and their employees. In terms of quality improvement, individuals with disabilities might not be considered customers of the state agency unless the agency were also providing direct support services, or unless the agency could clearly define what other products and services it was providing to them. However, it is easy to see that by doing a better job of meeting the needs of their own direct customers, they will have a great impact on the quality of services received by the individuals with disabilities they wish to support.

It is most useful to be very specific in defining customers. For example, a service provider's customers are not *all* individuals with disabilities; rather, they are the specific individuals with disabilities to whom they are providing services. Likewise, its employer-customers are not the general business community; rather, they are the specific businesses (and the people who work within those businesses) who are currently using, or are likely to use, the organization's support services. Organizations that refer to customers in vague, general terms do not clearly understand who their customers are and, thus, can neither seek their input nor develop long-term relationships with them. An organization cannot be customer-driven unless it first knows very clearly who its specific customers are.

DELIGHTING THE CUSTOMER

Customers are important to an organization because they provide the resources it needs to stay in business, and the market for the goods and services the organization produces. However, customers also are important because they can give the organization valuable information on how to *improve* its goods and services, or the processes used to produce those goods and services. Customers define quality.

Customer Definitions of Quality

Customers most likely will continue to purchase those things that meet or exceed their definitions of quality. Understanding its customers' definitions of quality leads an organization to do a better job of meeting the customers' needs. Companies that have taken on the philosophy and methods of Continuous Quality Improvement work hard to develop open channels of communication with customers, to understand customer definitions of quality, and to develop customer loyalty. Companies consistently look for ways to meet their customers' expectations. More than that, however, they look for ways to *delight* their customers, providing everything their customers ask for and more.

Quality experts believe that, if an organization, whether it is a manufacturer of copier machines or a rehabilitation agency, is going to stay in business, be financially stable or profitable, and achieve its mission of continuous improvement, then it must recognize that *the quality it seeks must be defined by its customers* (e.g., Deming, 1986; Feigenbaum, 1983; Scholtes, 1988; Scholtes & Hacquebord, 1987). In a company that manufactures copier machines, it is easy to see how this applies. Customers want a copier that does not break down, makes clear copies, is fast and easy to use, offers a variety of features, and is reasonably priced. The company that is able to manufacture copiers that meet and exceed these customer expectations, as well as to anticipate their customers' future desires, will sell the most copiers. In the world of business, customers usually have a choice. If they take a copier from Company A and over the years are not happy with the product or service provided, they are free to take their next copier from Company B or C. One of the barriers to a quality transformation in rehabilitation and supported employment services is that this free market choice often is not available to customers. Only larger communities have more than one employment service provider. Even then, in too many communities the choice is narrowed down quickly to which provider has an available service slot or which provider agrees to take on another individual needing services. Thus, individuals with disabilities and funders often have no choice. Without the demands of such a market, where customers are free to go to another supplier if their definitions of quality are not met, service provider agencies become more focused on business transactions than on understanding and meeting their customers' expectations.

DEFINING YOUR ORGANIZATION'S CUSTOMERS

Because the role of customer is based on the relationship with an organization, each organization must define its own specific list of customers. Taking time with a group of board members, managers, or staff members to define your organization's customers is a good first step for developing their customer awareness and becoming customer-driven. Here are some suggestions for working with a group to define your organization's customers:

1. Discuss the definition of customer from an industry perspective. Use a strict definition of customer as "someone who buys and receives products or services."
   A. Given that definition, ask staff members to list who actually buys products and services from your organization. Ask them to be very specific. For contracted work, for example, do not allow them to list "businesses," but ask them to list the specific businesses that are paying for and receiving goods or services.
   B. If possible, list the actual individuals within those businesses who provide the orders and receive the goods and services.
   C. Note that by this definition, unless individuals are paying directly for the services they receive, they might not be considered customers.
2. Ask the group to expand upon the industry's definition of customer. What are other characteristics of a customer (e.g., someone who has future wants and needs)? Given this expanded definition, ask the group to expand the customer list. It may be useful also to introduce the definition of supplier and use the format in the chart in Figure 3.1 showing sample supplier and customer roles. Use this strategy if the group is confusing—or confused about—the functions of supplier and customer.
   A. Again, ask them to be very specific, listing individuals within categories or groups.
   B. Ask them to identify for each customer the goods or services that are designed for and distributed to them by your organization. Be careful not to mix quality standards (e.g., customer expectations regarding reliability or accuracy) with actual products or services.
   C. You may wish to discuss the distinction between primary and secondary customers, as presented in this text, if it is useful in helping the group to focus on a few types of customers who represent those most significant to the primary activity of the business. However, do not force this distinction if it is not needed or useful.
3. Present the definition of customer from the perspective of Continuous Quality Improvement: "whoever is next in line in a process." Discuss how that fits with the customer list already generated. Invite the group to expand the customer list given this definition.
   A. The group may need assistance and examples to see themselves and other employees of the organization as customers.
   B. Ask the group to consider a specific part or parts of the organization, and then identify that group's customers and the products or services it provides to those customers. For example, who are the customers of the production facility, the front office staff, the top managers, the van drivers?

(continued)

DEFINING YOUR ORGANIZATION'S CUSTOMERS (*continued*)

    C.   Discuss how this definition of customer supports becoming customer-driven and assists in adoption of an emphasis on continuous improvement.

4.   In a related activity, it may be useful to develop an exhaustive list of the goods and services that are generated by your organization. Include everything from data sheets to reports, purchase orders to invoices, and so forth. Once the list is compiled, ask the group to identify the customers for each item. Are there products or services in the original list that have no customers? Has the group identified a full list of products or services for each of the customer groups defined above?

5.   Once the group has settled upon a list of types of customers (e.g., individuals receiving support services, employers offering jobs, funders purchasing support services, and the employees of the organization), use this list consistently whenever the need to discuss customers arises. For example, a plan to solicit customer feedback should identify which customer group feedback will be solicited from or offer strategies for soliciting feedback from all customer groups.

Diverse Customer Definitions of Quality

That successful copier manufacturing company also understands that its machines are used by a variety of customers, for example, small and large offices, print shops, and business service centers, to name a few. Each customer is likely to have a different perspective on quality. Each may have different requirements for size, speed, cost, and features. The manufacturer, therefore, designs different copiers to meet these needs and is able to sell even more.

Each of the defined customer groups served by rehabilitation and supported employment service providers has a very different customer perspective; indeed, definitions of quality may differ widely *within* each group, as well. The challenge is to address these different perspectives in a way that will delight each of the customers. Understanding the different perspectives requires that an organization specifically identify its customers, and the products or services each is receiving. As indicated above, broad customer categories such as "the business community" or "all people with disabilities" are not useful. The more specifically and clearly an organization is able to define its customers, and the specific products or services it provides to them, the more accurately it will be able to identify how those customers define quality.

Leading Customers into the Future

Organizations seeking excellence do far more than simply meet their customers' expectations. They create products and services that will lead their customers into the future. Although customers may always be right, customers are not always on the edge of innovation. Express mail, color copiers, facsimile machines, and, a century ago, even telephones are all examples of products or services developed by companies or individuals that created a market demand, that created customer expecta-

In *A Passion for Excellence*, Tom Peters and Nancy Austin present an example of a grocery store in which, during a customer focus group meeting, one customer complained that the store did not sell "fresh fish." The store's management knew they sold fresh fish, but, by listening to the customer, they learned an important lesson. They discovered that the customer defined "fresh fish" as fish that is on ice in a refrigeration case, rather than wrapped in plastic, in supermarket packaging. As a result, the store added a "fresh fish" counter with a refrigeration case and doubled its fish sales, with no reduction in the sales of prepackaged fish (Peters & Austin, 1985).

tions—that led their customers into the future. The development of these products and services may have been the result of trying to meet the needs of a very few of their customers, for example, customers who needed faster methods of communicating information. However, most offices in the 1950s and 1960s relied on carbon paper, typewriters, and mimeographs, and had not even conceived of such things as facsimile machines. The developers of facsimile machines not only delighted their customers who wanted faster methods of communicating written information, they also led the majority of their customers into the future.

Changeover from facility-based to supported employment services is a reflection of being responsive to customers, including leading some customers into the future. The federal government, which provides funds for state programs and special projects, has defined supported employment as a valued service for individuals with severe disabilities. Similarly, most states have applied for and received federal grants for the purpose of increasing the number and range of supported employment opportunities available to their residents with various disabilities. These federal and state initiatives have grown from the concerns of individuals receiving services; of their families, advocates, and friends; and of involved professionals. The concerns are related to dissatisfaction with the lack of employment outcomes in the previously existing service system, dissatisfaction with the enforced segregation of facility-based services, and so forth.

In developing supported employment initiatives, the federal government and the states were being responsive to subgroups of *their* customers. Facility-based rehabilitation organizations that are changing their way of operating to focusing on supporting individuals in jobs in community settings are listening to the input they are receiving from some of their customers, as well. Through this shift, rehabilitation organizations will lead some of their customers into the future. These are the customers who had not yet envisioned the benefits of full lives in integrated settings for people with severe disabilities, and who had grown accustomed to the presumed security of a sheltered setting. Leading these customers into the future will require rehabilitation organizations to use carefully planned strategies to introduce them to the new service, illustrate its benefits, and demonstrate how supported employment will better meet their wants and needs.

BECOMING A CUSTOMER-DRIVEN ORGANIZATION

Most rehabilitation organizations face several barriers to becoming customer-driven, achieving a quality transformation, and pursuing changeover to supported employment. Some of these have already been discussed: a lack of clarity about who the customers are; the history of a lack of free-market choice by customers; conflicting feedback from customers; and the presence of some customers who have not come to understand the benefits of integrated employment strategies. However, one of the most significant barriers to becoming customer-driven is an organizational culture in which employees and managers alike exhibit negative attitudes about one or more of the organization's customer groups.

Employee Roles and Attitudes Toward Customers

What does a customer obsession mean if you are the director of an activity center for 60 people that has been operating in a timber town in a rural county for 35 years, and you want to changeover the organization to supported employment? What does a customer obsession mean if you are an employment training specialist and your job is to support three or four people who are working in different departments of a large electronics company? Quality improvement experts say that, to become customer-driven, each person in an organization, whether the top manager, the receptionist, a job coach, or a rehabilitation specialist, must be clear about who his or her customers are, how those customers define quality, and how he or she, as an employee, can exceed those customer expectations. Each staff person must clearly understand his or her role in achieving quality and look for new and better ways to delight the customers. Each employee must take responsibility for improving products, processes, and services, regardless of specific job descriptions and assigned duties, and without assigning blame to others. Unfortunately, such a pervasive customer obsession is seldom observed in rehabilitation organizations, supported employment agencies, or the public sector.

In too many states and communities, rehabilitation and supported employment agencies have developed an adversarial relationship with one or more of their primary customer groups. And this adversarial relationship stands in the way of using customer definitions to improve quality. Certainly, many service provider organizations have an inadequate relationship with the government agencies responsible for funding and for ensuring quality in programs. This may be true for any of a variety of reasons, such as a history of the funder continually requiring more of the provider without increasing funding levels; a record of lack of follow-through on commitments made by the funder; experience with external evaluations conducted by the funder's regulatory or certification staff that were not helpful in solving provider problems; or simply that it is easy to use the funder-as-bad-guy attitude as a way to create a team spirit: "It's us against them so let's stick together." Yet, if an obsession with delighting customers is one of the basic tenets proposed by quality experts, such attitudes on the part of rehabilitation and supported employment agencies place significant barriers in the road to quality improvement.

Even employer-as-customer definitions of quality are often viewed as petty nuisances. I once visited a supported employment job site in a company where cans and bottles were sorted, crushed, and then sold as scrap. The production manager of that company had just finished explaining one reason for their quality requirements to me: If plastic bottles were mixed with the cans, the entire semi-trailer truck load of crushed cans could be rejected by the scrap dealer at a loss of thousands of dollars for the recycler. I then observed the supported employee working on the final quality control point on the conveyer belt to the can crusher, the position where any remaining plastic bottles had to be removed. The worker did not watch the cans as they moved by and paid attention only when something became stuck, making a noise. There was no question that plastic bottles could have moved past him. When I went over to talk with the job coach (who was an employee of the supported employment agency) and asked a general question about the customer's required quality levels and the employee's performance, she said, "Can you imagine? They expect him to have 100% quality, and all they do here is recycle cans!" I was appalled at the lack of concern for the customer's definition of quality. Evidently, so was the employer. For a variety of reasons, shortly after that visit, the placement was lost.

> "Help employees everywhere to see 'customers' as real living, breathing, human beings who actually purchase, use and care about the product." (Scholtes & Hacquebord, 1987, p. 22)

Similar stories could be recounted about adversarial relationships or customers-as-nuisances with respect to other primary and secondary customer groups of rehabilitation service providers. Most agencies could write a book listing the complaints by employees about the individuals with disabilities whom they support; the arguments that have occurred between residential support staff members or advocates and their own staff; and the periods of dissension between "rehab" and production within the staff of the rehabilitation agency itself. But the negative stories that persist about customers work against developing the customer orientation needed to achieve a quality transformation.

In rehabilitation and supported employment, a culture that values customers must replace one that permits or even encourages employees to complain about them. Staff members at all levels of the organization must come to understand the importance of customers, as well as their own roles in achieving customer satisfaction. Staff members must learn to listen to customers, in order to understand their customers' definitions of quality. Their goal should be to exceed the expectations of the organization's customers, not merely to meet them. Employees should give customers reason to boast about how much they benefit from what the organization does for them. This achievement will require a basic change in the culture of most organizations.

Strategies for Becoming Customer-Driven

The literature of quality improvement is replete with examples of how companies ensure that a focus on customers pervades their organizations. Indeed, some quality improvement experts even reject the notion of markets in favor of referring to customers, for customers are imagined by their employees as real people, and markets are seen as abstract numbers and charts. The best companies use a variety of strategies to embed a customer-focus in their organizations. Several of these, adapted from *A Passion for Excellence* (Peters & Austin, 1985) and other sources, are listed below. Keep in mind your organization's various customer groups as you consider this list. Do not try to implement all of these strategies at once; but, as you add them one by one, you will notice a significant change in the organization toward becoming customer-driven.

1.   *Implement an organizational philosophy about customers.*   Develop a statement that defines the organization's customers and how the organization perceives and treats its customers. It may be part of the organization's mission and values statement, or a statement that stands alone. (See Chapter 2 for an example.)

Provide copies of it to all employees. Use it as part of the orientation package for new employees. Reinforce it at every opportunity.

2. *Watch your language.*   Use a language of respect when speaking about, or interacting with customers. Stop participating in negative storytelling about customers. Let employees know that negative attitudes toward customers will no longer be tolerated.

3. *Communicate about customers often.*   Use every opportunity with employees to communicate about customers. Include feature stories about working with customers in newsletters and annual reports. Report about joint problem-solving task forces, and discuss customer feedback at staff meetings. Try to tie every significant step that the organization takes to how it will affect the customers.

4. *Provide training to all employees about customers.*   All employees—receptionists, bookkeepers, supervisors, trainers, and so forth—need training in understanding who the organization's customers are, the importance of the various customer groups to the organization, how to interact with them, and how to respond to customer feedback and complaints. Do not assume that all employees understand about customers. Give the most training to employees with the greatest interaction with customers, but train everyone. The activity presented above, "Defining Your Organization's Customers," may be useful during this training to help employees gain better understanding about customers.

5. *Celebrate good examples of a customer focus.*   Give attention to employees who do a good job of being customer-driven. Talk about specific examples in newsletters and staff meetings. Hold mini-parties as customer service celebrations. Visibly reward the staff members who do it best.

6. *Arrange visits with customers.*   When your organization's customers include other organizations (e.g., the state or county funder or residential support providers), do everything you can to bring the staffs of the two organizations together. Arrange for staff members from all levels of your organization to visit theirs, and vice versa.

7. *Make it a rule to make only achievable promises to customers.*   Employees must understand that it does a disservice to customers for employees to make promises

One rehabilitation agency has been carrying out a joint project to improve relationships with a local residential provider. The two organizations have traded a few staff members for short periods, traveled together and shared rooms at conferences, formed joint problem-solving groups, shared training—in short, done everything they could to bring their two staffs together. The result has been remarkable. Instead of the typical adversarial relationship between home and work providers, communication channels have been opened, staff members from each organization understand the others' needs better, and they have been able to work together to share resources and solve mutual problems. The people who are really benefiting from this exchange, however, are not only the two staffs, but also the people with disabilities whom they support. Because the two organizations are working together rather than complaining about each other, the typical problems between supported employment and home providers (e.g., transportation and work hours) have been solved in much better ways.

that they are not absolutely sure they can keep. Customers must be able to count on what your organization says it can deliver and when. Whether it is submitting a report for the funder or delivering a box of widgets, be sure that staff members make only achievable promises. And then be sure that all promises to customers are kept.

8. *Measure customer satisfaction often.* To improve their performance in the eyes of their customers, organizations must collect reliable information on what various types of customers need and want from the company's products or services. Rehabilitation and supported employment organizations probably have done best at viewing persons with disabilities as customers of their services, and yet our collective ability and experience in soliciting input from this customer group are lacking as well. Developing a customer obsession requires that organizations actively and regularly pursue customer input at all levels. Therefore, staff and board members alike must become expert at listening to customers when they give input, asking questions of customers to solicit that input, and using the input to improve their personal or organizational performance from the customer's perspective. Make it a regular habit to solicit customer feedback. Teach board and staff members to use all direct customer interactions as an opportunity to solicit feedback on how they or the organization is doing. The following section of this chapter offers suggestions on specific strategies for soliciting customer input.

9. *Use a variety of different methods to solicit customer input.* Do not rely on any one method for soliciting customer feedback. Although face-to-face interactions are great, also use written or telephone methods as well.

10. *Make sure that each function or department also measures customer satisfaction.* Help the different parts of your organization to take a customer focus in the things that they do. Begin by defining that department's customers and then measuring their satisfaction. Start with the management team. Once they are consis-

A manufacturing firm in the Northwest agreed to hire an individual with severe disabilities. When the area production supervisor and a human resource management staff person were asked by the support organization, "How will we all know when we have achieved providing you with a successful employee?", their answers were simple and to the point:

"Good employees here get along with co-workers and are real producers . . . . We don't want to get involved in doing 'make-work.' We need employees who will be at work reliably, who work at a rate that won't interfere with production schedules, and who make good parts."

"What do you mean when you say 'get along with co-workers'?"

"We want them to be like any other employee; they don't need to be friends with everyone, but they should be friendly and try to get to know other workers. We like all of our employees to join a quality circle team, too. They don't have to, but it shows they can get along with others and care about the company."

These answers gave the support organization clear information on this customer's definition of quality in supported employment—a definition that was based on the outcomes of the service.

tently measuring and responding to their customers' input (including that of their employees), you may begin to expand to other areas of the organization.

11. *Involve all employees with customers.*   Make sure that all employees have an opportunity to interact directly with customers on a regular basis. Have everyone participate in gathering and analyzing customer feedback about the organization's performance. Give employees from all levels and parts of your organization a chance to see how your products or services work for the customer. Make sure that everyone in the organization understands what the customer wants and also understands his or her personal role in delighting customers.

12. *Make sure that all managers work shifts of direct contact with customers on a regular basis.*   Tom Peters and Nancy Austin (1985) recommend that managers work full shifts of customer contact for at least 1 week per quarter. This makes sure that managers directly experience how the organization's systems are working for the various customer groups, directly receive their feedback, and see clearly what it is like to perform their employees' jobs. Managers must stay close to customers in order to lead a customer-driven organization.

13. *Establish joint problem-solving task forces with major customers.*   A good way to improve relationships with a major customer is to work with the customer in solving mutual problems. Sharing resources and expertise, staff members from each organization come to know each other better, understand the pressures each is under, and arrive at solutions satisfactory to both.

14. *Recognize customer complaints as opportunities.*   To become customer-driven, organizations must learn to treat customer complaints as opportunities to receive information about how to improve performance, rather than problems to be suppressed as soon as possible. Although it is difficult to listen to negative feedback, it is an important source of improvement ideas. To ensure exposure to complaints, when soliciting input, include customers you know are disgruntled with your service, as well as those who are happy with it. Teach staff to look for the opportunities in what they say. Employees need to understand that it is the customer's perception that counts. Support employees for responding right away to a complaint, without trying to blame someone else for the problem. Make sure that information about complaints received is given to everyone in the organization, and then discuss the improvement opportunities they represent. After a problem with a customer has been handled, communicate with him or her to learn whether the improvement is satisfactory.

15. *Help staff to understand that customers are partners.*   Employees must come to view customers as partners in the organization's success rather than its adversaries or nuisances in the way of doing business. Treat customers as partners yourself, and staff likely will follow your lead.

16. *Question everything you do.*   Make it a habit continually to question everything you do for customers—both internally and externally. Consider how you can make the product or service work better for them. Continually question whether the organization or you as an individual are doing the right things. Avoid ruts at all cost. Encourage employees throughout the organization actively to look for ways to improve performance.

Quality experts often talk about "making the customer come alive" for employees in all parts of the organization. Employees must come to understand that customers are real people who experience pressures and demands—who, in many cases, must meet the needs of their own customers. In addition, it is important for employees to recognize their own individual roles in satisfying customers for the organization.

Soliciting Customer Input

Your customers should boast about how much they benefit from what you do for them. To achieve this goal, you must collect reliable information on what they need and want from your products or services. In doing so, you will find out whether your services and processes are on target and gain valuable information on how to improve them. Begin by focusing internally: on products, services, and employees-as-customers. Doing so will give everyone a chance to practice soliciting input, as well as assist in improving internal operations before increasing the demands and expectations of external customers.

Identify Customers   Clearly identify specific customers and the products or services that are delivered to them. It might be helpful to carry out the activity presented previously, "Defining Your Organization's Customers." Who are the customers of different parts of your organization? What *individuals* in other organizations actually receive the products or services? Speculate about what each customer is likely to say about the organization's or department's services. What do you think you will find out about their needs? Comparing your individual guesses with what you learn is a good way to assess how well you know your customers.

Decide from Which Customers To Collect Information   Plan how the organization will actually gather information. From which customers will you seek information? From which potential customers? It is important to consider each group separately, and even to consider specific representatives of each group separately. For example, the head of a state's developmental disability services agency is likely to give different input than a county staff person who is responsible for monitoring that agency's contracts for services. But, both have valuable perspectives that will assist an organization in defining quality. Try to select individuals from different parts of customer organizations: a case manager and the contracts officer from the county's developmental disability office; a program manager and a direct care staff person from a residential support provider. Select individuals who are visionary, who are opinion leaders, or who are pivotal to the success of your organization. Be sure to include individuals who are dissatisfied with your organization, as well as those who are happy with it.

Plan the Questions To Be Asked   A rehabilitation or supported employment agency needs to know how its customers view its product or service. What accomplishments and features of the service are important to them? What are their expectations? How well has your organization been meeting those? What else would they like? How do they use your product or service? What are *their* customers' expectations of them? What problems do customers have with the product or service? How can your organization determine whether it is meeting the customers' expectations? How easy is it to do business with your organization? How can you make it easier? Try to find out about how the customers perceive their interactions with individuals from your organization, not only how they perceive the quality of the product or service itself. In developing the list of questions, consider what kinds of information you need from customers to help you take action to improve the product or service.

Plan How the Information Will Be Collected   What manner will you provide for the customers to tell you what they need? How will the information be collected?

Many methods are possible. Do not rely solely on formal, written customer surveys; take advantage of informal face-to-face interactions as well. For major customer groups, you might form an ongoing "customer focus group," inviting representatives to meet with a few employees intensively on a regular basis to discuss how things are working. Try individual face-to-face or telephone interviews, either following a predetermined set of questions, or asking a few opening questions and then following the customer's lead from there. Use open-ended how, what, and why questions to the greatest extent possible rather than simply yes/no or forced multiple choice questions. If you are concerned that customers are not telling you how they really feel, consider hiring a consultant on occasion to conduct the interviews.

Consider how the results and feedback received will be summarized and analyzed. Determine what format will be useful for collecting the information that might facilitate summary and analysis during or after data collection. Chapter 10, on quality improvement tools, offers several formats that may be very useful in collecting, summarizing, and analyzing information from customers.

Try to involve all employees in receiving customer feedback. Consider how to ensure that board members, managers, supervisors, counselors, direct service staff, and support staff receive direct information from customers. Directly connecting individuals at all levels of an organization to customer input is one very effective strategy for creating an obsession with customers that permeates the organization. Train employees in allowing customers to speak first and in "naive listening," so that they hear what the customer is saying unfettered by their own biases. Employees must learn to treat the customer's view as more important than their own. Train all members of your organization to view every interaction with a customer as an opportunity to gain information on that individual's definition of quality, as well as an opportunity to gather feedback on how well the organization is doing in meeting that customer's expectations. Quality improvement experts view all direct interactions with customers as "moments of truth," when the success of the organization is at stake.

Take Action on the Customer Input that Is Received   If your organization solicits feedback from customers, it is important to take action on that feedback and to let customers know what will happen as a result of their input. How will the actions taken as a result of the feedback be communicated to the customers who provided it? Giving information back to customers will help ensure their continued willingness to provide feedback, as well as demonstrating that your organization is responsive to their concerns.

Report the results of the feedback surveys to everyone in your organization. Make sure that everyone understands what the customers are saying about performance. Use staff meetings to discuss the customer feedback and to strategize possible actions. Implement the simple changes right away. Form quality improvement groups to work on more complex problems. Help all staff members to understand their personal roles in responding to the customer feedback and in achieving customer satisfaction.

Finally, be sure to evaluate the process of soliciting and analyzing customer input that was used. How can it be improved the next time? Try to involve everyone who participated in soliciting customer feedback in evaluating and improving the process. In doing this, you will be demonstrating the Shewhart Cycle (see Chapter 2)—Planning, Doing, Checking, and Acting—in improving the process of soliciting feedback from customers.

Deal with Conflicting Feedback   With multiple customers, like those in supported employment, anticipate receiving conflicting information on quality features from different customer groups. Which of these is most important? Where is a reasonable balance between them? There is no single answer. In some cases, an organization may not encounter differing definitions of quality: Remember that a major problem for one customer is likely to be a major problem for others. Meeting the special needs of one customer group does not mean that an organization necessarily must stop providing a service that meets the needs of another. Instead, meeting a customer's needs may lead to an expansion in the products or services that the organization offers to its customers.

Some Words of Caution

Begin developing a customer focus in your organization with a focus on employees-as-customers. Use the staff's own experiences as customers in your organization to begin to develop a customer orientation. Practice the recommendations for soliciting customer input with employees as customers before moving to external customers. It is important that you do not attempt to solicit input from external customers until the organization is prepared to deal with it. Customers will learn that your organization does not care about their input, if they see no response to it. Perhaps even more important, however, is that your employees will feel frustrated and abused if they must listen to negative input from customers when the organizational culture and systems are not in place to help them deal with doing so. Refer to Chapter 4 for information on changing the organizational culture, Chapters 6 and 11 for information on supporting staff performance, and Section III for quality improvement methods and tools for strategies that should be implemented long before you begin actively and intensively to seek the input of external customers. This chapter appears in Part I of this book because it presents a fundamental concept of Continuous Quality Improvement. However, to be fair to your employees, do not try to implement its recommendations fully until your organization is well along in its quality transformation.

REFERENCES

Deming, W.E. (1986). *Out of the crisis.* Cambridge: Massachusetts Institute of Technology, Center for Advanced Engineering Study.
Feigenbaum, A.V. (1983). *Total quality control.* New York: McGraw-Hill.
Juran, J.M. (1989). *Juran on leadership for quality.* New York: Free Press.
Peters, T., & Austin, N. (1985). *A passion for excellence: The leadership difference.* New York: Warner Books.
Scholtes, P.R. (1988). *The team handbook: How to use teams to improve quality.* Madison: Joiner Associates, Inc.
Scholtes, P.R., & Hacquebord, H. (1987). *A practical approach to quality.* Madison: Joiner Associates, Inc.

ADDITIONAL READINGS

Boothe, R. (1990). Who defines quality in service industries? *Quality Progress, 23*(2), 65–67.
Brache, A.P., & Rummler, G.A. (1988). The three levels of quality. *Quality Progress, 21*(10), 46–51.

Crom, S.E. (1990). Total quality and customer value; Part 2: The 10 steps in conducting a Customer Value Analysis. *P&IM Review with APICS News, 10*(10), 32, 36.

Crom, S.E. (1990). Total quality and customer value; Part 3: Shure Brothers, Inc.—A case study in conducting a Customer Value Analysis. *P&IM Review with APICS News, 10*(11), 38.

Patterson, J.W., & Engelkemeyer, S. (1989). A company cannot live by its quality alone. *Quality Progress, 22*(8), 25–27.

Zemke, R. (1989). Putting the service back into public service. *Training, 26*(11), 42–49.

CHANGEOVER FROM FACILITY-BASED TO COMMUNITY-BASED EMPLOYMENT SERVICES

APPLICATIONS OF QUALITY IMPROVEMENT STRATEGIES

Part II of this book builds upon the fundamental principles of Continuous Quality Improvement discussed in Chapters 2 and 3. In addition, Part II introduces some of the basic tools of the approach within the context of changeover to supported employment. The chapters in this Part establish the foundation for the instrument titled *Self-Assessment Guide for Changeover to Supported Employment*. This guide is designed primarily for use by facility-based service providers seeking to changeover at least a part of their services to supported employment. This change has been referred to as "conversion" by many rehabilitation professionals. However, the term "changeover" has been chosen for use in this text.

Chapter 4 begins Part II with a discussion of changeover and the organizational factors affecting change to supported employment. This chapter also offers perspectives on how the principles of Continuous Quality Improvement apply to the issue of changeover from facility-based services to supported employment. Chapter 5 presents troubleshooting, a strategy commonly used in industry settings to localize the root causes of problems. It offers a valuable method for use by human service organizations, whether or not they are undergoing changeover to supported employment.

Chapter 6 introduces the Performance Engineering Matrix for analyzing problems related to performance of an individual staff person or group, and identifying cost-effective solutions to those problems. The Performance Engineering Matrix emphasizes that most performance problems are the result of issues in the systems in which staff members work, rather than the result of deficits in the staff persons themselves. Chapter 7 presents the instrument, *Self-Assessment Guide for Changeover to Supported Employment*, along with strategies for implementing it in an organization making planning decisions related to changeover.

Both troubleshooting and the Performance Engineering Matrix are quality improvement strategies and may be applied to many situations unrelated to changeover or to supported employment. However, the techniques are introduced here within the context of changeover. Later chapters of this book present other examples of applications for troubleshooting and for the Performance Engineering Matrix, as well as other tools of Continuous Quality Improvement.

While Part II specifically addresses the issues and processes related to changeover from facility-based rehabilitation services to community-based supported employment services, its principles and methods may be applied in other arenas. Changeover could be used to refer to any significant modification in the direction, structures, culture, or methods of any organization. Such changes could be designed for a state vocational rehabilitation agency, a local vocational rehabilitation branch office, a community mental health program, or a county volunteer association. In any case, many of the principles and tools offered in Part II may be adapted for use whenever substantial changes are required in the fabric of an organization.

Chapter 4

Changeover to Supported Employment

Challenges and Strategies

"People don't resist change, they resist *being* changed." (Scholtes & Hacquebord, 1987, p. 10)

In the context of this book, changeover is the process through which a facility-based vocational program restructures some or all of its resources and methods to implement a community-based employment program that ensures ongoing support for individuals with severe disabilities. This process poses great challenges. However, if an organization understands and addresses those challenges, changeover can be successful. Part II of this book uses changeover as an example to demonstrate how Continuous Quality Improvement offers an approach to managing massive organizational change.

THE CHALLENGE OF CHANGEOVER TO SUPPORTED EMPLOYMENT

Running a community-based employment program is very different from running a facility-based one. Each program is operated on different assumptions and values, requires different staff filling different types of roles, and is challenged by different issues.

Differences in Assumptions, Beliefs, and Values

Supported employment programs are based on the assumption that providing support in natural environments will result in immediate and desirable personal and employment-related gains. Those who promote supported employment programs believe, for example, that every individual can work in a community job given the

This chapter incorporates material from Chapter 1, "Changeover," and Chapter 2, "Culture, Management, and Implementation," appearing in Albin, J.M., and Magis-Agosta, K. (1989). *Self-assessment for changeover to supported employment: A troubleshooting approach.* Eugene: University of Oregon, Technical Assistance Brokerage. The author wishes to thank Kristen Magis-Agosta for her work on the earlier version, and Oregon's Mental Health and Developmental Disability Services Division for agreeing to allow those chapters to be incorporated in this text.

appropriate types and amounts of support, and that individuals with disabilities should have the opportunity to choose community employment. Furthermore, proponents of community-based employment believe that it enhances an individual's participation in the community, development of relationships with other community members, and maximization of individual competence (e.g., Bellamy, Rhodes, Mank, & Albin, 1988; Gardner, Chapman, Donaldson, & Jacobson, 1988; Kregel & Wehman, 1989; Parent et al., 1989; Sowers & Powers, 1991).

These views, held by supported employment advocates, differ greatly from those of most facility-based rehabilitation programs. Facility-based programs are designed on the assumption that an undefined period of training and experience in a structured facility will result in future employment gains, through *preparing* individuals for eventual community placement. Through work tasks—both paid and simulated—performed in the facility setting, it is expected that participants will learn the general work skills needed to prepare them for real jobs in competitive settings (e.g., Parent et al., 1989). Individuals with disabilities are expected to progress through a service continuum of pre-employment training, work adjustment, job placement, and time-limited support services that will lead to independent, paid employment in competitive jobs (Bellamy, Rhodes, Bourbeau, & Mank, 1986).

Proponents of facility-based services, for example, maintain that skills such as work attendance, response to supervisor directions, attention to task, productivity, and development of work habits are best learned through work adjustment training *prior to* entry into the real world of work. They believe that work in sheltered settings is more resistant to economic downturns than is work in supported community jobs. They believe that facilities offer the structured settings that are best suited for protecting individuals with disabilities from harm, for controlling behavioral excesses, and for remediating behavior problems. In other words, they view facilities as a safe place where service providers can work with individuals with disabilities whose behavior may be viewed as inappropriate based on typical community norms (e.g., National Association of Rehabilitation Facilities, 1988).

It must be said that, for years, "sheltered workshops," as they are often called, also have offered opportunities to work in community settings, primarily through work crews and independent job placements (National Association of Rehabilitation Facilities, 1988). The primary differences between those services and those of supported employment are the severity of disability of the individuals targeted for service, the amount and frequency of ongoing support provided, and the degree of emphasis on social integration and other employment outcomes. The primary difference between sheltered workshops that offer supported employment and *changeover* to supported employment is that, in the former, the services are viewed as part of an array of services offered by the rehabilitation organization, rather than as necessitating a basic and dramatic shift in how those organizations do business. For this reason, organizations that offer supported employment services simply as an added part of an existing array of services are viewed, for the purposes of this text, as closer in values and structure to facility-based programs than to programs undergoing changeover.

For any of a variety of reasons, however, many organizations that previously offered only facility-based services are now implementing a change of all or part of their operations to community-based supported employment services. For each organization, the reasons for the change are different. For some, the change is due to pressures from state funders, advocates, individuals with disabilities, or the profes-

CONFLICTS BETWEEN BASIC
BELIEFS OF SUPPORTED EMPLOYMENT AND FACILITY-BASED SERVICES

Supported employment services	Facility-based services
Providing support in natural environments will result in immediate and desirable personal and employment gains.	An undefined period of training and experience in a facility will result in future employment gains.
Every individual can work in a community job given the appropriate types and amounts of support.	Individuals need preparation in facilities before they can deal with community placement.
Individuals with disabilities should be given the opportunity to choose community employment.	Through paid and simulated work tasks, participants will learn general work skills needed for real jobs in real settings.
Community employment is critical to enhancing an individual's participation in the community, to developing relationships, and to maximizing individual competence.	Progress through a continuum of pre-employment training, work adjustment, job placement, and time-limited support services will lead to independent employment in competitive jobs.
Placement in sheltered settings masks the effects of economic downturns with simulated work tasks.	Work in sheltered settings is more resistant to economic downturns.
Sheltered settings congregate people with unusual behaviors together, increasing the likelihood of unacceptable behaviors that might not be displayed in more natural settings.	Sheltered settings protect individuals from harm and offer a place where service providers can work to improve unacceptable behaviors and needs in skill areas.

sional community. For others, the change may be due simply to a desire to be viewed as an agency that offers innovative services. Hopefully, for most, however, the change is due to a belief in the advantages offered to service recipients by community-based employment over facility-based services, including having the opportunity to enjoy lifestyles in which they are more integrated in the community. Changeover to integrated, community-based employment services requires a strength of commitment that can derive only internally from a belief that it is the right thing to do, rather than from a set of external pressures or concerns with image. Like the transformations that companies undergo in adopting Continuous Quality Improvement, changeover must reach into the heart and soul of an organization.

However, such changes do not come easily. During changeover from facility-based to community-based supported employment services, the organization must endure a period of time in which it will directly confront basic differences in assumptions and values within its own organization. Even organizations that choose to add supported employment to an array of services—rather than undergo changeover—may experience these conflicts, albeit to a lesser extent. Changeover will raise many fundamental questions in an organization and may lead to conflict among those persons involved in different parts of the program. Those holding a new vision of what is possible are likely to clash with those who want to protect the status quo.

Changeover requires that the organization reexamine its mission in order to support a changed set of attitudes, beliefs, and values of its members. To achieve changeover most effectively, all members of the organization must understand and support the new direction. Just as with the principles of Continuous Quality Improvement presented in Chapter 2, an organization undergoing total changeover must "create a unity of purpose" toward achieving that end. Managers must lead all members of the organization in the new direction through a variety of strategies, including revising the organization's mission so that it leads the change, incorporating the mission in everything that is done by the members of the organization, and behaving in new ways that support the new direction.

Differences in Roles

Supported employment programs require many individuals to assume roles that are different from those needed in facility-based programs. Vocational staff members, accustomed to working with the support and assistance of their facility-based peers, are asked by supported employment programs to work more independently in training and supporting individuals in community jobs, arranging transportation, negotiating with employers and co-workers, facilitating relationships at work, and so forth. Thus, during changeover, management and other personnel must identify the needed changes in roles, deal with any resistance or reluctance to change roles, and provide the training and support to staff members and others to help them assume these new roles during the changeover process.

In supported employment, families and residential personnel may assume greater involvement more often than is possible, or needed, in facility-based programs. Families and residential providers may assist in identifying individual job interests; networking to locate possible jobs; and providing support to individuals related to maintaining their jobs, including providing transportation and adjusting home schedules to accommodate different work schedules. Although some of these functions may also be provided to support facility-based services, their frequency or intensity may be much higher in supported employment.

Supported employment also reaches into the community and its businesses to redefine the roles of employers, their employees, and other community members. Formerly, employers and others provided support for rehabilitation objectives for individuals with severe disabilities primarily through donations or by subcontracting work to rehabilitation agencies. These methods resulted in little or no contact between employers and the individuals with disabilities who were performing the work. However, in supported employment, the significance of the potential contribution that each stakeholder will make to supported employment outcomes is still being discovered. As our collective experience and skills related to supported employment expand, personnel in supported employment organizations are utilizing new ways to involve employers, co-workers, and others in defining jobs and in providing the supports needed by individuals with severe disabilities who are working in regular job settings. Co-workers are befriending and advocating for individuals with disabilities (e.g., Mank, Rhodes, & Sandow, 1991; Rusch, Johnson, & Hughes, 1990) and receiving training in support methodology to eliminate the need for job coaching (Mank et al., 1991). Indeed, many of the methods available for expanding the roles of employers and co-workers in supported employment parallel systems and roles that are already in place in business settings for their employees without apparent disabilities. These include leadership in promoting supported employment with other divisions or departments in a company, or with other businesses, and involving training departments, employee assistance programs, trade associations, and unions in providing support to workers with disabilities (Rhodes, Sandow, Mank, Buckley, & Albin, 1991).

When an organization providing facility-based services first enters into supported employment, its staff members must learn about who can help in achieving the goal of community employment (e.g., company personnel and family members), their interests and influences, and how to work with them in new ways. Changeover, therefore, requires a change in how rehabilitation agencies approach and interact with businesses and other community members, as well as how they support and supervise their staffs.

With the dispersion of staff into diverse community locations, expansion of roles, and other factors, changeover to supported employment clearly requires that staff members be given greater autonomy. The Continuous Quality Improvement principle, "Empower Employees To Work To Achieve the Mission," as well as the strategies offered to implement this principle, provide valuable guidance to supported employment organizations, and to organizations undergoing a changeover to supported employment. More specific information on how to apply this principle in human service organizations is presented in Chapter 11.

Differences in Issues Faced

The issues faced by supported employment programs also differ from those faced by facility-based services. Facility-based services have long been plagued by problems with attracting, training, supervising, and maintaining qualified personnel. The ongoing staffing issues faced by most facility-based programs often are compounded in supported employment. Supported employment programs must find and maintain personnel who are skilled in a broader range of competencies, which include finding job opportunities, negotiating jobs, and advocating for promotions; trying to understand and become a part of a variety of businesses; facilitating the development of friendships; developing natural support structures; and using the best available training technology to increase worker independence at the work site.

With supported employment, staff scheduling and supervision also may become more difficult, particularly when jobs developed involve nonstandard work hours and sites that are geographically dispersed. Working alone in the community, staff members in supported employment may feel isolated from their peers, and organizations may have difficulty maintaining good communication with them.

Facility-based programs can deal with the problem of lost jobs (i.e., lost contracts) or reduced production work by scheduling downtime activities, such as simulated work tasks or classes, if other work tasks are not readily available in the facility. Jobs lost in supported employment are not recovered or replaced as easily. Supported employment organizations that work from an office, with no other facility for providing services, cannot rely on their own facility-based services as back-up in the event of job loss. Changeover, therefore, requires that rehabilitation organizations develop new or revised methods for managing personnel and for providing support in diverse settings. As described in Chapter 2, the Continuous Quality Improvement principle, "Use a Systematic Approach To Find Opportunities and To Improve Performance," and the many tools that principle represents, offer assistance to community-based programs and others in making effective decisions to identify and resolve problems. Some of the tools of Continuous Quality Improvement are presented in Chapters 5 and 6 and in Part III of this book.

The Challenge of Operating Dual Programs

The differences between supported employment programs and facility-based programs notwithstanding, changeover means starting a community-based employment program while simultaneously operating an existing facility-based program for a period of time. When one organization runs both programs, the constant changes being made may exacerbate existing tensions. Typically having to operate with inadequate public resources, rehabilitation organizations undergoing changeover find that competing demands on resources and management time result in a nearly continuous need to make trade-offs by taking resources from one program to assist the other. Having to deal with constant change and trade-offs, if not monitored closely, can lead to confusion, chaos, or even destabilization of the individual programs and of the organization as a whole.

Providing community-based employment services for people with disabilities, individually or in small clusters, requires restructuring of the organization as a whole: Existing staff must be retrained to gain the skills needed to work in community settings, management structures must be revised to support community employment, and resources tied to the facility must be gradually redirected.

- Will the organization continue to provide facility-based services to other individuals for whom supported employment may not be appropriate?
- What will we do with this building?
- How can we complete this in-house work order without our best workers?
- What will we do with this bus we own?

These are only a few of the questions that may arise regarding redirecting resources during the period of changeover.

THE THREE FACES OF CHANGEOVER: CULTURE, MANAGEMENT, AND IMPLEMENTATION

Both changeover to supported employment services and implementation of the principles of Continuous Quality Improvement bring about fundamental changes in the fabric of an organization. Yet, as shown in the case study presented in Chapter 13, both organizational changes may be undertaken simultaneously. Indeed, many of the strategies of quality improvement—such as those used to create a unity of purpose, develop a customer focus, and empower staff—used to promote a quality transformation will also support changeover to supported employment. In addition, the systematic methods employed in quality improvement to support decision-making are particularly useful for an organization suddenly faced with members of its staff working nearly independently from supervision in very dispersed community locations. Thus, the methods of quality improvement may even be viewed as a fundamental strategy for supporting changeover. However, either one requires a substantial change in how most organizations do business, and broad-based organizational change is not easy to accomplish.

Brager and Holloway (1978) indicated that three major factors must be addressed for change to occur: The organization must address the impact of change on people, on the organization's structure, and on technology. Thus, an organization can take the initiative to position itself for success through the continual evaluation and improvement of these critical factors. In this book, these critical factors are redefined as Culture, Management, and Implementation.

Culture refers to the character of the organization, the beliefs shared by its members, and the unwritten norms and rules that govern the actions of its members. Although difficult to define, and even more difficult to manage, the culture of an organization is a powerful force that can either support or obstruct change. Management includes the organization's formal mission and all its structures, including policies, procedures, and systems. Implementation includes those activities—the technology—necessary to run an employment program. These three factors are highly interrelated; changes in one will result in changes in the others. Culture both forms and is formed by an organization's management structures and implementation technology. Management structures reflect the organizational culture and technology. And the implementation technology is selected and guided by the organization's formal management structures and informal culture.

Because pursuing changeover implies constant change, continuously managing these three factors is critical to success. As an organization proceeds in its changeover, the predominance of any one factor and the variables within each factor change. For example, on the one hand, an organization just embarking on changeover usually must focus on its cultural aspects, building consensus on its new direction before it can hope to implement supported employment activities. On the other hand, organizations that have been actively involved in changeover may need to focus on improving implementation of community employment activities or on adjusting management structures to better support development of integrated employment.

The instrument, *Self-Assessment Guide for Changeover to Supported Employment*, presented in Chapter 7, is designed to facilitate the evaluation and improvement process. The instrument recognizes culture, management, and implementation as factors critical to the conversion process, and its design is based on principles and methods of Continuous Quality Improvement and performance technology. The remainder of this chapter presents and discusses each of these factors.

Culture

"Culture . . . is a pattern of beliefs and expectations shared by the organization's members. These beliefs and expectations produce norms that powerfully shape the behavior of individuals and groups in the organization" (Schwartz & Davis, 1981, p. 33). Each organization has a culture, a social energy, that defines its character, its style, its personality. This energy provides meaning to the organization's members. It directs and guides their actions, and it can be more powerful than any formal system in the organization. Organizational culture consists of two basic parts reflected by the history or saga of the organization and its current patterns of behavior. The way the organization was created, the personality of its founder, and legends about crisis situations in its past, for example, form the basis for the habits, traditions, and customs of an organization's culture. Through stories and the underlying pattern of relationships among organizational members, the culture also conveys the values, beliefs, and norms upon which the organization bases its daily operations.

Culture can be positive and constructive, or negative and destructive. On the one hand, a positive culture reinforces the mission of the organization. It effectively and efficiently meets the needs of the organization and its employees. A negative culture, on the other hand, can take several forms. It can diffuse social energy in many directions, leaving members confused about the organization's mission. It can deactivate social energy, leaving members apathetic or depressed about their jobs. Even worse, it can actively work against an organization's mission. Negative cultures, invisible in the formal organizational structure, can destroy an organization.

Cultural problems result when members of an organization continue behaving in ways that may have worked well in the past, but are currently counterproductive, or when members perpetuate a routine, going through the motions without questioning the reason for or effect of their actions. For example, managers and rehabilitation specialists may have grown accustomed to enforcing their goals, methods, and expectations based on their positions as "highly-trained professionals," rather than responding to input from consumers, advocates, and staff members who are more directly involved with issues. However, as community-based employment grows as a service option, these latter stakeholders are likely to become less willing to accept such top-down communication.

Cultural problems can lead to a situation in which an organization suddenly discovers that it has lost touch with its mission or that its mission is outdated from the perspective of its customers. Not meeting the needs of its customers may jeopardize an organization's very survival. These problems can go unheeded for some time. However, when the organization decides to change its course, existing cultural problems will be revealed. As Allen (1980) stated, "Cultural norms develop, teaching us what is expected, supported, and accepted by the people we live and work with. These norms exert a powerful pressure. . ." (p. 32). Therefore, an organization must constantly be aware of its culture and work to adjust that culture to support changes in the organization's mission or direction.

> "At the base of any strategic change process there must be a clear conception of what the organization is in relation to its wider context (its mission) and what it is aiming at (its vision)." (Berg, 1985, p. 299)

This analysis of culture is relevant for facility-based programs that choose to changeover to community-based employment programs. As previously discussed, community employment requires a set of values, assumptions, and expectations very different from those of facility-based programs. When an organization tries to make this shift in basic operating strategy, the change will reach into the very heart of its culture. If resulting issues are not addressed, efforts to changeover will be mitigated, if not fully stifled. Staff members may respond with apathy, resistance, or active rebellion, and mid-managers may continue to reward behavior that does not support changeover.

For changeover to succeed, the culture must support the gradual shift in operations to the community, changes in roles of staff members, and adjustments in basic values as well as in the vision of the future for the new organization. In a transformation that adopts Continuous Quality Improvement as a management philosophy, the culture must nourish the organization's improvement efforts; it must maintain a spirit that includes a focus on customers, an obsession with quality, a belief in team-work and problem-solving, a recognition of the importance of data and systematic methods, and a pride in individual and organizational accomplishments. For many organizations, firmly establishing these values in the informal culture will require a carefully considered approach.

Addressing changes in organizational culture requires that several conditions exist to support the change. First, the set of conditions in the general environment surrounding the organization must be supportive of change. Second, internal conditions must be arranged to support the change. Factors such as available management

---

NECESSARY CONDITIONS FOR SUPPORTING CULTURAL CHANGE

A. Conditions in the general environment surrounding the organization must be supportive of the change.
    Examples:
    - Threats posed by competition are within reasonable bounds.
    - The differences between the organization's culture and that of the environment surrounding the organization are perceived as modest, rather than threatening.
B. Internal conditions must be arranged to support the change.
    Examples:
    - Internal resources (e.g., management time, financial resources) are available to support the change.
    - The members of the organization are willing to live with the uncertainty of change.
    - Communication linkages exist between separate parts of the organization.
    - There is strong and stable leadership that is able to communicate interpretations of experiences and visions of the future.
C. Internal or external pressures may set the stage for cultural change.
    Examples:
    - There may be atypical performance demands from the organization's customers or the general public.
    - Customers may exert pressures to change the character of the organization.
    - Changes may take place in the size or complexity of the organization itself.
    - There may be pressures associated with environmental or internal uncertainties, such as labor market shortages, high turnover rates, actions of competitors, or reductions in financial resources.
D. It is necessary for the events that stimulate the onset of change to be triggered.
    Examples:
    - An innovation in the market that jeopardizes the organization's products or services may occur.
    - There may be technological breakthroughs that provide an opportunity for the organization to change or improve products or services.
    - New and more stringent governmental regulations may be enacted.
    - Change in the organization's management team may occur (adapted from Lundberg, 1985).

time and energy to invest in the change, and strong and stable leadership provide internal conditions that support cultural change. Third, internal or external pressures set the stage for cultural change. Increased performance demands or pressures from stakeholders, or changes in the size of the organization, might present sufficient tension to increase the likelihood of cultural change. Fourth, the cultural transition is usually precipitated by some internal or external "triggering event," such as the appearance of new technologies or a managerial change (Lundberg, 1985).

For many organizations undergoing changeover to supported employment, the stage was set for organizational change by similar conditions. The federal government and states, through various supported employment initiatives, and a relatively strong economy during the last half of the 1980s, provided a general environment that was conducive to change to supported employment. Indeed, in some states and communities, some rehabilitation organizations may have interpreted the initiatives as external pressures to change. Supported employment offered new strategies and methods for achieving employment outcomes for individuals who previously had been considered by the U.S. Department of Labor as "inconsequential" producers (Bellamy et al., 1986). Rehabilitation organizations around the country have responded to these conditions by initiating cultural and organizational change to supported employment.

Implementing an organization-wide change, such as changeover to supported employment services, is likely to require changes that go deep into an organization's culture, deep enough to change the points of reference for staff behavior. "If correctly performed it [a strategic change program] is a 'rite of renewal' by which the organization attempts to gain insight into the very reasons for its existence and to collectively reaffirm or renew itself" (Berg, 1983, p. 297). If changeover requires such a rite of renewal for changing the organization's culture, then several strategies will assist in that effort. Creating shared images or symbols of the change; using collective, group processes throughout the change; and expressing the change strategy as basic beliefs rather than simply as operational plans for action are three strategies that will support comprehensive organizational change. Organizational change—as a rite of renewal—must be approached as an undertaking that questions the corporate mission and vision and challenges the social and political system in an organization. The leaders of the organization must undertake such a strategy with the understanding that the outcome of the process of change cannot be entirely predicted. The cultural and organizational transformation of one organization, presented in Part III, offers a good example of how using such strategies affected cultural change during the continuing process of changeover to supported employment.

As indicated in Chapter 2, a shared vision is critical to achieving Continuous Quality Improvement. The best leaders and top managers understand that their roles are to create clear organizational images and to manage the meaning of those images, in order to create a shared vision. These roles are particularly important during periods of organizational change, when staff members need a concise understanding of their new direction. Peters and Waterman (1982) described "excellently managed" firms where leaders emphasize homogeneity on a few central dimensions, such as tolerating failure, concern for individuals, and openness. If leaders can build adherence to these values in the organization's culture, they reduce the chance for deviation from the mission or resistance to specific changes. In this way, the leaders are actually using the culture to assist in accomplishing management's

"A true strategic change program does not impose anything but makes people aware of and illuminates certain aspects of the culture in which they exist. . . . [B]y bringing values, principles, and behaviors to the surface, and by providing people with a framework with which they can interpret what they see, a creative and emancipatory process is started." (Berg, 1985, p. 298)

objectives and reducing the opportunities for deviations from the organization's course.

The executive director of a rehabilitation organization thus plays a vital role in the success, or failure, of the organization's changeover to supported employment, adoption of Continuous Quality Improvement principles and methods, or other fundamental change. Such changes may be initiated from the "lower" ranks, but only with great difficulty. And, if not supported by the top manager, most will fail.

Management

Management refers to the formal aspects of an organization, including its mission and administrative structures. If an organization is to function effectively, it needs a written mission and formal structures that are appropriately designed.

The mission of an organization establishes its philosophical foundations and sets the direction toward which it continually moves. If there is no clear mission or if the mission is outdated, it will make little difference how well particular structures and procedures have been designed; the members of the organization will not be moving in concert toward one overall objective. Rather, individuals will move in their own different directions and those directions will change as different people carry out their responsibilities.

Administrative structures formally align human and technical resources to move the organization in its intended direction. They guide performance via systems and procedures, tools and materials, and incentives. And they provide symbols that reflect the organization's basic values. If administrative structures are inappropriate or missing, individual and organizational performance will falter, and morale will be adversely affected. Furthermore, if these structures do not support the organization's mission, the mission cannot be served. Therefore, it is critical for an organization to have a clear mission and appropriate administrative structures that move the organization toward its mission effectively and efficiently.

The most difficult time to develop and maintain an appropriate mission and structures is during periods of rapid change and growth. However, periods of rapid change and growth, more than any other, require clarity of purpose and constant focus on direction. Without these, an organization could lose sight of its mission and could even degenerate into chaos. This should be of particular concern to organizations involved in changeover to supported employment.

Because changeover to community-based employment requires maintaining current facility-based operations while developing and implementing an entirely different service program, changes will be needed in management structures. The mission and administrative structures that worked for the facility-based program are not likely to work for the community-based program. Along with the organization's cultural values, assumptions, and expectations, therefore, the mission and administrative structures must be changed to support the community-based program. While changeover is occurring, two separate organizations will effectively be in operation—even while the organization attempts to adjust to the differences between them.

For changeover to be successful, an organization must clearly indicate in its mission statement that community-based employment is the expected outcome for individuals. In addition, it must design or revise administrative structures to realign resources to move the organization toward accomplishing its desired supported employment outcomes. Planning activities should include the development of strategies and implementation plans for supported employment. Personnel systems should promote hiring, supervision, and training procedures relevant to identifying, developing, and maintaining staff members who will be successful given the demands of supported employment settings. Resources, both from within the organization and from the community, should be adjusted to maximize integrated employment outcomes for individuals. Finally, organizational policies not specific to supported employment, as well as regulations imposed by external forces, should be reviewed for analysis of their potential effect on achieving supported employment outcomes. The principles and methods of Continuous Quality Improvement can assist in completing these changes.

Implementation

Implementation refers to the specific accomplishments and activities, that is, the outcomes and processes, involved in putting a supported employment program into practice. In addition to attending to culture and formal management structures:

> To provide successful supported employment, an organization must: 1) create the opportunity to perform paid work, 2) see that the work is performed according to the employer's requirements, 3) integrate employees with disabilities into the social and physical environment of the workplace, [and] 4) meet the employees' ongoing support needs. . . ." (Bellamy 1988, p. 28)

Changeover to supported employment, therefore, means that organizations accustomed to meeting employer or customer demands through facility-based programs must instead continuously generate individually specific employment opportunities, must facilitate opportunities for integration of individuals within work sites, and must adequately support all individuals in community employment.

The implementation activities in which an organization participates will shift as the changeover process matures. When changeover is started, the program will need to put basic systems in place, such as identifying individual interests, training, and support needs; selecting the service approaches to be used in developing supported employment; and establishing the necessary marketing strategies. With these initiated, the organization can start specific job development, job placement, and job training activities. As changeover proceeds, the organization can shift its attention to enhancing career development for individuals, including negotiating promotions, wage increases, and job changes, as well as assessing individual job satisfaction. During every phase, an organization should attend to improving its effectiveness and increasing its capacity to provide supported employment services. The principles and methods of Continuous Quality Improvement, presented throughout this text offer valuable strategies for doing just that.

The nature of changeover is everything its name implies. The organization's mission must be reviewed and a new mission identified and defined. Based on the new mission statement, changes to the organization's culture will have to be made to ensure that the cultural norms that support the new mission are encouraged and those that do not support it are discouraged or replaced. A large part of the success of the needed changes will depend on the design and development of a management structure that will support the mission of the organization. Effectively supported by the new management structures, the organization can begin to replace its facility-based program with supported employment services.

REFERENCES

Albin, J.M., & Magis-Agosta, K. (1989). *Self-assessment for changeover to supported employment: A troubleshooting approach.* Eugene: Univeristy of Oregon, Technical Assistance Brokerage.

Allen, R.F. (1980). The IK in the office. *Organizational Dynamics, 8*(3), 26–41.

Bellamy, G.T., Rhodes, L.E., Bourbeau, P., & Mank, D. (1986). Mental retardation services in sheltered workshops and day activity programs: Consumer benefits and policy alternatives. In F.R. Rusch (Ed.), *Competitive employment issues and strategies* (pp. 257–271). Baltimore: Paul H. Brookes Publishing Co.

Bellamy, G.T., Rhodes, L.E., Mank, D.M., & Albin, J.M. (1988). *Supported employment: A community implementation guide.* Baltimore: Paul H. Brookes Publishing Co.

Berg, P.O. (1983, August). *Corporate culture development: The strategic integration of identity, profile and image.* Paper presented at the meeting between the Nordic Schools of Business Administration, Copenhagen. As referenced in Berg, P.O. (1985). Organization change as a symbolic transformation process. In P.J. Frost, L.F. Moore, M.R. Louis, C.C. Lundberg, & J. Martin, *Organizational culture* (pp. 281–300). Beverly Hills: Sage.

Berg, P.O. (1985). Organizational change as a symbolic transformation process. In P.J. Frost, L.F. Moore, M.R. Louis, C.C. Lundberg, & J. Martin, *Organizational culture* (pp. 281–300). Beverly Hills: Sage.

Brager, G., & Holloway, S. (1978). *Changing human service organizations: Politics and practice.* New York: Free Press.

Gardner, J.F., Chapman, M.S., Donaldson, G., & Jacobson, S.G. (1988). *Toward supported employment: A process guide for planned change.* Baltimore: Paul H. Brookes Publishing Co.

Kregel, J., & Wehman, P. (1989). Supported employment: Promises deferred for persons with severe disabilities. *Journal of The Association for Persons with Severe Handicaps, 14*(4), 293–303.

Lundberg, C.C. (1985). On the feasibility of cultural intervention in organizations. In P.J. Frost, L.F. Moore, M.R. Louis, C.C. Lundberg, & J. Martin, *Organizational culture* (pp. 169–186). Beverly Hills: Sage.

Mank, D., Rhodes, L., & Sandow, D. (1991). *Training co-workers to teach job tasks to employees with mental disabilities.* Manuscript submitted for publication.

National Association of Rehabilitation Facilities. (1988). *Conversion: Restructuring for integrated community placement.* Washington, DC: Author.

Parent, W.S., Hill, M.L., & Wehman, P. (1989). From sheltered to supported employment outcomes: Challenges for rehabilitation facilities. *Journal of Rehabilitation, 55*(4), 51–57.

Peters, T.J., & Waterman, R.H. (1982). *In search of excellence: Lessons from America's best-run companies.* New York: Harper & Row.

Rhodes, L., Sandow, D., Mank, D., Buckley, J., & Albin, J. (1991). *Expanding the role of employers in supported employment.* Manuscript submitted for publication.

Rusch, F.R., Johnson, J.R., & Hughes, C. (1990). Analysis of coworker involvement in relation to level of disability versus placement approach among supported employees. *Journal of The Association for Persons with Severe Handicaps, 15*(1), 32–39.

Scholtes, P.R., & Hacquebord, H. (1987). *A practical approach to quality.* Madison, Joiner Associates, Inc.

Schwartz, H., & Davis, S.M. (1981). Matching corporate culture and business strategy. *Organizational Dynamics, 10*(1), 30–48.

Sowers, J., & Powers, L. (1991). *Vocational preparation and employment of students with physical and multiple disabilities.* Baltimore: Paul H. Brookes Publishing Co.

ADDITIONAL READINGS

Christensen, C.R., Andrews, K.R., Bowen, J.L., Hamermesh, R.G., & Porter, M.E. (1982). *Business policy: Text and cases.* Homewood, IL: Richard D. Irwin.

Frost, P.J., Moore, L.F., Louis, M.R., Lundberg, C.C., & Martin, J. (1985). *Organizational culture.* Beverly Hills: Sage.

Howes, N.J.R., & Quinn, R.E. (1978). Implementing change: From research to a prescriptive framework. *Group and Organizational Studies, 3*(1), 71–84.

Kilman, R.H. (1987). *Beyond the quick fix.* San Francisco: Jossey-Bass.

Kirkpatrick, D.L. (1985). *How to manage change effectively: Approaches, methods, and case examples.* San Francisco: Jossey-Bass.

Lynn, G., & Lynn, J.B. (1984). Seven keys to successful change management. *Supervisory Management, 29*(11), 30–37.

Nord, W.R. (1985). Can organizational culture be managed? A synthesis. In P.J. Frost, L.F. Moore, M.R. Louis, C.C. Lundberg, & J. Martin, *Organizational culture* (pp. 187–196). Beverly Hills: Sage.

Wallach, E.J. (1983). Individuals and organizations: The cultural match. *Training and Development Journal, 37*(2), 29–36.

Wehman, P., Kregel, J., & Shafer, M.S. (Eds.). (1989). *Emerging trends in the national supported employment initiative: A preliminary analysis of twenty-seven states.* Richmond: Rehabilitation Research and Training Center, Virginia Commonwealth University.

Wehman, P., & Moon, M.S. (Eds.). (1988). *Vocational rehabilitation and supported employment.* Baltimore: Paul H. Brookes Publishing Co.

Chapter 5

Troubleshooting Performance Problems

Too often, managers look for the right solution when they have not yet identified the right questions. And, all too often, staff people are held responsible for the problem and its solutions when the issue really lies within the systems in which they work. Quality improvement experts recognize that at least 85% of performance problems are due to systems issues—largely under the control of management—and only 15% are due to issues related to the staff themselves (e.g., Scholtes, 1988). Yet, too often, managers in rehabilitation and other human services behave as if most service problems must be the fault of the individual employees involved. As a result, the organization's limited resources are spent blaming employees, applying the wrong solution, assigning the wrong personnel (or the right personnel without the needed authority and support), and, in the end, *not* resolving the real problem.

If managers are to improve the performance of their organizations and employees, they must have effective strategies for analyzing performance problems and their causes, and for selecting appropriate solutions to those problems. This chapter presents the quality improvement strategy referred to as *troubleshooting performance problems*, drawn from the work of performance technologists such as Thomas Gilbert and Robert Mager.

PERFORMANCE

Unfortunately, we often confuse behavior with performance. But, performance is much more than behavior. *Performance* includes the results or products of the behavior, as well as the behavior itself. In most cases, we are most interested in *valuable* performance; that is, behavior that results in a valued outcome. Thomas Gilbert (1978) offered yet another level of definition of performance: *worthy* performance. To Gilbert, the performance of an organization, group, or individual is worthy when the value of the accomplishments achieved exceeds the costs—largely in behavior— required to achieve them. Therefore, the worth of performance increases as the value of the accomplishment increases and/or the costs invested to achieve those accom-

This chapter incorporates material from Chapter 3, "Troubleshooting," appearing in Albin, J.M., and Magis-Agosta, K. (1989). *Self-assessment for changeover to supported employment: A troubleshooting approach.* Eugene: University of Oregon, Technical Assistance Brokerage. The author wishes to thank Kristen Magis-Agosta for her work on the earlier version, and Oregon's Mental Health and Developmental Disability Services Division for agreeing to allow that chapter to be incorporated in this text.

TREK PERSONNEL SERVICES

James T. had just been hired by Trek Personnel Services as the new lead job developer. He decided to begin his first day by interviewing Spock, one of Trek's more experienced job coaches.

"Tell me, Spock. When I was hired I got the impression that things are not good around here in the job development area. Tell me what's up."

Setting down the newspaper he had been studying diligently, Spock responded, "We have all 36 people we are supporting in community jobs."

"Great! So, what's the problem?"

"The state isn't happy with the number of hours people are working each week. They say that it has to be at least 20, but that they would rather people worked 30 hours per week."

"That makes sense; it's hard to earn a decent living only working half time. So, did they have any recommendations?"

"No, not really; I guess they think that's our job. Anyway, the director decided to fire Sallye, the last person in your job. He really wanted a good review from the state and was mad that we didn't get an A+. He said it was all Sallye's fault. I just don't get it; I thought Sallye was really doing well and had developed great relationships with the companies we're working with. They liked her, I know. And she had developed a lot of jobs, good jobs with great pay—and good companies to work for, too. I'm afraid the same thing will happen to me. I'm starting to keep close watch on the want ads."

"How did the director decide it was her fault? Did he figure out why it is each person isn't working enough hours? What did she do wrong?"

"No. He just said she should have had them all working enough hours by now. He said it must be she wasn't working hard enough to find them the right kinds of jobs. She tried to explain: One person she's working with, Jane, is under doctor's orders to stay off her feet and to work no more than 3 hours a day. Also, that residential program said "no way" to the evening shift at the shopping center. That's too bad, too. We would have had some great jobs there. And the fact that the city bus route stops 2 miles short of that electronics company west of town is a real bummer."

"Hmmm."

"And then there's the scare about losing Social Security—SSI and SSDI payments. The director held a big parent meeting and told them they had to be careful or they could lose everything. So, the parents are really freaked out. He didn't tell them anything about the Social Security Work Incentives that are available—things like 'PASS Plans' and 'IRWEs.' Ever since that big parent meeting he held, when we meet with them at the individual planning meetings they say, 'Don't let John work more than 10 hours,' or 'No, Fred can't take a job that pays $7 an hour.' They're just plain scared."

"Oh, I see. That's some great troubleshooting the director did. I wonder how long it will be before I get the axe, too? Pass me the want ads, when you're finished with them, okay?"

plishments decrease. These distinctions are important, for often managers evaluate employees based on the behavior they observe, without regard to the value of the accomplishment or the cost of the behavior expended to achieve it. Instead, managers should view as most competent those staff persons who achieve valuable results while expending the least possible amount of costly behavior.

An accomplishment is an outcome or result achieved by an individual or organization. Outstanding knowledge, many hours of work, and great motivation to succeed are worthless if they do not lead to a desired accomplishment, or if their cost is greater than the value of the accomplishment achieved. For example, if a job developer knows everything there is to know about developing jobs, works 16 hours a day, and expresses a sincere desire to develop great jobs, but does not actually produce those jobs, then knowledge, work, and motivation are worth little to his or her employer. In fact, the employer has expended valuable resources at high cost with no return on investment. In addition, without additional analysis and information, the employer may waste yet more resources by providing training to the job developer, encouraging her or him to work harder, or trying to improve motivation to succeed. With the limited resources available to most rehabilitation and supported employment organizations, finding the best means of improving performance—of improving the worth of performance—is necessary to achieving organizational excellence.

TROUBLESHOOTING

Organizations wishing to improve the outcomes of the services they provide need a systematic way of diagnosing their problems. Using a troubleshooting approach to problem identification will lead managers in identifying the right problem in less time. *Troubleshooting* is a method of diagnosis that provides a systematic order in which to ask questions about improving organizational performance. It does not say anything about the nature of the organization: It assumes that the professionals involved already know the relevant details and simply helps in directing their questions.

The Game of "20 Questions"

Troubleshooting may be illustrated very simply by a variation on the two-person game of "20 Questions." In this game, one person thinks of something that is either animal or mineral, and the other must try to guess what it is. By asking "either/or" or "yes/no" questions and starting with broad categories (e.g., "Is it animal or mineral?", or "Is it bigger than a breadbox?"), the second person gradually narrows the possibilities. If the questioner is successful, the correct answer is revealed by fewer than the allotted 20 questions. Given the potentially infinite number of possible answers at the start of the game, and the limit on the number of questions, it is crucial that the questioner use a strategy that makes it possible to eliminate large segments of possibilities with each step.

While diagnosing problems in organizations is never as simple as a game of "20 Questions," the game demonstrates two valuable points:

1. Some sequences of questions about complex systems are more efficient than others.
2. Those who follow a systematic sequence are more likely to identify the true issue with the greatest efficiency (Mager, 1982).

A GAME OF "20 QUESTIONS"

1.	"Is it animal or mineral?"	"Mineral"
2.	"Is it bigger than a bread box?"	"No"
3.	"Is it natural or manmade?"	"Manmade"
4.	"Is it used by people?"	"Yes"
5.	"Is it used for work or for personal life?"	"Work"
6.	"Is it generally found inside or outside of buildings?"	"Usually inside"
7.	"Does it require electricity to be used?"	"No"
8.	"Is it most likely to be used in an office?"	"Yes"
9.	"Is it likely to be used in all offices?"	"No"
10.	"Is it likely to be used in only certain occupations?"	"Yes"
11.	"Is it likely to be used in your occupation, rehabilitation?"	"Yes"
12.	"Is it mostly made of paper?"	"Yes"
13.	"Is it something that has writing or printing on it?"	"Yes"
14.	"Is it a book?"	"Yes"
15.	"Is it this book?"	"Yes"

No other questions needed.

Troubleshooting performance in an organization applies these points. First, the organization must clearly define its desired accomplishment. (In the "20 Questions" example, the desired accomplishment was identifying an item.) Second, the troubleshooter must evaluate the major factors or subaccomplishments of performance leading to that accomplishment (as, in the example, the initial questions were designed to eliminate large segments of possibilities). When one area is identified in which improvement would have the greatest impact on performance (comparable, in the example, to the revelations provided by the responses), the troubleshooter must proceed to focus on analyzing the major components of that area. The troubleshooting process continues until the activity that will lead to the greatest improvement in performance at the lowest cost is identified.

Troubleshooting Trees

The troubleshooting process may be depicted visually using a "troubleshooting tree" format, which displays the relationships between each level and the major branches of the tree. In the troubleshooting tree depiction of the game of 20 Questions (see Figure 5.1), it is clear that at each branch, other branches could have been chosen. Each of the branches that was not selected represents a number of other possibilities that were eliminated, and, thus, are not shown on this tree. In the example game of "20 Questions," the questioner was able to identify the correct answer in only 15 questions. Using a strategy in which the answer to each succeeding question reduces the remaining possibilities by half, the questioner could reduce the number of possibilities from near infinity down to one, with both minimal effort and great accuracy.

The *Self-Assessment Guide for Changeover to Supported Employment*, presented in Chapter 7, is a tool designed to assist in implementing troubleshooting for analyzing problems in changeover to supported employment. Rather than presenting a comprehensive survey of best practices in supported employment, the guide ties practices to performance outcomes and uses a troubleshooting methodology for analyzing performance problems—that is, for analyzing problems in achieving desired outcomes. The logical structure of the guide may be represented using a troubleshooting tree format, as shown in Figure 5.2. Changeover, the desired overall accomplishment, is listed first, followed by the three major "segments of possibilities" or factors related to successful changeover to supported employment: culture, management, and implementation. At lower levels of the tree, each of these major factors may be subdivided into two or more categories, and so forth.

TROUBLESHOOTING CHANGEOVER TO SUPPORTED EMPLOYMENT

Using the troubleshooting strategy embedded in the *Self-Assessment Guide for Changeover to Supported Employment* (Albin & Magis-Agosta, 1989), an organization is able to identify the issues having the greatest impact on the performance problems associated with changeover. The organization first determines which organizational factor (i.e., Culture, Management, or Implementation) is presenting the largest barrier to success in changeover. Having chosen one, the organization then looks at the major *areas* in that factor and chooses the one whose improvement would result in the greatest improvement in performance. After choosing the area (e.g., *relationships*), the organization then analyzes the *components* relevant to the chosen area and selects the one whose improvement would lead to the greatest overall improvement in performance.

In any organization pursuing changeover, issues may exist in Culture, Management, *and* Implementation, and in many areas and components of each. Throughout the troubleshooting process the organization identifies the *one* area, component, or activity that is expected to lead to the *greatest* overall improvement in performance. In this way, the strategies and resources used by the organization to improve performance are focused on activities that are tied directly to performance outcomes and have a high likelihood of creating the greatest impact with the least cost. By using the troubleshooting process continuously, the organization will go on identifying other performance barriers in other aspects of the organization and will prioritize activities for improving performance.

Organizations are interactive and interrelated. That is, every part of an organization is related and a change in one affects the others in some way. Therefore, the *Guide* does not advocate attention to one area exclusively. Rather, it attempts to make problem diagnosis more efficient and effective. Given the relative scarcity of resources, organizations undergoing changeover to supported employment must invest resources in areas that promise the greatest return. The *Guide* helps organizations do just that. However, if the organization implements a strategy related to one identified barrier, and still does not see an improvement in performance, it may be that another part of the organization is not working well. Therefore, an organization should troubleshoot changeover frequently, either by using the *Self-Assessment Guide*, or by simply applying the general troubleshooting process. In this way, an organization will be able to identify and address the ever-changing challenges faced in pursuing changeover to supported employment.

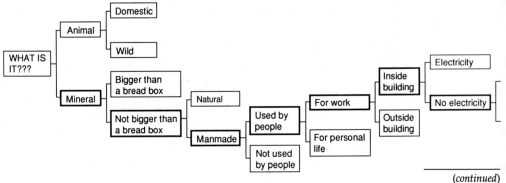

(continued)

Figure 5.1. The game of "20 Questions" depicted in a troubleshooting tree format.

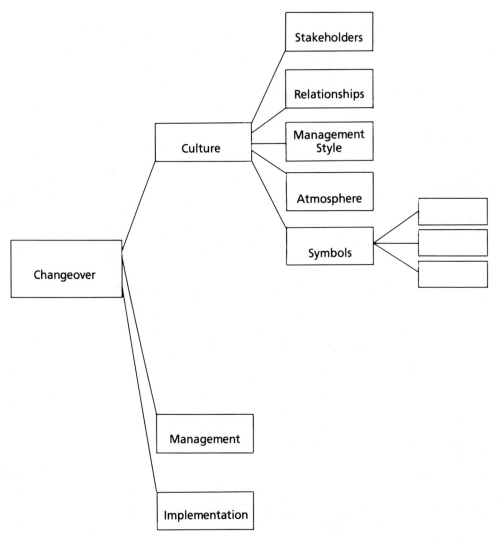

Figure 5.2. The *Self-Assessment Guide for Changeover to Supported Employment* depicted in a troubleshooting tree format.

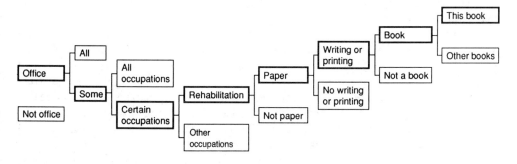

Figure 5.1. (*continued*)

INFORMATION SOURCES FOR TROUBLESHOOTING

Troubleshooting is a process, or strategy, for performance improvement that can be applied to many different situations in human service organizations or in public sector agencies. It is much more than the *Guide* presented in Chapter 7. That *Self-Assessment Guide for Changeover to Supported Employment* provides an extensive template for troubleshooting problems related to changeover from facility-based services to supported employment services. Other, less complex performance templates are presented in later chapters.

Robert Mager defines *trouble* as "an opportunity for improvement" (Mager, 1982, p. 8) and *troubleshooting* to include diagnosing or locating the trouble, as well as the intervention used to treat or "clear" the trouble. The troubleshooter in human service or public sector settings, therefore, should hunt for causes of performance deficits *and* act to eliminate those causes.

TROUBLESHOOTING: INFORMATION SOURCES

- *Use personal experience.* Use knowledge based on prior experience and/or directly work the process or system at issue.
- *Interview those most directly involved.* Talk with those who are closest to the issue, who may be working the process or system on a daily basis, or who have direct experience with the issue; listen carefully, and "naively," to what they say.
- *Use aids to troubleshooting.* Develop or find applicable performance templates, such as the tool, *Self-Assessment Guide for Changeover to Supported Employment.*
- *Use a systematic search process.* Start with larger, more general categories of information, and work toward more specific factors.
- *Use data to move through the search.* Use data and information generated by the system or process, as well as information obtained from observation, interviews, and the like to guide the search.
- *Make use of errors and unsuccessful interventions.* Consider what has *not* worked in the past as a valuable source of information; analyzing why an intervention did not work can help to move the troubleshooter to a better solution.

The purpose of troubleshooting is to improve performance by moving from symptoms of performance deficits (i.e., outcomes or accomplishments that are unsatisfactory) to the causes of the trouble with the least amount of time and effort. While the details of a specific troubleshooting sequence may vary, the general strategy is the same: move from general to specific, eliminating unrelated factors, using data and information to show the way. In this way, troubleshooting provides a strategy to help the troubleshooter move from a place of uncertainty regarding where the problem lies, to certainty. By the end of the troubleshooting process, the troubleshooter has eliminated factors that are not related to the targeted performance area, in order to home in on the ones that are. Through the troubleshooting strategy of moving systematically from the intended outcome through related systems and processes, it is possible to target the action most likely to result in improved performance. In this way, resources can be directed where they are likely to have the greatest impact.

TROUBLESHOOTING TREK PERSONNEL'S PROBLEMS

When we last saw James T. (who had just been hired by Trek Personnel Services as the new lead job developer) he was talking with Spock about the events that had led to the firing of the last lead job developer.

"Sallye sure got a raw deal out of all this, didn't she?", Spock complained, handing over the newspaper.

"Yeah. I'm afraid the same thing is going to happen to me, if I don't figure out how to do some quick troubleshooting and get some results."

"What do you mean?"

"At my last job, I learned a technique for prioritizing what I do by analyzing my biggest problem. Let's try it together."

"Okay. So, what is your biggest problem?"

"No question, right? The people we're supporting in jobs aren't working enough hours."

"Right."

"So, what are the biggest things that would have to be in place if we were to succeed in getting enough work hours?"

"Well, there would have to be good jobs that offered enough work hours—enough jobs for all of the people we're supporting. But the people we support would also have to be available to work those hours."

"What do you mean by good jobs?"

"A job that matches the person's interests and criteria for a job."

"Right. So, if we need both jobs and people available, which one is the biggest problem?"

"I think we haven't had much trouble with finding jobs that are 20 hours a week or more. In fact, as I told you, we had to let several go. Right now, we have four people who are job-sharing two jobs in order to get the work done because none of them is able to be at work as long as the employer wants someone. No, I'd say getting the jobs isn't much of a problem. But we do have a terrible time filling jobs. The work

---

(continued)

TROUBLESHOOTING TREK PERSONNEL'S PROBLEMS (*continued*)

hours are too long, or the time of day is wrong, or there is a conflict with the Special Olympics, or we don't have a job coach available, or . . ."

"Hold it. So, the biggest problem isn't getting the jobs, it is with getting people to fill the jobs?"

"Right, that's what I said."

"Sallye really did get a bum deal. She was fired for not developing jobs, when the real problem was getting people to fill those jobs. Okay, let's keep going. What are the most important things we need to have in place in order to get people to fill those jobs?"

"We need to have a staff person available to work with the company to provide the training and other supports needed for the job to work, and we need an individual interested in the job who will be there for the required hours."

"Which of those is the bigger problem?"

"We used to have a terrible time keeping up with the new jobs; job coaches just couldn't seem to fade from their sites. But that isn't as much of a problem anymore. Sallye began working with employers as she was developing jobs, talking about how she could support *them* to support their new employees with disabilities. It seemed to make sense to the businesses. Now, our job coaches are training co-workers and supervisors at the companies to provide support, and so they fade from job sites much faster. Of course, there still are problems and we have to talk with companies a lot to help them if they have an issue to be dealt with, but some of the companies are doing most of the *direct* support themselves. Coming up with support is still a problem sometimes, but it isn't the biggest one. No, I'd say the problem is really with getting the people with disabilities to be available for jobs that are 20 hours a week or more."

"What do you think the biggest issues are there?"

"Like I started to tell you before, there are a lot of them. The work hours are too long, or it's not the right time of day for the group home, or it conflicts with Special Olympics, or the doctor says no, or parents don't want them to make too much money and jeopardize their Social Security. Sometimes it is just because the bus doesn't go to the job site at the right times, or at all."

"It sounds to me like there are three basic reasons why people aren't available to work the number of hours we need them to work: lack of available job support, lack of agreement by the home provider or family that working 20 hours or more is important, and lack of appropriate transportation. From what you said, the first issue—job support—isn't really the big problem any more. I'm sure we could do it more effectively, but that can wait until we have the biggest problem solved first. Of the other two issues, how many people do you think are affected? How many jobs are less than 20 hours a week because of transportation issues, and how many because of home-related reasons?"

"Let's see. We haven't been able to develop jobs at the electronics company because of the bus route. I'd say we'd be able to get five or six jobs there; that's what Sallye said, based on her meetings with them. It's a pretty large company with several buildings on the same campus. People could work in different parts of the company—shipping and receiving, component prep, hardware, inventory, final assembly, cables. Sallye had three jobs at the shopping center, but they would have been

(*continued*)

TROUBLESHOOTING TREK PERSONNEL'S PROBLEMS (*continued*)

from 2 P.M. to 8 P.M., and the residential provider said no. Of our 36 people, eight people are working at least 20 hours per week, so that leaves 28 who aren't. Three of them are working shortened hours because of transportation problems. The other 25 aren't for a variety of reasons: there's Jane and her doctor's orders so she is job-sharing with John; 10 of them live in places supported by that same residential provider who says no to evening hours. At least half of the 25 aren't working more because their families are afraid of losing Social Security. It's a real mixture."

"It sounds to me like we should do two things to have an impact on how many hours a week our folks are available to work."

"Two things? Only two things? How do you figure that?"

"Simple, you just told me what to do. It sounds like at least 12 people aren't working longer hours because of questions about Social Security. That is our biggest group. So, first, let's find out more about that Social Security issue, and get some better information to the families. If they are afraid of something, we should deal with it and figure it out, instead of pretending it isn't there. Second, I think we should do some consensus-building and joint problem-solving with the residential providers about community-based employment. It sounds like another 10 or so people aren't working longer hours because the residential providers don't share the same vision of what is possible or haven't figured out how to support it. We could help with that by working together with the residential staff and a few family members to come up with ideas to get around their problems. And if we can't, at least we will understand better when they do say no. Maybe there are things that we could do differently that would allow them to support our folks working 20 hours or more a week, especially when it comes to those 'non-standard' work hours. What do you think?"

"You're the captain, sir. Let's go." (See Figure 5.3.)

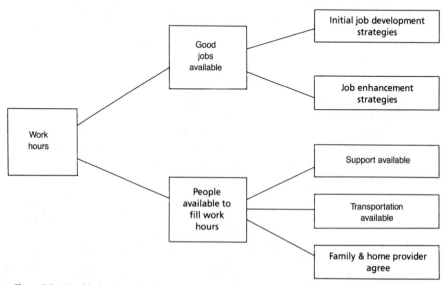

Figure 5.3. Troubleshooting tree representing James T.'s approach to Trek personnel's problems.

A TROUBLESHOOT AT THE OK CORRAL

The rehabilitation specialist at QRS Employment Services had a problem. The job coaches usually failed to collect and report data required by the individual support plan, which caused problems during program reviews conducted by the funder. Asked to intervene and "make those job coaches do their jobs," the executive director, instead, followed a rehabilitation specialist as he prepared for, attended, and followed-up after an individual planning team meeting.

At the same time, the job coaches (several of whom worked at the 10 OK Corral Westernwear stores throughout the county) were complaining that the annual individual support plans, developed by the rehabilitation specialists in team meetings, were not useful to them. In fact, they knew very little about what was really on them. But, the rehab specialists continually wanted the job coaches to give them some data. "Don't those rehab people know we have better things to do with our time?" So, the executive director began asking questions—asking rehab specialists about what they needed to make their jobs work well, and asking job coaches the same thing. Being a very wise director, she also asked how they could make the individual plans work better for everyone involved. And, she listened very carefully for the meaning in their answers.

Being lucky as well as wise, the director had just purchased a copy of the book, *Quality Improvement in Employment and Other Human Services*. She took a few moments to review the chapter on troubleshooting to prepare for continued work on the problem. Maybe it would give her some clues.

Her next step was to determine two major categories in which to begin troubleshooting. She decided those categories should be: first, what the organization has to offer to support job coaches in doing a good job with individual plans, and second, the job coaches themselves. She knew that the cause of the problem just had to be related to one or the other.

Based on her interviews and observations, the director decided that the problem probabl̲ ̲ ̲ ̲ ̲ ̲ ̲ ̲ ̲ h the job coaches. After all, they all clearly wanted to do a g̲c̲ ̲ ̲ ̲ ̲ ̲ ̲ ̲ ̲ ̲ ̲ ̲ ̲ ̲ ̲ ̲ ̲ ̲ ̲aration and experience to do that. But she had observed ̲ ̲ ̲ ̲ ̲ ̲ ̲ ̲ ̲ ̲ developed and had reviewed information available for ̲ ̲ ̲ ̲ ̲ ̲s, she discovered the following data:

̲ngs for	0 plans
̲ing objectives for	0 plans
̲ctives as useful and helpful in	1 plan
the reason objectives had been selected for	3 plans
̲gress, including graphs for	0 plans
̲efined in	7 plans
̲job setting in	8 plans
̲ ̲ ̲ easily compiled and graphed in	7 plans

The rehab specialists told the director that they could not understand why the job coaches did not do a better job. After all, they had given the job coaches a 2 hour

(continued)

A TROUBLESHOOT AT THE OK CORRAL (*continued*)

training session on the importance of individual plans and keeping data. They had even talked about the county's program review process. But after the training, the job coaches still did not turn in the data. "Aha!" exclaimed the director. "They tried training, but that did not work this time to fix the problem. That is good information to have. The problem must be something other than lack of training."

The director already had decided that the real problem was in the system and not in the job coaches. To her, that meant the problem had to be in the information flow between job coaches and rehab specialists, or the forms and procedures available for data collection. The job coaches had received training, so that could not be it. Based on all of the information collected, she decided that the job coaches had no input into the objectives and received no feedback on the data they did provide. Her troubleshooting job was nearly done. Now, how was she going to get those folks to talk to each other more, so they could get a dialogue going for both setting objectives and giving feedback? (See Figure 5.4.)

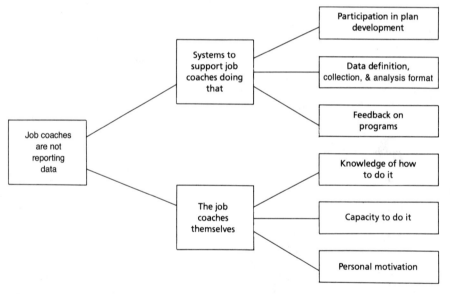

Figure 5.4. Troubleshooting tree representing the approach used for problems at QRS Employment Services.

Troubleshooters find causes by collecting and interpreting data and information at each step along the way. In doing so, they apply the principles of Continuous Quality Improvement. They use personal experience—from previous experience in similar situations and from actually working in the targeted process itself. They interview the staff members or others who are closest to the problem. They respect their knowledge and listen to them very carefully, for troubleshooters understand that the person who works a process every day knows that process best. Effective troubleshooting requires good information about the process. Later chapters provide further information on selecting measures for troubleshooting and offer several tools for data collection, display, and analysis that will facilitate the troubleshooting process.

Troubleshooting offers a powerful tool for staff members at any level of an organization. It helps staff members to select the actions and solutions most appropriate to identified problems. Because it works backwards from the outcomes desired to the root causes, troubleshooting ensures that the chosen solution will have an impact on the problem. Chapter 6 offers a specific troubleshooting aid—The Performance Engineering Matrix—which is designed to assist in finding solutions to problems in individual performance.

REFERENCES

Albin, J.M., & Magis-Agosta, K. (1989). *Self-assessment for changeover to supported employment: A troubleshooting approach.* Eugene: University of Oregon, Technical Assistance Brokerage.

Gilbert, T.F. (1978). *Human competence: Engineering worthy performance.* New York: McGraw-Hill.

Mager, R.F. (1982). *Troubleshooting the troubleshooting course: Or debug d'bugs.* Belmont, CA: David S. Lake.

Scholtes, P.R. (1988). *The team handbook: How to use teams to improve quality.* Madison: Joiner Associates, Inc.

Chapter 6

The Performance
Engineering Matrix

Finding Solutions

> "Solutions to problems are like keys in locks; they don't work if they don't fit." (Mager & Pipe, 1984, p. v)

Troubleshooting, discussed in Chapter 5, offers one strategy for localizing the target of repairs that are needed to improve the performance of an organization, department, group, or individual. Troubleshooting focuses on making the most important changes first. It does so by first identifying the outcome that is most unsatisfactory, then identifying the processes and activities that are the most direct causes of that outcome, and finishing by identifying the factors that will be most effective in changing that outcome. Thus, troubleshooting helps service organizations and others find the process or performance factor with the potential to yield the greatest amount of improvement in the outcome for the least cost.

For determining more specifically which variable, or barrier, deserves attention, this chapter presents another troubleshooting method: The Performance Engineering Matrix. Based on the work of Thomas Gilbert (1978), the Performance Engineering Matrix provides organizations with a guide to locating and prioritizing the causes of performance failures, and a strategy for selecting the most cost-effective means of addressing them. The Matrix is most useful in analyzing the performance of an individual staff person, though it may be applied at other levels as well. When the broader troubleshooting methods presented in Chapter 5 have identified issues that seem to be related to one or a few staff members, applying the Performance Engineering Matrix can refine identification of possible causes and identify potential remedial actions.

This chapter incorporates material from Chapter 4, "The Performance Engineering Matrix: Finding Solutions," appearing in Albin, J.M., and Magis-Agosta, K. (1989). *Self-assessment for changeover to supported employment: A troubleshooting approach.* Eugene: University of Oregon, Technical Assistance Brokerage. The author wishes to thank Kristen Magis-Agosta for her work on the earlier version, and Oregon's Mental Health and Developmental Disability Services Division for agreeing to allow that chapter to be incorporated in this text.

THE ROLE OF SYSTEMS IN INDIVIDUAL PERFORMANCE

Performance, even at the level of an individual staff person, encompasses a mixture of different variables. Indeed, Dr. Joseph Juran recognized that the potential to improve performance lies mostly in the systems in which staff members must work, rather than in the staff members themselves (Scholtes, 1988). At least 85% of problems can be corrected only by changing processes and systems, while only approximately 15% are under an employee's control (Scholtes, 1988)—this statement has become a rule of thumb in Continuous Quality Improvement. Furthermore, quality experts such as Dr. W. Edwards Deming assert that it is largely the responsibility of management to ensure that processes and systems that support the work of the organization are in place. Therefore, looking for improved outcomes primarily by blaming individual staff members is, in most cases, useless. Understanding and living by the "85%–15% rule" is one way in which managers can adopt quality improvement principles in their organizations.

> **The 85%–15% Rule:** "At least 85% of the problems can only be corrected by changing systems (which are largely determined by management) and less than 15% are under a worker's control . . . ." (Scholtes, 1988, ch. 2, p. 8)

Unfortunately, many system problems are blamed on individual staff persons working in rehabilitation or community-based employment settings. A job developer who is blamed for being ineffective, while his or her scheduled development time is used by the organization for substitute coverage for the facility or job sites; a job coach who is unable to help a company to help a supported employee perform well in a job that does not match the employee's interests; or the staff person who developed that job but was never provided with a viable method for job analysis and job matching, are examples of staff members suffering from problems in the processes and systems in which they work. Blaming an individual, when the most significant causes of poor performance lie in the systems in which he or she is forced to work, has dire results: The staff member learns to hide problems, becomes distrustful toward management and the organization, and loses the motivation to work to accomplish the mission.

The Performance Engineering Matrix is a tool to assist managers and others in sorting out systems issues from individual employee issues, and to identify possible means of resolving them. Therefore, the Performance Engineering Matrix provides an organization with a specific method for embedding in its system the principle, "Empower Employees To Work To Achieve the Mission," which was presented in Chapter 2.

PERFORMANCE VARIABLES

According to T.F. Gilbert (1978), an individual's ability to achieve the accomplishments desired by the organization is a function of the presence of six immediate variables represented as The Performance Engineering Matrix (see Figure 6.1.). Within this matrix, the variables are divided into two categories: Environmental Supports and Personal Repertory of Behavior. *Environmental Supports* are the components of the work environment created and manipulated by management to support individ-

	Information	Instrumentation	Motivation
Environmental Supports	Data Guides Feedback Performance indicators	Instruments Tools Materials Resources Equipment Schedules Systems	Incentives Pay Bonuses Recognition Time off
Personal Repertory of Behavior	Knowledge Conceptual Basic Technical Basic skills Technical skills	Capacity Perceptual Physical Emotional Personal prosthetic devices	Motives Intrinsic Internal reasons why a person is doing the job

Figure 6.1. The Performance Engineering Matrix. (Adapted from Gilbert [1978].)

ual efforts to achieve the organization's desired accomplishments. A *Personal Repertory of Behavior* consists of the personal resources and characteristics that the individual brings to the job which directly affect the individual's ability to perform. To perform effectively, an individual must have access to the appropriate Environmental Supports in the form of *Information and Feedback; Tools, Equipment, Resources, and Procedures;* and *Incentives;* as well as possess the appropriate Personal Repertory of Behavior, including *Knowledge and Skills, Capacity,* and *Motives.* Each of these variables is described briefly below:

- *Environmental Supports: Information and Feedback*—Information or guides provided by an employer to support performance includes, for example, job descriptions or written procedures that clearly describe desired accomplishments and how to achieve them. Frequent, relevant *feedback* on a person's performance and data systems that provide feedback to staff provide other information mechanisms that may be used by employers to support performance.
- *Personal Repertory of Behavior: Knowledge and Skills*—Information that is within the person's repertory includes his or her own individual *knowledge and skills.* To perform well, a person must possess basic conceptual knowledge, that is, an understanding of the theories, concepts, and rationale behind desired accomplishments; an understanding of what constitutes good and bad performance; and the specific knowledge and skills required to perform the duty. Organizations use staff training as a strategy for changing a person's repertory of knowledge and skills.
- *Environmental Supports: Tools, Equipment, Resources, and Procedures*—The *instrumentation* provided by employers to support performance includes the equipment, tools, materials, systems, and other resources that an individual may use to achieve desired accomplishments. To work best, these *instruments* must be designed with human factors in mind and with the assistance of the individuals who will be using them.
- *Personal Repertory of Behavior: Capacity*—The *instrumentation* that is within the individual's personal repertory is referred to as *capacity* and includes areas such as *perceptual capacity* (the senses such as sight and hearing), *physical capacity* (the

ability to perform and sustain the body movements necessary to perform tasks), and *emotional capacity* (the personal emotions that support effective performance).

- *Environmental Supports: Incentives*—Employers may provide *motivation* for good performance by using the environmental support of *incentives* to reward individuals for achieving desired accomplishments. These supports may be given in the form of contractual, or formal, incentives such as pay and benefits, or in the form of noncontractual, or informal, incentives such as recognition, awards, or bonuses.
- *Personal Repertory of Behavior: Motives*—The *motivation* variable in an individual's personal repertory is referred to by Gilbert as *motives*. This variable represents the individual's intrinsic motivation to achieve the accomplishments desired by the organization. Incentives offered by the organization are most influential when they match the motives of individual employees.

APPLYING THE PERFORMANCE ENGINEERING MATRIX

Together, the six variables described above make up the Performance Engineering Matrix. Individuals in an organization cannot achieve desired organizational accomplishments most effectively unless all six variables are arranged appropriately. Therefore, once an organization has used a troubleshooting tree to prioritize a component or activity of concern, often the specific source of the performance failure is revealed to be related to one or more of these six variables. The task for the organization, then, is to determine which of these has the most impact as a source of the barrier to accomplishment and to select and implement strategies to remediate the problem.

Probe Questions are a set of questions designed to lead an organization through an analysis of the six variables of the Performance Engineering Matrix. By reflecting the variables represented in the Performance Engineering Matrix, Probe Questions help target the sources of problems. Thus, Probe Questions are simply a guide for completing detective work into possible causes of performance deficits. The questions may be applied to many situations, including problems arising in changeover from facility-based to supported employment services, or performance problems in other human service situations. They may be applied to the performance of managers, direct line staff, or supported employees.

PRIORITIZING ACTIONS

The Performance Engineering Matrix not only provides a guide for discovering the sources of the barriers to improved performance, it also assists in prioritizing these sources so that they receive attention and resources in order of priority. Because resources are limited, particularly for organizations attempting to changeover to supported employment services, establishing priorities should be based on an assessment of the relative cost-effectiveness of different strategies for improving performance. In other words, the question becomes: Which solution will yield the greatest improvement in the desired accomplishment at the least cost?

Performance technologists such as Thomas Gilbert, along with quality improvement experts, recognize that most performance deficits are related to issues in the environmental factors represented in the Performance Engineering Matrix. Most employees want to do a good job and, given the appropriate environmental supports, will do so. Thus, Gilbert indicates that the most cost-effective approaches to

SAMPLE PROBE QUESTIONS

Environmental Supports: Information and Feedback
- Is there a description of what is expected of performance (e.g., a job description)? Does the responsibility fit the person's job?
- Are clear and relevant performance guides present that list the methods expected to be used? Are good examples available?
- Is relevant and frequent personal feedback available about the adequacy of performance? Is the feedback selective and specific, related to the defined expectations of performance? Is the feedback positive and constructive so people can learn from it?
- Do the data and information systems provide relevant, accurate, timely, readily accessible, and simple feedback on performance? Are the information systems used?

Environmental Supports: Tools, Equipment, Resources, and Procedures
- Are systems or procedures in place to support performance?
- Are adequate resources (e.g., tools, supplies, materials, assistance) available to support performance? Are they appropriate, reliable, efficient, safe?
- Do the working conditions (e.g., interruptions, noise, space, or time) support performance?
- Have the tools, procedures, and so forth been adapted to best support the capacities of the individual performing the job?

Environmental Supports: Incentives
- Are adequate financial incentives to good performance available (e.g., competitive pay, bonuses, or raises)? Are they timely, frequent?
- Are nonmonetary incentives available (e.g., recognition, responsibilities, days off)? Are they timely, frequent?
- Are career development opportunities offered?
- Is there an absence of punishment for performing well?
- Is there an absence of hidden incentives to perform poorly?

Personal Repertory of Behavior: Knowledge and Skills
- Do the members of the organization have the knowledge to perform well? Does this knowledge include an understanding of the "big picture," the difference between good and bad performance, and the technical concepts?
- Do the members of the organization have the specific technical or specialized skills to perform well?
- Do they have needed basic or general skills?
- Has previous training been provided in this area? Did it result in improved performance?

Personal Repertory of Behavior: Capacity
- Do the organization members have the ability to learn to fulfill the responsibility?
- Are organization members free of emotional limitations that would interfere with performance?
- Given appropriate prosthetics or adaptations, do organization members have sufficient physical capacity to perform the job well?
- Have organization members with the appropriate capacity been selected for performing this responsibility?

Personal Repertory of Behavior: Motives
- Did organization members have the desire to fulfill the responsibility when selected?
- Has the desire to fulfill the responsibility endured? (Adapted from Gilbert [1978].)

THE GARDENER, PART I

Jane Smith works as a gardener for the Greens, a wealthy family with a very large estate, and has been assigned responsibility for the flower beds on the grounds. Jane knows everything there is to know about gardening and works 16 hours a day. However, for all of her hard work, the flower beds are not producing very well. Her employer is understandably unhappy, having expended the cost of her salary with little return on that investment. Being an enlightened manager, Mrs. Green knows that she needs to analyze the sources of the problem before deciding on a course of action. So she proceeds to ask herself, and Jane, some Probe Questions to find those sources. Those Probe Questions and the answers Mrs. Green received are presented below.

Probe Questions about Environmental Supports	Answers
Information:	
Is there a description of the garden and guides for completing different parts of the job?	"Yes, in fact the landscaper left a very detailed drawing of what the flower beds should look like."
Does Jane get feedback on her performance?	"Yes, Mrs. Green comments at least once each week."
Instruments:	
Do procedures exist to guide performance (e.g., how to plant, how to treat the soil)?	"Yes, we have quite a library of gardening books in the shed."
Does she have all the right tools, chemicals, and other things she needs, and are they working well?	"No, I don't think so. The fertilizer you got from cousin Fred burned the soil, and I really could use a composter and other equipment."
Incentives:	
Are raises and promotions based on achieving high quality flower beds?	"Well, no. I just get my salary and a raise every year."
Are informal recognition and bonuses available for achieving bountiful flower beds?	"No. I never really get any of that. What kind of recognition?"

Probe Questions about the Personal Repertory	Answers
Knowledge:	
Does Jane understand how her performance affects the image of the family in the neighborhood?	"Yes, I know that how the estate looks is important in the community."
Does she have the needed knowledge and skills to produce bountiful flower beds?	"I have a degree in horticulture from Whatsamatter U. and graduated top in my class! My senior project was flower beds."

(continued)

THE GARDENER, PART I (*continued*)

Capacity:

Can Jane see and hear well enough to care for the flower beds?	"Yes, no problems there."
Can she lift, carry, use her hands, and so forth to attend to the beds?	"Yes, I'm strong as an ox."
Is she patient? Does she like working alone?	"Yes, I believe so."

Motives:

Does she care about producing bountiful flower beds?	"Well, no, if you want to know the truth. I used to love working on flower beds, but things have been going so badly here that I really don't know anymore."

Reviewing the answers to her various questions, Mrs. Green noticed that there were three variables from the Performance Engineering Matrix acting as sources of the problem of ugly flower beds:

- *Environmental Supports: Tools, Equipment, Resources, and Procedures*   Jane does not have the appropriate tools and materials to work well.
- *Environmental Supports: Incentives*   Jane is not rewarded, formally or informally, for good work. In fact, she gets raises whether or not the flower beds look beautiful.
- *Personal Repertory of Behavior: Motives*   Jane does not seem to care much any more about producing bountiful flower beds. Her low motivation seems to be related to her lack of accomplishment with the flower beds.

Mrs. Green now has some ideas about where to turn to improve the flower beds on her property. But she isn't sure which variable to address first.

barriers to success involve improving environmental deficiencies. In general, he says that modifying or creating information, instruments, or incentive systems is cheaper than providing training, developing methods to improve personal capacities, or influencing a person's internal motives. Moreover, he states that modifying environmental supports provides a higher probability that the organizational accomplishments will be achieved than do attempts at modifying personal characteristics (Gilbert, 1978).

Gilbert recommends the following order in which to prioritize direction of the organization's limited resources for improving performance:

1. *Information*   Examine the data provided to personnel. "Improper guidance and feedback are the single largest contributors to incompetence in the world of work . . . " (Gilbert, 1978, p. 91). By simple addition or revision of guides and feedback, many problems may be addressed in a very cost-effective manner.
2. *Instruments*   Examine the instruments, including the tools, systems, processes, and resources used to complete required tasks. If the instruments are deficient,

improvement efforts should be focused there. It is a waste of resources to train people to use ineffective processes and systems. Many of the tools of Continuous Quality Improvement, presented in later chapters, offer strategies for improving the processes through which staff members work.

3. *Incentives*   Look at the incentives provided by the organization to reward employees for their accomplishments. Referring to incentives, Gilbert says, "The most fundamental and simple concept of engineering competence seems to have been virtually abandoned . . . " (p. 91). People need to be rewarded for achieving organizational accomplishments. Rewards may be as simple as a pat on the back in recognition of a job well done. But without incentives to perform well, finding the motivation for achieving the organization's desired outcomes is much more difficult.

4. *Training*   Assess the need for training. While it is important continually to offer training opportunities, training is *not* always the best solution to specific performance problems. Skills learned through training cannot be used if the appropriate environmental supports are not present or are ineffective. Hence, it is important to ensure that all environmental supports are in place before implementing training strategies as the primary method of performance improvement. The Probe Questions from the Performance Engineering Matrix will help the organization avoid reliance on training as a solution when environmental supports really need attention. It is a waste of resources, for example, to train people to use tools that are inadequate for the job or to provide training to help staff memorize information that could be developed into a simple guide.

5. *Capacity*   If the four variables described above are in place, analyze a person's capacity to perform. There may be a need for adaptations to be developed (an environmental support, rather than a change in the person's repertory) to accommodate the person's inability to perform appropriately.

6. *Motivation*   Finally, consider the individual's internal motivation to succeed. As indicated above, incentives work best when they match an individual's motives for working. However, sometimes an organization is unable to provide the incentives a particular individual needs. If all other appropriate environmental and personal variables are intact and seem to work with other personnel, but the person is still not motivated to perform well, there are two choices: invest resources into influencing the person's internal motivation, or hire a different person for the job who *is* motivated to perform well.

The costs of adjusting a person's capacity and internal motivation to succeed can be very high. Counseling, for example, is expensive and carries no guarantee of success. Decisions to put resources into either area should be made with caution. The costs of adjusting these can be so great, in fact, that Gilbert recommends that a person's capacity and internal motivation be used as important criteria for initial hiring, rather than primarily the individual's knowledge and skills. This hiring guideline also applies to organizations that are undergoing changeover to community-based employment or other significant organizational changes requiring some of the existing staff to be reassigned into new roles. During changeover, selecting staff to work in new roles who are motivated to work in community employment settings and who seem to have the capacity to do so will greatly facilitate the changeover effort. Given the environmental supports of good information and feedback, effective tools and resources, and adequate incentives, staff members selected for new roles based on their capacity and motivation are most likely to make the changeover to community-based employment succeed.

Prioritizing actions according to the variables of the Performance Engineering Matrix will work in most situations. However, when the guidelines do not quite fit, analyze the potential solutions to determine where to focus attention and resources. Consider trying the following steps:

1. Using the Probe Questions from the Performance Engineering Matrix, identify potential solutions for each source of the performance barrier.
2. Determine the cost that might be associated with each of the solutions, including direct costs, staff time, and the indirect—less measurable—costs.
3. Estimate the value of the expected impact of each of the possible solutions on the barrier, as well as the impact on the other variables in the Performance Engineering Matrix.
4. Select the source on which to focus, based on the solution that promises the greatest effect for the least cost.
5. Finally, do not assume that performance problems can be solved by application of any one solution. Often, performance problems are the result of many factors, and only a combination of different solutions will resolve the problem. In any case, it makes sense to start by attacking the factor that seems to have the greatest impact on the problem. But often other solutions will be necessary as well.

Each of the Probe Questions from the Performance Engineering Matrix addresses a factor related to competent performance. A board or staff member may be having difficulty with a responsibility related to changeover or to implementing sup-

---

THE GARDENER, PART II

As you recall, Mrs. Green noticed that there were three variables from the Performance Engineering Matrix acting as sources of the problem of ugly flower beds:

- *Environmental Supports: Tools, Equipment, Resources, and Procedures*   Jane does not have appropriate tools and materials to work well.
- *Environmental Supports: Incentives*   Jane is not rewarded, formally or informally, for good work. In fact, she gets raises whether or not the flower beds look beautiful.
- *Personal Repertory of Behavior: Motives*   Jane does not seem to care much any more about producing bountiful flower beds. Her low motivation seems to be related to her lack of accomplishment with the flower beds.

Following Gilbert's recommendations, Mrs. Green decided to give Jane the equipment and supplies she needed immediately. She also decided to come up with a way to reward Jane for improving the flower beds. Because it is the beginning of the growing season, Jane will have the next few months with good tools and materials, and lots of attention whenever things are looking good. But she knows that if Jane's motives related to working on the flower beds do not improve, Jane may decide to leave. If Jane does leave, however, better equipment, supplies, and a reward system *should* help the *next* gardener to do a better job.

ported employment due to one or more of the factors listed in these questions. Therefore, a "No" answer to any of the Probe Questions begins to define the solution that is needed to improve performance.

Often it takes only a few minutes to analyze the information system issue by applying the Probe Questions, and even less time to choose a strategy based upon the answers to them. This is so because, basically, the Probe Questions themselves define possible solutions.

IDENTIFYING RESOURCES TO IMPLEMENT THE STRATEGY

The solutions identified through the Probe Questions represent some simple strategies for improving performance that are applicable to an organization pursuing changeover to supported employment services, or to other human service organizations. Other tools related to performance improvement are presented in later chapters. In implementing these or other solutions, there are several possible resources an organization may use:

- *Look at the organization's internal resources.* In many situations, identified solutions may be implemented simply by use of the resources already available in the organization. Other staff members or board members may possess the knowledge and skills to design and implement solutions for improving environmental supports and for providing training to staff.
- *Find another organization in changeover that performs the targeted activity well.* Gilbert recommends observing the methods of exemplary performers, that is, individuals who are achieving the desired accomplishment at the lowest cost in terms of both money and time. Therefore, if the activity that will lead to the greatest improvement in an organization is, for example, an improved method for communicating with staff who are working in dispersed locations, look for another organization that has already attacked that issue. In observing their methods, talk with members of their staff about what works and does not work. Ask the person most involved with their communication systems to spend time with your staff.
- *Obtain technical assistance.* Many groups, such as universities, private consulting firms, state associations, and state or federally funded projects, provide technical assistance related to organizational management, organizational culture, and implementing supported employment. Technical assistance is most effective when the organization requesting assistance is very clear about its needs; identifies an appropriate technical assistance provider with the capacity, knowledge, and skills to meet those needs; and schedules sufficient time for the technical assistance provider to understand the issues, provide support, and provide follow-up to assist with implementation of the recommendations.
- *Obtain training for staff members.* Some of the activities and solutions derived through a self-assessment process of changeover may be very new to all staff in the organization. Staff may require training in basic concepts or in information or skills directly related to implementing selected solutions. Technical assistance groups, professional associations, community colleges, and universities are good sources of training. However, be a wise consumer of training. Simply sending staff to a seminar on a topic that seems related to the issue at hand is likely to result in frustration. Be sure that the selected seminar offers content and training formats appropriate to the desired outcomes. Furthermore, provide follow-up on

XYZ REHABILITATION CENTER

At a recent board meeting, board members complained that the reports they were receiving did not provide the information they need to make decisions about change-over to more integrated employment services. As the board members discussed the issue, they realized that they had each felt the same way for the past few months, but had never said anything about it. However, they and the staff present at the meeting agreed that if more relevant data and information were available, the organization could move much more quickly through the changeover process. Thus, they agreed that this was the area of greatest need and asked Bill Jones, the executive director, to address the information system. Immediately, Bill wrote himself a note to talk with John Smith.

According to his job description, as assistant director for XYZ Rehabilitation Center, John Smith is responsible for establishing and maintaining the information system of the organization. His job description indicates that the information system is to give the managers and board members access to timely, accurate, and well-organized data for making decisions. Bill wondered, "Is the problem here that John is not doing his job? Or is the board's dissatisfaction due to causes outside John's control?"

The next day, before calling John in, Bill decided to analyze this issue using the Probe Questions from the Performance Engineering Matrix. Following are summaries of his thoughts on each probe topic area:

RESPONSES TO PROBE QUESTIONS

Environmental Supports: Information and Feedback

1. John's job description clearly specifies his responsibility with respect to the information system and gives clear expectations for that system.
2. John has access to other information systems from similar agencies. However, no specific model has been identified that is focused on decisions for changeover.
3. No, John has not been given feedback that his information system is not providing data relevant to changeover. In fact, in the past, the accuracy and completeness of the system have been praised both by Bill and by the board members.

Environmental Supports: Tools, Equipment, Resources, and Procedures

1. John has access to computers and has more than adequate resources for maintaining the information system.
2. Procedures for revising the system are established.
3. While all staff are overworked, generally John's working conditions are comfortable.
4. No, a system is not in place that adequately addresses changeover information needs. The current system was designed for the facility-based program and was purchased from QT Computer Systems.

Environmental Supports: Incentives

1. A variety of monetary and nonmonetary incentives are available and have been given to John to encourage and reward good performance.

(continued)

XYZ REHABILITATION CENTER (*continued*)

2. There are no known punishers for performing well or incentives for performing poorly.

Personal Repertory of Behavior: Knowledge and Skills

1. John is very knowledgeable and skilled with respect to computers and actually implemented the existing information system, adapting QT's system to XYZ's particular needs.
2. No, Bill does not know if John knows enough about the types of information needed for changeover decisions.

Personal Repertory of Behavior: Capacity and Motives

1. John clearly has adequate capacity and motivation for fulfilling this responsibility well. He usually does very well with special assignments.
2. There is no reason to believe that another person should be selected to assume this responsibility.

Reviewing his thoughts, Bill saw that he had answered "No" in the following categories of Probe Questions:

Environmental Supports
 NO   Information and Feedback
 NO   Tools, Equipment, Resources and Procedures
 ____   Incentives

Personal Repertory of Behavior
 NO   Knowledge and Skills
 ____   Capacity
 ____   Motives

The answers Bill gave to the Probe Questions basically defined the potential solutions to the problem of the information system. He had a few choices:

1. Give John some feedback based on the board's discussion related to the issues with the information system, and suggest someone he might contact to find a good sample system and to give him ideas.
2. Purchase a new information system that does address the information needs of his board with respect to changeover.
3. Send John to a training seminar on changeover to supported employment to teach him more about the kinds of information that might be needed to assist with changeover decisions.

Because feedback seemed to be an inexpensive and potentially effective solution, Bill decided to apply that strategy first. Besides, he could not find a seminar that directly addressed information systems for changeover, and QT Computer Systems had not heard about supported employment yet.

SAMPLE SOLUTIONS DEFINED BY PROBE QUESTIONS

I. Environmental Supports
    A. Information and Feedback
        1. Revise job descriptions to include specific definitions of responsibilities related to outcomes.
        2. Develop or purchase guides that assist staff to carry out each of the steps needed to fulfill the defined responsibility well.
        3. Establish clear expectations for performance, and share these with staff.
        4. Provide frequent, constructive feedback on performance that is specific and relevant and that compares performance with the defined expectations.
        5. Establish and use an information system that provides relevant, accurate, timely, accessible, and simple feedback on performance. Eliminate measures that are not used for decision-making.
    B. Tools, Equipment, Resources, and Procedures
        1. Document a system or procedure that is to be used by members of the organization. Review the system for effectiveness and apply quality improvement methods.
        2. Make sure that the appropriate procedure or system is being used for the situation.
        3. Provide the resources (e.g., tools, supplies, materials) needed to perform the responsibility well. Review these resources to ensure that they are appropriate, reliable, efficient, and safe.
        4. Arrange for working conditions (in regard to factors such as interruptions, noise, space, comfort, time) that support completion of tasks. When possible, eliminate distractions and other barriers to doing a good job.
        5. Adapt specific tools, resources, and procedures to support the capacities of the individual performing the job.
    C. Incentives
        1. Arrange available incentives (including bonuses or raises) so they are available for good performance, are timely, and are frequent.
        2. Develop nonmonetary incentives (e.g., recognition, responsibilities, days off). Use them frequently and in a timely manner.
        3. Identify individual career development interests and make opportunities for career development activities available.
        4. Review existing formal and informal personnel procedures to ensure that there are no punishers for performing well.
        5. Review existing formal and informal personnel procedures to ensure that there are no hidden incentives to perform poorly.
II. Personal Repertory of Behavior
    A. Knowledge and Skills
        1. Include members of the organization in discussion and decision-making regarding alternative courses of action.

(continued)

SAMPLE SOLUTIONS DEFINED BY PROBE QUESTIONS (*continued*)

    2. Provide ongoing training opportunities related to general concepts and basic skills to members of the organization.

    3. Provide training opportunities that provide knowledge of the "big picture," an understanding of the difference between good and bad performance, and the technical concepts needed to perform well.

    4. Provide training opportunities that are designed to include practice with feedback in order to help staff develop the specific technical or specialized skills needed to perform the job well.

    5. Provide opportunities to practice new skills in multiple settings with immediate feedback on performance.

    6. Select a different person for the job, with the knowledge and skills to perform the responsibility well.

B. Capacity
    1. Identify or design prosthetic devices to assist the employee to perform well.
    2. Select a different person for the job, with the physical, intellectual, and emotional capacity to fulfill the responsibility well.

C. Motives
    1. Provide supports such as counseling and values discussion to influence an individual's motives.
    2. For this job select a different person, one with the motivation to perform well.

site for staff persons who have attended seminars to help them apply their newly learned knowledge or skills in real work settings. For example, follow-up may entail a discussion with the staff person, a presentation by the person to other staff, or opportunities to practice skills in the natural setting *with feedback* provided. Some groups providing training seminars also offer on-site follow-up support to participants.

Improving an organization's outcomes with respect to changeover likely will involve many different solutions and performance strategies that are implemented throughout the changeover period. No one strategy will remediate all problems. Rather, a commitment to constant improvement of an organization's performance—that is, the outcomes, taking into account the cost of attaining them—will lead to a culture of growth and development, innovation, and change that will provide a better work experience both for staff members and for individuals in community-based employment.

REFERENCES

Albin, J.M., & Magis-Agosta, K. (1989). *Self-assessment for changeover to supported employment: A troubleshooting approach.* Eugene: University of Oregon, Technical Assistance Brokerage

Gilbert, T.F. (1978). *Human competence: Engineering worthy performance.* New York: McGraw-Hill.

Mager, R.F., & Pipe, P. (1984). *Analyzing performance problems or you really oughta wanna*. Belmont, CA: David S. Lake Publishers.

Scholtes, P.R. (1988). *The team handbook: How to use teams to improve quality*. Madison: Joiner Associates, Inc.

ADDITIONAL READINGS

Gilbert, T.F. (1982). A question of performance Part I: The PROBE Model. *Training and Development Journal, 36*(9), 21–30.

Gilbert, T.F. (1982). A question of performance Part II: Applying the PROBE Model. *Training and Development Journal, 36*(10), 85–89.

Zemke, R. (1982). *Figuring things out*. Reading, MA: Addison-Wesley Publishing Co.

Self-Assessment Guide for Changeover to Supported Employment

Applying Troubleshooting and the Performance Engineering Matrix to the Process of Changeover

Troubleshooting and the Performance Engineering Matrix are strategies that may be used in any situation in which an individual or group is trying to determine the best course of action to take for the greatest impact on improving performance. An organization may apply these strategies easily and informally, whenever performance is lacking, simply by asking a series of questions similar to those presented in the preceding chapters. Little specialized training is needed. Indeed, most people can increase their ability to use these strategies merely through practice.

This chapter offers a more formal example of implementing troubleshooting and the Performance Engineering Matrix through the *Self-Assessment Guide for Changeover to Supported Employment*. The *Guide* has been included for two reasons: to illustrate yet another specific application of these troubleshooting strategies, and to do so by offering a tool designed specifically to assist organizations undergoing the complex process of changeover to more integrated employment services. This chapter, therefore, should offer additional support to individuals who feel uncomfortable with their ability to use troubleshooting strategies without more formal guidance. For those who are completely unsure about how to do troubleshooting, the *Guide* is a good place to start. However, it is only a tool. Troubleshooting is a flexible process that does not require formal assessment instruments such as the *Guide* and can be done easily and quickly, with or without a written tool.

This chapter incorporates material from the Introduction and Chapter 5, "Using the Self-Assessment Instrument," appearing in Albin, J.M., and Magis-Agosta, K. (1989). *Self-assessment for changeover to supported employment: A troubleshooting approach.* Eugene: University of Oregon, Technical Assistance Brokerage. The author wishes to thank Kristen Magis-Agosta for her work on the earlier version, and Oregon's Mental Health and Developmental Disability Services Division for agreeing to allow those chapters to be incorporated in this text.

The *Self-Assessment Guide for Changeover to Supported Employment* (which is presented in the Appendix at the end of this chapter) supports stepping back from the daily grind of operations in a rehabilitation program to troubleshoot issues and prioritize actions to keep the organization moving forward in changeover. Chapters 5 and 6 give background information on the specific processes involved in implementing the *Guide*, and it is important to read them prior to attempting to use it. In addition, while reading through this chapter, it will be useful to refer to the *Guide* often to understand its structure clearly, as well as to see how it can assist in changeover.

FEATURES OF THE GUIDE

The *Self-Assessment Guide for Changeover to Supported Employment* serves as an example of one way to implement the troubleshooting methods of Continuous Quality Improvement. It was designed to offer a structure to support specific troubleshooting efforts related to organizational changeover from facility-based to community-based employment services. As such, it offers a troubleshooting tree for changeover. The *Guide* was designed to be applicable to a variety of unique rehabilitation organizations, each with very different histories, organizational structures, styles, expertise, and environments, as well as to be applicable across a range of potential approaches to providing employment supports. Furthermore, the *Guide* should be useful to organizations that are at different points in the changeover process including those that are only beginning to consider the benefits of changeover, as well as those that have already changed a large portion of their services from facility- to community-based operations. The *Guide* can also be expanded. Any organization should feel free to add items or otherwise revise it to better meet particular needs.

In designing the *Self-Assessment Guide for Changeover to Supported Employment*, it was clear that there were many things that it would *not* be able to do. For example, a focus on changeover meant that new, start-up organizations likely would not find the tool useful. In addition, organizations that have completed the changeover process may not find it helpful with respect to assistance in ongoing management of their activities. Even for organizations pursuing changeover, the *Guide* and its accompanying materials do not provide prescribed solutions to specific problems. Instead, the *Guide* offers help in organizing the questions for analyzing issues. In addition, the tool does not teach users how to implement the solutions chosen to address identified issues, but helps to ensure that the most cost-effective solutions are selected.

The specific content and process of the *Self-Assessment Guide for Changeover to Supported Employment* are designed to reflect fundamental principles and strategies of Continuous Quality Improvement. Because it uses self-assessment rather than relying primarily on an external evaluation process, the *Guide* empowers service provider organizations and builds ownership of changeover in their staff members. This chapter includes information that will allow members of service provider organizations to apply the instrument to troubleshoot changeover without additional assistance, if desired. Through its self-assessment process, the *Guide* takes advantage of the in-depth knowledge held by an organization's members, rather than relying primarily on short-term external consultants to analyze changeover needs. Thus, the methods used in the *Guide* encourage collaboration and team-building in organizations. Most important, however, the tool should lead to decisions and actions that make the best use of limited resources and that are effective in achieving im-

---

FEATURES OF THE *SELF-ASSESSMENT GUIDE FOR CHANGEOVER TO SUPPORTED EMPLOYMENT*

- Uses a self-assessment strategy.
- Focuses on changeover.
- Applies to a variety of rehabilitation organizations.
- Applies across differing approaches to providing employment with support.
- Useful at different points in the changeover process.
- Uses a troubleshooting approach.
- Assists with prioritizing next steps.
- Leads to decisions and action.
- Encourages collaboration and team-building.
- Increases the effectiveness of external consultants.
- Goes beyond identifying training and technical assistance needs.
- Provides explanatory materials and instructions for use.
- Supports efforts continually to improve outcomes, systems, and processes.

---

provements in changeover. And, if it is used repeatedly, it provides a process that can lead to continual improvement of organizational performance through changeover.

At times, however, organizations should also look beyond their own personnel for additional expertise—both for an external perspective to support the self-assessment process, and for assistance in remedying the identified issues. It is recommended that an organization occasionally invite an outside consultant to participate in the self-assessment process. Someone who is familiar with the methodology of the instrument, but who is not embedded in the organization, may be very useful in providing fresh perspectives on promoting changeover. This consultant may be a member of another organization that is also using this self-assessment process, or another individual who is familiar with it. Whoever is invited to participate, however, the process should be embraced by, and led by a member of the organization pursuing changeover. Indeed, the *Guide* can be used to help outside consultants

---

WHAT THE *SELF-ASSESSMENT GUIDE FOR CHANGEOVER TO SUPPORTED EMPLOYMENT* WAS NOT DESIGNED TO DO

- Assist in the formation of new, start-up organizations.
- Support ongoing management of organizations after changeover.
- Provide prescribed solutions to specific problems.
- Teach users how to implement the solutions chosen.
- Rely solely on external evaluation, training, and technical assistance for answers to performance problems.

assist an organization more effectively, by focusing their efforts on issues that will have the greatest impact on improving overall performance.

Too often, organizations assume that the answers to their dilemmas lie in obtaining additional staff training or technical assistance. However, as discussed in Chapter 6, training is not always the best solution for performance problems. Therefore, the *Self-Assessment Guide for Changeover to Supported Employment* goes beyond identifying training and technical assistance needs by assisting organizations to recognize when other performance improvement strategies to promote change might be more cost effective.

STRUCTURE OF THE GUIDE

The *Self-Assessment Guide for Changeover to Supported Employment* has been divided into three major sections, representing the three factors previously discussed with respect to organizational change: *Culture, Management,* and *Implementation.* Section I, *Culture,* deals with the character and style of the organization; Section II, *Management,* includes the formal mission statement and structures that form the foundation of the organization; and Section III, *Implementation,* addresses the specific activities necessary to implement supported employment. Table 7.1 depicts all the elements of the *Guide.*

Each section includes several different levels, as depicted in the troubleshooting tree shown in Figure 7.1. This figure places the organizational outcome of Changeover at the first level of the troubleshooting tree. The Sections (Culture, Management, and Implementation) are the second level of the tree, representing the primary

Table 7.1. Elements of the *Self-Assessment Guide for Changeover to Supported Employment*

Element	Definition	Location in *Guide*
Sections	Culture, Management, and Implementation—the three major factors in changeover to supported employment	Section I: Culture Section II: Management Section III: Implementation
Areas	Significant outcomes or accomplishments related to each Section	Part A of each Section
Components	The systems, processes, steps, or issues making up each Area	I Culture: Part B II Management: Part B III Implementation: Part B-1
Activities	The processes or steps for putting Components in place—The *Guide* has defined Activities only in Section III, Implementation.	III Implementation: Part B-2
Probe Questions	Factors addressed by the Performance Engineering Matrix—The same Probe Questions are applied to all Sections of the *Guide.*	Part C of each Section
Summary Worksheets	Sample format for tracking decisions made as an organization proceeds through the self-assessment and changeover process	The *last page* of each Section

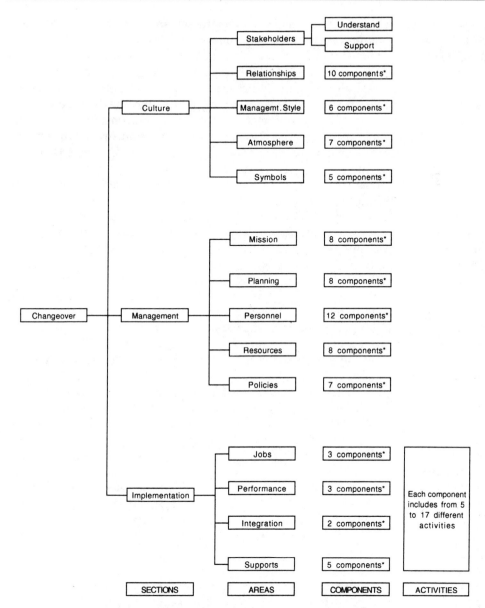

Figure 7.1. Levels of the troubleshooting tree from the *Self-Assessment Guide for Changeover to Supported Employment.* (*See *Guide* for details.)

accomplishments of a changeover effort. The next three levels, described below, are labeled *Areas, Components,* and *Activities.* Throughout this chapter, to reduce possible confusion, this terminology is used consistently to refer to each respective level of the troubleshooting tree.

Each Section of the troubleshooting tree has been divided into four or five Areas at the third level. These Areas represent significant outcomes or accomplishments the organization is attempting to achieve in Culture, Management, and Implementation. Implementation, for example, includes Areas related to developing jobs, meeting employer specifications, achieving integration, and providing ongoing support to meet individual needs. Areas are presented in *Part A* in each Section of the *Guide*.

The Areas of each Section have been divided into important Components at the fourth level of the tree. These are the issues that make up each Area; they could be viewed as systems, processes, or steps for achieving the outcome described by the Area. They define a part of the task of achieving the desired outcome in more specific detail. For example, in the Implementation Section, Integration Area, two Components are presented: 1) identifying or enhancing opportunities for integration, and 2) using strategies to increase actual social integration. Components are presented in *Part B* in the Culture and Management Sections of the *Guide*, and in Part *B-1* of the Implementation Section.

In the Implementation Section only, the troubleshooting tree has been taken to a fifth level, referred to as *Activities*. In this way, the Implementation Section related to supported employment has been taken to a greater level of detail than either of the others. Activities are the processes or steps that are necessary to put the Components in place to achieve the organization's accomplishments. For example, the Activities in the Implementation Section under Area 1: Integration, related to the Component on identifying and enhancing opportunities for integration, include: analyzing communication requirements, conducting ecological assessments, developing relationships between support personnel and co-workers, and restructuring the work environment to improve physical integration. Activities are presented in *Part B-2* of the Implementation Section only.

Two additional elements are included with each Section of the *Guide*: Part C of each Section presents the *Probe Questions*, based on the Performance Engineering Matrix described in Chapter 6. The Probe Questions are applied to the Component or Activity that, through the troubleshooting process, was selected as the greatest barrier to improved performance. The purpose of the Probe Questions is to assist in identifying the sources of that barrier. A Summary Worksheet is provided at the end of each section. As decisions are made, they may be recorded here so that they are not lost during the process. The Summary Worksheets provided in the *Guide* in the Appendix to this chapter are only samples. Feel free to revise them or create others that are more applicable to your organization's needs.

USING THE *SELF-ASSESSMENT GUIDE* FOR CHANGEOVER TO SUPPORTED EMPLOYMENT

Using the *Self-Assessment Guide for Changeover to Supported Employment* should be a relatively simple process. Following are several recommendations to help an organization begin using the *Guide* and maintain an effective self-assessment process as changeover proceeds.

Steps for Using the *Guide*

To use the *Guide* follow its format: Start with the three major Sections, prioritizing to identify the one most likely to have the greatest impact, then troubleshoot through the levels of that Section until the Performance Engineering Matrix Probe Questions can be applied.

STEPS FOR USING THE *SELF-ASSESSMENT GUIDE FOR CHANGEOVER TO SUPPORTED EMPLOYMENT*

Step 1. Determine whether troubleshooting should proceed first within the Culture, Management, or Implementation Sections. Make this decision based on which Section is likely to have the greatest impact on improving performance. (It might be helpful to review Part A [Areas] for each Section of the *Guide* in making this decision.)

Step 2. Determine which Area within that Section will lead to the greatest improvement in performance, by completing Part A of the chosen Section. If you are using Part A as a survey, instructions are listed at the top of Part A in each Section for each person who will be responding to the survey. Compile their responses by counting the number of "1" and "2" votes received by each item to determine which Area should be addressed first.

Step 3. Determine which Component in that Area will lead to the greatest improvement by completing Part B of the chosen Section. (In the Implementation Section, this is Part B-1.) *Use only the pages from Part B that apply to the Area selected in the previous step; ignore the rest for now.* See Step 2, above, if you are using Part B as a survey. For the Culture and Management Sections, this step should lead to identifying the biggest barrier to improved performance.

Step 4. If your organization has chosen to troubleshoot the Implementation Section, then determine which Activity in that Component will lead to the greatest improvement by completing Part B-2 of Implementation. Again, use only the pages for Part B-2 that apply to the specific Component selected through Step 3, above; ignore the rest for now. See Step 2 if you are using Part B-2 as a survey. Whether decided by group consensus, by a survey, or by one individual, this step for the Implementation Section should lead to identifying the biggest barrier to improved performance.

Step 5. Apply the Probe Questions to the selected Component (from the Culture or Management Section) or Activity (from the Implementation Section) to identify the possible sources of the performance barrier. The Probe Questions are included in Part C of each Section.

Step 6. Based on the sources of the barrier identified in Step 5, consider potential solutions and prioritize actions for removing the barrier and improving performance.

Step 7. Identify appropriate resources and implement the prioritized solutions.

Step 8. Repeat the above steps until changeover is completed.

Tips

- See Chapter 5 for additional information on the troubleshooting process used in Steps 1-4, and Chapter 6 for background information on Steps 5-7.
- When the meaning of an Area or Component is not clear, read ahead in the *Guide* to understand better where current decisions are leading.
- Review available data and use the knowledge of the individuals most directly involved with an item to help to make decisions.
- When making decisions about particular items, be sure to consider *all parts* of that item.

(continued)

STEPS FOR USING THE *SELF-ASSESSMENT GUIDE FOR CHANGEOVER TO SUPPORTED EMPLOYMENT* (continued)

• Solutions implemented to address the originally identified barriers may create change in other parts of the organization as well as in the Areas to which they were applied. Therefore, after implementing solutions in Step 7, it will probably be necessary to repeat the entire troubleshooting process to identify a new Section, Area, Component, and Activity of greatest concern.

Making Decisions During the Process

Using the *Guide*—or any troubleshooting process—requires that a series of decisions be made at several points in the process. Who participates in making these decisions and when and how these decisions are made are important questions that must be addressed by any organization involved in this process. A few guidelines are suggested here to support making good decisions throughout the troubleshooting process. Also, later chapters in Part III of this book offer several quality improvement strategies and tools that may be used to support decision-making during troubleshooting.

    Decisions About Potential Impact Throughout the troubleshooting process, the organization is asked to determine which Section, Area, Component, or Activity presents the greatest barriers to achieving accomplishments. In most cases, pick the item in which organizational or individual performance currently is the *farthest* from desired levels or that will lead to the highest value in improved outcomes, given the cost. If this is done, changes are likely to have the greatest impact. However, it is important also to consider the potential impact that changes in this item might have on other items. If, for example, troubleshooting the Implementation Section is necessary because there are not enough jobs, the existing employers are not satisfied, few people are achieving social integration, and other support services are disorganized and fragmented, the task is to choose the one Area in which changes likely will have the greatest impact on improving overall performance. In one organization, the Area with the greatest impact might be improving performance to meet employer-as-customer expectations, especially if improved employer satisfaction could be expected to lead to improved integration (someone who is doing a good job may be accepted more readily), and more jobs (recommendations from pleased employers are a good source for job leads). In another organization, it might be the fragmented support services—such as confusing telephone calls to the employer from the residential support provider, or Special Olympics practice that is scheduled to occur during work hours—that are the major issues reducing employer satisfaction.

    Strategies for Making Decisions An organization using the *Guide* must determine who should be involved in making the decisions required throughout the troubleshooting process and what methods will be used for making decisions. There are several options, and each may be useful at different points in the self-assessment. A few are discussed below:

1. One person with an accurate, broad-based view of the organization might make decisions on behalf of the organization. For example, which Section (i.e., Culture, Management, or Implementation) to troubleshoot, or which source identified from the Performance Engineering Matrix to target first are decisions that might be made by one person who is coordinating the overall process. Decisions made in this way have the advantage of being made quickly, but carry with them significant disadvantages related to building staff ownership and involvement, which may be critical concerns. Some decisions are simple, however, and are not worth the time that would be necessary to gather broader-based input.

2. All members of the organization might participate in decision-making. For example, if Culture has been selected for troubleshooting, distribute copies of Part A of the Culture Section to everyone. Compiling the responses or reaching partial or full agreement in a group meeting can give everyone a say in determining *which* Area of Culture should be chosen for attention. Once the Area is selected, copy and distribute the appropriate page or pages from Part B in the Section that lists the Components of the prioritized Area to allow members of the organization to continue the troubleshooting process. Note that only one level of the *Guide* should be distributed at a time and that *only* the page or pages from Part B (or B-1 and then B-2) that apply to the selected Area (and Component) need be used. Ignore the rest for now.

   To facilitate using pages from the *Guide* as a survey to obtain broad-based input, the appropriate pages of the *Guide* include written instructions for those who will be completing it. At each level of the *Guide*, compile individual survey responses by counting the number of "1" and "2" votes received by each item.

3. A team of individuals representing different groups, divisions, or roles in the organization might make decisions on behalf of the full organization. This strategy might work in larger organizations or in organizations that are farther along in the changeover process. If this strategy is selected, the composition of the team should be considered carefully, for the view of an organization held by a job coach or crew supervisor is very different from that of a rehabilitation manager, and each of these views is important to the changeover process. Thus, an effective team might be composed of a team coordinator, a person receiving employment services, the director or assistant director, a marketer, a job coach, a facility-based supervisor, and the bookkeeper. Strategies discussed in Number 2, such as distributing copies of the appropriate pages of the *Guide* to all team members and compiling responses from team members, or holding group meetings to reach consensus, should also be used in a team approach to decision-making. Later chapters in this book present strategies for developing teams for improving performance.

4. An external consultant could be employed to do an overall review of the organization and to recommend which Section and Areas should be addressed first. While the *Guide* is clearly designed to support a self-assessment process, it is recommended that an individual external to the organization participate in the process at least once a year. Such an individual is less likely to fall subject to "groupthink"—in which, for example, members of a group refrain from objecting to a decision because no other members of the group are objecting (Gaegler,

1989)—and may be able to offer new insights about the organization that are difficult to see from within. However, view the external consultant as a *participant* in the process, rather than as its leader.

5.   A mixture of the above approaches may be used. For example, copies of pieces of the *Guide* could be distributed for broad-based input for the management team or a changeover planning team. That team might then make the decisions themselves based on the input received and their own more global view of the organization and its resources. In another organization, all members of the organization might be asked to participate in one decision for each "round" of troubleshooting, with a smaller, cross-departmental team empowered to make the other decisions.

An organization may develop other options, as well. According to quality improvement experts, however, it is important to use the knowledge of the individuals most directly involved with an issue to help make decisions. They will have the most information about the item and care the most that a good decision is made. In addition, because changeover is such a demanding objective with significant impact at all levels of an organization, it requires the strong support of the people who will feel its impact. Therefore, it is recommended that decision-making during changeover include at least a team of participants, with information being shared with, and input obtained regularly from all members of the organization. In that way, the self-assessment process itself can assist in building a culture of support for changeover, teamwork, problem-solving, and communication. As more members are represented on the team, the decisions made will reflect a more holistic view of the organization, from differing vantage points. In addition, participation in decisions builds ownership of the changeover process to supported employment and increases investment in success.

Of course, each strategy also has its drawbacks. A simple count of votes on a survey of all staff to determine the item that would have the greatest impact could result in a skewed view if, for example, the staff is heavily weighted with job coaches or composed mostly of facility-based floor staff. In such cases, the decisions made would overwhelmingly lean toward the larger group, when the problems identified by the smaller group actually might be of equal or greater concern to the organization. For many organizations, meetings of the entire staff to reach consensus may be not only arduous, but too costly to use very often. And, as organizations proceed through changeover and staff members are dispersed into various community locations and work different hours, it may become less and less possible to hold full staff meetings on a regular basis. Yet, the *Guide* offers a good way to open discussions about different parts of the organization, and it is recommended that parts of the *Guide* be discussed whenever possible in small or large group meetings.

Whenever possible, use objective data for supporting decision-making throughout the troubleshooting process. Avoid making decisions based on the status of the individual in the organization who happened to offer a decision, the loudness with which the idea was presented, or the time during the meeting when it was offered. It is unlikely that the best decision is always the idea of the executive director, the only idea that could be heard, or simply the last thing that was said at the meeting. Section III, Implementation, suggests several performance indicators for each of its four major Areas to assist with determining which Area requires immediate attention. Use these to support opinions of those involved with making the decision regarding which Area to address first. Utilize data to support decisions in other Sections and levels of the *Guide* as well. The remaining chapters of this book suggest strategies for using information and offer additional tools and techniques for supporting decision-making.

COORDINATING THE TROUBLESHOOTING PROCESS

Implementing the self-assessment process will go more smoothly if one individual is selected to coordinate the process in an organization. Once a coordinator is selected, has read the chapters in Part II of this book, and understands the approach used by the *Guide*, an organization may begin the troubleshooting process.

The Role of the Self-Assessment Coordinator

The coordinator of the self-assessment process is very important to its success. The coordinator must become very knowledgeable about the strategies of troubleshooting, including the Performance Engineering Matrix. Reading Parts I and II of this book and fully understanding their content should help. The coordinator may also wish to pursue the Additional Readings on troubleshooting listed at the end of this chapter. In addition to the basics of troubleshooting, the coordinator must under-

ROLE OF THE SELF-ASSESSMENT COORDINATOR

- Learn about troubleshooting, the Performance Engineering Matrix, and the *Guide* by reading relevant chapters and recommended readings, and talking with others who have used these strategies.
- Explain the process and its purpose to all members of the organization, but particularly to those who will be participating in the self-assessment.
- Determine, for each step of the process, who will be involved in providing input and in making troubleshooting decisions.
- Select the methods that will be used for decision-making for each step of the troubleshooting process. For example, methods might include surveys to obtain input or group meetings to reach consensus.
- Facilitate group meetings in which the self-assessment process is discussed or carried out.
- When pages of the self-assessment instrument will be completed by several people or the full staff, coordinate copying and distributing the relevant pieces. Make sure participants clearly understand the instructions. Compile and report the results.
- Give participants in the process frequent and clear feedback about the value of their input.
- Communicate clearly, openly, and regularly about the process and its outcomes with anyone interested in your organization, including staff, board members, and members of the community.
- Be available to discuss the organization's experience with others interested in changeover to supported employment.

stand appropriate applications of the *Guide*, the values and assumptions underlying the approach, the structure of the instrument itself, and information on how to implement it. It is recommended that the coordinator talk with someone from another organization who is experienced in using the *Guide*, if such a person is available, in order to obtain further insights into its application. It is important that the self-assessment coordinator become well-versed in the material in order to lead the troubleshooting process. This knowledge will allow the coordinator to explain the process to others involved with the organization, particularly those who are participating in completing portions of the *Guide*. It is not necessary that all participants in the process read the material in Parts I and II of this book if the coordinator is able to teach them how to proceed through the process.

The coordinator should also be responsible for planning how the self-assessment will be implemented: How many people will participate in providing input and making decisions during each step of the troubleshooting process? How will they be selected? What strategies—that is, a survey using the forms provided, a set of interviews, or a group meeting—will be used for making decisions at various points in the process? What quality improvement tools for data collection and analysis would be most useful for making decisions? Will there be more than one group of troubleshooters functioning at one time? How will all members of the organization be given a chance to participate? How will information about the status of the self-assessment process be disseminated? The coordinator likely will wish to obtain input from others in making these decisions, but it is the coordinator who must know when to raise the questions and which questions to raise.

This person will also organize the logistical details of implementing the troubleshooting process. When portions of the self-assessment instrument are to be completed by several people, the coordinator must see to copying, distributing, and collecting the relevant pieces. The coordinator probably should also be responsible for compiling the results when the self-assessment is performed as a survey. When the self-assessment is conducted through group meetings, the coordinator may be the most appropriate person to facilitate those meetings. Whether using a survey, a meeting, or other means, however, it is important that the coordinator ensure that participants in the process understand the instructions for the self-assessment, as well as the meaning of particular items on it.

Perhaps the most fundamental role of the coordinator, however, involves communication. The coordinator must communicate clearly, openly, and regularly with all concerned about the process and its outcomes. Give participants in the process clear feedback about the value of their input and the status of the process. Report regularly to all staff, whether or not they are participants in the self-assessment. This communication must include individuals outside the organization, as well as those inside it. An organization undergoing changeover to supported employment needs the support of its community and state, and community members and state personnel are likely to have many questions about how the process is proceeding. As the coordinator grows in experience with troubleshooting and the *Guide*, he or she might also wish to be available to discuss the organization's experience with others beginning to use the instrument.

Who Should Be Coordinator?

The role of the coordinator should be filled by someone who is personally committed to the concept of changing over to community-based employment at least a part of the organization's facility-based services. The coordinator should be someone who is well-respected in the organization and is good at communicating with others. The coordinator should not have a defensive attitude and should treat issues raised as opportunities to work on concerns, rather than as attacks upon the coordinator, the organization, or its members. This is especially important because, in the process of troubleshooting, if staff feel that issues raised are not respected or are handled defensively, the process will not work. The self-assessment coordinator should also have some power in the organization to be able to get things done. However, this person need not be the executive director, an upper-level manager, or even a member of the staff. Some organizations may find it useful to invite a person outside of the staff to initiate the process, and then rely on an internal coordinator after that. There is no one answer. Consider the style and culture of your organization and work from there.

DEALING WITH MAKING DECISIONS

The self-assessment instrument is designed to be used repeatedly, in an ongoing process to improve the performance of an organization in changeover. Therefore, do not labor over decisions. Instead, at each level select the Area whose improvement the collective best guess indicates would lead to the greatest improvement in performance. Use data when they are available to support the decision, and use the knowledge of the people most directly involved in that Area. However, if the Area selected is not in order of priority, this is not a big problem; very likely on the next troubleshooting round the highest priority Area will be selected, or, if not then, on the following troubleshooting round.

Following are suggestions for the situation in which the decision on where to begin the self-assessment process just cannot seem to be made. These apply particularly to organizations that are at a relatively early stage in the changeover process:

1. Using the Management Section of the *Guide*, review the formal mission of the organization. Does it clearly support and lead the organization toward changeover? If not, spending the time to involve all members of the organization in revising the mission statement is an excellent starting point.
2. If the mission statement is adequate to lead the change, begin by using the Culture Section, then move to Management, and finally to Implementation. As described in previous chapters, the Culture of an organization must support change if changeover is to be successful.
3. In the Culture Section, start with the Area related to *stakeholder attitudes* then move to *symbols* or *management style*.
4. In the Management Section, once the Area related to *mission* has been addressed, move to the one on *planning*.
5. In the Implementation Section, start with the Area related to *supports* to lay the groundwork for *developing jobs*, then move to *work requirements*.

Make the troubleshooting process easy, light, and fun. Build it into how the organization operates on a regular basis. Use it at different organizational levels: for making decisions about improvements in the organization as a whole, or for troubleshooting at a particular job site. Do not put it on a shelf. Do not turn it into an overwhelming project. Just do it.

APPLYING THE *SELF-ASSESSMENT GUIDE FOR CHANGEOVER TO SUPPORTED EMPLOYMENT* TO TREK PERSONNEL'S PROBLEMS

James T., the new lead job developer, and Spock, a job coach, at Trek Personnel first appeared in Chapter 5 as they were trying to identify solutions to their biggest problem: insufficient work hours in community jobs. James T. used his knowledge and skills in troubleshooting to select solutions that were likely to have the greatest impact on improving work hours. However, if he had *not* had those skills, he could have used the *Guide* as he interviewed Spock. Try doing that yourself—finding your way through the levels and pieces of the *Guide* based on the information that was presented in Chapter 5. In this example, particularly when considering the Probe Questions (Part C of each Section), think of the family members and home providers as if they are the staff person with whom you are using the Probes. After you have finished compare your results with the following description.

Step	Result	Reasons
Select the Section	Implementation	Trek clearly has issues in other Sections as well—based on Sallye's firing—but the work hours problem is more immediate. (And it probably would not be a good idea for James T. to *start* in his job by trying to change the director's management style [Culture] or personnel systems [Management].)
Select the Area	Support	According to Spock, developing jobs was not a problem, and he reported no complaints from employers about performance, or from anyone about integration outcomes.
Select the Component	Individuals are *matched* with appropriate jobs *and* Consumers and advocates are *satisfied* with employer, job, and support organization	If you are unsure about which Component to choose, select two or three Components. Look at Part B-2 if you are not sure about what is included in a Component. These two seem to be closest to the problem.
Select the Activity	1. From *"matched"*: Utilize strategies to ensure family/residential provider commitment to community employment in general, as well as to the specifically selected job. 2. From *"satisfied"*: Provide opportunities for families and residential providers to address real or presumed issues and barriers related to integrated employment.	When Spock's information is used to review these two Components of Implementation in the *Guide,* these two items stand out. Spock described parental fears of loss of Social Security benefits as directly affecting about half the people with less than 20 hours of work per week. The other issues were a mixture of lack of support from home and problems faced by the home.

(continued)

110

APPLYING THE *SELF-ASSESSMENT GUIDE FOR CHANGEOVER TO SUPPORTED EMPLOYMENT* TO TREK PERSONNEL'S PROBLEMS
(*continued*)

Probe Questions

Environmental Supports

__X__ IA. Information and Feedback

Trek Personnel has limited *information* about Social Security, does not keep track of the financial effects of working, and has sponsored only one meeting on Social Security in the past year. No meetings have been held on "vision and values" beyond individual planning meetings.

__X__ IB. Tools, Equipment, Procedures

There is no system evident for regularly sharing information, and communication seems to be limited to individual planning meetings.

____ IC. Incentives

Reducing fears and barriers should offer natural incentives for stakeholders without additional effort.

Personal Repertory of Behavior

__X__ IIA. Knowledge and Skills

Parents, Trek's personnel, and others seem to lack knowledge and skills related to Social Security and work incentives.

__X__ IIB. Capacity

There may be capacity barriers for home providers related to nonstandard work hours. Some of these might be solved by adaptations made by Trek to assist.

____ IIC. Motivation

This is not an apparent issue. There is no reason to believe that the homes and families do not want the individuals to do well.

Select Solutions

IA. Environmental Supports: Information and Feedback
1. Develop/locate basic guides on Social Security and work incentives.
2. Discuss issue of Social Security individually or in another group meeting.
3. Discuss values and vision regarding community-based employment.
4. Summarize and give feedback on the experience of others related to the financial impact of working.

IB. Environmental Supports: Tools, Equipment, and Procedures
1. Develop a system to provide, on a regular basis, information to parents, families, and others regarding Social Security and the financial impact of working.
2. Develop procedures to improve ongoing communication about vision and values with stakeholders.

IIA. Personal Repertory of Behavior: Knowledge and Skills
1. Offer training related to Social Security and work incentives on a regular basis to staff, families, and others.

IIB. Personal Repertory of Behavior: Capacity
1. Develop a representative team consisting of Trek employees, home providers, and family members to identify and address any capacity barriers faced by the homes related to community-based employment.

The *Self-Assessment Guide for Changeover to Supported Employment* provides a system to improve the performance of an organization that is changing its services from facility-based to community-based supported employment. It will be effective only if it is used repeatedly and if the decisions made regarding performance improvement strategies lead to *action*. By using the approach presented in this *Guide*, an organization can focus its attention to make improvements, prioritize actions, and, hopefully, make the very difficult process of changeover a little easier. It is worthwhile. The result of all this work will be a giant step forward in offering opportunity to people with severe disabilities.

REFERENCES

Albin, J.M., & Magis-Agosta, K. (1989). *Self-assessment for changeover to supported employment: A troubleshooting approach.* Eugene: University of Oregon, Technical Assistance Brokerage.

ADDITIONAL READINGS

Gaegler, M.A. (1989). Overcoming groupthink. *Journal for Quality and Participation, June,* 86–89.

Gilbert, T.F. (1978). *Human competence: Engineering worthy performance.* New York: McGraw-Hill Book Company.

Gilbert, T.F. (1982). A question of performance Part I: The PROBE Model. *Training and Development Journal, 36*(9), 21–30.

Gilbert, T.F. (1982). A question of performance Part II: Applying the PROBE Model. *Training and Development Journal, 36*(10), 85–89.

Mager, R.F. (1982). *Troubleshooting the troubleshooting course: Or debug d'bugs.* Belmont, CA: David S. Lake Publishers.

Mager, R.F., & Pipe, P. (1984). *Analyzing performance problems or you really oughta wanna.* Belmont, CA: David S. Lake Publishers.

Scholtes, P.R. (1983). *The team handbook: How to use teams to improve quality.* Madison: Joiner Associates, Inc.

Zemke, R. (1982). *Figuring things out.* Reading, MA: Addison-Wesley Publishing Co.

Appendix

Self-Assessment Guide for Changeover to Supported Employment

After determining the Section in which to proceed with troubleshooting, determine which Area within that Section will lead to the greatest improvement in performance, by completing Part A of the chosen Section. Determine which Component in that Area will lead to the greatest improvement, by completing Part B of the chosen Section. Use only the pages from Part B that apply to the specific Area selected through Part A; ignore the rest of Part B for the time being. Finally, apply Part C only to the one or two Components (or Activities) selected through Part B.

SECTION I: CULTURE

This section of the self-assessment tool addresses the informal, cultural aspects of your organization. In some organizations, this culture encourages innovation, communication, and joint problem-solving, while in others these are discouraged. If there seems to be little consensus in your organization, or if you feel like you are working alone without the support of your peers, complete this section.

PART A: TARGET THE AREA OF GREATEST NEED IN CULTURE

*Consider each **area** listed below. Determine which area(s) impede your organization's ability to change over services to integrated employment. Select the **one** area in which you believe changes would have the greatest impact on improving performance. (If these areas are not clear, refer to Part B of this section for a further description of each.)*

Areas of Culture

____1.   Do all *stakeholders* share a vision that supports accomplishing changeover to integrated employment?

Stakeholders are specific individuals who have some sort of a vested interest in your organization. Whether employees or community members, stakeholders are individuals who will both be affected by and have an impact on the course of changeover. Therefore, their understanding and support are vital to accomplishing any large scale change. Changeover to integrated employment is such a change.

____2.   Are *relationships* within the organization characterized by teamwork and problem-solving?

Organizations that have embraced quality improvement principles understand that improving individual relationships within the organization is a powerful strategy to support achieving the mission. Therefore, in these organizations, employees are treated—and treat each other—as customers, communication flows freely across departmental and hierarchical boundaries, and individual members work together in teams to identify and solve mutual problems.

____3.   Does the *management style* of the organization support accomplishing integrated employment?

Although it may be possible to make some changes in organizations working from "lower levels" of the structure, the active support and leadership of top management is vital to achieving lasting, organization-wide change. The vision set by leaders and the way in which they interact with and support employees set the course of the organization during changeover.

____4.   Does the *atmosphere* support accomplishing integrated employment?

An organization's culture includes many intangibles: unwritten rules of behavior, expectations, shared values, beliefs. These intangibles seem to create a large part of the atmosphere in which employees work.

_____5.   Do the *symbols*, language, and public image used with individuals and groups both inside and outside of your organization support changeover to integrated employment?

The culture of an organization is passed on through its members by means of various symbols and images, largely created through the use of language. An organization with a culture that supports changeover to integrated employment makes good use of symbols, language, and a public image that will support such a change.

PART B: PRIORITIZE COMPONENTS WITHIN THE AREA OF GREATEST NEED

> *Read through each of the **components** of this area, listed below. Write "NA" next to any item that is already substantially in place and therefore will not need immediate attention. For the others, consider which ones would result in the greatest overall improvement in performance* **if** *they were in place. Rank those with 1 = the most important item, 2 = the next most important.*

Area 1.   Do all *stakeholders* share a vision that supports changeover to integrated employment?

Stakeholders are specific individuals who have some sort of a vested interest in your organization. Whether employees or community members, stakeholders are individuals who will both be affected by and have an impact on the course of changeover. Therefore, their understanding and support are vital to accomplishing any large scale change. Changeover to integrated employment is such a change.

Recommendation: For each component in this area, consider each stakeholder group separately, for the issues and strategies that might be used to address those issues will likely vary with different groups.

Components

_____   All **stakeholders** have a basic understanding of the rationale behind integrated employment and how it differs from other, facility-based services.
- _____   Board members
- _____   Top management staff
- _____   Middle management staff
- _____   Direct service staff
- _____   Other support staff
- _____   Employees with disabilities
- _____   Family members and advocates
- _____   Funders
- _____   Case managers and vocational rehabilitation counselors
- _____   Residential providers
- _____   Employers
- _____   Others _____

_____   The attitudes and values of all **stakeholders** support changeover to integrated employment services.
- _____   Board members
- _____   Top management staff
- _____   Middle management staff
- _____   Direct service staff
- _____   Other support staff
- _____   Employees with disabilities
- _____   Family members and advocates

_____ Funders
_____ Case managers and vocational rehabilitation counselors
_____ Residential providers
_____ Employers
_____ Others _____
_____ Systems exist to regularly maintain and improve communication between the
organization and its stakeholders related to its mission, values, and direction.
_____ Other _____

PART B: PRIORITIZE COMPONENTS WITHIN THE AREA OF GREATEST NEED

> *Read through each of the **components** of this area, listed below. Write "NA" next to any item that is already substantially in place and therefore will not need immediate attention. For the others, consider which ones would result in the greatest overall improvement in performance **if** they were in place. Rank those with 1 = the most important item, 2 = the next most important.*

Area 2.   Are *relationships* within the organization characterized by teamwork and problem-solving?

Organizations that have embraced quality improvement principles understand that improving individual relationships within the organization is a powerful strategy to support achieving the mission. Therefore, in these organizations, employees are treated—and treat each other—as customers, communication flows freely across departmental and hierarchical boundaries, and individual members work together in teams to identify and solve mutual problems.

Components

_____   Employees are treated as customers, and interactions among them are recognized as customer interactions.

_____   Every member of the organization, including direct care and support staff, is valued as having a function and knowledge critical to achieving the organization's goal.

_____   Members of the organization work cooperatively and collaboratively as a team, supporting each other, exchanging knowledge, and sharing resources to achieve a common goal.

_____   Strategies are used to build consensus, for example, when introducing planned changes to members of the organization. Collective group processes are used whenever possible to build support for change.

_____   People within the organization approach problem identification and solution as workable challenges rather than insurmountable barriers.

_____   Conflicts among members of the organization are dealt with openly and directly to achieve reconciliation.

_____   Two-way communication regularly and freely occurs across formal hierarchical boundaries.

_____   Positive, constructive, informal feedback on performance occurs freely across any formal hierarchical boundaries. Employees acknowledge efforts, encourage each other, and give recognition for accomplishments.

_____   The organization forms and supports small work groups to pursue specific issues, and utilizes their results. Work groups bring together individuals from different parts or levels of the organization and with different experience and skill backgrounds relevant to the task at hand.

____ Members of the organization who are recognized as experts take responsibility to teach others what they know.

____ Other _____

_____

PART B: PRIORITIZE COMPONENTS WITHIN THE AREA OF GREATEST NEED

> *Read through each of the **components** of this area, listed below. Write "NA" next to any item that is already substantially in place and therefore will not need immediate attention. For the others, consider which ones would result in the greatest overall improvement in performance **if** they were in place. Rank those with 1 = the most important item, 2 = the next most important.*

Area 3.   Does the *management style* of the organization support accomplishing integrated employment?

Although it may be possible to make some changes in organizations working from "lower levels" of the structure, the active support and leadership of top management is vital to achieving lasting, organization-wide change. The vision set by leaders and the way in which they interact with and support employees set the course of the organization during changeover.

Components

_____   Managers instill ownership of ideas, methods, and outcomes in staff and delegate authority and responsibility to members of the organization who are best qualified and most knowledgeable, rather than by hierarchical status. In this way, managers support decision-making by the individuals in the organization who are closest to an issue.

_____   The organization, at all levels, operates proactively, rather than in a reactive, crisis-management mode. Attention is focused on the factors and activities that will have the greatest impact on improving performance.

_____   Management provides support both for personal needs and professional growth. Managers recognize that "staff are customers, too" and take steps to increase their job satisfaction so they can work for achieving the organization's vision. This includes using effective strategies to prevent or decrease burnout.

_____   Management recognizes the organization's varying needs during changeover and addresses the ongoing trade-offs between facility-based and community-based services, consistently balancing in favor of integrated employment. The important role of the facility in supporting the changeover is clear.

_____   Top managers demonstrate active and visible leadership for changeover and for constant improvement. Managers behave as mentors and examples to others.

_____   Managers recognize that most problems are due to the systems in which people work, rather than the people themselves. Therefore, they use strategies to identify and troubleshoot systems issues and to support staff performance, rather than blaming individual staff for problems.

_____   Other _____

PART B: PRIORITIZE COMPONENTS WITHIN THE AREA OF GREATEST NEED

*Read through each of the **components** of this area, listed below. Write "NA" next to any item that is already substantially in place and therefore will not need immediate attention. For the others, consider which ones would result in the greatest overall improvement in performance **if** they were in place. Rank those with 1 = the most important item, 2 = the next most important.*

Area 4.   Does the *atmosphere* support accomplishing integrated employment?

An organization's culture includes many intangibles: unwritten rules of behavior, expectations, shared values, beliefs. These intangibles seem to create a large part of the atmosphere in which employees work.

Components

_____   In everything they do, members of the organization demonstrate respect for individuals with disabilities.

_____   Innovation and its essential elements, such as flexibility, questioning, risk-taking, and creativity, are characteristic of the organization.

_____   Members of the organization demonstrate high energy and commitment to quality and to changeover.

_____   The organization pursues constant improvement of services through ongoing refinement of processes and procedures, applying systematic methods and routinely using data for decision-making.

_____   Managers and employees alike believe that members of the staff want to do a good job, and given adequate environmental supports, will do so. All members of the organization seek to drive out fear, recognizing mistakes as opportunities to learn rather than as occasions for blame.

_____   The organization's members assume individual ownership of quality, taking responsibility for improving products and services. Individuals pursue quality improvements in small ways every day.

_____   Members of the organization are customer-driven, frequently seeking and responding to customer definitions of quality. All members of the organization value customers, rather than viewing them as nuisances or adversaries.

_____   Other _____

PART B: PRIORITIZE COMPONENTS WITHIN THE AREA OF GREATEST NEED

> *Read through each of the **components** of this area, listed below. Write "NA" next to any item that is already substantially in place and therefore will not need immediate attention. For the others, consider which ones would result in the greatest overall improvement in performance **if** they were in place. Rank those with 1 = the most important item, 2 = the next most important.*

Area 5.   Do the *symbols*, language, and public image used with individuals and groups both inside and outside of your organization support changeover to integrated employment?

The culture of an organization is passed on through its members by means of various symbols and images, largely created through the use of language. An organization with a culture that supports changeover to integrated employment makes good use of symbols, language, and a public image that will support such a change.

Components

_____   The organization is respected as a valued business in the local economic community that provides opportunities and professional services to community members.

_____   All interactions and materials confirm the competence and dignity of individuals with disabilities.

_____   All interactions with the community support the mission of the organization to increase integrated employment for people with disabilities.

_____   The organization uses a common language and other symbols that present cultural images supporting change to integrated employment. Change strategies are communicated to organizational stakeholders as basic beliefs rather than simply as operational plans.

_____   Staff orientation programs include a discussion of the organization's history, values, traditions, symbols, language, and future directions.

_____   Other _____

PART C: ANALYZE THE COMPONENT: PROBE QUESTIONS

Note here the **component** that offers the greatest opportunity to improve performance (as defined in Part B), from the prioritized area of culture:

_____

_____

Who will be given the responsibility for leading efforts for improving that?

_____

Issues related to changeover may be very complex and require group problem-solving methods. Additional strategies and tools for problem-solving and improving performance are presented elsewhere. However, when the performance issue appears to be linked with an individual staff member, or when the problem-solving group is not sure of what to do next, the Performance Engineering Matrix's Probe Questions are a good place to start.

---

*Below is a series of **probe questions** based on each variable of the Performance Engineering Matrix. The probe questions are designed to help you to analyze the issues related to this component. Apply the questions to the component you noted above, thinking in terms of the individual or group that will be responsible for leading improvement in that activity within your organization. Score each question as follows:*

NA = Not applicable
YES = Yes, this is substantially in place and therefore is not a concern at this time.
NO = No, this is not in place and therefore may need to be addressed at this time.
DK = Don't know

Probe Questions

IA.   Environmental Supports: Information and Feedback

NA YES NO DK   Is there a description of what is expected of performance, including clear and measurable guidelines for performance, for example, a job description? Does the responsibility fit with the rest of the job?

NA YES NO DK   Do clear and relevant guides exist for performance, that list the expected methods to be used? Are good examples available?

NA YES NO DK   Is relevant and frequent personal feedback available about the adequacy of performance? Is the feedback selective and specific, related to the defined guidelines for performance? Is the feedback educational, that is, positive and constructive so people learn from it?

NA YES NO DK   Do the data and information systems provide relevant, accurate, timely, readily accessible, and simple feedback on performance, and are they used?

NA YES NO DK   Do ongoing opportunities exist for open discussion of values, working relationships, policies, procedures, issues, and so forth?

IB.   Environmental Supports: Tools, Equipment, Resources, and Procedures

NA YES NO DK   Are systems or procedures in place to support performance and are they efficient, effective, and appropriate to the situation?

NA YES NO DK   Are adequate resources (e.g., tools, supplies, materials, schedules, assistance) available to support performance? Are they appropriate, reliable, efficient, safe?

NA YES NO DK   Do the working conditions (e.g., interruptions, noise, space, or time) support performance?

NA YES NO DK   Have the tools, procedures, and so forth been adapted to best support the capacities of the individual performing the job?

IC.   Environmental Supports: Incentives

NA YES NO DK   Are adequate financial incentives (e.g., competitive pay, bonuses, or raises) made available for good performance? Are they timely, frequent?

NA YES NO DK   Are nonmonetary incentives (e.g., recognition, titles, responsibilities, days off) made available for good performance? Are they timely, frequent?

NA YES NO DK   Are career development opportunities offered for good performance?

NA YES NO DK   Is there an absence of punishment for performing well?

NA YES NO DK   Is there an absence of hidden incentives to perform poorly?

NA YES NO DK   Do the organization's members recognize that most problems are systems problems, rather than individual performance issues, and handle incentives accordingly?

IIA.   Personal Repertory of Behavior: Knowledge and Skills

NA YES NO DK   Do the members of the organization have the knowledge to perform well, including understanding the "big picture," the difference between good and bad performance, and the technical concepts?

NA YES NO DK   Do the members of the organization have the specific technical or specialized skills to perform well?

NA YES NO DK   Do members of the organization have needed basic or general skills?

NA YES NO DK   Has previous training been provided to members of the organization in this area? Did it result in improved performance?

IIB.   Personal Repertory of Behavior: Capacity

NA YES NO DK   Do the organization members have the ability to learn how to fulfill the responsibility?

NA YES NO DK   Are organization members free of emotional limitations that would interfere with performance?

NA YES NO DK   Given appropriate prosthetics or adaptations, do organization members have sufficient physical capacity to perform the job well?

NA YES NO DK   Have organization members with the appropriate capacity been selected for fulfilling this responsibility?

IIC.   Personal Repertory of Behavior: Motives

NA YES NO DK   Did organization members have the desire to fulfill the responsibility when selected?

NA YES NO DK   Has the desire to fulfill the responsibility endured?

---

*If the items discussed in the **probe questions** are not present or effective in your organization, you need to create or modify them. Using the following list, check off the variables for which you indicated "NO" in answer to one or more of the probe questions.*

I.   Environmental Supports
   A.   _____   Information and Feedback
   B.   _____   Tools, Equipment, Resources, and Procedures
   C.   _____   Incentives
II.   Personal Repertory of Behavior
   A.   _____   Knowledge and Skills
   B.   _____   Capacity
   C.   _____   Motivates

Congratulations! You are well on your way to defining a strategy to improve the changeover of your organization to supported employment. Refer to the text to assist you in selecting the variable on which to focus, the performance improvement strategy (solution), and the resources that may be used to address this issue. As you select these, record them onto the Culture Summary Worksheet and begin implementing them.

*You may continue troubleshooting by applying the **probe questions** to the next prioritized **component** within the **area** of greatest concern. However, do not attempt to address more than one or two issues at a time. Instead, implement the selected performance improvement strategies and watch for positive changes. Then repeat the self-assessment process to prioritize the next item of concern.*

CULTURE: Summary Worksheet

Enter the organization's major decisions onto this worksheet as you proceed through the troubleshooting process. Feel free to use this as a suggested format and retype to provide more or less space, to add or delete information, and so forth. The purpose of this worksheet is only to help the coordinator of the self-assessment process keep track of decisions.

A.   Note the chosen **area** of greatest need from Part A:

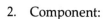

B.   List the selected **components** here from that area, as prioritized in Part B, with the most significant first. Complete the rest of the items as you finish Part C and finish selecting performance improvement strategies.

   1.   Component:

      Person responsible:

      Solution(s) and resources:

   2.   Component:

      Person responsible:

      Solution(s) and resources:

   3.   Component:

      Person responsible:

      Solution(s) and resources:

SECTION II: MANAGEMENT

This section of the self-assessment tool addresses formal management structures of your organization. In some organizations, these structures do not address supported employment or do not offer the flexibility needed to successfully change services to supported employment. If your own organization seems to be "getting in the way" of expanding community-based employment, complete this section.

PART A: TARGET THE AREA OF GREATEST NEED IN MANAGEMENT

*Consider each **area** listed below. Determine which area(s) impede your organization's ability to changeover services to integrated employment. Select the **one** area in which you believe changes would have the greatest impact on improving performance. (If these areas are not clear, refer to Part B of this section for a further description of each.)*

Areas of Management

_____1.   Does the organization actively pursue accomplishing a *mission* that includes integrated employment as an expected outcome?

The mission of an organization should lead its members toward integrated employment and continuous improvement of service to its customers. To be most effective in providing direction for prioritizing organizational and individual goals, strategies, and activities, the mission must be embedded throughout the organization.

_____2.   Do *planning* activities include and effectively promote changeover?

Changeover to integrated employment reaches into all corners of an organization. Strategic planning is needed to ensure that the organization both is poised to take advantage of opportunities and is prepared to address issues that may arise during the changeover process.

_____3.   Do *personnel* systems address and facilitate changeover?

Formal personnel systems in organizations pursuing changeover often require significant changes to provide for the flexibility needed to satisfy the varying demands of working in diverse community settings.

_____4.   Are organization and community *resources* developed, adjusted, and used to facilitate changeover?

Rehabilitation organizations have long relied upon a combination of community resources to maintain, expand, or improve operations. During changeover to integrated employment, existing resources must be adjusted and new resources may need to be identified to support new ways of doing business.

_____5. Do other organization *policies*, procedures, and external regulations facilitate changeover?

Changeover to integrated community employment requires flexibility. Too often, internal or externally controlled policies and procedures place barriers in the path of change.

PART B: PRIORITIZE COMPONENTS WITHIN THE AREA OF GREATEST NEED

*Read through each of the **components** of this area, listed below. Write "NA" next to any item that is already substantially in place and therefore will not need immediate attention. For the others, consider which ones would result in the greatest overall improvement in performance **if** they were in place. Rank those with 1 = the most important item, 2 = the next most important.*

Area 1. Does the organization actively pursue accomplishing a *mission* that includes integrated employment as an expected outcome?

The mission of an organization should lead its members toward integrated employment and continuous improvement of service to its customers. To be most effective in providing direction for prioritizing organizational and individual goals, strategies, and activities, the mission must be embedded throughout the organization.

Components

____ The existing mission statement is reevaluated at least annually with respect to its applicability for leading organizational change to community-based employment and continuous improvement. The re-evaluation process encourages the involvement of all members of the organization and representatives of its various customer groups.

____ The mission statement both clearly indicates community-based employment as an expected outcome and is formally incorporated throughout all levels and parts of the organization, for example, in job descriptions, staff meetings, and planning.

____ Board members' activities effectively support accomplishing a mission that includes integrated employment through their roles in planning and evaluation.

____ The formal structure of the organization (i.e., the organizational chart, including the allocation of staff resources, lines of communication, and so on) is organized to facilitate accomplishing a mission that includes integrated employment.

____ The decisions and activities within the organization related to integrated employment are coordinated across involved personnel to yield effective outcomes.

____ Formal links are established with the community and state (e.g., business community, other service providers, state personnel, funders, local planning council, families, advocates, consumers) to foster achieving a mission that includes integrated employment.

____ The formal strategies for building positive public relations support achieving a mission that includes integrated employment.

____ The organization regularly seeks information from its various customer groups on their definition of quality related to the mission and on the organization's performance. The organization takes action to improve performance on the mission based on customer input.

____ Other _____

PART B: PRIORITIZE COMPONENTS WITHIN THE AREA OF GREATEST NEED

> *Read through each of the **components** of this area, listed below. Write "NA" next to any item that is already substantially in place and therefore will not need immediate attention. For the others, consider which ones would result in the greatest overall improvement in performance **if** they were in place. Rank those with 1 = the most important item, 2 = the next most important.*

Area 2.   Do *planning* activities include and effectively promote changeover?

Changeover to integrated employment reaches into all corners of an organization. Strategic planning is needed to ensure that the organization both is poised to take advantage of opportunities and is prepared to address issues that may arise during the changeover process.

Components

_____   The board and staff of the organization have considered the impact of change-over to community-based employment with respect to all aspects of the organization and are implementing strategies to ensure organizational stability over time.

_____   Goals and objectives are established that will lead to achieving the mission and changeover to integrated employment and that reflect customer input.

_____   Effective strategies to promote changeover are identified as part of the plan.

_____   Implementation plans (e.g., budget allocations, staff assignments, timelines, contingency plans) are established and are effective for achieving desired objectives related to integrated employment. Plans include redirecting resources from facility-based to community-based employment services.

_____   An efficient information system that permits board, staff, and others to measure performance is available and is used effectively to make decisions.

_____   Objectives, strategies, and/or implementation plans are regularly reviewed and adjusted to improve performance.

_____   All management planning activities are based on the Shewhart Cycle (Plan-Do-Check-Act) to ensure continuous improvement.

_____   The organization's members use systematic approaches to find improvement opportunities and to improve performance.

_____   Other _____

PART B: PRIORITIZE COMPONENTS WITHIN THE AREA OF GREATEST NEED

> *Read through each of the **components** of this area, listed below. Write "NA" next to any item that is already substantially in place and therefore will not need immediate attention. For the others, consider which ones would result in the greatest overall improvement in performance **if** they were in place. Rank those with 1 = the most important item, 2 = the next most important.*

Area 3.   Do *personnel* systems address and facilitate changeover?

Formal personnel systems in organizations pursuing changeover often require significant changes to provide for the flexibility needed to satisfy the varying demands of working in diverse community settings.

Components

_____ Job descriptions adequately assign and describe responsibilities for implementing integrated employment.

_____ Staff recruitment, selection, and hiring procedures result in a cadre of staff with the motivation and capacity for implementing integrated employment.

_____ Incentives for performance (e.g., pay levels, promotions, raises, bonuses, recognition) promote improved performance related to implementing integrated employment.

_____ Other personnel policies and procedures support implementing integrated employment in a variety of settings.

_____ Staff orientation and initial training foster staff commitment, knowledge, and skills related to achieving integrated employment.

_____ The organization has identified needed changes in staff roles, implemented strategies to work with staff members who are resistant to role changes, and provided support to assist staff members to assume new roles.

_____ Formal mechanisms for communicating with staff (e.g., staff meetings, written memos) are designed to promote changeover to integrated employment and to reduce the isolation of staff members working in dispersed locations.

_____ Staff members have access to training, conferences, and forums on integrated employment to increase knowledge, skills, and flexibility related to identified implementation needs.

_____ Staff members are skilled in methods for collecting and analyzing data to support systematic methods for decision-making and troubleshooting. Data that are collected are used.

_____ Staff schedules provide the flexibility required to meet the support needs of individuals working in community jobs.

_____ Management provides support to personnel so that decisions can be made by those most directly involved with an issue.

_____ Personnel systems include procedures to ensure continuous improvement.

_____ Other _____

PART B: PRIORITIZE COMPONENTS WITHIN THE AREA OF GREATEST NEED

*Read through each of the **components** of this area, listed below. Write "NA" next to any item that is already substantially in place and therefore will not need immediate attention. For the others, consider which ones would result in the greatest overall improvement in performance **if** they were in place. Rank those with 1 = the most important item, 2 = the next most important.*

Area 4.   Are organization and community *resources* developed, adjusted, and used to facilitate changeover?

Rehabilitation organizations have long relied upon a combination of community resources to maintain, expand, or improve operations. During changeover to integrated employment, existing resources must be adjusted and new resources may need to be identified to support new ways of doing business.

Components

_____ The organization has identified and secured financial resources (e.g., through mental health, developmental disability, or vocational rehabilitation agencies, private sector foundations, or other sources) to support extra costs of changeover.

_____ The organization has secured other community resources (e.g., through professional and fraternal organizations, or generic services) to support changeover needs.

_____ The organization has established relationships with colleges, universities, and technical assistance organizations to support immediate and ongoing training and technical assistance needs.

_____ Integrated transportation options have been identified and are utilized to support individual participation in integrated employment. Transportation is not a barrier to working.

_____ The organization is implementing a plan for utilization or "disposal" of all or part of the physical facility to reduce overhead costs due to unneeded space.

_____ The organization is implementing a plan for performance or "disposal" of any existing subcontracts (including equipment and inventory) performed inside the current facility, given the reduced facility-based labor force after changeover. If a small facility-based program will be continued, the plan includes, for example, the anticipated capacities to perform work, the type and amount of work to be maintained, and strategies for increasing integration.

_____ In cooperation with the community, the organization has identified strategies to be implemented if workers lose jobs.

_____ Systems for managing the organization's resources include procedures to ensure continuous improvement.

_____ Other _____

PART B: PRIORITIZE COMPONENTS WITHIN THE AREA OF GREATEST NEED

> *Read through each of the **components** of this area, listed below. Write "NA" next to any item that is already substantially in place and therefore will not need immediate attention. For the others, consider which ones would result in the greatest overall improvement in performance **if** they were in place. Rank those with 1 = the most important item, 2 = the next most important.*

Area 5.   Do other organization *policies*, procedures, and external regulations facilitate changeover?

Changeover to integrated community employment requires flexibility. Too often, internal or externally controlled policies and procedures place barriers in the path of change.

Components

_____   Funder requirements that specifically interfere with changeover to supported employment have been identified and negotiations completed for their revision or waiver.

_____   Procedures used to meet external evaluation or accreditation requirements have been adjusted to facilitate changeover.

_____   Procedures used to meet requirements of the state or county mental health or developmental disability agency have been adjusted to facilitate changeover.

_____   Procedures used to meet requirements of the state's vocational rehabilitation agency or local offices have been adjusted to facilitate changeover.

_____   Procedures used to meet requirements of the Department of Labor and those of the equivalent state agency have been adjusted to facilitate changeover.

_____   Other policies and operating procedures specific to the organization have been adjusted to facilitate changeover.

_____   Systems are in place to ensure the continuous improvement of the organization's policies and procedures.

_____   Other _____

_____

PART C: ANALYZE THE COMPONENT: PROBE QUESTIONS

Note here the **component** that offers the greatest opportunity to improve perfor-mance (as defined in Part B) from the prioritized area of management:

_____

_____

Who currently has responsibility for implementing that? _____

Issues related to changeover may be very complex and require group problem-solving methods. Additional strategies and tools for problem-solving and improving perfor-mance are presented elsewhere. However, when the performance issue appears to be linked with an individual staff member, or when the problem-solving group is not sure of what to do next, the Performance Engineering Matrix's Probe Questions are a good place to start.

---

*Below is a series of **probe questions** based on each variable of the Performance Engi-neering Matrix. The probe questions are designed to help you to analyze the issues related to this component. Apply the questions to the component you noted above, thinking in terms of the individual or group that is responsible for that activity within your organization. Score each question as follows:*

NA = Not applicable
YES = Yes, this is substantially in place and therefore is not a concern at this time.
NO = No, this is not in place and therefore may need to be addressed at this time.
DK = Don't know

Probe Questions

IA.   Environmental Supports: Information and Feedback

NA YES NO DK   Is there a description of what is expected of performance, includ-ing clear and measurable guidelines for performance, for exam-ple, a job description? Does this responsibility fit with the rest of the job?

NA YES NO DK   Do clear and relevant guides exist for performance, that list the ex-pected methods to be used? Are good examples available?

NA YES NO DK   Is relevant and frequent personal feedback available about the adequacy of performance? Is the feedback selective and specific, related to the defined guidelines for performance? Is the feedback educational, that is, positive and constructive so people learn from it?

NA YES NO DK   Do the data and information systems provide relevant, accurate, timely, readily accessible, and simple feedback on performance, and are they used?

NA YES NO DK   Do ongoing opportunities exist for open discussion of values, working relationships, policies, procedures, issues, and so forth?

IB. Environmental Supports: Tools, Equipment, Resources, and Procedures

NA YES NO DK   Are systems or procedures in place for fulfilling this responsibility and are they efficient, effective, and appropriate to the situation?

NA YES NO DK   Are adequate resources (e.g., tools, supplies, materials, schedules, assistance) available to fulfill the responsibility? Are they appropriate, reliable, efficient, safe?

NA YES NO DK   Do the working conditions (e.g., interruptions, noise, space, or time) support fulfillment of this responsibility?

NA YES NO DK   Have the tools, procedures, and so forth been adapted to best support the capacities of the individual performing the job?

IC. Environmental Supports: Incentives

NA YES NO DK   Are adequate financial incentives (e.g., competitive pay, bonuses, or raises) made available for good performance? Are they timely, frequent?

NA YES NO DK   Are nonmonetary incentives (e.g., recognition, titles, responsibilities, days off) made available for good performance? Are they timely, frequent?

NA YES NO DK   Are career development opportunities offered for good performance?

NA YES NO DK   Is there an absence of punishment for performing well?

NA YES NO DK   Is there an absence of hidden incentives to perform poorly?

NA YES NO DK   Do the organization's members recognize that most problems are systems problems, rather than individual performance issues, and handle incentives accordingly?

IIA. Personal Repertory of Behavior: Knowledge and Skills

NA YES NO DK   Does the person have the knowledge to perform well, including understanding the "big picture," the difference between good and bad performance, and the technical concepts?

NA YES NO DK   Does the person have the specific technical or specialized skills to perform well relevant to this responsibility?

NA YES NO DK   Do they have needed basic or general skills?

NA YES NO DK   Has previous training been provided to this person in this area? Did it result in improved performance?

IIB. Personal Repertory of Behavior: Capacity

NA YES NO DK   Does the person have the ability to learn how to fulfill the responsibility?

NA YES NO DK   Is the person free of emotional limitations that would interfere with performance?

NA YES NO DK   Given appropriate prosthetics or adaptations, does the person have sufficient physical capacity to perform the job well?

NA YES NO DK   Has the person with the appropriate capacity been selected for fulfilling this responsibility?

IIC. Personal Repertory of Behavior: Motives

NA YES NO DK   Did the person have the desire to fulfill the responsibility when selected?

NA YES NO DK   Has the desire to fulfill the responsibility endured?

---

*If the items discussed in the **probe questions** are not present or effective in your organization, you need to create or modify them. Using the following list, check off the variables for which you indicated "NO" in answer to one or more of the probe questions.*

I.   Environmental Supports
   A.   ____   Information and Feedback
   B.   ____   Tools, Equipment, Resources, and Procedures
   C.   ____   Incentives
II. Personal Repertory of Behavior
   A.   ____   Knowledge and Skills
   B.   ____   Capacity
   C.   ____   Motivates

Congratulations! You are well on your way to defining a strategy to improve the changeover of your organization to supported employment. Refer to the text to assist you in selecting the variable on which to focus, the performance improvement strategy (solution), and the resources that may be used to address this issue. As you select these, record them onto the Management Summary Worksheet and begin implementing them.

*You may continue troubleshooting by applying the **probe questions** to the next prioritized **component** within the **area** of greatest concern. However, do not attempt to address more than one or two issues at a time. Instead, implement the selected performance improvement strategies and watch for positive changes. Then repeat the self-assessment process to prioritize the next item of concern.*

MANAGEMENT: SUMMARY WORKSHEET

Enter the organization's major decisions onto this worksheet as you proceed through the troubleshooting process. Feel free to use this as a suggested format and retype to provide more or less space, to add or delete information, and so forth. The purpose of this worksheet is only to help the coordinator of the self-assessment process keep track of decisions.

A.   Note the chosen **area** of greatest need from Part A:

_____

B.   List the selected **components** here from that area, as prioritized in Part B, with the most significant first. Complete the rest of the items as you finish Part C and finish selecting performance improvement strategies.

  1.   Component:

      Person responsible:

      Solution(s) and resources:

  2.   Component:

      Person responsible:

      Solution(s) and resources:

  3.   Component:

      Person responsible:

      Solution(s) and resources:

SECTION III: IMPLEMENTATION

This section of the self-assessment tool addresses specific strategies and activities directly related to implementing community-based employment. If your organization, as a whole, agrees that change to integrated employment is a desirable outcome but you do not quite know how to effect it or are having difficulty achieving the outcomes you desire, complete this section.

PART A: TARGET THE AREA OF GREATEST NEED IN IMPLEMENTATION

*Consider each **area** listed below. Determine which area(s) impede your organization's ability to changeover services to integrated employment. Select the **one** area in which you believe changes would have the greatest impact on improving performance. (If the content included in these areas is not clear, look ahead to Parts B-1 and B-2 for lists that describe each area more fully.)*

*A few suggested indicators are listed below each area to help in selecting the area with the greatest potential for improving performance. Complete these to help determine the area of greatest need: that is, the area in which the data are furthest from where you would like them to be. The indicators listed, if collected regularly, would give one perspective from which to evaluate the success of integrated employment in an organization on an ongoing basis. Feel free, however, to adjust these or add others that are more meaningful. **For many of the indicators, it will be necessary to establish a time period (e.g., 1 year, 6 months, 1 month) or a point in time at which to look at the data**.*

Areas of Implementation

____1.   Are sufficient integrated employment opportunities available to provide *jobs* for all individuals for whom integrated employment is a targeted outcome? Do the employment opportunities that are developed and maintained meet the definition of supported employment (i.e., the jobs developed are paid, *permit* social integration, provide at least 20 hours per week of work, and *allow for* ongoing support)?

Successful changeover from facility-based to community-based services requires that an organization work with community businesses both to develop new job opportunities and to maintain them. To be most successful, the organization must consistently have a sufficient number of appropriate job opportunities available to meet the employment needs of all individuals wishing to work who are served by the organization.

Suggested Indicators

____a.   Number and/or percentage of all individuals served by the organization who have access to integrated, community-based employment each week

____b.   Number and/or percentage of all individuals served by the organization who are in jobs that meet the supported employment definition (see above) ____c.   Number and/or percentage of individuals in jobs *offering* wages and benefits that are commensurate with those for co-workers without disabilities in similar positions, and are not productivity-based

____d.   Number of hours of paid work performed by individuals with disabilities working in community-based work sites

____e.   Number and/or percentage of individuals in employment settings and jobs that are highly valued by the community and that enhance the image of the individual

____f.   Number and/or percentage of community jobs lost (during a defined period of time) and reasons for job loss

____2.   Does *work performance* meet employer/customer expectations?

In integrated employment, the employer must be viewed as a customer. Therefore, the support organization must recognize and respond to the employer's expectations—or definition of quality—for work performance and related factors.

Suggested Indicators

____a.   Duration of employment for individuals in community-based jobs

____b.   Monthly wages earned by individuals with disabilities working in community-based work sites

____c.   Number and/or percentage of jobs in which the individual is meeting rate/productivity expectations of the employer/customer

____d.   Number and/or percentage of jobs in which the individual is meeting the quality expectations of the employer/customer

____e.   Number and types of complaints related to individuals' performance, received from employer/customer or others

____f.   Summary of employer-as-customer satisfaction surveys or interviews

____3.   Are individuals socially *integrated* with peers without disabilities?

Supported employment was largely developed as a vehicle to decrease the congregation of individuals with severe disabilities, as well as their segregation from typical social environments. However, the goal of social integration is not met by mere physical presence in regular work settings. Rather, the goal is to assist in supporting individuals with disabilities in expanding their social networks and relationships with peers who are not also "service recipients." *Meaningful* social integration results from expanding the number and diversity of people in an individual's life who care and who participate in the mutual relationships that are typical of friends.

Suggested Indicators

Note: For each indicator within this area, do not consider staff of the support organization when identifying "people without disabilities."

____a.   Number and/or percentage of individuals working *in proximity* to people without disabilities (within the same work area for most of the working hours)

____b.   Number and/or percentage of individuals who *frequently* interact at least casually (e.g., exchange greetings or jokes) with people without disabilities during work and/or break times

____c.   Number and/or percentage of individuals who have extended *both* the network of people with whom they interact and their significant relationships, within or outside of the work place, as a result of this job

___d. Number and/or percentage of individuals who work in sites with no more than one other individual with disabilities in same work area

___e. Summary of surveys or interviews with service recipients (and/or their advocates) related to their satisfaction with integration and social relationships

___4. Are ongoing *supports* that meet individual needs provided?

Individuals with severe disabilities may require diverse numbers and types of supports to allow them to work successfully in integrated settings. Supports must be tailored to each individual's changing needs, but may be provided by any of a number of different people: employers and co-workers, neighbors and friends, family members or advocates, or members of the more formal "service system."

In addition, individuals with disabilities are likely to be most successful if they and the people in their lives who care about them, including service providers, can agree on the importance of work, an appropriate vision of what is possible, and strategies for achieving that vision.

Suggested Indicators

___a. Number and/or percentage of individuals in community-based jobs (or targeted for supported employment) for whom all needed supports (e.g., financial, medical, transportation, family, appropriate clothing) are available and delivered as needed

___b. Number and/or percentage of individuals in community-based jobs for whom the employer, supervisor, and co-workers provide for support needs

___c. Number and/or percentage of individuals in community-based jobs who have achieved promotions or job enhancement related to career development

___d. Number and/or percentage of individuals in community jobs and their advocates who are satisfied with their job and the support provided; summary of satisfaction surveys or interviews

PART B-1: PRIORITIZE COMPONENTS WITHIN THE AREA OF GREATEST NEED

> *Read through each of the **components** of this area, listed below. Write "NA" next to any item that is already substantially in place and therefore will not need immediate attention. From the others, **select the one** that would result in the greatest overall improvement in performance **if** it were in place.*

Area 1. Are sufficient employment opportunities available to provide *jobs* for all individuals for whom integrated employment is a targeted outcome?

Successful changeover from facility-based to community-based services requires that an organization work with community businesses both to develop new job opportunities and to maintain them. To be most successful, the organization must consistently have a sufficient number of appropriate job opportunities available to meet the employment needs of all individuals served by the organization who wish to work.

Components

_____ New **prospective** job opportunities or employers/customers are continuously identified. (Consider whether the number of these "prospects" is always significantly larger than the number of individuals who are candidates for integrated employment.)

_____ **Actual** job commitments that appropriately match the interests and needs of individuals and meet or exceed the definition of supported employment, are secured from employers/customers. (Consider whether the number of appropriate job commitments is at least equal to the number of individuals who are candidates for integrated employment.)

_____ Appropriate job commitments from employers/customers are maintained over time through strong relationships among the support organization, the employers/customers, and the worker. (Consider the longevity of the commitments from each employer/customer.)

_____ Other _____

PART B-1:   PRIORITIZE COMPONENTS WITHIN THE AREA OF GREATEST NEED

> *Read through each of the **components** of this area, listed below. Write "NA" next to any item that is already substantially in place and therefore will not need immediate attention. From the others, **select the one** that would result in the greatest overall improvement in performance **if** it were in place.*

Area 2.   Does *work performance* meet employer/customer expectations?

In integrated employment, the employer must be viewed as a customer. Therefore, the support organization must recognize and respond to the employer's expectations —or definition of quality—for work performance and related factors.

Components

____   Work systems are organized for performance. (This component reflects larger "production management" issues that may need to be addressed in particular for group placements or for small businesses that are operated by the support organization.)

____   Work to be performed is organized to facilitate individual performance. (Consider activities such as task design, adaptations, and material handling related to individual performance of jobs.)

____   Individual worker performance is developed to meet employer/customer expectations and performance is maintained over time. (This component includes direct training and support, which may be provided by the employer, co-workers, support agency staff, or others.)

____   Other _____

PART B-1:   PRIORITIZE COMPONENTS WITHIN THE AREA OF GREATEST NEED

> *Read through each of the **components** of this area, listed below. Write "NA" next to any item that is already substantially in place and therefore will not need immediate attention. From the others, **select the one** that would result in the greatest overall improvement in performance **if** it were in place.*

Area 3.   Are individuals socially *integrated* with peers without disabilities?

Supported employment was largely developed as a vehicle to decrease the congregation of individuals with severe disabilities, as well as their segregation from typical social environments. However, the goal of social integration is not met by mere physical presence in regular work settings. Rather, the goal is to assist in supporting individuals with disabilities in expanding their social networks and relationships with peers who are not also "service recipients." **Meaningful** social integration results from expanding the number and diversity of people in an individual's life who care and who participate in the mutual relationships that are typical of friends.

Components

____   Effective strategies are used to identify and enhance the physical and social integration **opportunities** for individuals with disabilities.
____   Effective strategies are implemented and evaluated to increase the meaningful social integration of individuals with disabilities.
____   Other _____

PART B-1:   PRIORITIZE COMPONENTS WITHIN THE AREA OF GREATEST NEED

> *Read through each of the **components** of this area, listed below. Write "NA" next to any item that is already substantially in place and therefore will not need immediate attention. From the others, **select the one** that would result in the greatest overall improvement in performance **if** it were in place.*

Area 4.   Are ongoing *supports* that meet individual needs provided?

Individuals with severe disabilities may require diverse numbers and types of supports to allow them to work successfully in integrated settings. Supports must be tailored to each individual's changing needs, but may be provided by any of a number of different people: employers and co-workers, neighbors and friends, family members or advocates, or members of the more formal "service system."

In addition, individuals with disabilities are likely to be most successful if they and the people in their lives who care about them, including service providers, can agree on the importance of work, an appropriate vision of what is possible, and strategies for achieving that vision.

Components

_____ Individuals are matched with appropriate jobs.

_____ Logistical activities that must be completed prior to initiation of employment (e.g., transportation arrangements and Social Security, Department of Labor, and tax forms) are completed.

_____ Individual support needs are coordinated and implemented through, for example, continuous reassessment, individual service plans, and communication with other stakeholders.

_____ Consumers and advocates are satisfied with the employer, job, and support organization.

_____ Career development is achieved for each individual over time.

_____ Other _____

PART B-2: SELECT THE ACTIVITIES TO IMPROVE PERFORMANCE

Area 1. Are sufficient employment opportunities available to provide *jobs* for all individuals for whom integrated employment is a targeted outcome?

Component: New *prospective* job opportunities or employers/customers are continuously identified.

> *Read through each of the **activities** related to this component and area of Implementation, listed below. Write "NA" next to any item that is already substantially in place and therefore will not need immediate attention. For the others, consider which ones would result in the greatest overall improvement in performance if they were in place. Rank those with 1 = the most important item, 2 = the next most important.*

Activities To Improve Performance

____ Define the quality parameters of desirable jobs (e.g., working conditions, type of work, hours of employment, who provides supervision, longevity of job, opportunities for advancement), based on individual interests of candidates for integrated employment and your organization's values.

____ Perform and update public and private sector market analysis based on defined quality parameters and career interests of candidates for integrated employment.

____ Develop and adjust marketing plan, including, for example, market identity and location, objectives, selected strategies, evaluation system, resources, and contingency plans. Consider both public and private sector markets.

____ Develop marketing materials to support plan.

____ Implement marketing plan, including making marketing contacts to develop potential job opportunities.

____ Build long-term relationships with businesses, sharing a vision of inclusion for people with disabilities and supporting the business in leading the effort.

____ Develop and maintain a business advisory board to advise staff and extend networks for marketing.

____ Implement networking strategies to identify potential employers/customers.

____ Provide presentations on integrated employment to employers, business associations, and civic groups to increase community awareness.

____ Develop and maintain an information system to evaluate marketing efforts.

____ Maintain employer/customer files.

____ Incorporate methods to support continuous improvement in all systems and processes related to this component.

____ Other _____

PART B-2:   SELECT THE ACTIVITIES TO IMPROVE PERFORMANCE

Area 1.   Are sufficient employment opportunities available to provide *jobs* for all individuals for whom integrated employment is a targeted outcome?

Component: *Actual* job commitments that appropriately match the interests and needs of individuals and meet or exceed the definition of supported employment, are secured from employers/customers.

> *Read through each of the **activities** related to this component and area of Implementation, listed below. Write "NA" next to any item that is already substantially in place and therefore will not need immediate attention. For the others, consider which ones would result in the greatest overall improvement in performance if they were in place. Rank those with 1 = the most important item, 2 = the next most important.*

Activities To Improve Performance

____   Establish a process for developing jobs, negotiating job commitments, and developing long-term relationships with employers/customers. Through the process, support businesses in taking the lead in identifying their interests, needs, and capabilities.

____   "Qualify" potential job opportunities or employers/customers based on a job development checklist and decision rules; assess employment sites based on desired quality parameters (e.g., good working conditions, stable settings, opportunities for advancement).

____   Work with employer to complete job analysis for all jobs to include, for example, job tasks, time studies, schedules, employer/customer expectations, low frequency job events, social interaction opportunities. Integrate results of job analyses with planning and performance.

____   For subcontract relationships, develop and submit bid; rebid as appropriate.

____   Match individual interests and needs with specific jobs developed.

____   Negotiate job commitments with employers/customers (including, e.g., working conditions, type and location of work, hours of employment, who provides training and other support, longevity of job, opportunities for advancement). Emphasize application of typical company policies and routines.

____   Develop and implement written agreements defining responsibilities and commitments based on negotiations, as appropriate.

____   Utilize job creation or modification strategies when appropriate; negotiate desired quality parameters of job.

____   Establish and maintain payment mechanisms for all employees that meet the requirements of the Fair Labor Standards Act and its amendments. Advocate for pay and benefits that are commensurate with other employees doing similar work, and are not productivity-based.

_____ Incorporate methods to support continuous improvement in all systems and processes related to this component.

_____ Other _____

PART B-2:   SELECT THE ACTIVITIES TO IMPROVE PERFORMANCE

Area 1.   Are sufficient employment opportunities available to provide *jobs* for all individuals for whom integrated employment is a targeted outcome?

Component: Appropriate job commitments from employers/customers are maintained over time through strong relationships among the support organization, the employers/customers, and the worker.

*Read through each of the **activities** related to this component and area of Implementation, listed below. Write "NA" next to any item that is already substantially in place and therefore will not need immediate attention. For the others, consider which ones would result in the greatest overall improvement in performance if they were in place. Rank those with 1 = the most important item, 2 = the next most important.*

Activities To Improve Performance

_____ Build relationships with employers/customers based on honesty and trust beginning with initial meetings. Build employer capacity to lead the effort to incorporate individuals with disabilities into the context of their company.

_____ Plan and implement strategies (including communication, problem-solving, and crisis management) for maintaining strong employer/customer relations.

_____ Maintain contact with employers/customers during job vacancies or interruption of work.

_____ Define and implement methods for assessing employer/customer satisfaction with individual, trainer, and support organization.

_____ Analyze employer/customer satisfaction and modify strategies to improve employer/customer commitment.

_____ Assist the employer/customer to recognize the contribution that the individual makes to the employment setting.

_____ Define and deliver employer/customer support services related to work systems or employee services as requested by the employer/customer.

_____ Negotiate for modifying job responsibilities if appropriate, and modify any written agreements.

_____ Develop and implement procedures to interview employers/customers in the event of job loss. Utilize information collected to improve future services.

_____ Incorporate methods to support continuous improvement in all systems and processes related to this component.

_____ Other _____

PART B-2:   SELECT THE ACTIVITIES TO IMPROVE PERFORMANCE

Area 2.   Does work *performance* meet employer/customer expectations?

Component: Work systems are organized for performance.

*Read through each of the **activities** related to this component and area of Implementation, listed below. Write "NA" next to any item that is already substantially in place and therefore will not need immediate attention. For the others, consider which ones would result in the greatest overall improvement in performance if they were in place. Rank those with 1 = the most important item, 2 = the next most important.*

Activities To Improve Performance

____   Complete capacity planning (e.g., technical skills, financial resources, labor requirements).

____   Arrange physical location for performing work that offers opportunities for community integration.

____   Complete process design, layout, and workflow to facilitate performance.

____   Complete work allocation/schedule across workers to maximize earnings for individuals with disabilities.

____   Plan and purchase material requirements to meet customer obligations.

____   Maintain inventory control.

____   Utilize appropriate materials handling procedures, including packaging and shipping.

____   Design and implement quality assurance procedures, including specifications, methods, and performance records.

____   Utilize appropriate business procedures such as invoices and accounts management.

____   Establish and maintain production information and control system to permit monitoring and adjusting production procedures to improve performance.

____   Incorporate methods to support continuous improvement in all systems and processes related to this component.

____   Other _____

PART B-2:   SELECT THE ACTIVITIES TO IMPROVE PERFORMANCE

Area 2.   Does work *performance* meet employer/customer expectations?

Component: Work to be performed is organized to facilitate individual performance.

> *Read through each of the* **activities** *related to this component and area of Implementation, listed below. Write "NA" next to any item that is already substantially in place and therefore will not need immediate attention. For the others, consider which ones would result in the greatest overall improvement in performance if they were in place. Rank those with 1 = the most important item, 2 = the next most important.*

Activities To Improve Performance

Note: The activities listed below may be performed by the employer or co-workers, members of the support organization, or others. However, it is important to ensure that the company is supported in leading the effort, and that the support organization work for increasing the company's capacity to perform these functions.

____ Utilize job analysis information to organize work for performance (including, e.g., sequencing tasks, organizing materials).

____ Analyze flexibility of employer/customer regarding job modifications, task design, and adaptations. Support employer/customer, as needed, to accomplish all planned changes.

____ Design each task to facilitate performance (e.g., determine how to perform task, arrange work station, select tools and equipment).

____ Design, implement, and adjust job adaptations and fixtures to assist individual performance.

____ Obtain necessary resources for designing and developing modifications, job adaptations, or fixtures.

____ Perform ongoing job analysis to ensure adequate performance.

____ Incorporate methods to support continuous improvement in all systems and processes related to this component.

____ Other _____

PART B-2:   SELECT THE ACTIVITIES TO IMPROVE PERFORMANCE

Area 2.   Does work *performance* meet employer/customer expectations?

Component: Individual worker performance is developed to meet employer/ customer expectations and performance is maintained over time.

> *Read through each of the **activities** related to this component and area of Implementation, listed below. Write "NA" next to any item that is already substantially in place and therefore will not need immediate attention. For the others, consider which ones would result in the greatest overall improvement in performance if they were in place. Rank those with 1 = the most important item, 2 = the next most important.*

Activities To Improve Performance

Note: The activities listed below may be performed by the employer or co-workers, members of the support organization, or others. However, it is important to ensure that the company is supported in leading the effort, and that the support organization work for increasing the company's capacity to perform some or most of these functions.

_____   Complete specific analysis of individual tasks that require training and identifying natural cues and consequences.

_____   Analyze job to identify general case training needs.

_____   Design and implement general case training strategies if needed.

_____   Implement training strategies that are appropriate to the employment setting to increase accuracy or rate of performance.

_____   Design and implement procedures to maintain performance over time.

_____   Establish an information system and procedures for documenting and reviewing employee performance.

_____   Analyze performance over time (including employer/customer feedback) and adjust training and support strategies to improve performance. Provide retraining when required.

_____   Design and incorporate self-management procedures.

_____   When subminimum wages are paid, utilize fair methods of assessing productivity; meet the requirements of the Department of Labor. Advocate for non-productivity-based wage payments that are commensurate with that of other employees performing similar work.

_____   Design, implement, and adjust procedures to improve productivity to match the expectations of the environment.

_____   Utilize strategies to fade trainer support, based on performance data.

_____   Identify and utilize natural long-term supports in the work environment while implementing individual training and support strategies.

_____   Provide support to the employer, supervisor, and/or co-workers to implement methods for improving and maintaining individual performance.

____ Incorporate methods to support continuous improvement in all systems and processes related to this component.

____ Other _____

PART B-2: SELECT THE ACTIVITIES TO IMPROVE PERFORMANCE

Area 3. Are individuals socially *integrated* with peers without disabilities?

Component: Effective strategies are used to identify and enhance the physical and social integration *opportunities* for individuals with disabilities.

> *Read through each of the **activities** related to this component and area of Implementation, listed below. Write "NA" next to any item that is already substantially in place and therefore will not need immediate attention. For the others, consider which ones would result in the greatest overall improvement in performance if they were in place. Rank those with 1 = the most important item, 2 = the next most important.*

Activities To Improve Performance

Note: As with all support activities, efforts by support organization personnel to expand social integration outcomes must be implemented with care. Indeed, recent research has shown that the presence of a job coach or support person is likely to have a significant effect: **decreasing** the amount of integration that is achieved. Therefore, support organization staff must take care to support the company and its employees in efforts to achieve full inclusion for their co-worker with disabilities.

_____ Analyze work- and non–work-related communication requirements and opportunities in the employment setting.

_____ Conduct ecological assessments (as a part of job analysis) to identify existing physical and social integration opportunities in and around the workplace.

_____ Match clothing and style of support personnel and the individual to the work setting.

_____ Develop relationships between support personnel, co-workers, and supervisors.

_____ Provide information to co-workers, home providers, and others to support participation in social events and activities both at and outside of work.

_____ Continuously seek opportunities to restructure work environment (including location of work station) or supports to increase opportunities for social integration; negotiate needed changes with employer/customer as needed.

_____ Identify co-workers or others in the work environment who, based on their informal social position, might be able to increase the acceptance by others of the individual with disabilities.

_____ Incorporate methods to support continuous improvement in all systems and processes related to this component.

_____ Other _____

PART B-2:   SELECT THE ACTIVITIES TO IMPROVE PERFORMANCE

Area 3.   Are individuals socially *integrated* with peers without disabilities?

Component: Effective strategies are implemented and evaluated to increase the meaningful social integration of individuals with disabilities.

> *Read through each of the **activities** related to this component and area of Implementation, listed below. Write "NA" next to any item that is already substantially in place and therefore will not need immediate attention. For the others, consider which ones would result in the greatest overall improvement in performance if they were in place. Rank those with 1 = the most important item, 2 = the next most important.*

Activities To Improve Performance

Note: As with all support activities, efforts by support organization personnel to expand social integration outcomes must be implemented with care. Indeed, recent research has shown that the presence of a job coach or support person is likely to have a significant effect: **decreasing** the amount of integration that is achieved. Therefore, support organization staff must take care to support the company and its employees in efforts to achieve full inclusion for their co-worker with disabilities.

____ Identify the discrepancy between opportunities for physical and social integration and the actual outcomes experienced by individuals with disabilities.

____ Identify co-workers or others interested in assisting with support for individuals with disabilities.

____ Develop and provide orientation to co-workers at the employment setting (if appropriate) that enhances the image of individual(s).

____ Define and utilize strategies to reduce the amount and types of unnatural supports used to maintain performance, when feasible.

____ Provide training and support to assist individuals to use community stores and other resources near the workplace.

____ Provide training and support to individuals and others to enhance integration during work, breaks, lunch, or other nonwork times.

____ Provide assistance to facilitate and maintain relationships with other employees.

____ Design appropriate communication strategies, including augmentative systems, to assist individuals to meet work-related communication requirements and to interact with others in their work environment.

____ Provide training and support to the individual and co-workers to utilize selected communication systems while providing task or other training.

____ Incorporate methods to support continuous improvement in all systems and processes related to this component.

____ Other _____

PART B-2:   SELECT THE ACTIVITIES TO IMPROVE PERFORMANCE

Area 4.   Are ongoing *supports* that meet individual needs provided?

Component: Individuals are matched with appropriate jobs.

> *Read through each of the **activities** related to this component and area of Implementation, listed below. Write "NA" next to any item that is already substantially in place and therefore will not need immediate attention. For the others, consider which ones would result in the greatest overall improvement in performance if they were in place. Rank those with 1 = the most important item, 2 = the next most important.*

Activities To Improve Performance

Note: As in other areas and components, it is important that the support organization provide support to the company interested in hiring a person with disabilities. Therefore, some of these activities should be performed by the company (just as they would with their other employees), but with extra assistance available from the support organization.

_____   Target individual candidates for integrated employment, including those with more challenging physical and intellectual disabilities.

_____   Identify (with assistance of the individuals, staff, family members, and interested others) the job interests, desired quality parameters, and needs of targeted candidates for integrated employment. Use information to develop résumé.

_____   Utilize strategies to ensure family/residential provider commitment to community employment in general, as well as to the specifically selected job.

_____   Match individuals with jobs based on, for example, job development and analysis information, interests, skills, and needs of the individuals.

_____   Incorporate methods to support continuous improvement in all systems and processes related to this component.

_____   Other _____

PART B-2:   SELECT THE ACTIVITIES TO IMPROVE PERFORMANCE

Area 4.   Are ongoing *supports* that meet individual needs provided?

Component: Logistical activities that must be completed prior to initiation of employment (e.g., transportation arrangements and and Social Security, Department of Labor, and tax forms) are completed.

> *Read through each of the **activities** related to this component and area of Implementation, listed below. Write "NA" next to any item that is already substantially in place and therefore will not need immediate attention. For the others, consider which ones would result in the greatest overall improvement in performance if they were in place. Rank those with 1 = the most important item, 2 = the next most important.*

Activities To Improve Performance

_____ Develop standard list of pre-employment logistics to be addressed.

_____ Complete referral and eligibility determination process for support from vocational rehabilitation.

_____ Identify and implement procedures to secure any other available financial resources to support employment (e.g., through federal job training initiatives, the Social Security Administration, or a developmental disabilities agency).

_____ Provide training and support to individuals to utilize integrated transportation options to and from work, as appropriate, including riding with co-workers.

_____ Assist with job interview if necessary.

_____ Assist employer to complete work site orientation for individual with disabilities.

_____ Notify members of individual planning team of impending job.

_____ Complete tasks on pre-employment checklist for each individual placed.

_____ Incorporate methods to support continuous improvement in all systems and processes related to this component.

_____ Other _____

PART B-2:   SELECT THE ACTIVITIES TO IMPROVE PERFORMANCE

Area 4.   Are ongoing *supports* that meet individual needs provided?

Component: Individual support needs are coordinated and implemented through, for example, continuous reassessment, individual service plans, and communication with other stakeholders.

> *Read through each of the **activities** related to this component and area of Implementation, listed below. Write "NA" next to any item that is already substantially in place and therefore will not need immediate attention. For the others, consider which ones would result in the greatest overall improvement in performance if they were in place. Rank those with 1 = the most important item, 2 = the next most important.*

Activities To Improve Performance

_____ Assess short- and long-term support and training needs with respect to integrated employment and individual service planning.

_____ Assemble individual planning group at least annually in cooperation with case manager.

_____ Develop individual plan, including goals, objectives, methods, measures, and responsible parties.

_____ Review performance data against individual plan and adjust strategies or plan as needed.

_____ Develop individual training and behavior support methods required by plan.

_____ Develop and implement strategies to increase employer/co-worker involvement in providing support to individual at the work site.

_____ Establish and update schedules for providing individual support.

_____ Implement strategies to support individual expression of preferences and choices whenever feasible.

_____ Coordinate individual financial benefits to minimize financial disincentives for working.

_____ When appropriate, coordinate adult education opportunities with supported employment job.

_____ Identify and facilitate provision of supports (e.g., transportation, job development, training) through the family, social network, or service system.

_____ Develop (and implement when needed) an individual resource and support plan to deal with potential job loss.

_____ Coordinate with local schools to begin to transfer employment support for students transitioning from school to adult services, well before school eligibility ends.

_____ Provide information to schools to ensure that students are well prepared for integrated employment and leave school with a paid job.

_____ Develop (and implement when needed) emergency or crisis procedures.

_____ Assist individual to access generic services as needed.
_____ Incorporate methods to support continuous improvement in all systems and processes related to this component.
_____ Other _____

PART B-2:   SELECT THE ACTIVITIES TO IMPROVE PERFORMANCE

Area 4.   Are ongoing *supports* that meet individual needs provided?

Component: Consumers and advocates are satisfied with the employer, job, and support organization.

> *Read through each of the **activities** related to this component and area of Implementation, listed below. Write "NA" next to any item that is already substantially in place and therefore will not need immediate attention. For the others, consider which ones would result in the greatest overall improvement in performance if they were in place. Rank those with 1 = the most important item, 2 = the next most important.*

Activities To Improve Performance

_____ Develop and implement strategies to assess the satisfaction of the individual with disabilities and his or her advocate with the employer, job, and support organization.

_____ Implement procedures to adjust or change to a new job when the individual and his or her advocates are dissatisfied.

_____ Maintain good communication with families and residential providers regarding each individual's job, changes, and needs.

_____ Provide opportunities for open dialogue with families and residential providers to address real or presumed issues and barriers related to integrated employment.

_____ Develop and implement separation interview procedures. Utilize information to improve future services.

_____ Establish customer relationships with families, residential providers, and others, soliciting and responding to their feedback to improve performance.

_____ Incorporate methods to support continuous improvement in all systems and processes related to this component.

_____ Other _____

PART B-2:   SELECT THE ACTIVITIES TO IMPROVE PERFORMANCE

Area 4.   Are ongoing *supports* that meet individual needs provided?

Component: Career development is achieved for each individual over time.

> *Read through each of the **activities** related to this component and area of Implementation, listed below. Write "NA" next to any item that is already substantially in place and therefore will not need immediate attention. For the others, consider which ones would result in the greatest overall improvement in performance if they were in place. Rank those with 1 = the most important item, 2 = the next most important.*

Activities To Improve Performance

____   Provide or arrange for re-employment assistance to individuals changing jobs.

____   Refine individual career preferences over time through analysis of work experiences, observation, tours, or other means appropriate to the individual.

____   Pursue opportunities for job enhancement or promotion (e.g., changes in job responsibilities, location, pay, benefits, employment status).

____   Utilize job loss as an opportunity to pursue individual career development.

____   Utilize time (particularly downtime) in the facility-based program prior to community placement to access the community.

____   Utilize volunteer positions on a time-limited basis and only when they support career development objectives, paid positions cannot be found, and they are in valued and integrated settings where people typically volunteer. Volunteer positions support career development objectives if they develop marketable skills, lead to employment or are used to supplement paid work experiences, and do not interfere with resources to develop paid work.

____   Incorporate methods to support continuous improvement in all systems and processes related to this component.

____   Other _____

PART C: ANALYZE THE ACTIVITY: PROBE QUESTIONS

Note here the **activity** that offers the greatest opportunity to improve performance (as defined in Part B-2), from the prioritized **area** and **component**:

_____

_____

Who currently has responsibility for implementing that? _____

Issues related to changeover may be very complex and require group problem-solving methods. Additional strategies and tools for problem-solving are presented elsewhere. However, when the performance issue appears to be linked with an individual staff member or when the problem-solving group is not sure of what to do next, the Performance Engineering Matrix's Probe Questions are a good place to start.

---

*Below is a series of **probe questions** based on each variable of the Performance Engineering Matrix. The probe questions are designed to help you analyze the issues related to this activity. Apply the questions to the activity you noted above, thinking in terms of the individual or group that will be responsible for that activity within the organization. Score each question as follows:*

NA   = Not applicable
YES = Yes, this is substantially in place and therefore is not a concern at this time.
NO   = No, this is not in place and therefore may need to be addressed at this time.
DK   = Don't know

Probe Questions

IA.   Environmental Supports: Information and Feedback

NA YES NO DK   Is there a description of what is expected of performance, including clear and measurable guidelines for performance, for example, a job description? Does the responsibility fit with the rest of the job?

NA YES NO DK   Do clear and relevant guides exist for performance, that list the expected methods to be used? Are good examples available?

NA YES NO DK   Is relevant and frequent personal feedback available about the adequacy of performance? Is the feedback selective and specific, related to the defined guidelines for performance? Is the feedback educational, that is, positive and constructive so people learn from it?

NA YES NO DK Do the data and information systems provide relevant, accurate, timely, readily accessible, and simple feedback on performance, and are they used?

NA YES NO DK Do ongoing opportunities exist for open discussion of values, working relationships, policies, procedures, issues, and so forth?

IB. Environmental Supports: Tools, Equipment, Resources, and Procedures

NA YES NO DK Are systems or procedures in place for fulfilling this responsibility and are they efficient, effective, and appropriate to the situation?

NA YES NO DK Are adequate resources (e.g., tools, supplies, materials, schedules, assistance) available to fulfill the responsibility? Are they appropriate, reliable, efficient, safe?

NA YES NO DK Do the working conditions (e.g., interruptions, noise, space, or time) support fulfillment of this responsibility?

NA YES NO DK Have the tools, procedures, and so forth been adapted to best support the capacities of the individual performing the job?

IC. Environmental Supports: Incentives

NA YES NO DK Are adequate financial incentives (e.g., competitive pay, bonuses, or raises) made available for good performance? Are they timely, frequent?

NA YES NO DK Are nonmonetary incentives (e.g., recognition, titles, responsibilities, days off) made available for good performance? Are they timely, frequent?

NA YES NO DK Are career development opportunities offered for good performance?

NA YES NO DK Is there an absence of punishment for performing well?

NA YES NO DK Is there an absence of hidden incentives to perform poorly?

NA YES NO DK Do the organization's members recognize that most problems are systems problems, rather than individual performance issues and handle incentives accordingly?

IIA. Personal Repertory of Behavior: Knowledge and Skills

NA YES NO DK Does the person have the knowledge to perform well, including understanding the "big picture," the difference between good and bad performance, and the technical concepts?

NA YES NO DK Does the person have the specific technical or specialized skills to perform well relevant to this responsibility?

NA YES NO DK Does the person have needed basic or general skills?

NA YES NO DK Has previous training been provided to this person in this area? Did it result in improved performance?

IIB. Personal Repertory of Behavior: Capacity

NA YES NO DK   Does the person have the ability to learn how to fulfill the responsibility?

NA YES NO DK   Is the person free of emotional limitations that would interfere with performance?

NA YES NO DK   Given appropriate prosthetics or adaptations, does the person have sufficient physical capacity to perform the job well?

NA YES NO DK   Has the person with the appropriate capacity been selected for fulfilling this responsibility?

IIC. Personal Repertory of Behavior: Motives

NA YES NO DK   Did the person have the desire to fulfill the responsibility when selected?

NA YES NO DK   Has the desire to fulfill the responsibility endured?

---

*If the items discussed in the **probe questions** are not present or effective in your organization, you need to create or modify them. Using the following list, check off the variables for which you indicated "NO" in answer to one or more of the probe questions.*

I.   Environmental Supports
    A.   ____   Information and Feedback
    B.   ____   Tools, Equipment, Resources, and Procedures
    C.   ____   Incentives
II. Personal Repertory of Behavior
    A.   ____   Knowledge and Skills
    B.   ____   Capacity
    C.   ____   Motivates

Congratulations! You are well on your way to defining a strategy to improve the changeover of your organization to supported employment. Refer to the text to assist you in selecting the variable on which to focus, the performance improvement strategy (solution), and resources that may be used to address this issue. As you select these, record them onto the Implementation Summary Worksheet and begin implementing them.

    *You may continue troubleshooting by applying the **probe questions** to the next prioritized **activity** within the **component** and **area** of greatest concern. However, do not attempt to address more than one or two issues at a time. Instead, implement the selected performance improvement strategies and watch for positive changes. Then, repeat the self-assessment process to prioritize the next item of concern.*

IMPLEMENTATION: SUMMARY WORKSHEET

Enter the organization's major decisions onto this worksheet as you proceed through the troubleshooting process. Feel free to use this as a suggested format and retype to provide more or less space, to add or delete information, and so forth. The purpose of this worksheet is only to help the coordinator of the self-assessment process keep track of decisions.

A.   Note the chosen **area** of greatest need from Part A:

_____

B.   List the **components** here from that area, as prioritized in Part B-1, with the most significant first. For each, list the **activity** you selected to improve performance (Part B-2). Complete the rest of the items as you finish Part C and finish selecting performance improvement strategies.

   1.   Component:

        Activity:

        Person responsible:

        Solution(s) and resources:

   2.   Component:

        Activity:

        Person responsible:

        Solution(s) and resources:

   3.   Component:

        Activity:

        Person responsible:

        Solution(s) and resources:

PART III

TOOLS AND TECHNIQUES

BUILDING BLOCKS FOR QUALITY IMPROVEMENT EFFORTS

Troubleshooting and the Performance Engineering Matrix are tools that can be used to support an organization's efforts to implement Continuous Quality Improvement or to achieve changeover to integrated employment. By themselves, they offer powerful techniques to support organizational change. However, Continuous Quality Improvement also relies on many other methods to support planning, data collection, and data analysis. Part III of this book focuses on these additional tools, and the processes and concepts underlying them.

Chapter 8 offers performance templates, which are guides for planning, measuring, and troubleshooting to improve performance. Also known as tree diagrams or accomplishment models, performance templates are more formal, written versions of the troubleshooting methodology presented in Chapter 5. Chapter 8 includes several examples of performance templates to demonstrate their utility for planning and troubleshooting performance. In addition, it suggests a perspective on defining quality parameters based on customer input.

Chapter 9 provides background material on systematic methods for improving performance. This chapter presents the steps of a basic quality improvement process, as well as introducing information on forming quality improvement teams. Chapter 10 offers several specific tools often used in organizations implementing quality improvement methods. Ranging from tools that support creativity and development of new projects to tools that assist in analyzing actual performance, this chapter provides additional methods that can be used to implement the fundamental principle, "Use a Systematic Approach To Find Opportunities and To Improve Performance." Part IV of this book includes methods for employing these tools and processes to initiate an organization-wide quality transformation.

Chapter 8

Performance Templates

Guides for Planning, Measuring, and Troubleshooting To Improve Performance

Organizations are complex. Whether or not they are aware of it, staff members and managers alike are constantly making decisions about how they will spend their time. They move from one activity to another, from one priority to another, and from one crisis to the next, juggling time throughout the day. To have a hope of success, staff members need systematic strategies to assist them to focus on achieving the organization's mission, to troubleshoot performance problems, and to select from a potentially infinite range of possible activities those to receive attention. Without systematic strategies to assist managers and staff to negotiate the muddy waters of service delivery and systems change, their energy might be diffused through trying to perform better by working harder, attempting to do more, and extending slim resources too far.

Performance templates are tools that offer managers and other staff members a means of working smarter not harder. As such, they offer a specific method that may be used to implement one of the fundamental principles of Continuous Quality Improvement: "Use a Systematic Approach To Find Opportunities and To Improve Performance." The purpose of this chapter, then, is to describe how to develop and use performance templates to address performance improvements systematically.

PERFORMANCE TEMPLATES DEFINED

A performance template could be viewed as simply a written representation of a troubleshooting process—one that is written to allow it to be used repeatedly. Because it is written down, a performance template is somewhat more formal than the flexible troubleshooting process that was described in Chapter 5. In addition, troubleshooting is very much a reactive process: By moving through the levels of a troubleshooting tree, it is possible to identify existing performance issues and to select strategies for improving performance in response to those issues. Performance templates, however, offer important proactive assistance as well. The process of developing a performance template may be used to plan for a new venture, to develop responsibilities in a new work group, or to organize and prioritize the tasks for achieving a desired goal.

Thus, performance templates have a variety of potential uses in many different parts of an organization, whether the organization is an employment service provider, a public sector agency, a private sector business, or an ad hoc work group. These applications, several of which are described later in this chapter, all revolve around three primary functions: planning, measuring, and troubleshooting in order to improve performance.

The *Self-Assessment Guide for Changeover to Supported Employment* presented in Chapter 7 provides one example of a complex performance template. That *Guide* meets the definition of a performance template in that it is written and it could be represented as a troubleshooting tree. Clearly, it can be used to assist an organization to plan for changeover to more integrated employment services. Furthermore, it offers a format for evaluating performance: either through the subjective opinions of those who respond to the parts of the *Guide* as a survey, or through objective, quantitative measures such as those that are suggested in Section III, Implementation. Additional quantitative measures could be defined by its users as well.

Elements of Performance Templates

In its simplest form, a performance template is an organized list of the major accomplishments and activities that must be in place for achieving a desired outcome. Sometimes referred to as an *accomplishment model, job model, decision tree,* or *tree diagram,* this list is organized in a very specific way: Each activity is tied directly to a higher order outcome. Because of this, depending on their use and the nature of the desired accomplishments, performance templates may be very simple, consisting of only two levels, or quite detailed, with several levels listed for obtaining the desired accomplishment. These levels will be referred to as the *mission, mission accomplishments, responsibilities, duties,* and *logistics* in the following discussion.

Missions   Performance templates must always begin with a singular *mission.* This mission must clearly state the overall outcome or accomplishment that the organization, work group, or individual is attempting to achieve. As described in Chapter 2, an organization's mission must lead its quality improvement efforts. However, the term "mission" may be applied in different ways, so long as it reflects the overall outcome that is sought. For example, missions, purposes, or overall outcomes may be defined for smaller work groups or individual employees, as well as for organizations. "Birthday Cake Made from Scratch" is an example of the mission that might be undertaken by a single individual. If Trek Personnel's mission is "Integrated Jobs with Support," "Appropriate Jobs Developed" might be the mission of the department in which job developer James T. and job coach Spock work. The organization's mission provides the context within which organizations, departments, or work groups exist. It describes the larger purpose and provides meaning for organizational or group effort. A focus on improving performance on the basis of the mission is the basis of Continuous Quality Improvement efforts.

As discussed in Chapter 2, missions should be short and very outcome-oriented. Rather than the lengthy statements typical of rehabilitation organizations, missions for performance templates should consist of a few words that can be remembered easily by staff. This way, the mission is able constantly to remind staff members of

SAMPLE PERFORMANCE TEMPLATES FOR THE
ACCOMPLISHMENT: BIRTHDAY CAKE MADE FROM SCRATCH

SAMPLE #1: A SIMPLE PERFORMANCE TEMPLATE

Desired Accomplishment: Birthday Cake Made from Scratch

I. Ingredients Assembled
II. Cake Baked
III. Cake Decorated
IV. Kitchen Cleaned

SAMPLE #2: A DETAILED PERFORMANCE TEMPLATE

Desired Accomplishment: Birthday Cake Made from Scratch

I. Ingredients Assembled
   A. Recipe Selected
      i. Determine the birthday person's favorite type of cake.
      ii. Review favorite cookbooks.
      iii. Choose a recipe that fits needs.
   B. List completed of needed ingredients for cake, frosting, and decorations
   C. Ingredients available in kitchen gathered
   D. Shopping trip completed for missing ingredients
      i. Prepare list.
      ii. Take money.
      iii. Travel to store.
      iv. Locate listed items.
      v. Check-out.
      vi. Travel home.
II. Cake Baked
   A. Cake ingredients mixed together
      i. Gather equipment and utensils.
      ii. Measure ingredients.
      iii. Mix according to directions.
   B. Baking Completed
      i. Preheat oven.
      ii. Set timer.
      iii. Bake cake.
      iv. Test for doneness.
      v. Remove from oven and cool.
         a. Set on cooling rack.
         b. Set timer for cooling time.
         c. Remove from cake pan.
         d. Set onto serving plate.
III. Cake Decorated
   A. Frosting ingredients mixed together
      i. Gather equipment and utensils.
      ii. Measure ingredients.
      iii. Mix according to directions.

(continued)

**SAMPLE PERFORMANCE TEMPLATES FOR THE
ACCOMPLISHMENT: BIRTHDAY CAKE MADE FROM SCRATCH
(continued)**

    B. Cake Frosted
       i. Gather equipment and utensils.
      ii. Apply frosting base.
     iii. Clean frosting from spatula and beaters.
    C. Birthday decorations added
       i. Plan location of decorations.
      ii. Apply decorations.
     iii. Add birthday candles.
IV. Kitchen Cleaned
    A. Baking and decorating utensils cleaned
       i. Fill dishpan with dish soap and water.
      ii. Wash dishes.
     iii. Rinse dishes.
     iv. Dry dishes.
    B. Dishes, utensils, and ingredients put away
    C. Counters, stove top cleaned

their purposes in the organization. A mission should remind staff members of the overall outcome that they are individually or collectively trying to achieve, rather than the behavior that they expend to achieve it. Furthermore, a mission must be reconcilable with everything that the organization or work group does. In effective organizations, everthing that is done leads to accomplishing the mission. If staff are involved in activities that are not reconcilable with the mission, they should question either the activities or the mission. Missions should also assist organizations or work groups to evaluate how well they are doing. Therefore, missions should be defined in a way that supports identifying specific measures of quality, but—to maintain clarity and simplicity—should not directly include those definitions of quality. Additional information on measuring quality with respect to missions and performance templates is presented later in this chapter.

Thomas Gilbert (1978) developed a technique for determining if the mission has been well-defined. Originally presented as the "ACORNS Test," his method has been adapted here for use in reviewing or developing missions for performance templates. The ACORNS Test uses those features of a mission that make it useful for leading an organization: that the mission defines an *accomplishment* rather than a behavior, that it represents an accomplishment over which the participants have some *control*, that it reflects the *overall objective* of the organization, that this objective is *reconcilable* with everything the organization does, that it can be measured (*numbers*) in some way, and, finally, that it is *short and simple*.

Mission Accomplishments The next level of performance templates defines the *mission accomplishments*, that is, the major accomplishment areas of an organization, individual, or group. Tied to achieving the mission, this level of the template specifies the major desired outcomes of the organization or work group. These out-

THE ACORNS TEST FOR MISSIONS

Use this test when establishing or reviewing the mission for an organization or the purpose for a work group, project, and so forth:

A ccomplishment
C ontrol
O verall objective
R econcilable
N umbers
S hort and simple

USING THE ACORNS TEST

Apply the ACORNS Test by asking and answering a series of questions about a defined mission statement. Adjust the statement as needed to better meet the requirements defined by the questions.

A Is it an *accomplishment* or outcome and not a description of behavior? Does it clearly direct you toward a result?
C Is it something over which the organization or work team generally has *control*? Or does performance depend primarily on the efforts or impact of others?
O Is it the *overall objective* for this project or organization or is there some other objective above it?
R Is it *reconcilable* with the (other) things that the organization or project is doing and with the overall mission of the organization (if you are looking at a project or team mission)?
N Is it useful for defining measures of success? Is there a way in which you can determine how successful you are in achieving it? How do you know if you are doing well? This does not mean that you have to be able to turn it into *numbers*; qualitative or other sorts of measures may be appropriate also.
S Is it *short and simple*? Is it easy to understand and to remember? Will it help the group to stay focused on where it is heading?

Potential pitfalls: Failing to differentiate between behavior and accomplishment; identifying an accomplishment over which the group truly has little control; writing a paragraph to describe the major values and/or activities instead of using a few words (adapted from Gilbert [1978]).

comes are what must be in place in order for the mission to be achieved. In the example, "Birthday Cake Made from Scratch," "Ingredients Assembled," "Cake Baked," "Cake Decorated," and "Kitchen Cleaned" are the mission accomplishments. "Jobs Developed and Maintained," "Work Performance Requirements Met," "Integration Achieved," and "Ongoing Support Provided" are the mission accomplishment areas of the mission "Supported Employment Implemented."

Most often, the top two levels of a performance template are written in accomplishment language rather than in a way that reflects the behaviors being performed. "Birthday Cake Made from Scratch" focuses on the accomplishment that will remain after the behavior of *making* a birthday cake from scratch is completed. Similarly, "Cake Decorated" identifies the result of the activities that must be performed to accomplish the objective of a cake that is decorated for a birthday. While such phrasing may sound awkward at first, using accomplishment language for the top two levels (or more) of a performance template reminds its users that the accomplishments are valued over the costly behavior that must be expended to achieve them.

Responsibilities, Duties, and Logistics   Lower levels of an organization's performance templates reflect *responsibilities* that often may be used to define the separate roles of members of the group. The third level reflects *duties, tasks,* or *skills* that each member performs to fulfill defined responsibilities. This level of the performance template usually reflects behaviors that are performed by staff members, rather than projecting their accomplishments. Therefore, they are usually written in action phrases such as, "Gather equipment and utensils," "Measure ingredients," and "Mix according to directions," rather than in accomplishment language. Finally, a *logistical* level may be included in performance templates to define the resources required to complete tasks, including implementation schedules, materials, and other supports. However, performance templates should be built only to a level of detail sufficient to support staff performance. Templates that are too detailed are cumbersome to use, at best. In addition, staff members may resent such detailed specification of their activities, preferring to maintain more control and opportunity for creativity.

According to Gilbert (1978), fine-tuning the definition, particularly at higher levels of the template, allows better definition of and communication concerning competent performance. In addition, at whatever level we might wish to draw conclusions about performance, it is necessary to begin by identifying its context at higher levels. Therefore, in rehabilitation and community-based employment services, we can evaluate the competence of an employee in the performance of a specific duty— or behavior—only when that duty is taken in the context of the higher level responsibility, mission accomplishment, and, ultimately, the organization's mission. Thus, it is necessary always to consider the overall cultural goal and the organization's defined mission accomplishments, in addition to the behavior of an individual. These higher levels of a performance template provide a context in which to view behavior, for a behavior cannot be evaluated without consideration of the outcomes it is designed to achieve.

Key Performance Templates

These levels can be applied to devising performance templates for organizations, departments, projects, or individuals. In its most basic form—referred to here as a "Key Performance Template"—the template must include two levels: 1) a definition of the overall mission or purpose of the organization, project, or job; and 2) the mission accomplishments within that mission.

PERFORMANCE TEMPLATE: ICON EMPLOYMENT SERVICES

ICON Employment Services, located in Alexandria, Virginia, utilizes its performance template for a variety of purposes, including annual planning and organizational performance reviews. Originally established in 1985 with the purpose of becoming a catalyst for systems change in the Northern Virginia region, ICON Employment Services has become both a regional technical assistance center for supported employment and a provider of supported employment services to citizens of Northern Virginia.

At its simplest level, ICON's performance template consists of four mission accomplishments. This level is useful for ICON's staff in that, for example, it supports organizing information for public relations materials, for new staff orientation, and for presentations describing the organization. However, for other uses, ICON applies a more detailed performance template. In this template, the four mission accomplishments are subdivided into more detailed levels identifying responsibilities, duties, and resources, as needed. ICON's detailed performance template is provided in the Appendix at the end of this chapter.

Performance templates offer a flexible structure for conceptualizing organizations, projects, or issues. Initially developed in cooperation with the staff of the Employment Projects at the Specialized Training Program, University of Oregon, the basic structure of ICON's performance template has remained largely unchanged since its first use. However, specific strategies, activities, and resources have changed as regional and local priorities have shifted. For example, the first item on the template, "Establish an array of affiliated employment sites," originally reflected ICON's emphasis on developing a network of new, freestanding organizations to become supported employment providers. Now, however, it includes developing supported employment job opportunities supported directly by ICON Employment Services itself. Thus, the lower levels of the performance template in this area of organizational performance have shifted, as well.

Furthermore, ICON Employment Services now offers both individual and small group employment in integrated settings, and the organization is structured with these options managed by different coordinators. Taking ICON's Key Performance Template as the base mission accomplishments, these coordinators are able to build more specific templates for planning and monitoring their own departments' performance.

DEVELOPING PERFORMANCE TEMPLATES

The process of developing a performance template is as important as the template itself, for through the analysis process, staff members learn the relationships between activity—or behavior—and outcomes and obtain a method for measuring performance that will assist in troubleshooting. Through developing performance

---

KEY PERFORMANCE TEMPLATE FOR ICON EMPLOYMENT SERVICES

MISSION: EXPAND SUPPORTED EMPLOYMENT IN THE MID-ATLANTIC REGION

Mission Accomplishments:

1. Array of affiliated employment sites established.
2. Regional supported employment direct service delivery improved.
3. Local, state, and national attention to supported employment increased.
4. Fiscal and management stability established and maintained.

templates, staff members learn a strategy for analyzing diverse projects or performance problems and also develop greater ownership and understanding of the template defined.

A Group Process for Developing Performance Templates

Although there is no single way to develop a performance template, the sequence of steps listed below has been useful. The process presented assumes that the template is being developed by a group with one member acting as a facilitator and recorder. Try this process and then adjust the steps to best meet your needs.

Step 1. Define the mission or purpose. The first, and probably most important, step in devising a performance template is to reach consensus on the purpose or mission of the organization, project, or group for which the template is being developed. This step is important to ensure that all group members are thinking about reaching the same goal, are working in the same direction, and are guided by a unified vision of their ultimate purpose. Seemingly a simple task, this step may turn out to be the most difficult one in the process. The difficulty usually arises from uncovering differences in perceptions of the objectives, as well as in the values that underlie them. Review the information in Chapter 2 about missions, and apply the ACORNS Test to evaluate and improve any missions that are proposed.

Step 2. Identify relevant customers. Who are, or will be, the customers? What have they identified as being important to them in terms of overall outcome? Maintaining a focus on customers and their input is central to any quality improvement effort. Devising a performance template, therefore, must include consideration of customers and the information they provide regarding the mission. If no clear customer for a project can be identified, why do it? Avoid the tendency to accept answers such as "the general public"; group members must be as specific as possible in defining customers. For example, "the business community" is probably not an accurate description of an organization's business customers, but a list of the 8, 18, or 58 businesses with which the organization actually does business would be. Reviewing the information about customers presented in Chapter 3 might be useful in completing this step.

Step 3. Brainstorm. Ask group members to list anything that comes to mind that might have to be in place to accomplish the defined mission. What activities must be carried out? What resources are required? Members likely will list quite a variety of items. For example, in defining a performance template for a new supported employment component of a facility-based program, the list that staff provide might range from small items such as, "We need data collection forms to determine if workers are doing a good job," to larger items such as, "We need enough community jobs available for people to fill." An important part of brainstorming is recording items without judgement. Redundant or insignificant items will be eliminated or combined, and specific wording of items can be improved during the next step in the process.

Step 4. Select the mission accomplishments. Ask group members to review the brainstormed list to identify any major groups or categories of items, or items that seem to encompass several others on the list. From these select a few items (usually no more than two to four) that represent the most significant accomplishment areas in achieving the defined purpose. Ask questions like, "What are the few most important things that must be in place in order to achieve this mission?" The process used for organizing ideas into an *Affinity Diagram*, presented in Chapter 10, may be useful during this step.

Step 5.   Organize the brainstormed list into a performance template. Once the mission accomplishment areas have been selected, it is usually a fairly simple task to organize remaining items into the multiple levels of a performance template. Encourage participants to eliminate or combine items when appropriate. Do not worry if there are items that might fit into more than one category. Take the best guess, or duplicate the item, and be willing to revise the template when the template development process, or the project at hand, is better understood. Throughout Steps 4 and 5, be alert to keep from mixing in words with the accomplishments, responsibilities, and so forth, that actually define quality requirements or measures for them. For example, an accomplishment for a training department (of an organization or a state) might be "Training Delivered." Words such as "effective" or "relevant" or "sufficient" would define requirements for measuring the *quality* of the training delivered, rather than defining the *outcome* of training delivered. See the following section, "Performance Templates and Measuring Performance: Definitions of Quality" for an in-depth discussion of how to build methods for evaluating quality into performance templates.

Developing Performance Templates with or for One Staff Person

Performance templates are not only useful for work groups or organizations. They are also valuable when designed to be used by a single staff person for planning, evaluating, and troubleshooting to improve performance. Use a similar process to assist an individual staff person in developing a performance template for his or her own job. Try a series of questions such as:

- What is your purpose? What are you trying to accomplish in your job? What is the most important overall achievement that you are working for?
- For whom are you doing this? Who receives the benefits of or outcomes from what you do?
- What are the most important things that have to be in place or that you must accomplish in order to achieve this outcome?
- How do you do those things? What are the major activities you do to achieve this outcome?
- How do you know when you have done a good job? What are your measures of success?

PERFORMANCE TEMPLATES AND MEASURING PERFORMANCE: DEFINITIONS OF QUALITY

From a quality improvement perspective, there are two fundamental purposes of measuring performance, whether in rehabilitation programs, manufacturing industries, or elsewhere:

1. To determine if performance meets or exceeds the customers' definition of quality
2. To identify means for improving performance toward that definition of quality

Given these purposes, performance measurement changes from an onerous task performed for little reason other than providing reports, to one that is vital for taking action toward fulfilling customer expectations. A rehabilitation organization undergoing changeover to supported employment, then, should regularly measure its performance against its customers' (e.g., its recipients of service, community employers, funding agents, and staff members) definitions of quality. Performance templates can assist in organizing that effort.

Quality Dimensions, Measures, and Targets

Many customers respond with fairly vague statements when asked about their quality expectations. For example, customers of a fast food restaurant are likely to say that they want their food "fast" and "hot." These customers are defining the general *dimensions* of timeliness and temperature as the quality features that are important to them. They are unlikely to say, "Check the temperature in degrees Fahrenheit" to define a *measure,* and probably would not even know what their preferred *target* temperature might be using that measure. (Imagine a customer returning an order saying, "I prefer hamburgers that have an internal temperature of 157° F.")

This example demonstrates three perspectives of quality definitions: *quality dimensions,* the general features of quality ("temperature" in this example); *measures,* the unit of measurement or measurement tool ("degrees Fahrenheit"); and *targets* or *standards,* the specific level of outcome desired or needed ("157° F") (see Table 8.1).

Quality dimensions refer to the general characteristics or features of quality, such as "accuracy," "timeliness," "novelty," "volume," or "temperature." For a particular accomplishment or behavior, one or more general dimensions of quality may be relevant. A fast food customer is interested in the timeliness, temperature, cost, and taste of the order; an owner of a fast food restaurant with a supported employee may be most concerned with that employee's courtesy to customers and consistency in work. Each of these represents a general dimension of quality.

Measures define the specific unit of measurement that will be used to assess performance against the requirement, such as "errors per thousand units" or "number of customer complaints" for accuracy; "cubic feet" or "number of units produced" for volume; "degrees Centigrade" or "degrees Fahrenheit" for temperature. For any defined quality dimension, several different units of measurement are possible. Selecting a specific measure or measures depends on the dimension being measured, the nature of that dimension, and the resources and capabilities of the measurer.

Part of the difficulty of performance measurement is that much of what we do in human services is difficult to measure quantitatively, that is, numerically. However, the measures selected need not be numerical; *qualitative* or *descriptive* measures are very useful as well. For example, customers may be asked to judge the acceptability

Table 8.1.   Defining measurements of quality

Perspective	Definition	Fast food example
Dimensions	General dimensions of quality	Temperature
Measures	Units of measurement	Internal temperature in degrees Fahrenheit
Targets	Specific level of performance required or desired	157°F

of a hot dog's temperature ("Is it hot enough?"), to rank several items from best to worst, or simply to state their opinions about a product or service.

Targets define the *actual level* of performance that is expected—or demanded—for a specific measure. When required, for example, through state or federal regulation, these may be referred to as *standards* for performance. (The term "standards" is also used in government regulations to include processes—e.g., requirements for service providers to use the process of individual service planning, to have procedures for fire drills, or to maintain an annual program of staff training. Process-oriented standards are discussed further below.) These targets may reflect objective measures or more subjective ones. For example, "No more than two errors per thousand units" or "An average of less than one complaint per 500 orders processed" might be used as a target for accuracy; and "At least 98% of the customers interviewed will judge the hamburger to be 'hot enough'," as a target for temperature.

Too often, organizations and individuals confuse the different perspectives of measurement, trying to compare general quality dimensions with targets or units of measure. Keeping these perspectives clear is important to developing a performance evaluation system for an organization, project, or department, particularly because specific quality dimensions, measures, and targets are likely to change with the changing perspectives of customers. Thus, it is useful to define these quality measures separately from the mission, accomplishments, responsibilities, duties, and so forth listed in the basic framework of the performance template, but to include them in the template.

Quality Dimensions, Measures, and Standards in Supported Employment

While some customers offer only general *dimensions* of quality, others are very specific and provide guidance relevant not only to these dimensions, but also to measures and even specific standards, as well. The federal and state governments offer good examples. The federal government has the role of customer when it provides funding to states and other recipients for supported employment. As a customer, the federal government has provided very detailed definitions of quality for supported employment through a variety of different documents (e.g., in its regulations on supported employment and requests for proposals for state systems change grants). Some states have refined these definitions even further.

General dimensions of quality, such as "paid work," "integrated settings," and "ongoing support" are defined with units of measurement and, in most cases, specific standards for performance. Such specificity in its definition of quality allows the federal government or states clearly to define instances in which supported employment does and does not exist, as a basis for funding and regulation. Setting aside any disagreements with the specific measures or standards the federal or state governments have selected (e.g., "Why not require 40 hours per week?" or "Shouldn't only individual jobs count?"), this strategy of precise definition makes very clear what will and will not fall within the definition of quality (see Table 8.2).

Changing Definitions of Quality

Defining the three perspectives of quality performance must be viewed as an ongoing process. Whenever customers offer clear direction for quality dimensions, measures, and standards for performance, remain alert for changes in customer expecta-

Table 8.2. Quality dimensions, measures, and standards that have been defined for supported employment

Dimension	Measure	Sample standard
Paid work	Hours of paid work per week	At least 20 hours of paid work per week
Integration	Number of individuals with disabilities grouped together	No more than eight individuals with disabilities grouped together
Regular work settings	Sites in which persons without disabilities are employed	At least 50% of individuals at the work site do not have apparent disabilities
Ongoing support	Number of support visits per month	At least two support visits per month

tions. Continue to adjust the definition of quality used to evaluate performance based on customer feedback. When customers offer little direction beyond their general dimensions of quality, use customer feedback as a guide for selecting appropriate performance measures and targets. Determine these through further interaction with customers or through best guesses of relevant measures. Expect that you will need to translate customer expectations into dimensions and measures that are meaningful in your organization. Be open to adjusting the specific dimensions, measures, and targets selected based on further customer feedback.

One of the current quality dimensions of employment services, integration, offers a good example of changing definitions of quality. Early definitions of quality for the integration of individuals with severe disabilities looked primarily at the dimension of physical integration. Measures often reflected the number of instances during a day or week that an individual went into a community setting from a facility, or the number of people without disabilities present in a targeted setting. As dialogues with consumers and their advocates continued, however, these measures, and even the dimension of physical integration, were found to be inadequate. As a result, an entirely different quality dimension was established—that of *social integration.*

As a dimension of quality, social integration is much more difficult to measure. Is the best measure the number of social interactions a person experiences during a typical work day? The number of personal conversations? The number of people without disabilities who have established relationships with the individual that extend beyond the work place? Or is it the individual's answer to the question, "Are you satisfied with the quality of your opportunities to be with other people both at work and away from work, and the quality of the relationships you have with them?" Any or all of these could be used to measure the quality dimension, social integration. It is only through ongoing dialogue with individuals receiving services, their families, and advocates, that we can select appropriate measures to assess performance, and adjust those measures to better reflect their changing definitions of quality.

USING PERFORMANCE TEMPLATES TO MEASURE PERFORMANCE

General quality dimensions, measures, and targets offer perspectives on measurement that may be used in a performance template. Each of these perspectives may be defined at each of the various levels of the template, and more than one dimension, measure, or target may be defined for each component at each level. However, based on the approach of Continuous Quality Improvement, it is often most beneficial to define only the dimensions and measures for various components of the performance template, leaving targets largely undefined.

There are several disadvantages to setting specific, numerical standards for performance. Dr. W. Edwards Deming (1986), in his principles for management transformation, states the need for eliminating numerical standards in several ways:

> Eliminate targets, slogans, exhortations, posters, for the work force that urge them to increase productivity. . . . "Do it right the first time" . . . is just another meaningless slogan. . . . [N]umerical goals set for other people, without a road map to reach the goal, have effects opposite to the effects sought. . . . Eliminate numerical quotas for the workforce. . . . A quota is a fortress against improvement of quality and productivity. . . . [P]ut in their place intelligent supervision. . . . Eliminate numerical goals for people in management. . . . Management by numerical goal is an attempt to manage without knowledge of what to do, and in fact is usually management by fear. . . . (Deming, 1986, pp. 65–76)

Dr. Deming's warnings are based on a concern that is stated very eloquently in his 10th point for quality transformations:

> What is wrong with posters and exhortations? They are directed at the wrong people. They arise from management's supposition that the production workers could, by putting their backs into the job, accomplish zero defects, improve quality, improve productivity, and all else that is desirable. The charts and posters take no account of the fact that most of the trouble comes from the system. (Deming, 1986, p. 66)
>
> Such exhortations only create adversarial relationships, as the bulk of the causes of low quality and low productivity belong to the system and thus lie beyond the power of the workforce. (W.E. Deming, as quoted in Scholtes, 1988, ch. 2, p. 4)

Thus, Dr. Deming's concerns are that standards too often are defined almost capriciously, reflecting levels of performance that may be unrelated to the capacity of the organization's systems and resources to achieve those standards, and unrelated to the outcomes the organization has actually experienced. Standards such as these cause increased fear among employees, adversarial relationships, and lowered morale, because it is the employees who are blamed for failing to achieve those standards. These damaging effects rob employees of their spirit to work for the company, as well as robbing the company of the full potential of employee performance.

But there is another issue with performance standards. Those that are set too low, such as "minimum compliance standards" often used by governmental regulatory agencies, promote mediocrity because they encourage organizations and individuals to stop trying to push for better performance once they are achieved. The supported employment standard defined in the early years of the initiative—20 hours of paid work per week—offers a good example. Many organizations, perhaps because of their funding and staffing constraints, developed jobs that offered only 20 hours per week, and no more. These service providers even split full-time jobs into two 20-hour jobs, to allow them to bring more people into integrated employment, while still meeting the supported employment standard for the amount of paid work.

Process Standards

Regulatory bodies also set standards for *processes* they believe to be necessary to achieve desired outcomes. Individual service planning, record-keeping, and procedures for handling medications, for example, are often defined by states to ensure quality. Specific standards may be necessary in some arenas, such as ensuring that service providers attend to the health and safety needs of the individuals they are supporting in work. Whenever reasonable, though, it is recommended that organizations decrease their reliance on specific performance standards in favor of supporting continuous performance improvement along agreed upon quality dimensions. Therefore, the remainder of this chapter focuses on quality dimensions and measures, leaving out, at least for now, the notion of standards for performance.

Performance Templates as a Measurement Framework

Performance templates offer a framework for measuring the quality of performance by linking the performance of duties directly to achieving the mission accomplishments of the work group or organization, and, ultimately, to the overall mission.

Defining the quality dimensions and measures for a performance template provides an evaluation plan for a work group, department, or organization. Define dimensions and measures for the topmost levels of the performance template, that is, for the mission or purpose and the mission accomplishments. Measuring performance of the mission accomplishments identifies assessment of the performance of the overall mission. Use these measures regularly to assess its performance. Significant deficits in one mission accomplishment suggest that the area is one in which the greatest performance improvements can be made. This is the basic strategy for troubleshooting. The following list summarizes measurement guidelines:

- Use a performance template to structure an evaluation plan for individual, group, or organizational performance.
- Determine quality performance based on customer definitions of quality.
- Select specific performance requirements and measures based on customer input and best guess.
- On an ongoing basis, adjust requirements and measures used to assess quality based on changing customer expectations and feedback, as well as better guesses.
- Avoid setting numerical standards for staff performance.
- Use a performance template as a guide for the sequence for measuring performance.
- Take initial measurements at the topmost level—the mission—of defined outcomes to determine first the area of performance requiring the most attention.
- Measure staff behavior only after taking higher level measures—that is, measures of mission accomplishments or the overall mission—that indicate a need for improving performance.
- Collect data on measures only for the purposes of assessing actual performance against the customer definition of quality and for determining the best way to improve performance.
- Stop collecting data when they are no longer used for making decisions and taking action.

Using a performance template as a guide provides a sequence for measuring performance. Just as the *Self-Assessment Guide for Changeover to Supported Employment* began first with decisions regarding more global questions before leading to analyzing specific activities, a similar sequence should be used in measuring performance.

CASE STUDY: AN INTERVIEW WITH A STATE
DIRECTOR OF DEVELOPMENTAL DISABILITY SERVICES

A group of community employment service providers decided that they did not have clear information from one of their customers, the state's director of developmental disability services, about his definition of quality for services. To remedy this problem, the group prepared a set of questions and invited the director to their next meeting. Questions asked included:

- What products and services overall does your office purchase?
- If you could buy any employment service, what would its features be?
- Which of our products and services meet your expectations?
- How do you know when products or services meet your expectations? What information do you look at?
- What products or services would you like to purchase from us in the future?
- What features do our competitors give you that you would like us to provide, as well?
- What requirements set by your superiors can we help you satisfy?

The director gave some very clear statements during the interview that helped the group to understand his definition of quality better. Some of those statements are presented below:

- We are looking for supports for people with disabilities in making a contribution to their communities. That includes employment for many, but where employment opportunities are not available, we want to support people contributing to their communities in other ways. A dramatic shift we would like to see is for vendors to become providers of training and technical assistance to businesses, rather than providing only direct support to individuals with disabilities.
- We prefer individuals to be in work environments where they are better compensated and have opportunities to be more integrated and more productive. The traditional notion of standards for services is irrelevant. Once health, rights, and safety standards are met, we are looking for wages, benefits, consumer and family satisfaction, and so forth. We value vendors who are challenging themselves to improve their performance and to come up with innovative ways to change the way they do business, at less cost. The demands on me are to support as many people as possible at the local level at a minimal cost, and then to talk about quality.

From these interview responses, the group learned many things about the director's definition of quality for their services. For example, he listed three different services that he is willing to purchase: 1) direct employment services, 2) technical assistance services to businesses to support individuals they employ, and 3) alternatives to employment that allow individuals to contribute to their communities. He defined a wide range of important quality dimensions for these services, including: cost, wages, benefits, integration, safety, health, rights, consumer satisfaction, and innovation. However, through these he gave little direction for specific units of measurement. Some of his quality dimensions are easy to translate into units of measurement, for example, "wages" into "dollars earned per month," or "cost" into "dollars per person served." However, he provided no consumer satisfaction survey questions

(continued)

**CASE STUDY: AN INTERVIEW WITH A STATE
DIRECTOR OF DEVELOPMENTAL DISABILITY SERVICES (*continued*)**

for the group to use, no definition of integration, and no measure of innovation. For these, the service providers must make a "best guess" to be adjusted based on future feedback from him. Furthermore, he did not assist the service providers to define lower levels of the performance template: the responsibilities, duties, and so forth. If he had, these would be listed in columns to the right of the Quality Measures shown in Table 8.3, which summarizes his responses.

Table 8.3. Draft performance template based on initial interview with the state agency director. Mission: People with Disabilities Supported To Contribute to Their Communities

Accomplishments	Quality dimensions	Quality measures
Direct employment services purchased	Cost	Cost in dollars per month per person served
	Wages and benefits	Dollars earned per month; dollar value of benefits
	Integration	
	Safety, health, rights	Minimal standards
	Consumer and family satisfaction	Surveys and interviews
	Innovation	
Technical assistance services to businesses purchased	Cost, wages, benefits, integration, safety, health, rights, consumer and family satisfaction, innovation	See above
Alternatives to employment	Allow contribution to community	
	Cost	Cost in dollars per month for services provided
	Consumer and family satisfaction	Surveys and interviews

There is little reason for measuring a behavior or activity if the higher level measurements—at the mission accomplishment or overall mission levels of the template—have not been taken. Indeed, even then, it is necessary to measure only those behaviors that, based on the template, are related to the outcome that is targeted for improvement. Thus, following a performance template, after measuring accomplishments at the highest level, one eliminates unnecessary data collection by continuing to measure further down only one level until it is possible to make a decision about the best strategy for improving performance. Continuous Quality Improvement methods suggest that it is important to limit data collection to only the purpose of making decisions and taking action. Using a performance template as a guide for data collection should help to do just that.

PERFORMANCE TEMPLATE FORMATS

Templates for planning, measuring, or troubleshooting performance components may be presented in variations of three basic formats: 1) troubleshooting trees,

2) outlines, or 3) charts. Each has similar features. However, they each begin with a singular statement of the overall mission or the mission accomplishment, which is then subdivided (or stratified) into its major components. Each format may present as few as two levels (the single mission plus one additional level) or several, with each level moving to greater detail and more specific activities, tactics, or resources. They each may also include specific measures to assist with troubleshooting, although some formats offer less space for addressing measures and other detail. Each format attempts to represent the direct relationship between specific activities performed by individual employees and the outcomes desired.

Figure 5.2 presented the performance template underlying the *Self-Assessment Guide for Changeover to Supported Employment* in a troubleshooting tree format. The advantage of this format is that it offers a visual representation of the levels of the template and their relationships to achieving the mission accomplishments and overall mission of the organization or project. It is most useful in assisting a staff person to understand the nature of troubleshooting: moving systematically through the levels of the tree to identify the root cause of a problem. Its disadvantage is the amount of space required to depict complex structures, projects, or systems. In addition, this format limits the number of words that can be used to describe each level of the tree. Thus, it is difficult to include specific measures for each level. However, when it is used in combination with one of the other basic formats, this format helps staff members to understand the relationships between specific activities and targeted outcomes and is a powerful tool to help them use a more systematic approach in their jobs.

Any performance template could be organized as simply an outline, as in the "Birthday Cake Made from Scratch" example, or the pages of the *Self-Assessment Guide for Changeover to Supported Employment*. This approach has the advantage of being familiar in format to those who have never previously developed or used a performance template, and it is not limited by space. Each level of the outline may be written as a clear, descriptive statement and may include measurement information or other guides as well, such as specific data sources or references to other materials to support staff performance. Outlines can easily present several levels of outcomes and activities, as shown in the detailed version of the template for "Birthday Cake Made from Scratch."

The disadvantage of presenting a performance template in an outline format, however, is that it does not provide a compelling, visual image of the relationship among activities and the desired outcomes. It may be most useful to use both a multi-level outline and a troubleshooting tree format to depict the same performance template. In this way, staff persons may use the troubleshooting tree to represent the relationship between activities and outcomes and refer to the outline for greater detail on specific elements.

The *chart* format offers a compromise between the troubleshooting tree and outline formats. At least at the top two or three levels, a chart such as that in Figure 8.1 allows greater detail than a troubleshooting tree, yet still provides a visual display of the relationships among items.

PERFORMANCE TEMPLATE APPLICATIONS

Performance templates have many possible uses and some examples of these are included with this chapter.

Mission:

Mission accomplishments	Responsibilities	Duties
1.0	1.1	1.1.1
		1.1.2
Quality dimensions:		1.1.3
Quality measures:		
	1.2	1.2.1
		1.2.2
—	—	—
—	—	—

Figure 8.1. Sample chart format for a performance template. (Where the dashes appear the chart would continue with 2.0, 2.1, 2.1.1, and so forth.)

A General Framework To Help Organize
Thinking About a Problem, Project, or Desired Outcome

The process of developing a performance template offers a strategy to support both thinking creatively and organizing diverse ideas and activities to reveal their relationship to achieving desired outcomes. As such, the exercise of developing the performance template is an excellent method for newly formed work groups to explore and organize their tasks; for training the staff to think analytically; or for bringing a level of coherence to an existing, out-of-control department or project.

EXAMPLES OF USES FOR PERFORMANCE TEMPLATES

DEFINING, PLANNING, MEASURING, AND/OR TROUBLESHOOTING:

- The mission accomplishments, responsibilities, and duties in the organization as they relate to the organization's overall mission
- The mission accomplishments, responsibilities, and duties for a work group as they relate to the purpose of the group
- The roles of individual staff persons and how they contribute to achieving the mission accomplishments
- An employer's definition of quality and the activities that work toward achieving that definition
- Agendas for staff meetings and formats for staff reports to help the staff maintain a focus on activities directly related to achieving their work group's purpose or the organization's mission
- The components—and the relationships among them—of a process or system in the organization, such as a staff substitute system
- The major components of a statewide system for achieving changeover to supported employment or transition from school to adult life
- The marketing plan for changeover to supported employment
- A new business venture
- Problems faced by staff in job sites
- Staff orientation and training systems
- Back-up systems for job loss

Tying the Work of a Department or Work Group to the Organization's Mission

A performance template for an organization begins with the organization's mission and desired outcomes. By defining the major responsibilities and duties in achieving these desired organizational outcomes, a performance template may be used to define departmental responsibilities. Furthermore, a template developed for a department or work group must begin with the group's desired outcomes. Together, the purposes and desired outcomes of the separate work groups must fulfill the organization's mission. An example of how one organization used performance templates to clarify responsibilities within work groups and their relationship to the organization's mission is presented in Chapter 13.

Organizing Individual Responsibilities for Achieving a Larger Purpose

A performance template developed for an organization, project or department involving more than one staff person may be used for defining individual roles and responsibilities, as well. Because the template is organized around major desired accomplishments and the activities required to lead to those accomplishments, it is a relatively simple task to subdivide the template to devise individual job descriptions.

Tied to the larger template, these individual-level template/job descriptions assist staff persons clearly to recognize their roles in achieving the larger purpose, as well as to understand the relationship between their roles and the roles of others. Using a performance template for defining job descriptions offers a strategy for reducing duplication of effort, in addition to its benefits in planning, measuring, and trouble-shooting performance.

Developing a Specific Performance Plan for an Organization, Project, Department, Work Group, or Individual

Once developed, a performance template can serve as both a guide for project planning and decision-making and a reminder of the relationships between various activities and the desired outcome. Thus, with a performance template in place, developing specific plans for achieving an objective or purpose becomes an easier task. Following the structure of the performance template and utilizing data gathered based on the template in making strategic decisions leads managers and staff persons in designing performance plans tied directly to improving performance.

Establishing the Basis for an Evaluation System for Measuring Group or Organizational Performance

Performance templates begin with defining the overall mission and desired accomplishments or outcomes of an organization, group, or individual. They elaborate on these accomplishments by connecting them systematically with the major activities necessary to achieve each. Thus, they form a framework for defining performance evaluation measures at the highest level—overall mission—as well as at the lower levels of responsibilities, duties, and tactics defined for achieving the mission. Using templates, therefore, it is possible to define specific, objective performance measures for activities that are directly tied to achieving desired accomplishments. In this way, using a performance template offers a format that focuses attention on the highest level outcome, but provides direction for more detailed data collection when performance issues are identified.

Troubleshooting a Specific Performance Problem

Because they provide a strategy for organizing the relationship between specific activities and desired outcomes, as well as a framework for devising an evaluation system, performance templates offer a guide for identifying the root causes of specific performance problems. By identifying the outcome that is not being achieved, and systematically reviewing performance at each lower level, the template becomes a troubleshooting tree for making a decision about how to remediate performance problems. Part II of this book presented detailed information about the use of the *Self-Assessment Guide for Changeover to Supported Employment* as a troubleshooting tree.

Communicating Information Concerning the Components of an Organization or Project

Performance templates are organized and straightforward. Because of this, they offer a useful way to arrange information on the overall scope of an organization or project. New staff, colleagues, advocates, and the general public will find refreshing clarity in the information presented through the top levels of a performance template. Project proposals or reports may also be designed along the lines of a performance template.

Whether used as a systematic guide for troubleshooting and improving performance, or as a strategy for planning new work groups, performance templates define the components that lead to fulfilling larger purposes. Thus, measuring performance in those components to determine the next course of action offers an approach that gives both managers and staff persons a basis on which to make decisions for improving performance.

SEARCHING FOR THE PERFECT PERFORMANCE TEMPLATE

The best way to learn about developing and using performance templates and their requirements and measures is through reviewing examples of templates developed for various purposes, along with practicing developing them for different situations. Throughout this chapter, as well as in others, several sample templates are provided for issues on levels ranging from individual to statewide. Review these to see how some useful performance templates have been devised for a range of situations. Do not assume, however, that these templates would apply to all similar situations, or that these are the only ways to analyze the situations presented. Practice developing templates. Do not wait to use templates as a performance improvement strategy until you are sure that you can do so appropriately. Try using them right away. Start with simple projects before taking on defining a template for an organization or department. Do not assume that there is only one correct way to devise a particular performance template. Performance templates, like all aspects of organizational and individual behavior, are subject to continuous improvement.

REFERENCES

Deming, W.E. (1986). *Out of the crisis*. Cambridge: Massachusetts Institute of Technology, Center for Advanced Engineering Study.

Gilbert, T.F. (1978). *Human competence: Engineering worthy performance*. New York: McGraw-Hill.

Scholtes, P.R. (1988). *The team handbook: How to use teams to improve quality*. Madison: Joiner Associates, Inc.

ADDITIONAL READINGS

Albin, J.M., & Magis-Agosta, K. (1989). *Self-assessment for changeover to supported employment: A troubleshooting approach*. Eugene: University of Oregon, Technical Assistance Brokerage.

Boothe, R. (1990). Who defines quality in service industries? *Quality Progress, 23*(2), 65–67.

Brache, A.P., & Rummler, G.A. (1988). The three levels of quality. *Quality Progress, 21*(10), 46–51.

Brassard, M. (1990). *The memory jogger +™*. Metheun, MA: GOAL/QPC.

Brethower, D.M. (1982). The total performance system. In R.M. O'Brien, A.M. Dickinson, & M.P. Rosow (Eds.), *Industrial behavior modification: A management handbook*. New York: Pergamon.

Mager, R.F. (1982). *Troubleshooting the troubleshooting course: Or debug d'bugs*. Belmont, CA: David S. Lake Publishers.

Detailed Performance Template for ICON Employment Services

MISSION: EXPAND SUPPORTED EMPLOYMENT IN THE MID-ATLANTIC REGION.

1.0. Array of affiliated employment sites established
    1.1. Establish the organization's internal capacity to support the development of employment sites.
        a. Develop the internal capacity to create and support employment opportunities directly.
            i. Develop financial resources.
            ii. Develop skilled personnel, materials, and systems.
        b. Develop the internal capacity to support the development or spin-off of free-standing organizations to support integrated employment opportunities.
            i. Develop skilled personnel, materials, and systems for providing support.
            ii. Develop funding and support for new organizations through regional networks with funding agents, advocates, and others interested in developing new supported employment organizations.
    1.2. Develop sites.
        a. Develop job sites directly.
            i. Develop marketing plan.
            ii. Develop employer relationships.
        b. Develop sites for freestanding organizations.
            i. Complete planning activities.
            ii. Complete start-up checklist.
    1.3. Maintain sites.
        a. Perform direct support functions to employers, co-workers, and employees with disabilities.
            i. Support job analysis and initial training.
            ii. Support employer and co-workers to maintain job satisfaction.
        b. Perform support functions for freestanding organizations.
            i. Support sites in identifying support needs.
            ii. Adjust site support functions based on feedback and performance.
2.0. Regional supported employment direct service delivery improved
    2.1. Plan activities for improving regional direct service delivery.
        a. Prioritize regional needs for improving direct service delivery.
            i. Identify target customers.
            ii. Conduct market analysis.
        b. Adjust plan based on previous performance evaluation.
            i. Analyze performance evaluations.
            ii. Analyze impact of previous activities.

    2.2. Conduct training and technical assistance.
        a. Develop technical assistance and training to match regional needs.
           i. Develop materials, schedules, and systems.
           ii. Develop personnel and other needed resources.
        b. Provide training and technical assistance according to plan and contract.
           i. Complete logistical arrangements.
           ii. Conduct activities.
    2.3. Evaluate performance of accomplishment.
           i. Establish evaluation mechanisms, schedules, and targets.
           ii. Implement activities.
3.0. Local, state, and national attention to supported employment increased
    3.1. Provide information to consumers, service providers, advocates, and others, including the general public.
        a. Complete public relations activities including presentations, tours, and newsletters.
           i. Develop materials and resources for conducting public relations activities.
           ii. Develop strategic plan for public relations activities.
        b. Respond to all requests for information.
    3.2. Influence government priorities
        a. Monitor government activity related to supported employment.
           i. Identify mechanisms for monitoring activity.
           ii. Implement monitoring system.
        b. Participate in public forums, task forces, and panels.
           i. Select strategic activities.
           ii. Schedule participation.
4.0. Fiscal and management stability established and maintained
    4.1. Plan and implement management operations to meet desired performance levels.
    4.2. Monitor and adjust management operations to meet desired performance levels.

Chapter 9

Concepts and Processes To Support Quality Improvement

Continuous Quality Improvement is much more than a philosophy. It suggests a variety of methods for taking systematic approaches to planning and problem-solving to support improved individual and organizational performance. This chapter steps back for a moment from specific tools—such as performance templates and troubleshooting—to expand on some of the broader concepts and processes behind the fundamental quality improvement principle: "Use a Systematic Approach To Find Opportunities and To Improve Performance."

As described in Chapter 2, using a systematic approach suggests that on an ongoing basis organizations compare their actual performance with the mission, identify and prioritize problems, analyze processes, identify the greatest opportunity for improvement, plan and implement interventions, and evaluate strategies implemented. This chapter, therefore, begins by returning to the basic quality improvement strategy, the Shewhart Cycle. In addition, it presents some of the other fundamental concepts behind the principle of using systematic methods and offers a standardized quality improvement process that may be applied to a range of different types of performance problems.

BASIC CONCEPTS OF A SYSTEMATIC APPROACH

The quality improvement process described later in this chapter will be easier to understand after a few of the basic concepts addressed by quality experts are introduced. For more in-depth information on these concepts, the reader is referred to the many excellent references listed at the end of this chapter.

The Shewhart Cycle Versus Linear Thinking

More than any other method presented in this book, the Shewhart Cycle represents the primary strategy of quality improvement: Plan, Do, Check, Act. **Plan** for quality improvement based on data; implement (**do**) the plan (through a pilot study, if appropriate), **check** to see what happens, then use the information gained to adjust the plan and **act** to install the new approach into daily operations. Also referred to as the Deming Cycle (Deming, 1986) or P-D-C-A, the Shewhart Cycle reflects the ongoing nature of improvement: constantly evaluating the results of previous actions to incorporate that information into improving the next round of planning.

In rehabilitation services, personnel often work in a linear fashion: implementing one decision to solve a pressing problem, then moving on to implement another. Planning is seldom data-based, and once planning decisions are implemented, data revealing the impact of those decisions are rarely evaluated and used to ensure future gains. Using a crisis management approach, many organizations concentrate their efforts on fixing mistakes and problems rather than on preventing them. Organizations committed to implementing the Shewhart Cycle, however, develop a spiral of quality improvement, continuously building even better strategies and results upon previous improvements.

Processes: Complexity, Variation, and Stability

Organizations, including those in human services, require that countless diverse tasks be performed each day. In quality management, personnel learn to look on these tasks as *steps in a process*. A process is the sequence of tasks directed toward accomplishing a specific outcome (Scholtes, 1988). Every organization uses thousands of processes to accomplish its work. Thinking of the myriad tasks as steps in processes helps staff members to see how various tasks are related and how performance on one influences the success of others.

> A process is the sequence of tasks directed toward accomplishing a specific outcome (Scholtes, 1988).

It may be easiest to understand the concept of processes in a manufacturing environment, where subcomponents and products move from one assembly step to another until the final product is completed. Each work station on an assembly line completes another step (or steps) in the process. Usually, many different processes are required to produce a completed product. Thus, in making a computer, separate processes are used to assemble any internal wire harnesses, circuit boards, and mechanical assemblies, and mold and screen print the outer case and keys. Each of these processes includes several steps. For example, completing a wire harness may require that the wires be cut to length, stripped, terminated, and inserted into connectors before they are assembled into a finished harness and inserted into the computer.

However, other business functions beyond manufacturing, including those in human services, involve processes as well. Both for-profit and not-for-profit organizations perform processes that result in, for example, hiring a secretary, managing incoming payments, and distributing paychecks. Likewise, organizations providing services such as community-based employment support perform processes in completing their work. The steps required to identify potential job opportunities, to analyze the work and social requirements of jobs, to respond to employer requests, to provide an orientation to co-workers, or to complete a billing to the vocational rehabilitation agency are processes that lead to the outcomes: developed jobs, analyzed jobs, requests responded to, oriented co-workers, and billing completed.

Thinking in terms of processes helps staff members to understand that, because the work of the organization consists of a set of processes, improvement requires improving processes. Improved processes lead to improved outcomes, which means improved productivity (Deming, 1986; Scholtes, 1988). Manufacturing firms regularly assess the performance of processes to ensure uniformity, to increase efficiency, and to prevent errors. In wire harness assembly, a company might measure the length of wires to determine if they are being cut uniformly, or if the measuring and cutting step is not working. Inspection that identifies a wire that has been cut too short may save later rework costs for either discarding or having to reassemble a harness that does not reach far enough when inserted into the computer at final assembly. Such inspection reflects a quality control approach to ensuring good performance. However, *improving the process* so that the capability of the process makes it feasible that no wires would be cut too short is the objective of quality improvement.

Personnel in human services are not accustomed to thinking in terms of pro-

At one agency, community support staff frequently complained about the lack of cleanliness and the dress of supported employees at job sites. A quality improvement team composed of job developers, job coaches, and a rehabilitation specialist was formed to address the issue of worker appearance. Team members felt overwhelmed by the issue and unsure about how to improve it. However, when asked questions such as: "How are workers and their families informed of and provided feedback about appearance?", or "What systems and procedures are in place now?", they discovered that their organization had a series of processes to deal with such issues.

Transition meetings to review requirements on entering a new job, informal supports provided by job coaches to give information about appearance, individual service planning meetings to set goals when formal programs were needed, and formal training or behavior programs implemented and monitored to improve appearance—all had been defined by the organization, but were not consistently provided or were not understood by the job coaches. Team members and managers alike were amazed at the discovery. When reviewing the diagram (Figure 9.1) that identified the process links, they could see that pieces of the processes did not occur; even though they were available, they were not used consistently. The resolution was obvious. Simply ensuring that the established processes were implemented consistently had a dramatic impact on the problem.

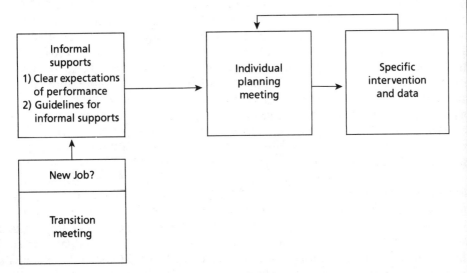

Figure 9.1. Sample diagram of agency processes related to worker appearance.

cesses. Thus, one challenge to rehabilitation agencies is to recognize the structure in the work they do, that is, identify the processes that are necessary to desired outcomes. Identifying processes allows analysis of those processes to discover ways in which to improve them and, thereby, to improve the outcomes, including the productivity of the organization.

Complexity in Processes   Processes are often confounded by *complexity*. Complexity in a process refers to inclusion of unnecessary steps which make a process more complicated but add no value to the resulting product or service. Usually complexity is added to processes to compensate for problems or errors, rather than plans being made for improvement of the process so that it will work flawlessly. Quality inspection points, delays built into the system, breakdowns, inefficiencies, and variation in materials all add complexity to processes. State and federal bureaucracies

> "Complexity is a general term for unnecessary work—anything that makes a process more complicated without adding value to a product or service." (Scholtes, 1988, ch. 2, p. 9)

offer extreme examples of complexity in processes—such as requiring several levels of signatures on purchase orders even though the orders represent only small amounts of money, or the lengthy processes required to carry out recruiting and hiring new personnel.

Variation in Processes   Quantum physicists and cosmologists suggest there is an inherent randomness in the universe (Davies, 1983). *Variation* occurs in everything—including individual characteristics and the behavior and outcomes of organizations (Nolan & Provost, 1990). There is variation in income level, hair length, and height of people. There is variation in the size and structure of organizations. And there is a natural and random variation in all processes. This variation in processes results in a natural variation in the actual outcomes those processes are able to achieve.

The concept of variation can be illustrated very simply with the example of the process of driving to work. Suppose the drive typically requires about 20 minutes. Measuring the exact length of time between leaving home and arriving at work over a 2-week period, however, would reveal that the exact length of time varies: one day—17½ minutes, another day—23 minutes, another day—19 minutes, and so forth. But the driver is so accustomed to this variation that she simply says, "It takes about 20 minutes to drive to work." Dr. Deming and other statisticians refer to the causes of such natural variation as *common causes*. These common causes of variation occur because of the system or process; that is, they are actually built into the way in which the process works (Deming, 1986). The variation experienced by the driver is the result of a number of different factors that are actually part of the system, including how much traffic she encounters, how fast it is moving, the number of red lights, and the waiting time at stop signs. She encounters these variations every day, and the sum of their effects results in the length of time of the drive to work. These variations are built into the process, and the driver has little control over them. If she continues to follow the same route, she cannot change the number of stop signs or stop lights, the waiting time at stop lights, or the amount of traffic; only the city's traffic planners can. Thus, this driver should not be blamed for variation in driving time that is due to common causes in the system, and so, not under her control.

But what if there is construction on the road, reducing four lanes of traffic to one, or an accident that closes the highway for 30 minutes? Or she runs out of gas, or she must return home for an important file that she forgot? In these cases the trip to work will take much longer than the typical 20 minutes—resulting in further variation. Such causes of variation are referred to as *special causes*—those fleeting, local, and, sometimes, person-specific causes of variation in outcomes.

This distinction between common and special causes of variation is central to understanding what is required to improve the performance of processes. Managers make decisions every day that are based on the variation they observe in performance outcomes: 2 months of decreasing bills, 1 week of fewer behavioral incidents, 1 year of high staff turnover, double the numbers of copies made on the photocopier from one month to the next, four late bills for services, an increase in the number of jobs developed or lost. Do these data represent a trend? What actions should be taken to improve performance? *Should* actions be taken to improve performance? Who is to blame for the variation?

Dr. Deming estimates that as much as 94% of variation is due to common causes, and only 6% to special causes (Deming, 1986). Common causes belong to the system and processes being used; because of that, they fall within the responsibility of management. Such variation is not controlled by the workers in the process, just as the typical variation experienced in driving time to work is not controlled by the driver. Blaming the driver is useless. Blaming employees for variation that is most likely the result of common causes is worse than useless—it instills fear, confusion, distrust, and resentment in employees. It places huge barriers in the way of supporting employees to work to achieve the mission. If Dr. Deming is right, then organizations will find their greatest opportunities for improving the performance of processes through reducing the common causes of variation—the causes that are unrelated to individual employees.

Stability in Processes   It is impossible to remove all variability from processes. However, our goal should be to reduce the amount of variation as much as possible. Continuous Quality Improvement offers processes and tools for doing so. These tools (see Chapter 10 for some of them) are used first to isolate and eliminate special causes of variation, bringing a process "under statistical control," then to attack the common causes. Attacking the common causes of variation can be done only through the use of systematic methods to address issues in the process itself.

A process that is *under statistical control* is said to be *stable*: The range of its variation is predictable. In this case, although functioning with only common causes of variation operating, the process will still exhibit variations in its output. Taking action to adjust to these variations, based on a single data point, will most likely make the performance of the process worse, rather than better. This effect is far from intuitive; rather, it is shown through application of statistical methods beyond the scope of this text. Suffice it to say that it is the *patterns* evident in data—rather than any specific data point—that should be used for making decisions to "tamper" with the process (Deming, 1986).

An organization may take two approaches to reducing variability in processes: ensuring that all staff implementing a particular process use the same standardized procedures, materials, equipment, and so forth, and studying processes by collecting and analyzing data to identify potential sources of variation. The first may be addressed, at least in part, through implementation of the Performance Engineering Matrix discussed in Chapter 6: providing environmental supports such as clear job aids, guides and feedback on performance, standardized tools and resources, incentives for performing processes accurately, or training in implementing the process.

The second approach is carried out through the use of other processes and tools of quality improvement, including those presented later in this chapter and in Chapter 10.

Systems and Systems Thinking

Systems consist of a group of related processes (Scholtes, 1988). Most organizations have sets of processes organized into more complicated systems to accomplish, for example, financial management or hiring. Community-based employment service providers have systems for developing jobs, working with employers, and coordinating individual support needs. Indeed, community rehabilitation organizations operate within larger systems of state funding and regulation. The importance of "systems thinking" (Senge, 1990) is that it requires personnel to see the patterns involved in interrelated actions and results across different processes. Unfortunately, systems are much more difficult to study and improve than an individual process, because of the number of different processes—and therefore steps—involved in them. Indeed, often the parts of a system can be totally disconnected in time and space—as in the effect of actions of the Federal Reserve System in Washington, D.C., on local home mortgage rates in Pocatello, Idaho. But instead of understanding the puzzling interrelationships of a system, "we tend to focus on snapshots of isolated parts of the system, and wonder why our deepest problems never seem to get solved" (Senge, 1990, p. 7).

A PROCESS FOR QUALITY IMPROVEMENT

Improving the performance of processes requires application of systematic methods. Continuous Quality Improvement offers a sequence of steps that may be followed to accomplish this. While presented in different ways by different authors (e.g., GOAL/QPC, 1988; Goodman, 1990; Juran, 1986; Mosgaller, n.d., 1990; QIP, Inc., 1986; Rhodes, Albin, Mank, Sandow, & Buckley, 1989; Scholtes, 1988) with variations in the specific number and sequence of steps, each version of the quality improvement process expands upon the Shewhart Cycle of Plan-Do-Check-Act. One simplified version of a quality improvement process is presented here. This process may be carried out by an individual or by a team of staff members and others. Guidelines for selecting a project, and for selecting project team members when the project will be carried out by a group, are presented later in this chapter.

Step 1. *Define the Problem* The first step is defining the problem, which requires development of a statement that describes the identified problem in terms of what occurs and where and when it occurs. It is often useful to draw a picture of the process, as well as a graph of its current results. A variety of tools such as workflow diagrams or detailed and possibly top-down flowcharts to show process complex-

A QUALITY IMPROVEMENT PROCESS

Step 1.   Define the problem.
Step 2.   Analyze possible causes.
Step 3.   Collect data to identify a root cause.
Step 4.   Select strategies for improvement.
Step 5.   Implement improvement strategies.
Step 6.   Complete data analysis.
Step 7.   Plan for continuous improvement.

ities are very useful for describing the existing process. Many different data display techniques also may be used to describe the problem. During this phase, team members should understand how the problem affects achieving the mission, as well as how it affects customers. Any customer feedback that is available on the problem should be provided to the problem-solvers at this time.

Step 2. Analyze Possible Causes   The second step involves team members brainstorming to identify possible causes for the problem and analyzing their potential influence on quality. During this step select any of the various brainstorming techniques described in Chapter 10, such as the Cause and Effect Diagram, to define potential causes. Use the knowledge of staff members who are the most directly involved with a problem to identify all of its possible causes. For each cause identified, seek the cause of that cause, until the most basic causes for the specified process performance problem are suggested. The result of this step should be a complete picture of the different causes that *could be* related to the problem being studied. This step is important to expand the way in which the problem-solvers view possible causes and relationships.

Step 3. Collect Data To Identify a Basic Cause   After developing an understanding of the range of possible causes to the problem, go to Step 3 and collect and analyze data to determine the most important cause—the root cause, which has the greatest impact on performance. Check sheets, scatter diagrams, Pareto analyses, and other data collection and display tools are useful at this step. Issues related to what data should be collected and how to plan for data collection are described later in this chapter. Do not be tempted to skip this step, assuming that, just because you thought of it, a potential cause must be the real one. Whenever possible, verify your best guess with data.

Step 4. Select Strategies for Improvement   There may be many different strategies that may be used to improve performance. However, the better the previous data collection step is completed, the better the information will be for Step 4, in which a solution is selected for the defined problem. Indeed, the data themselves may lead to a specific solution. How that solution will be implemented, however, may require creative and innovative strategies. Thus, techniques such as the various brainstorming methods, including Affinity Diagrams, are likely to be useful during this phase of the project. If several different strategies are generated, techniques are also available to help with narrowing the list of possible strategies to select one that is most likely to be successful.

This step of the quality improvement process also requires careful planning of how the selected solution will be implemented, and how its effects will be measured and analyzed. What measures will be used to assess the outcomes of the project? These quality indicators should be used to reflect the results achieved by the process both before and after improvement strategies are implemented. Quality improvement teams should use the input available from customers, from the managers who established the team, and from their own discussions to select the specific quality indicators. They may also choose to select the specific level of change desired for each quality indicator. Methods such as check sheets, Pareto analyses, and various graphing techniques will be needed by a quality improvement team during this phase of its project.

Step 5.   Implement Improvement Strategies   After the planning process, go to Step 5 and implement the selected improvement strategy. During this step, be sure to check that the solution is actually implemented as planned and to record performance data defined during Step 4 for evaluating the effect of the improvement strategy.

Step 6.   Complete Data Analysis   After a predefined period, go to Step 6 to evaluate the success of the selected improvement strategy and determine whether the strategy succeeded in reaching targeted goals. Data display methods that make the patterns in the data highly visible are particularly useful during this step. If goals have been reached, proceed to Step 7. If the goal has not been achieved, return to a previous step to reanalyze the problem and determine if additional improvement strategies are warranted.

Step 7.   Plan for Continuous Improvement   Although the improvement goal has been reached, and the strategy for improving performance has proved successful, the improvement process is not yet complete. Step 7, the final step, is just as important as any of the others because it carries out the last step of the Shewhart Cycle (Plan-Do-Check-**Act**): acting to embed the new strategies in the organization, expanding them to other parts of the organization if appropriate, and planning for how the organization will continuously build upon the improvements achieved in this process. For example, if improving a staff orientation process in one part of the community employment program is found to result in reduced staff turnover, then during Step 7 it would be documented and expanded to other parts of the organization. Furthermore, methods for ongoing evaluation and improvement of the performance of that program would be defined. Sometimes this step leads to taking on another root cause or selecting a higher improvement goal for the same project. How will staff involved in carrying out the process be trained to improve it continuously? What data will be reviewed to ensure that the process continues to work properly? These and similar questions should be answered by the individual problem-solver or project team before they complete work on one cycle of the ongoing spiral of quality improvement.

The Team Handbook (Scholtes, 1988) offers excellent information about specific strategies that may be combined in carrying out this overall quality improvement process. It details strategies such as how to localize recurring problems, how to streamline a process, and how to develop appropriate solutions.

Common Mistakes in Implementing a Quality Improvement Process

The quality improvement process described above is deceptively simple. At each step along the way, however, individuals and quality improvement teams alike make

QUALITY IMPROVEMENT PROCESS CASE STUDY:
REDUCING LATE ARRIVAL AT WORK

Judy has been having trouble getting to work on time, at 8:00 A.M. Although her boss has not said anything about it yet, she has decided she needs to take action and improve. Judy recently attended a seminar on Continuous Quality Improvement and decided to try to apply systematic methods from that seminar to her problem. Here is how she proceeded, step by step:

DEFINE THE PROBLEM—LATE ARRIVAL AT WORK

For the past month, Judy has arrived at work early or on time only four times out of 20 work days. She is afraid that continued problems with being late will affect her job and cause dissatisfaction among her co-workers and boss.

The major steps involved in her process for going to work are:
Get Up
1. Set alarm clock.
2. Get up when the alarm rings.
Get Ready for Work
1. Shower, dress.
2. Eat breakfast.
3. Feed the dog.
Drive to Work
1. Select route.
2. Follow route.

For the last 2 weeks, Judy kept data on what time she got up, left the house, and arrived at work:
Get Up
  6:29   ///
  6:30   ///// ///// //
  6:31   ////
  6:32   /
Leave for Work
  7:24   /////
  7:25   ///// /////
  7:26   ///
  7:28   //
Arrive at Work
  8:00   /////
  8:01–8:05   /
  8:06–8:10   //
  8:11–8:15   //
  8:15–8:20   ////
  8:21–8:25   ////
  8:26–8:30   ///

Based on these data, Judy decided that the biggest cause of variation of her arrival time must be related to the drive between home and work. Therefore, she redefined the problem as: **Reducing the variation in driving time between home and work.**

(continued)

QUALITY IMPROVEMENT PROCESS CASE STUDY: REDUCING LATE ARRIVAL AT WORK (*continued*)

ANALYZE POSSIBLE CAUSES

Judy asked a friend to help her to brainstorm possible causes for that variation and came up with quite a list. They reviewed the list to identify which items seemed to be most worthwhile to pursue further:

- The amount of traffic
- How fast traffic is moving
- The number of traffic lights
- The number of red lights
- The waiting time at red lights
- The number of stop signs
- The waiting time at stop signs
- Construction
- Special stops along the way (e.g., for donuts, to mail letters)
- Which route she takes to work

COLLECT DATA TO IDENTIFY A ROOT CAUSE

Judy decided to collect data on some of these for the next 2 weeks while she was driving (see Table 9.1). She was late for work during these 2 weeks, 7 out of 10 days. She discovered that one of the three routes she typically took to work had only half as many red lights and stop signs as did each of the others. None of the routes had construction during the 2 weeks she collected data. However, she did see that every day that she had to make a special stop along the way, she was late.

SELECT STRATEGIES FOR IMPROVEMENT

Judy decided on two improvement strategies, based on these data:

Table 9.1. Driving to work data

Day	Route A, B, C[a]	Special Stop	Traffic Speed	Arrival Time
1	A	Mail	Moderate	8:15
2	A	—	Moderate	8:00
3	B	Mail	Moderate	8:08
4	A	Donuts	Moderate	8:22
5	C	—	Moderate	7:55
6	B	Mail	Moderate	8:16
7	A	Pick up laundry	Moderate	8:10
8	B	—	Moderate	8:00
9	C	Mail	Moderate	8:06
10	B	Donuts	Moderate	8:10
Totals	A: 4 B: 4 C: 2	Stops: 7		Late: 7 times

[a]ROUTE A: 10 traffic lights, 6 stop signs, no construction. ROUTE B: 9 traffic lights, 7 stop signs, no construction. ROUTE C: 5 traffic lights, 3 stop signs, no construction.

(continued)

QUALITY IMPROVEMENT PROCESS CASE STUDY:
REDUCING LATE ARRIVAL AT WORK (*continued*)

1. Start using route "C" every day. It is not quite as pretty as the other two, but she would rather get to work on time.
2. Reset her alarm to get up 10 minutes earlier on the days when she knows that she will be making a special stop on the way to work.

IMPLEMENT IMPROVEMENT STRATEGIES

Judy decided to implement the first strategy right away, and collect data for 2 more weeks.

COMPLETE DATA ANALYSIS

Judy's data indicated that, with route "C," she was late to work only 4 out of 10 days. In addition, she was never more than 8 minutes late. The new route seemed to be an improvement.

PLAN FOR CONTINUOUS IMPROVEMENT

Judy wanted to do better, however, and decided to implement her second strategy: resetting her alarm clock 10 minutes earlier on the days when she knew she would have to make a special stop on the way to work. She would also continue keeping data on arrival time to see if this worked or if she needed to take more steps to improve her performance.

---

mistakes that reduce or block the effectiveness of the process. A few of the more common errors are described below:

1. *Failing to define the problem carefully:* Often, the problem selected is not understood in the same way by all involved with improving it. Therefore, taking time to describe the problem carefully, to draw diagrams and graphs, and to identify when it does and does not occur will save valuable time later in the process.
2. *Rushing to a solution before taking time to understand all possible causes of the problem:* One of the greatest barriers to quality improvement is a person who believes he or she knows the answer to a problem without making the effort to investigate the possible causes. Jumping to define a solution as soon as the problem is identified blocks creativity and innovation in problem-solving; it does not take advantage of the information provided by taking data on the process to identify the potential causes of the problem.
3. *Ignoring or discounting data:* The power of quality improvement methodology comes in large part from its reliance on systematic methods and data-based decision-making. When an organization fails to collect data, discounts data that are collected, or chooses to ignore the data, it is not capturing the power that quality improvement methods offer. Staff members must learn to make the most effective use of data by taking action based on what the data tell them.
4. *Failing to test the solution and analyze results to see if they match those expected:* Sometimes individuals or teams carrying out a quality improvement project put great energy into collecting data to identify the root cause and into planning for imple-

menting the solution. However, they fail to collect data and determine if the solution selected actually resulted in the outcomes expected. Completing all steps
of the quality improvement process is essential to ensuring its effectiveness.

5. *Moving on to another improvement project without first embedding continuous improve-
    ment in the current project:* The quality improvement process—like the Shewhart
    Cycle—is not "complete" until the steps for improvement to continue are de-
    fined and implemented. Organizations or individuals who are anxious to move
    on to another problem-solving cycle without planning for continuous improve-
    ment of the last likely will find that any gains made are transitory.

Each of these mistakes grows out of a lack of the discipline needed to continue to
focus on carefully moving through the process, overcoming any urge to take a short-
cut. Other mistakes that may be made in implementing this quality improvement
process are described later in this chapter under "Common Mistakes in Selecting
Projects."

QUALITY IMPROVEMENT TEAMS

Continuous Quality Improvement encompasses methods that may be implemented
on a daily basis by individual staff members of any organization. However, on occasion, problems encountered are too difficult or multi-faceted to be improved through
the work of a single employee. In these situations, companies adopting quality improvement methods form teams of employees and sometimes other persons to carry
out the quality improvement project. While costly in terms of time, teams have the
benefit of bringing a variety of perspectives and skills to the problem at hand. This
section of the chapter presents information on team members and team operation.
Additional information on management roles in supporting team performance and
on special considerations in forming the initial quality improvement teams are presented in Chapter 12.

Selecting Team Members

Quality improvement teams, or project teams, should consist of no more than three
to seven members. Their role is to work together to accomplish the steps of the quality improvement process in addressing a specific problem. The specific team members, either volunteers or management appointees, should represent all aspects of
the process under study and include individuals who directly perform parts of
the process. For example, a quality improvement team to increase the timeliness of
billing to the vocational rehabilitation agency might include a job coach who sub-
mits information on service hours, the bookkeeper who transfers information onto
the appropriate billing forms and records, and a manager involved in approving
the bills.

Quality improvement teams may also include individuals outside the organization—especially customers—who are affected by the problem being studied. Thus,
the billing team, above, might invite a person from the vocational rehabilitation
agency who receives the organization's bills and authorizes payment. Similarly, a
team to improve the individual service planning process should include a case manager and advocate or individual receiving services, as well as employees from the

rehabilitation program involved with different aspects of individual service planning. A team addressing complaints from residential providers about improving efficiency of transporting workers, might include parents and residential staff, in addition to employment program staff.

Teams can work effectively with members from different departments, shifts, work areas, ranks, or professions. Indeed, cutting across such formal and informal boundaries is likely to improve the outcome of the project and is required in addressing problems that cut across those boundaries. Such cross-divisional teams offer an opportunity to break down barriers to communication, which supports another fundamental principle of quality improvement: "Empower Employees To Work To Achieve the Mission."

In establishing a quality improvement team, managers may choose not only to select the individuals who will form the team, but to identify a team leader, as well. The *team leader* is the person who will be responsible for arranging logistics, running meetings, and so forth. In some organizations, the managers may choose to allow the team to select its own leader, or allow the team leader to rotate. However, rotating team leaders may result in a disorganized team with poor leadership, fragmented records, and ineffective results. The important role of team leader involves working with both the management staff and other advisors in planning and evaluating the progress of the team, in addition to the "simpler" tasks of handling the logistics of meetings. Therefore, treat the selection of a team leader seriously.

Team Operation

The basic operation of a project team, beyond carrying out the steps of the quality improvement process, requires methods similar to those necessary for effective operation of any work group.

- Teams must have a clear *purpose*. Managers who establish a project team must clarify for team members why they have been asked to work together, and what they are expected to achieve.
- Team members may need *training* to help them perform their task. This training should encompass quality improvement principles, quality tools, or the quality improvement process itself, if not yet understood by the team members.
- Teams should have *scheduled meetings*, usually 1–3 hours in length, which members treat as "sacred." Inconsistent attendance by some members of a project team undermines effectiveness.
- Using a *structured agenda*, that includes topics, time guidelines, and actions required, is a practical strategy to help teams stay focused. Before the end of each meeting, the team should take time to draft the agenda for the next meeting.
- Teams that are facing troublesome discussions or that have difficulty staying focused need the help of a skilled *meeting facilitator*. A good facilitator may, for example, act as a gatekeeper to ensure that all team members have an opportunity to contribute to the discussion, summarize statements or discussion, check for consensus, request clarification from members when needed, manage the time, and assist the group to deal with conflicting positions. Team members may choose to rotate the role of meeting facilitator or may have to bring in an outside facilitator who can remain more objective about the discussion.
- *Meeting records*, including the agenda, minutes, and an action list, are useful to remind team members of decisions and assignments.

- Completing a *meeting evaluation* after each session will obtain feedback from participants that can be used to improve subsequent meetings.

Many texts (and consultants) are available offering guidance for how to manage small groups and meetings (e.g., Cathcart & Samovar, 1988; Phillips & Elledge, 1989; Scholtes, 1988). These texts offer techniques useful for quality improvement teams, as well.

SELECTING A QUALITY IMPROVEMENT PROJECT

Quality improvement processes and tools can be applied easily to hundreds of different processes operating in any organization. The question is which process to choose. For example, in community-based employment, quality improvement projects may address performance issues related to a particular job site or supported employee, a department within the organization, or the organization as a whole. Chapter 5, on troubleshooting, and Chapter 7, on the *Self-Assessment Guide for Change-over to Supported Employment,* offer strategies for selecting improvement projects. Listed below are a few additional guidelines:

Project Selection Guidelines

1. *The proposed project should be a concern to many people.* Choose a project that reflects an issue that is of concern to more than one or two people in the organization and that addresses recurring issues. Everyone on the project team (except an outside facilitator) should probably be concerned by the issue. Quality improvement projects require hard work and careful attention. Because they will serve as a training ground, the first projects implemented will suffer from a variety of inefficiencies that will slow their completion. Therefore, so that the project does not die from simple lack of attention, select a project that is likely to affect both the managers and the quality improvement team members.
2. *The proposed project should be related to improving performance of the mission.* Because there are so many possible targets for improvement in any organization, and the cost in personnel time of using a project team can be high, it is wise to choose projects that are directly tied to improving mission accomplishments. Use troubleshooting methods, starting with the mission, to identify the areas offering the greatest opportunities for improved performance.
3. *The proposed project should be important to the organization's customers.* Select a project that will affect meeting the needs of the organization's customers. Early in a project, team members should describe any known customer expectations regarding the process or problem. Discussing customers first helpss team members to maintain a customer focus and to understand customer definitions of quality throughout the quality improvement project. Chapter 3 presents strategies for obtaining customer input.
4. *The proposed project should address a single process, rather than large systems.* While there are times when organizations must address issues of larger systems, narrowing down a project to focus on the process that is most problematic in a system is recommended. Lengthy projects, addressing complex systems, require great discipline and expertise to complete. Instead, choose a project that has

clear start and end points and has anticipated benefits that are far greater than the project's potential costs.

5. *The proposed project should have a high likelihood of success.* Very early in an organization's experience with quality improvement methods, it is important to select improvement targets that offer a good chance of success. As stated earlier, sticking with the quality improvement process requires discipline, and employees are best rewarded for this discipline by seeing the benefits of their work. Thus, choose projects that are important but also will likely lead to success for team members.

Other factors may be of particular importance in project selection, especially early in an organization's experience with implementing methods of Continuous Quality Improvement. The support of key personnel or overall employee receptivity to the project, for example, might override other criteria. Whether teams generate

---

SAMPLE CHECKLIST FOR PROJECT SELECTION

When you are having trouble deciding which of several possible improvement projects to undertake, try using a set of guidelines to help narrow the list. Begin with the guidelines listed below to build your own checklist for evaluating potential projects. It may not be possible to satisfy all of the criteria listed, and some may be more important than others at different stages in the quality transformation of an organization.

The questions on a selection checklist may be used in different ways. For example, you may simply answer each question "Yes" or "No," or choose to assign judgment ratings (e.g., on a 3-point scale) for how well each project option meets that criterion. If a few of the criteria are more important than others, and the selection is a particularly difficult or important decision, it may be necessary to use "Decision Matrices" and "weighted" methods to make the selection. See Chapter 10 for further information on these methods.

IS THE PROPOSED PROJECT:

_____ Important to all members of the project team and to others in the organization?
_____ Related to a recurring problem?
_____ Related to improving performance on the mission?
_____ Important to the organization's customers?
_____ Addressing a single process rather than a larger system?
_____ One that has a relatively high likelihood of success?
_____ Supported by key personnel?
_____ Likely to be received well by employees overall?
_____ Related to a problem rather than justifying a particular solution?
_____ Related to a process that will not be changing soon, anyway, even if it were not studied?
_____ A managable size, not too large and ambitious?
_____
_____
_____

project ideas by simply brainstorming ideas for possible areas of improvement, or by troubleshooting the organization's mission accomplishments, managers must determine the specific criteria to be used for evaluating ideas in order to prioritize the areas to be targeted. The sample checklist for project selection offers one strategy for doing so. Chapter 10 also offers tools to help with prioritizing from a list of options.

Common Mistakes in Selecting Projects

Mistakes that organizations just beginning a quality transformation commonly make involve ignoring part of the quality improvement process, or selecting the wrong project, too many projects, or too large a project. Some mistakes along these lines include (Scholtes, 1988):

1. *Jumping to a solution rather than studying the problem in the process:* In their haste, managers may assume that they already know what revisions are needed to improve a process. In selecting a project, they will tell the team what solutions to implement rather than help the team choose which process or issue to study. For example, one organization well into the quality improvement transformation had difficulties meeting U.S. Department of Labor guidelines for frequency of performing time studies for establishing productivity rates when subminimum wages are payed. The managers asked one improvement team to design a training program on the assumption that staff did not know enough about performing the time studies. Instead, the team surveyed staff to discover the root cause of the problem and found that staff *did* know how to do time studies but had a problem with the time required to perform the number of time studies for all of the different tasks defined for each work location. The better solution, therefore, was reanalyzing the jobs into fewer separate tasks for time study purposes, or working with employers to reduce the number of people on subminimum wage certificates.

   It may be that the solution identified by the managers actually would be the best method to use. If that is the case, the managers should believe that the quality improvement team will arrive at that conclusion through studying the process. Therefore, be careful to select *problems* for study; this allows the team the freedom to discover and implement the most creative and best solutions.

2. *Picking a process that will soon be changing anyway for other reasons:* Quality improvement projects require time and effort. Therefore, selecting for study a process that is, or soon will be, in transition is a waste of resources. For example, one organizaton chose to study its processes to ensure meeting state developmental disability agency regulations for employment services. However, the state agency had announced several months before that it was in the process of revising its regulations and on-site review procedures. Therefore, a project to ensure meeting regulations and review procedures would have been wasted effort until the state announced its new methods.

3. *Selecting a project that is too large and ambitious:* In quality transformation efforts, managers select projects that they expect will have significant impact on the organization. However, too often, they are too eager and choose a project that addresses a system—a set of separate processes—rather than a single process. For example, a project that looks at recruitment for job coach positions is more likely to meet with success than a project that is designed to study the entire system for hiring new employees into any part of the organization. Define a project care-

fully and precisely to maximize the chance of success. After completing that project, the team can move methodically on to another to improve other pieces of the system, with the motivation derived from a successfully completed project behind them.

DATA AND QUALITY IMPROVEMENT

> "Get into the habit of discussing a problem on the basis of the data and respecting the facts as shown by them." (Ishikawa, 1983, p. 5.)

Data provide powerful information for team members and managers using a scientific approach. In the quality improvement process defined earlier in this chapter, data are necessary to perform many of the improvement steps. Properly defined, collected, and analyzed data are essential to making good decisions for taking action to improve performance. Indeed, providing a basis for taking action is the only reason for collecting data. And only through carefully defining the uses of data to be collected will appropriate data measures, data collection methods, and data analyses be identified.

Uses of Data

Data provide a clear, unbiased view of problems, helping those involved to determine and describe the actual facts of a situation. Rather than basing decisions solely on opinions—particularly the opinions of the one who happens to talk the loudest or is the last to speak during a meeting—using data offers a way to see a situation clearly, separate from personal biases. Data provide a method to assess whether decisions made led to the desired result and whether activities carried out are yielding expected outcomes. They may help with identifying possible causes of problems and determining which cause is the most important. Also, they are useful for identifying a method for evaluating various alternative courses of action as part of development of implementation plans. And data provide a basis on which to adjust plans in order to improve performance.

Types of Data

Data for quality improvement may take many forms and are not limited to hard, quantitative measures, such as the number of occurrences, the rate of occurrence, the duration of an event, the cost, the length, or the percentage of instances. Data also may consist of judgment points awarded by knowledgeable persons (e.g., the judges in a gymnastics competition); estimates of relative order (e.g., this one is softer than that one); opinions of those involved; qualitative analyses of interview records; and so forth.

These data may be collected for either of two primary purposes: 1) to measure the *outcomes, results, or effects* of processes or projects; or 2) to measure the actual materials, machines, methods, performance, or environmental factors involved in *the process itself*. Thus, *results data* might reflect, for example, the number and type of complaints received from employers, while *process data* might measure the training and support activities provided for the employer, employee, and co-workers.

REASONS FOR DATA COLLECTION

- Data provide powerful information to support a scientific approach.
- Data are required to complete many of the steps of the quality improvement process.
- Data provide a basis for taking action.
- Data help personnel to understand the facts of the situation, in an unbiased way.
- Data provide information on whether the selected course of action led to the desired results.
- Data provide a basis for analyzing the relationships among various potential causes and effects.
- Data help to evaluate alternative courses of action.
- Data help personnel to determine if outcomes match targets.
- Data provide information to support developing implementation plans.
- Data provide a basis on which to adjust plans in order to improve performance.
- Data measures may be selected to reflect the outcomes of a process or to measure various aspects of the implementation of individual steps of the process.

Planning for Data Collection and Analysis

To obtain data that will effectively support action, users must carefully plan for the type of data needed, the methods to be used for gathering it, and the procedures to be used for analysis. Spending time during a planning phase prior to data collection will result in data that are more reliable, more useful for the decisions to be made, and more easily interpreted. Indeed, data are viewed as information—that is, useful for decision-making—only after they have been organized to support decision-making.

Define the Purpose for Data Collection   The first step to obtaining good data is clearly defining the purpose for the data. What action will be taken based on the data received? How will the data be used? What will you achieve by collecting data? What are the goals for data collection? Be certain of the purpose.

Identify the Appropriate Data To Collect   Based on the purpose, define the actual measures that will reveal the information needed to take action. Will the data gathered actually reveal the facts you need for taking action? Are you considering extraneous data that will not be a part of decision-making? Keep data to a minimum to avoid data glut, unused data, and negative attitudes about data by staff. But select data measures that will provide all of the information needed to take action. In most cases, results data are needed first in order to direct team members to the process data that might be required.

Select the Appropriate Methods for Collecting, Analyzing, and Comparing the Data   There are many ways for data to be in error, even if the appropriate measures have been selected for the decision at hand. For example, the data collected may not be what was defined, the definition may not be clear enough so that data collectors collect the same data, the data collectors may not accurately follow defined procedures, or types of data may be combined when they should not be. Will the data collected actually measure what we want to measure: Are they valid? Will the

GUIDELINES FOR DATA COLLECTION

DEFINE THE PURPOSE FOR DATA COLLECTION

- What action will be taken based on the data received?
- How will the data be used?
- What will you achieve by collecting data?
- What are the goals for data collection?

IDENTIFY APPROPRIATE DATA TO COLLECT

- Will the measures selected actually measure what you think they will measure; that is, are the measures valid?
- Will the data gathered actually reveal the facts that you need for taking action?
- Are you considering extraneous data that will not be a part of decision-making?
- Will the measures selected provide all of the information needed to take action?
- Are measures of *results* being considered first, so that team members might be directed to the *process* data that might be required?
- Have you developed operational definitions of the measures to guide data collectors?

SELECT THE APPROPRIATE METHOD FOR COLLECTING, ANALYZING, AND COMPARING THE DATA

- Will the methods used reveal the information needed for taking action?
- Does the plan include providing training to the data collectors?
- Have you developed formats for data collection that are easy to use and not intrusive to the setting?
- Does the plan include combining data that really cannot be combined appropriately?
- How will the data collected be analyzed? What formats will be used? What methods?

COLLECT DATA IN A WAY THAT WILL SIMPLIFY LATER ANALYSIS

- Do data collection forms clearly record the nature of the data (e.g., date, recorder, location, and other variables that "define" the data)?
- Do data collection methods record the data so that they are easy to use and support automatic analysis?

PERIODICALLY REVIEW THE DATA BEING COLLECTED, COLLECTION METHODS, AND ANALYSIS PROCEDURES

- Are the data being collected actually being used effectively?
- Are the data being collected accurately, according to the definitions of the measures?
- Are the data being collected accurately, according to the planned methods?
- Are the data being analyzed accurately, according to the planned methods?
- Are different data collectors using the same methods and collecting reliable data?
- Are the data collection and analysis methods used actually revealing the information needed for taking action?
- What other measures, data collection methods, or analysis methods might be more appropriate?

data be collected in a consistent way: Are they reliable? Will the data collection and analysis methods used reveal the information needed for taking action?

Careful planning, therefore, must include developing operational definitions of the data to be collected and specific procedural steps and formats for collecting it. This phase should also include providing any necessary training to data collectors to ensure that accurate, reliable data are obtained. Finally, planning must include decisions on how to analyze data. Much of the data that organizations collect are useless only because planners fail to consider how data collected will be analyzed.

APPLYING QUALITY IMPROVEMENT CONCEPTS AND PROCESSES

This chapter has presented several fundamental—and difficult—concepts related to implementing systematic methods for improving performance; a basic quality improvement process; as well as guidelines for methods of project selection, team selection, and data collection. While Continuous Quality Improvement may be viewed by some as "just common sense," the concepts and methods introduced in this chapter provide some evidence of its profound nature and the discipline that implementing quality improvement methods requires. Chapter 10 continues the focus on systematic methods by offering a variety of tools that will be helpful during many steps of the process. Tools such as brainstorming, data collection, data display, and data analysis methods are needed actually to apply the concepts and processes introduced in this chapter.

REFERENCES

Cathcart, R.S., & Samovar, L.A. (1988). *Small group communication: A reader.* Dubuque: Wm. C. Brown Publishers.

Davies, P. (1983). *God and the new physics.* New York: Simon & Schuster.

Deming, W.E. (1986). *Out of the crisis.* Cambridge: Massachusetts Institute of Technology, Center for Advanced Engineering Study.

GOAL/QPC. (1988). *The memory jogger + ™: A pocket guide of tools for continuous improvement.* Methuen, MA: Author.

Goodman, A.L. (1990). The quality freeway. *Quality Progress, 23*(7), 39–42.

Ishikawa, K. (1983.) *Guide to quality control.* Tokyo: Asian Productivity Organization.

Juran, J.M. (1986). A universal approach to managing for quality: The quality trilogy. *Quality Progress 19*(8), 19–24.

Mosgaller, T. (1990, November). *Total quality management.* Presentation at the Region X Rehabilitation Conference, Salishan Lodge, Gleneden, Oregon.

Mosgaller, T. (n.d.). *TQC story format.* Madison: City of Madison.

Nolan, T.W., & Provost, L.P. (1990). Understanding variation. *Quality Progress, 23*(5), 70–78.

Phillips, S.L., & Elledge, R.L. (1989). *The team-building source book.* San Diego: University Associates.

QIP, Inc. (1986). *The transformation of American industry.* Miamisburg, OH: Productivity-Quality Systems, Inc.

Rhodes, L., Albin, J., Mank, D., Sandow, D., & Buckley, J. (1989). *A quality improvement project for supported employment:* Eugene: University of Oregon.

Scholtes, P.R. (1988). *The team handbook: How to use teams to improve quality.* Madison: Joiner Associates, Inc.

Senge, P.M. (1990). *The fifth discipline: The art and practice of the learning organization.* New York: Doubleday/Currency.

ADDITIONAL READINGS

Brown, M.G. (1989). How to improve performance with better data. *Performance and Instruction, 28*(3), 1–6.

Delbecq, A.L., & VandeVan, A.H. (1971). A group process model for problem identification and program planning. *Journal of Applied Behavioral Sciences, 7*(4), 466–491.

McCabe, W.J. (1989). Examining processes improves operations. *Quality Progress, 22*(7), 26–32.

Shewhart, W.A. (1939). *Statistical methods from the viewpoint of quality control.* Washington, DC: U.S. Department of Agriculture.

Chapter 10

Tools for Planning and Problem-Solving To Support Quality Improvement

The systematic methods of Continuous Quality Improvement incorporate concepts, processes, and specific tools that help organizations to find opportunities and to improve performance. This chapter presents some of the tools that may be used to implement the quality improvement process presented in Chapter 9. The techniques are roughly organized under three broad categories: 1) tools to support creativity in planning and problem-solving; 2) tools for analyzing processes; and 3) tools for data collection, display, and analysis. Each of the tools presented could be used during one or more different steps of the quality improvement process, and several steps may call for employing more than one of these tools. Some of the tools reflect commonly used methods, such as methods for brainstorming or graphing data. Others are less well-known to general audiences but are commonly found in texts of quality improvement methods (e.g., Brassard, 1989; Feigenbaum, 1983; GOAL/QPC, 1988; Ishikawa, 1983; Mizuno, 1988) and in companies implementing a Total Quality Management approach. The purpose of this chapter is to introduce some of the tools that are recommended by quality improvement experts, particularly tools most applicable to human services and rehabilitation settings. See the Additional Readings at the end of this chapter, or other texts on statistics, for further information on many of the concepts and tools presented in this chapter.

TOOLS TO SUPPORT CREATIVITY IN PLANNING AND PROBLEM-SOLVING

Many of the quality improvement tools presented later in this chapter have a statistical basis. In other words, they rely on numbers and data to support decision-making. Unfortunately, however, in rehabilitation, community employment, and many other fields, many decisions do not easily lend themselves to data-based methods. Planning for a new project or department, defining a job description for a new position, establishing a new customer feedback group, or designing a strategy for changing the organizational culture to be more supportive of community-based employment are all examples of activities that are unlikely to be planned entirely based on data. Yet, these activities still would benefit from some of the systematic methods suggested by quality improvement.

The following sections, therefore, present several methods grouped into three general categories related to creativity and problem-solving: 1) tools for developing options, 2) tools for narrowing possible choices, and 3) tools for proposing relationships. These tools support creativity and expansive thinking by personnel.

Tools for Developing Options

Brainstorming Brainstorming (see, e.g., GOAL/QPC, 1988; QIP, Inc., 1986; Scholtes, 1988) is a technique used very frequently in quality improvement processes as a method to help a group of people generate a long list of ideas. The technique is useful in a wide number of applications, including generating ideas for a newly planned project and developing a list of possible causes of an identified problem. Thus, brainstorming may be useful at any point in a quality improvement process where ideas need to be generated.

Brainstorming helps group members to make decisions feeling confident that they have examined as broad a range of alternatives as possible. Thus, the goal of the process is to produce a wide *variety* as well as a large *number* of ideas, through involving all members of the group in the process, ensuring that nothing is overlooked, and creating an atmosphere of openness. To be successful, brainstorming requires an environment in which participants feel free to be creative and not afraid to share

GUIDELINES FOR BRAINSTORMING

- Write the question or topic at the top of a flipchart or board to keep the group focused.
- Review the guidelines for brainstorming with the group at the start of the session.
- Do not allow evaluation or criticism of ideas.
- Stress quantity over quality.
- Encourage freewheeling, in which one member can supply several ideas in a row.
- Build on other ideas ("hitchhiking"); encourage combining and improving on them.
- Use questions or suggestions to push participants to open their thinking, for example:
  "Think in terms of the five senses."
  "Think in terms of a process."
  "Explore opposites."
  "Reach for radical ideas, the wilder the better."
- Write all ideas on a flipchart or board so that the whole group can easily scan them.
- Write the ideas in the words of the speaker; do not try to interpret them.
- Record all ideas, including those that are only slightly different from some previously listed.
- Number the ideas as they are added to the list so the group can push for higher numbers.
- Keep the session short: 5–15 minutes.
- Save any discussion of items until the brainstorming session is over.

"wild" ideas. Therefore, participants in brainstorming sessions must assume that all ideas have value and that all members of the group can contribute to the process. It is important, therefore, to allow no criticism, or even discussion of ideas, so that members feel free to release their creativity and do not inhibit their flow of ideas. Because ideas generate other ideas, try to produce as many ideas as possible during brainstorming, valuing quantity over quality.

Plan for a total of 5–15 minutes for the full brainstorming session, depending on the size of the group and the breadth of the topic. Begin the session by reviewing the guidelines for brainstorming with the group and defining the topic of the brainstorm, usually in the form of a question (e.g., "What are the possible ways of overcoming our transportation barriers?" or, "How could we ensure adequate incentives for staff performance?"). Allow the group a minute or two of silence to consider the topic, and then solicit ideas. Using an *Unstructured Brainstorming* approach, allow participants to contribute ideas as they come to mind. This approach encourages freewheeling by participants, but runs the risk of domination by a few very vocal members.

This basic approach to brainstorming may be modified in several ways. For example, one alternative is to ask follow-up questions that lead members in a direction, such as, "Think of the most expensive ways of doing it," or "What are the most outrageous ways to solve this one?". In *Structured Brainstorming*, ask participants to jot down their own ideas and then go around the room inviting ideas until everyone's list has been exhausted. In this form of brainstorming, although participants may "pass" on any round, even the most shy participants are likely to contribute. A few additional brainstorming methods are presented below.

The "66" Technique   The "66" Technique (see, e.g., Newstrom & Scannell, 1980) offers a strategy for getting everyone in a larger group involved in a discussion or brainstorming session. Divide the group into six-person teams, each identifying a recorder. Allow each team 6 minutes to discuss or brainstorm on a topic or issue and to record the results on newsprint to share with others. Each group may work on the same issue, or be assigned different issues. Be sure to define the topic specifically, so that the group will be able to deal with it in 6 minutes. Give the groups a 2-minute warning for concluding their discussion. Post results and, if time permits, ask groups to share their results.

Crawford Slip Method   In this brainstorming method (see, e.g., QIP, Inc., 1986; Scholtes, 1988), ask group members to work individually for approximately 10 minutes to write their ideas, one by one, on slips of paper. Then collect and categorize these slips, arranging and rearranging them in many ways to stimulate further thought on a subject or to find patterns and similarities. Because this method does not require participants to speak out their ideas, participants may be more open and generate an even larger number of ideas than through a more typical brainstorming process. The Crawford Slip Method is similar to the Affinity Diagram, presented below under "Tools for Proposing Relationships."

Force Field Analysis   Originally developed by Kurt Lewin, a psychologist who worked in the first half of the twentieth century, Force Field Analysis (see, e.g., GOAL/QPC, 1988) is a technique for identifying the *driving* (positive) forces and the *restraining* (negative) forces of any specified change. According to Lewin, change occurs if the driving forces, that are pushing for the change, are greater than the restraining forces that are blocking the change and supporting the status quo (GOAL/ QPC, 1988; see Table 10.1).

Table 10.1. Sample Force Field Analysis

"What are the forces related to top management adopting Continuous Quality Improvement (CQI)?"

Driving Forces				Restraining Forces
Desire to improve organizational culture	⟶	⟵		Fear of losing control and power
Interest in learning new things	⟶	⟵		Lack of time to invest in CQI
Interest of some employees who are requesting CQI	⟶	⟵		Lack of understanding of what adopting CQI really means
Desire to improve organizational performance	⟶	⟵		Disbelief in the effectiveness of the methods
—	⟶	⟵	—	
—	⟶	⟵	—	

Force Field Analysis offers a possible starting point for change, in that it pushes participants to be creative and to think about a wide range of factors related to the desired change. Using this process, participants may prioritize the relative factors on each side of the "balance sheet" and decide which should be addressed first. Other tools described below, particularly those related to narrowing a list of possible options, may be helpful at this stage.

Tools for Narrowing Possible Choices

During brainstorming, it is important to allow no criticism so that members do not screen ideas before offering them to the group. However, eventually it may be necessary to narrow down the list to a few ideas that seem to be the best possibilities, such as the one project to be addressed or the preferred strategy to implement first. One approach for narrowing choices is to gather data to support or eliminate choices. However, in the absence of such data, Evaluation Criteria, Decision Matrices, Multivoting, Nominal Group Technique, and Delphi Decision-Making, described below, are methods that may help.

Evaluation Criteria   Evaluation criteria (see, e.g., QIP, Inc., 1986) are standards that may be used to narrow the list of ideas. (The project selection guidelines, suggested in Chapter 9, are examples.) These criteria may be developed through brainstorming or be based on predetermined criteria such as customer requirements, cost, impact, or feasibility. Some organizations may find it useful to develop a standardized set of evaluation criteria that may be applied to common decisions (e.g., evaluation criteria for potential jobs that are identified or for deciding whether to take on new projects). Such a list also may be used as the core evaluation criteria, with others to be developed by the individuals directly involved in the specific decision at hand. Such core evaluation criteria may be developed to reflect the basic values or desired mission accomplishments of the organization.

One useful approach for generating evaluation criteria is to give each participant a few minutes to write down the criteria she or he thinks are important, then solicit these one by one from the group until everyone's list is exhausted. After the list is completed, ask the group to review the list, identifying any criteria they view as mandatory. Use this set of mandatory criteria to narrow the list of ideas. Compare each of the original ideas being considered with the list of mandatory criteria. If one of the original ideas does not meet any one of the mandatory criteria, eliminate it.

Even after the group has eliminated the choices that do not meet the mandatory criteria, the original list of choices may still need to be narrowed further. This may involve simply asking each participant to rate the remaining items, for example, giving each 1–3 points. Tallying the results should lead to a clear ranking of the top few items.

Decision Matrices   The idea ranking process based on a set of evaluation criteria, described above, is a simple process that may be used to help a group reach consensus on selecting a single idea from many. However, if the issue is complex, with many variables or criteria to be considered, a more detailed process may be needed. In this situation, consider using a *Prioritization Worksheet* or *Decision Matrix* (see, e.g., Brassard, 1989). After eliminating those ideas that do not meet the mandatory criteria, list the remaining options across the top of the worksheet, and the evaluation criteria down the left side (or vice versa). It may be useful to weight the criteria for importance (e.g., giving each criterion 1–10 weighting points). Rate each idea based on each of the criteria (e.g., again using a 1–10 point scale or by ranking the

---

EVALUATION CRITERIA: IDEA RANKING

1. Complete brainstorming or another process for developing a list of ideas related to a topic or problem.
2. Brainstorm once more to develop possible evaluation criteria.
3. Review the list of criteria and identify those that are perceived by the group as mandatory.
4. Review the list of ideas, eliminating any items that do not meet the mandatory criteria.
5. Evaluate the remaining ideas, giving each option, for example, 1–3 points.
6. Tally the scores given to each idea by the group members.
7. Select the item with the highest number of points.

Sample idea ranking results

Ideas	Member scores	Total rank	Top rank results
Idea #1	1,1,1,2	5	
Idea #2	3,1,1,1	6	
Idea #3	3,2,3,3	11	2
Idea #4	3,3,2,2	10	3
Idea #5	2,2,1,1	6	
Idea #6	1,1,1,1	4	
Idea #7	Did not meet mandatory criteria		
Idea #8	Did not meet mandatory criteria		
—			
—			
—			
Idea #20	3,3,3,3	12	1

items within each criterion). Multiply that by the weighting factor given to the criterion. Add together the resulting ratings across criteria for each idea. The idea receiving the highest overall score should be the best idea, according to the criteria considered.

The Decision Matrix described here is referred to as an "L-shaped Matrix." There are several other versions of Decision Matrices commonly used in quality improvement processes (e.g., T-Shaped, Y-Shaped, and X-Shaped Matrices, and those that combine Tree Diagrams with a Matrix). However, these are beyond the scope of this text. The reader is referred to Brassard (1989) for a more complete description of other versions of this tool.

Multivoting   Multivoting (see, e.g., Scholtes, 1988) provides another method for reducing the difficulty of narrowing a large list of ideas to a few, by using a series of votes. After brainstorming a list of possible ideas, review the list to combine items the group agrees are similar. If necessary, renumber the list. Ask individual participants to select a few of the ideas they would like to discuss further, listing the item numbers on a piece of paper. During this step, allow participants to choose a number of ideas that is equal to approximately one third of the total number of items on the list. Compile the votes (anonymously, by collecting written ballots, or by asking participants to call out the numbers of the selected items). Eliminate items receiving only a few votes. Repeat the process two to four times until only a few items remain. Discuss these as a group to identify the top choice, or take one last vote.

Nominal Group Technique   The Nominal Group Technique (see, e.g., GOAL/QPC, 1988; Scholtes, 1988) offers a method for obtaining input from a group of people in a structured format. Because it limits discussion, this process prevents any individual from dominating, encourages quieter members to participate, and results in a prioritized list of recommendations. However, because it constrains discussion of ideas and viewpoints, it does not benefit from the "cross-fertilization" effect of other brainstorming methods. Thus, Nominal Group Technique may be viewed by participants as being too mechanical. Nominal Group Technique is most effective when group members do not know each other well, when one or a few members tend to dominate discussion, or when a team is stuck on highly controversial issues. Nominal Group Technique provides a more structured approach to the Idea Ranking method described above, under "Evaluation Criteria."

Delphi Decision-Making   The Delphi Technique is another structured approach for achieving consensus in a decision-making process. It relies on using a panel, usually composed of informed experts, each with an interest in the problem at hand. Because it does not include discussion, the method may be used with panelists located geographically far apart. Ask panel members to make their best guess about an issue or solution, such as, "What are the important skills for an employment training specialist?" Compile results and report back to the panel. If responses are numerical (e.g., panelists rated listed items), calculate a group average and frequency distribution, reporting the results back to the panel. Repeat the process several times. Usually, panelists' opinions will converge over time, with the result being more accurate than many of the initial individual opinions.

Tools for Proposing Relationships

Affinity Diagram   The Affinity Diagram (see, e.g., Brassard, 1989) is a creative tool that gathers large numbers of ideas (or opinions, issues, and so forth) and orga-

NOMINAL GROUP TECHNIQUE

1. *Introduce and clarify the topic.* Ask an open-ended question, such as, "How can we provide better support for staff working in dispersed locations?" or "What are the barriers or problems in the Motel Crew Department?".
    *   Write the question on newsprint flipchart or distribute copies to each group.
    *   Answer questions to help participants understand the question, but do not allow this to develop into a discussion of the topic.
2. *Brainstorm individually.* Allow several minutes of quiet for group members to brainstorm individually and write down ideas. Do not allow whispering, talking, or joking.
3. *Collect ideas.* Take ideas one by one going around the group and record the ideas on a flipchart.
    *   Do not allow criticism, but members may ask for clarification of an item after the list has been recorded.
    *   Reword an item only if the person who originally proposed it agrees.
4. *Reduce the number of items to 50 or fewer.* This may be accomplished through combining items with others (if the originators agree) to condense the list, through Multivoting, and/or through allowing participants to remove any less serious items they added to the list.
5. *Rate the items individually.* During this step, ask participants to rate the importance of individual items on the list. Two options for a process of individual rating might be:
    a. *For longer lists:* Ask participants to rate, for example, only "one half plus one" (e.g., 15 items of a list of 28), or a number that reflects an even smaller percentage if the original list is very long (e.g., 10 items from a list of 50). Give each participant a number of 3" × 5" cards equal to the number of items they are to rate. Ask members to select the items they wish to rate from the list, writing one item per card.
    b. *For shorter lists:* Assign a letter designation to each item on the list (e.g., a list of six items would be lettered A–F). Ask members to list all of the letters on a piece of paper. Continue by asking participants to rate individual items.
6. *Compile individual scores.* For each item, record votes on the original list of items, and then total the scores. The item that receives the highest point total is the group's selection.

Although a deviation from the strict Nominal Group Technique, it may be helpful to review the results and discuss any serious objections. If all members agree on the importance of the top-rated item, proceed on it. If members do not agree, the Nominal Group Technique at least should have helped to narrow the list to two or three items.

nizes them into groupings based on the natural relationships between them (see Figure 10.1). Based on the KJ Method of anthropologist Jiro Kawakita (Brassard, 1989), and similar to the Crawford Slip Method (see, e.g., Fiero, 1992), the Affinity Diagram offers a tool for organizing "language data" in a relatively short length of time (e.g., Brassard [1989] reports producing and organizing more than 100 ideas in 30–45 minutes).

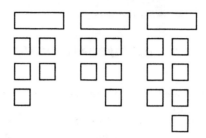

Figure 10.1. Affinity Diagram.

Use an Affinity Diagram when the ideas or thoughts are chaotic, when the overall issue seems too large or complex to grasp, or when the group needs to find new patterns of information or new solutions. Do not try to use this method, however, when the problem being addressed is relatively simple and its solution could be implemented quickly. Specific instructions for developing an Affinity Diagram are included in Appendix A, at the end of this chapter.

Cause and Effect Diagram   Also known as a Fishbone Diagram or Ishikawa Diagram (after its inventor, Kaoru Ishikawa, a pioneer of the quality control movement in Japan), the Cause and Effect Diagram provides a visual format for organizing, for example, possible causes of a problem or factors important to a successful project (see, e.g., Dew, 1991; GOAL/QPC, 1988; QIP, Inc., 1986; Scholtes, 1988; Walton, 1986). The diagram's format allows participants to see easily the relationship between factors or causes and the ultimate effect (see Figure 10.2). The Cause and Effect Diagram is an effective tool for analyzing processes or situations, as well as for planning, and is highly useful for dissecting complex problems. It may be developed by an individual or a group, using, for example, basic rules of brainstorming or the Crawford Slip Method.

Draw a Cause and Effect Diagram by placing the project, problem, or desired effect to the right of the diagram, and the inputs or possible causes for that effect on the left. Either brainstorm while adding items directly onto the appropriate spot on the diagram, or brainstorm a list and then position the resulting items later. For each "bone" that is added to the diagram, ask *why* to identify deeper causes. It is recommended that you ask *why* five times for each bone before moving on to the next. The purpose of repeating *why* is ultimately to seek the root cause of the defined problem.

The process of developing the Cause and Effect Diagram leads to detailed discussions of how the process or project under study works, and thus is most effective

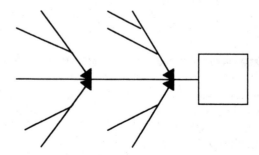

Figure 10.2. Cause and Effect Diagram.

DEVELOPING A CAUSE AND EFFECT DIAGRAM

1. Brainstorm a list of possible factors related to the issue or project, using any appropriate brainstorming technique.
2. Condense and categorize items on the list.
3. Enter the project or issue to be solved in a box at the right side of a piece of paper; draw a long horizontal line—a backbone—across the paper ending at the box.
4. Place category headings at the ends of large arrows pointing into the backbone. Headings might be, for example, equipment, personnel, methods, materials, measurement system, and environment.
5. Position the items from the brainstormed list onto smaller arrows that are drawn into each of those larger "bones." Add items representing subcategories or specific items, until the list of items is exhausted. (Alternatively, the group may brainstorm directly onto the diagram, rather than onto a separate sheet.)
6. For each "bone" of the diagram, ask "why," to identify its cause(s), until the "why's" no longer provide useful items.

---

after the process or problem has been well-defined. Therefore, it is especially useful to include participants in the group who work directly in the process under study. The diagram may be posted in a public area for a period of time before its results are used, and anyone should be encouraged to add other factors that come to mind. If the diagram is being constructed around a system, rather than a process, it is likely to become very complex, filling an entire wall. So, try to identify a simpler process for study (at least in initial diagrams), and allow plenty of time for pursuing each cause. It may be useful to do a less detailed diagram early in a project, and a more detailed one, reflecting only one part of the original diagram, once information has been collected to narrow the search for causes (see Figure 10.3).

The Cause and Effect Diagram identifies only *possible* causes or factors; it does not necessarily define actual causes. Therefore, it is useful to help define data collection categories. The diagram, however, most likely includes more items than would be efficient for collecting data on. To move to data collection, begin with larger groupings (the "major bones"), or ask group members temporarily to eliminate the most unlikely causes based on their own knowledge and experience. If necessary, use any of the methods described above for narrowing a brainstormed list.

Tree Diagram   Also referred to as *Performance Templates* or *Decision Trees*, the Tree Diagram was presented in detail in Chapter 8. (For additional information on Tree Diagrams, see, e.g., Brassard, 1989.)

Relationship Diagram   Also referred to as an *Interrelationship Digraph* (see, e.g., Brassard, 1989), the Relationship Diagram is used to support management and planning activities and explores the relationships between interrelated factors in complex problems or projects. Use a Relationship Diagram when the problem is complex and the interrelationships between ideas or factors are difficult to understand, and when the correct sequencing of activities is crucial. This diagram maps out the logical or sequential relationships among items and, unlike the Cause and Effect Diagram, is able to demonstrate multi-directional links. In addition, a Relationship Diagram in-

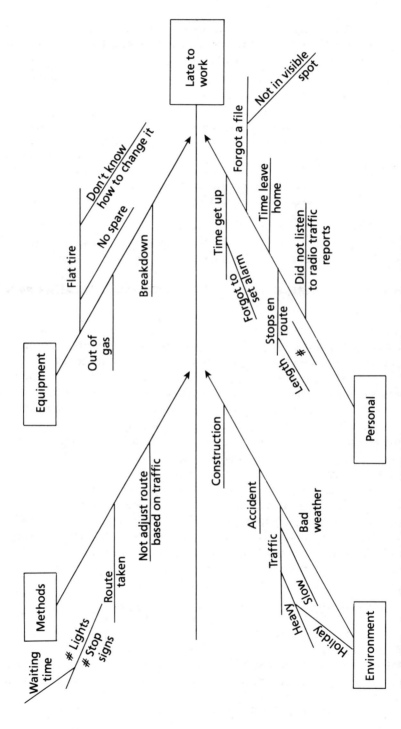

Figure 10.3. Sample completed Cause and Effect Diagram for the problem: "Late to Work."

dicates through its structure those factors or issues that are related to the greatest number of others, offering a basis for prioritizing activity. The Relationship Diagram is a good next step to complete after developing an Affinity Diagram or Cause and Effect Diagram, to help group members to look at further interrelationships among items. The specific steps required for developing a Relationship Diagram are provided in Appendix B, at the end of this chapter (also, see Figure 10.4).

TOOLS FOR ANALYZING PROCESSES

Troubleshooting

Troubleshooting to analyze processes to improve outcomes was presented in detail in Chapter 5, in the context of changeover to supported employment. However, troubleshooting has wide applicability in quality improvement. Troubleshooting is a method of diagnosis that provides a systematic order in which to ask questions about improving organizational or individual performance.

Flowcharts

Flowcharts offer schematic diagrams of a process or project and may be used to describe an existing situation or to plan a new, desired sequence. Four types of flowcharts are described here: Top-Down Flowcharts, Detailed Flowcharts, Workflow Diagrams, and Deployment Charts (see, e.g., GOAL/QPC, 1988; Juran, 1989; QIP, Inc., 1986; Scholtes, 1988; Walton, 1986).

Top-Down Flowchart   A Top-Down Flowchart provides a picture of the major steps of a process or project (see Figure 10.5). Use this type of flowchart to describe an existing process or to plan how a new process or project will operate. Construct a Top-Down Flowchart by listing the major step for groups of tasks across the top, with substeps below each. Depending on how the chart will be used, it may help to leave out extraneous detail, very small steps, or steps that do not add value to the process. However, if the project purpose is to decrease the complexity of a process, be sure to include every step required to reach the outcome.

Detailed Flowchart   A Detailed Flowchart defines most or all of the steps in a process, including inefficiencies and delays. The flowchart uses standardized symbols for different activities, such as a diamond for decision points, a rectangle for an action, and a circle for connecting points to other pages (see Figure 10.6). Use a Detailed Flowchart when a Top-Down Flowchart cannot represent all of the detail presented by the team, or when the process is complex with many branches or "if-then"

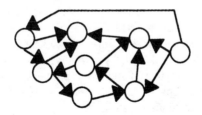

Figure 10.4.   Relationship Diagram.

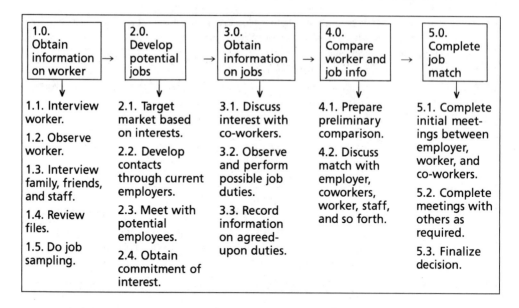

To construct a top-down flowchart
1.   List no more than 5–7 major steps or phases across the top of the page.
2.   Below each, list the significant substeps (again, no more than 5–7 under each major step.)
3.   Unless you are studying the complexity in a process, include only "useful" steps that move the process or project toward completion; do not list steps such as inspections, rework, and so forth.

Figure 10.5.   Top-Down Flowchart for a job matching process.

situations involved (see Figure 10.7). Constructing a detailed flowchart can be very useful in helping a team to reach agreement on the specific pieces and sequence of a process under study.

Workflow Diagram   A Workflow Diagram of the movement of people, materials, equipment, or information in a process is much like a picture obtained through time-lapse photography. Drawn on a floor plan of the area, the Workflow Diagram sketches the movements performed to complete the process. With such a diagram, employees can easily see any unnecessary or duplicated movements built into the process (see Figure 10.8). Particularly useful in analyzing inefficiencies at job sites, Workflow Diagrams can also be used in a rehabilitation organization, for example, by secretaries and bookkeepers to trace the flow of financial account information; by janitorial workers to chart the flow of work, equipment, and supplies; or by job coaches trying to develop a more efficient method for setting up a salad bar. Other versions of Workflow Diagrams, using symbols to depict various operations, are commonly used in manufacturing settings.

Deployment Chart   Deployment Charts combine information on the flow of the major steps of the process and the person who is responsible for performing each. Including only the *major* steps, as in the top level of the Top-Down Flowcharts, Deployment Charts help teams to identify who is responsible for what, and how they fit into the sequence of tasks (see Figure 10.9).

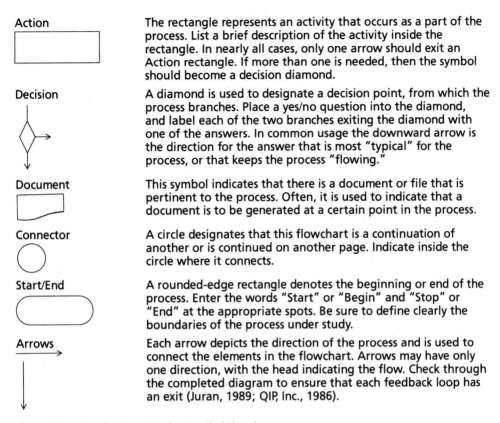

Action	The rectangle represents an activity that occurs as a part of the process. List a brief description of the activity inside the rectangle. In nearly all cases, only one arrow should exit an Action rectangle. If more than one is needed, then the symbol should become a decision diamond.
Decision	A diamond is used to designate a decision point, from which the process branches. Place a yes/no question into the diamond, and label each of the two branches exiting the diamond with one of the answers. In common usage the downward arrow is the direction for the answer that is most "typical" for the process, or that keeps the process "flowing."
Document	This symbol indicates that there is a document or file that is pertinent to the process. Often, it is used to indicate that a document is to be generated at a certain point in the process.
Connector	A circle designates that this flowchart is a continuation of another or is continued on another page. Indicate inside the circle where it connects.
Start/End	A rounded-edge rectangle denotes the beginning or end of the process. Enter the words "Start" or "Begin" and "Stop" or "End" at the appropriate spots. Be sure to define clearly the boundaries of the process under study.
Arrows	Each arrow depicts the direction of the process and is used to connect the elements in the flowchart. Arrows may have only one direction, with the head indicating the flow. Check through the completed diagram to ensure that each feedback loop has an exit (Juran, 1989; QIP, Inc., 1986).

Figure 10.6.   Standard symbols for Detailed Flowcharts.

TOOLS FOR DATA COLLECTION, DISPLAY, AND ANALYSIS

Many of the common tools used in Continuous Quality Improvement for data collection, display, and analysis are well-known in rehabilitation and other human services. Check Sheets or Tally Sheets, Time Plots, Dot Plots, and so forth are familiar to personnel who are accustomed to graphing data to make the patterns in them more obvious. Therefore, this section of the chapter only briefly reviews some of the familiar tools in this area, in order to provide greater detail on others—such as Pareto Analysis—that have not been commonly used in human services. Chapter 9 addressed some basic concepts related to data.

Tools for Data Collection

Check Sheets, or Tally Sheets, offer a tool for answering the question, "How often is X happening?" (See, e.g., QIP, Inc., 1986; Scholtes, 1988.) For a useful Check Sheet see Figure 10.10.

1. Develop an operational definition of the event or behavior being recorded, so that everyone collecting data is recording the same thing.
2. Design a clear, well-labeled form, with enough space for entering the data.

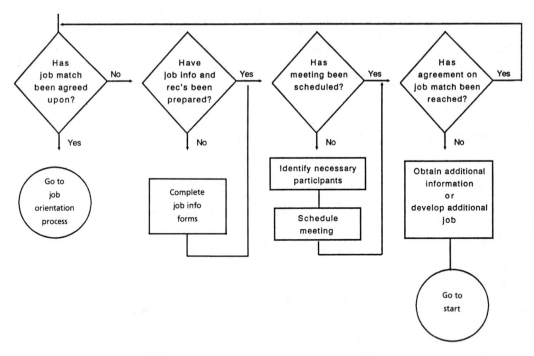

Figure 10.7. Detailed Flowchart for one part of a job matching process. (Rec's = recommendations.)

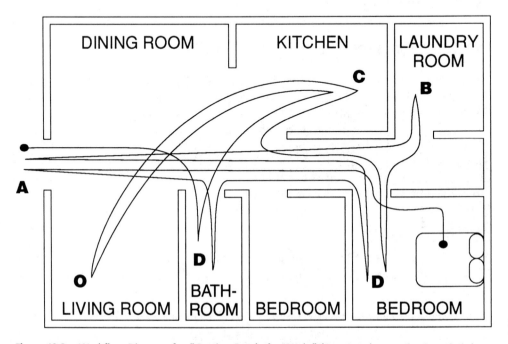

Figure 10.8. Workflow Diagram for "Getting Ready for Work." (A = Let dog out/in, B = Get clean clothes, C = Fix breakfast or lunch, D = Get ready, O = Other.)

Duty	Fred	Alice	Jean
Obtain worker information	X		
Develop potential jobs		X	O
Obtain job information		X	O
Compare worker and job information	X	O	O
Complete job match	X	X	X

Figure 10.9. Deployment Chart for job matching. (X = primary responsibility; O = advisor or assistant.)

Check Sheets also may be designed as a drawing of, for example, an object or room, when the location of the event being recorded is important. For example, the location of errors with pots and pans observed during each shift could be recorded on line drawings of the basic pan shapes; or the location of damage on shipping cartons could be marked onto a drawing of a box. Consider the factors that were determined possibly to be related to the effect being studied (e.g., from the Cause and Effect Diagram) in developing a Check Sheet that best captures data to support later decisions.

Tools for Data Display and Analysis

Time Plots   The most familiar of data display tools, referred to as *Time Plots* or *Run Charts*, present data trends as they appear over time (see, e.g., QIP, Inc. 1988; Scholtes, 1988; Walton, 1986). Thus, Time Plots simply present data plotted in the order in which they were collected (see Figure 10.11). Detecting changes that occur over time is a powerful method for analyzing patterns and making quality improvements in processes or outcomes.

Dot Plot   A Dot Plot displays each data point collected, presenting which values occur and how often (see, e.g., Scholtes, 1988). A method for visually displaying the range and frequency of measurements found along a single variable or dimension (e.g., length of time or wages), Dot Plots provide perhaps the simplest data

Complaint	Job Site #1	Job Site #2	Job Site #3	Total
Employee late to job	////		/	5
Error in job tasks	//	////	///	9
Slow	/	/	//	4
Job coach is in the way		////	/	5
Other		// Stopped working	/ Loud	3
Total	7	11	8	26

Figure 10.10.   Check Sheet for employer complaints in March.

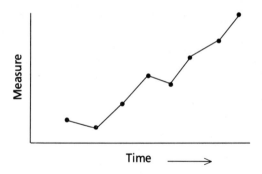

Figure 10.11. Time Plot.

display tool and can be completed and analyzed by staff with little training in statistical methods (see Figure 10.12). Dot Plots are quick to put together and indicate at a glance the range of measurements found, the average and most frequent values, as well as the pattern of distribution of scores.

Stem and Leaf Diagrams Similar to Dot Plots, Stem and Leaf Diagrams also may be used to present single variable data, but in a slightly different format—with the line and the measurement units presented vertically, on the left side of the diagram, and the individual data points entered in corresponding rows (see, e.g., Scholtes, 1988; Figure 10.13). In addition, rather than being represented by dots, each data point may be presented by its actual value, as shown in the example. In this example, the ages of 25 participants in a supported employment program range from 18 to 65. The advantage of Stem and Leaf Diagrams is that the actual value of each data point is readily available, unlike with dot plots.

Scatter Diagram Unlike Dot Plots and Stem and Leaf Diagrams, which present a single variable, Scatter Diagrams display the relationships between two variables (see, e.g., GOAL/QPC, 1988; Scholtes, 1988; Walton, 1986). Draw a Scatter Diagram by placing each variable along one axis and entering data points where the values of each pair intersect (see Figure 10.14). The pattern of the data points reveals whether there is a relationship between the variables. If data points are spread randomly around the diagram, the two variables are probably unrelated. If data points

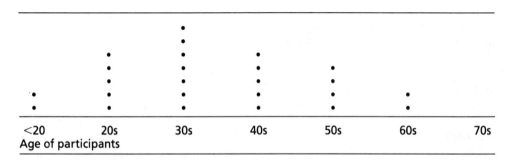

Constructing a Dot Plot:
1. Draw a horizontal line, marking it in units corresponding with data collection measures.
2. Place a dot above the value for each time it appears in the data set. (Data may be collected directly onto the Dot Plot.)

Figure 10.12. Dot Plot of age of supported employees.

Age of participants

```
6 | 1 5
5 | 3 3 5 7
4 | 1 2 2 5 6
3 | 2 2 2 3 4 4 5
2 | 1 1 2 3 6
1 | 8 9
```

Figure 10.13. Stem and Leaf Diagram depicting the actual age of each participant in one supported employment program. Ages range from 18 to 65.

clump together, for example, with the larger values of one variable associated with the larger values of the other, the variables are said to be "positively correlated"; that is, as one variable increases, so will the other. If larger values of one variable associated with smaller values of the other, they are said to be "negatively correlated"; that is, as one variable increases, the other decreases. In Figure 10.14 the age of participants is positively correlated with the number of months of employment on the current job.

Pareto Analysis   Pareto Analysis (see, e.g., GOAL/QPC, 1988; Relyea, 1989; Scholtes, 1988; Walton, 1986) is a tremendously useful and yet simple tool to use. It has applications both in selecting the most significant problem and in identifying solutions to problems. Used to separate the "vital few and the useful many" (Juran, 1989), this tool is based on an application of the Pareto Principle. Vilfredo Pareto, an Italian engineer and economist who lived at the turn of the 20th century proposed that, in complex situations, approximately 80% of the effects can be attributed to 20% of the factors involved. Also known as the "80/20 Rule," the principle was first applied to management by Dr. Joseph Juran, who urged managers to concentrate their efforts and attention on the factors in any situation that will have the greatest impact on the desired effect—the vital few—ignoring those having minor effects—the useful (but not vital) many.

Pareto Analysis provides a powerful tool and all staff members should know how to use it. Pareto Charts may be used to analyze reasons for job loss, causes of staff dissatisfaction and turnover, types of errors made, reasons for rejects in a manufacturing process, or hundreds of other issues related to supported employment (see Figure 10.15). Useful as a tool to build consensus on which issue to attack first, Pareto Analysis belongs in the tool box of any organization trying to implement principles of quality improvement.

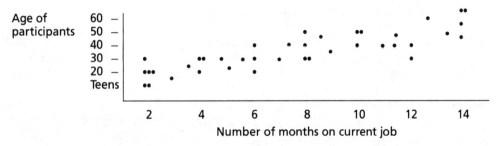

Figure 10.14. Scatter Diagram of the relationship between the age of participants and the number of months on their current jobs.

CONSTRUCTING A PARETO ANALYSIS CHART

1. Define data collection categories of roughly equivalent size. A Cause and Effect (Fishbone) Diagram may be used for identifying potential causes or factors.
2. Construct a Check Sheet for recording raw data on the frequency at which each data category is observed.
3. Collect data.
4. Draw a Bar Graph, with absolute or relative frequency on the left or vertical axis, and data categories on the horizontal axis.
   a. Use a scale for the vertical axis that will accommodate the data category with the greatest number or highest relative frequency; then divide the axis into equal intervals.
   b. Order data categories so that the one with the highest frequency appears first, the second highest second, and so forth, with the one with the lowest frequency last.
   c. Enter bars onto the graph to correspond with each data category, starting on the left with the highest bar. Draw other bars in order of descending size.
   d. Limit the number of bars on the chart to 10 or fewer. If more data categories were used, combine the trivial ones in an "Other" category as the last bar.
5. (Optional) Determine the cumulative percentages across categories, beginning with the highest frequency item. Enter a cumulative percentage axis at the right of the chart, and draw a line across the top of the chart indicating the cumulative percentage across items.
6. After completing one Pareto Chart, it is useful to perform a second analysis on the data category with the highest frequency. Follow the same procedure, identifying potential causes for that issue, collecting data on a Check Sheet, ordering the data by frequency, and constructing the chart.

Other Data Display Methods   Any basic text on statistics includes a variety of other means for displaying data (see Figure 10.16), and the reader is encouraged to refer to such texts if these additional methods are not familiar. *The Memory Jogger + *™ (GOAL/QPC, 1988) offers an excellent, pocket-size refresher (see also, e.g., QIP, Inc., 1986). *Histograms*, for example, display the frequency of measurement data along some continuous dimension, such as IQ scores, or thickness in inches. Thus, Histograms display the *frequency distribution* of the data along a single dimension. The shape of the Histogram offers information about the nature of the population from which the measures were taken: such as its variability or skewness. Histograms are a good tool for identifying whether a process is operating within specifications (such as average response time to emergency calls).

Bar Graphs look very much like Pareto Charts and Histograms. Bar Graphs may be presented horizontally or vertically, stacked (in which subcategories are stacked on top of each other), or as compound Bar Graphs, in which subcategories are placed next to each other.

Pie Charts are commonly used in popular publications, such as *USA Today*, because they are easy to interpret. In a Pie Chart, a circle is subdivided into sections based on the relative frequency of the categories. When using a Pie Chart, be sure to show each "slice" with its percentage and its label.

SAMPLE PROBLEM-SOLVING
SEQUENCE USING PARETO ANALYSIS

Quickie Employment Services is a supported employment program with 15 staff members providing support to 65 persons with disabilities in a wide variety of jobs, including bottle and can recycling crews at grocery stores, a small enclave doing janitorial work at a church, and individual jobs in businesses such as restaurants, nurseries, and a blue jeans factory.

Despite their efforts to find jobs that pay above minimum wage in order for the persons they support to realize reasonable incomes, quite a few of the employees have productivity-based jobs requiring special subminimum wage certificates. However, recently, managers have become concerned over their ability to keep up with the many different time studies that must be completed to meet Department of Labor regulations. They have begun trying to move people to new non-productivity-based jobs, but that process is slow.

Because of the significance of the issue, both in terms of compliance with the law and fairness to employees with disabilities, managers decided to implement a quality improvement project to improve their timely performance of time studies.

Initially, managers believed that the reason that time studies were not completed was that not all staff knew how to complete them. However, before they launched a staff training program, one manager, Pat, suggested that there might be other causes for the problem and that they should do a Pareto Analysis to identify the biggest issue. Thus, Pat defined a survey and distributed it to all staff who had responsibility for performing time studies to discover why staff thought they were not performing time studies as scheduled. She asked staff to record for each job site they supported why they had difficulty meeting the schedule for performing time studies.

When the surveys were completed, Pat compiled the results using a Tally Sheet:

Need training   / /

Too many separate tasks to do time studies on   / / / / / / / / / / / / /

No forms available   /

Need an extra staff at the site to perform   /

The procedure itself is complex and hard to do   /

Co-workers or employee with disabilities resents time studies   / /

Did not know the schedule for doing them   / / / / /

(continued)

SAMPLE PROBLEM-SOLVING
SEQUENCE USING PARETO ANALYSIS (*continued*)

From these data, she constructed a Pareto Chart:

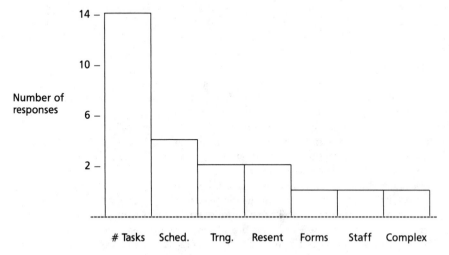

Pat presented the Pareto Chart at the next manager's meeting. Based on staff opinions, the biggest issue was *not* staff training, as had been guessed. The results indicated that the organization should look at how jobs were defined for time studies. If more tasks could be grouped together, fewer time studies would be required, and staff would be better able to meet the schedule.

Tools for Data Analysis

Stratification   Stratification refers to "splitting" or "cutting" data in different ways in order to reveal hidden patterns (see, e.g., GOAL/QPC, 1988; Scholtes, 1988). Stratification is the result of asking questions of data, and of looking for underlying patterns that may provide new insights into the data. Looking at data from different

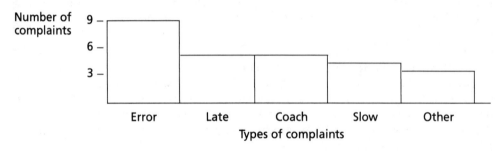

Figure 10.15.   Pareto Chart: Employer complaints in March (referring to Figure 10.10).

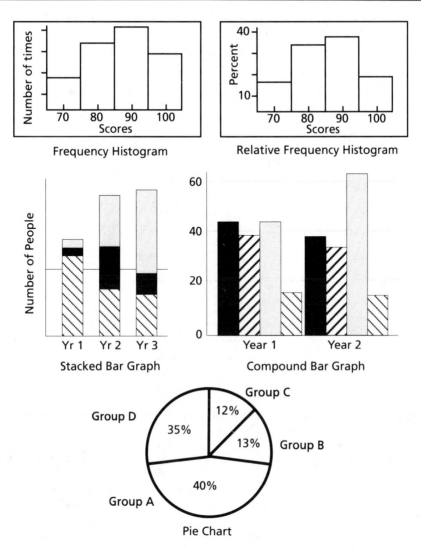

Figure 10.16. Other data display methods.

perspectives helps to localize a problem, to identify causes, and, thereby, to select improvement strategies. In stratifying data, consider the different factors that might influence the data. For example, could time of day affect performance? Does a substitute job coach change performance? Are data different between one job site and another? According to Scholtes (1988), it is useful to stratify both prior to data collection (to identify factors that are important to include on data collection forms), and afterward (to determine which factors actually affected the results). For example, in Figure 10.17, stratifying the employer complaint data from the Check Sheet presented in Figure 10.10, reveals that most of the problems, across all three job sites, occur during a specific time of day. This pattern was not evident from the original data; indeed, combining data across times of day masked this effect. However, with the information available from the stratified data, the job coach can better prioritize allocation of support time at the sites.

Stratification requires good detective work and an open mind willing to look at

Complaint	8 A.M.–11 A.M.	11 A.M.–2 P.M.	2 P.M.–5 P.M.	Total
Employee late to job (A.M., breaks, or lunch)		////	/	5
Error in job tasks	/	///////	/	9
Slow		///	/	4
Job coach is in the way		/////		5
Other		///		3
Total	1	22	3	26

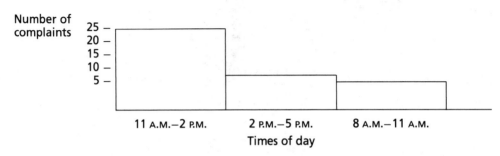

Figure 10.17. Employer complaints in March, stratified by time of day, with corresponding Pareto Analysis.

possible factors that might have an influence on the data. Day of the week, location, presence or absence of specific people in the environment, color of materials, and so forth, are all potential factors influencing the performance of a supported employee. Use stratification to help identify which factors are influencing performance.

Is/Is-Not Matrix Scholtes (1988) offers the Is/Is-Not Matrix as a tool to help with stratifying data. Based on the work of Kepner and Tregoe (1965, 1981), the Is/Is-Not Matrix helps to sort observations into patterns to support considering possible causes (see Figure 10.18).

Statistical Process Control Charts Control Charts (see, e.g., GOAL/QPC, 1988; Ishikawa, 1983; Mainstone & Levi, 1987; Nolan & Provost, 1990; QIP, Inc., 1986; Scholtes, 1988; Shainin, 1990; Walton, 1986) are statistical tools for monitoring and analyzing the performance of a process. Originally developed and applied to manufacturing processes (Deming, 1938, 1975, 1986; Shewhart, 1931, 1939), Control Charts are beginning to be applied in public sector and human service settings, as well (e.g., Demos & Demos, 1989; Mosgaller, 1990).

Control Charts depict the variation in a process, and the patterns of the data reveal whether special causes, or only common causes, of variation are operating (see Chapter 9). Although the Control Chart is somewhat similar to a Run Chart or Time Plot in appearance, it is both developed and interpreted in a totally different way: Data are entered into statistical formulas and plotted with "upper and lower control limits" to denote zones. It is the pattern of data points related to the zones that reveals whether the process is "in control" (i.e., operating consistently, although

Instructions: Identify the problem or situation you want to analyze. Use this matrix to organize your knowledge and information. Your answers should help you pinpoint the occurrence of the problem, and guide data collection so you can verify your conclusions/suspicions.

	Is Where, when, to what extent or regarding whom does this situation occur?	**Is Not** Where, etc., does this situation NOT occur, though it reasonably might have?	**Therefore** What might explain the pattern of occurrence and non-occurrence?
Where The physical or geographical location of the event or situation. Where it occurs or where it is noticed.			
When The hour, time of day, day of week, month, time of year of the event or situation. Its relationship (before, during, after) to other events.			
What kind or how much The type or category of event or situation. The extent, degree, dimensions, or duration of the occurrence.			
Who (Do not use these questions to blame.) What relationship do various individuals or groups have to the situation or event? To whom, by whom, near whom, etc., does this occur?			

Figure 10.18. The Is/Is-Not Matrix. (From Scholtes, P.R. [1988]. *The team handbook: How to use teams to improve quality.* Madison: Joiner Associates, Inc., ch. 2, p. 31; reprinted with permission.)

that does not necessarily mean it is operating well), or special causes of variation are affecting the process (see Figure 10.19).

There are several different types of Control Charts, and the specific methods for developing and interpreting them are well beyond the scope of this text. However, personnel in rehabilitation and other human services who have an interest in statistics will find valuable uses for Control Charts. The charts require a substantial amount of data to be reliable (e.g., at least 20–25 groups of samples) and can offer ways, for example, for state agencies such as vocational rehabilitation agencies to analyze variation in the cost of services across time, or in the outcomes that individual service providers are able to achieve. The reader is referred to one of the excellent

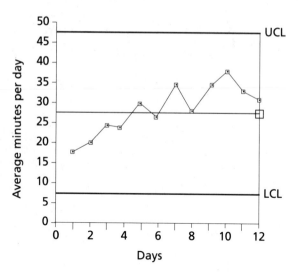

Figure 10.19. A Statistical Process Control Chart.

materials listed above for the statistical process for developing Control Charts, as well as for guides for interpreting them.

THE KEY: TURN DATA INTO INFORMATION THAT IS VISUAL AND FUN

Quality improvement methods rely on data to support decisions at every level of the organization. Unfortunately, organizations and individual staff members often make decisions in the absence of reliable and valid data, and because of this they spend too much time on trivial problems, select solutions that appear obvious but may have little to do with the actual cause of a problem, or otherwise waste valuable time and resources. In employment and other human services, board and staff members alike must learn to use data and statistical methods as tools to improve their decision-making and to use their time more effectively. In other words, they need to become skilled in methods for turning data into *information* that is useful to—and used for—decision-making.

The methods of Continuous Quality Improvement emphasize tools that make data very visual and easier to interpret and use. Charts, graphs, and tables are seen everywhere in a company that has embraced Total Quality Management. If available, teach staff members to use computers for maintaining, analyzing, and graphing data. Ask for data only when it will be used, and provide feedback to staff members on the result. But most of all, encourage staff members to start playing with data—have fun with it, ask questions of it, and get people accustomed to working with it. Begin regularly to ask of all staff, "Is that your opinion, or do you have data to support it?"

REFERENCES

Brassard, M. (1989). *The memory jogger* + ™. Metheun, MA: GOAL/QPC.
Deming, W.E. (1938). *Statistical adjustment of data.* New York: Dover Publications, Inc.

Deming, W.E. (1975). On some statistical aids toward economic production. *Interfaces, 5(4)*, 1–15.

Deming, W.E. (1986). *Out of the crisis*. Cambridge: Massachusetts Institute of Technology, Center for Advanced Engineering Study.

Demos, M.P., & Demos, N.P. (1989). Statistical quality control's role in health care management. *Quality Progress, 22(8)*, 85–89.

Dew, J.R. (1991). In search of the root cause. *Quality Progress, 24(3)*, 97–102.

Feigenbaum, A.V. (1983). *Total quality control*. New York: McGraw-Hill.

Fiero, J. (1992). The Crawford Slip Method. *Quality Progress, 25(5)*, 40–41.

GOAL/QPC. (1988). *The memory jogger + ™: A pocket guide of tools for continuous improvement*. Methuen, MA: Author.

Ishikawa, K. (1983). *Guide to quality control*. Tokyo: Asian Productivity Organization.

Juran, J.M. (1989). *Juran on leadership for quality*. New York: The Free Press.

Kepner, C.H., & Tregoe, B.B. (1965). *The rational manager*. New York: McGraw-Hill.

Kepner, C.H., & Tregoe, B.B. (1981). *The new rational manager*. Princeton: Princeton Research Press.

Mainstone, L.E., & Levi, A.S. (1987). Fundamentals of statistical process control. *Journal of Organizational Behavior Management, 9(1)*, 5–21.

Mizuno, S. (Ed.). (1988). *Management for quality improvement: The 7 new QC tools*. Milwaukee: Quality Press.

Mosgaller, T. (1990, November). *Total quality management*. Presentation at the Region X Rehabilitation Conference, Salishan Lodge, Gleneden, Oregon.

Newstrom, J.W., & Scannell, E.E. (1980). *Games trainers play: Experiential learning exercises*. New York: McGraw-Hill.

Nolan, T.W., & Provost, L.P. (1990). Understanding variation. *Quality Progress, 23(5)*, 70–78.

QIP, Inc. (1986). *The transformation of American industry*. Miamisburg, OH: Productivity-Quality Systems.

Relyea, D.B. (1989). The simple power of Pareto. *Quality Progress, 22(5)*, 38–39.

Scholtes, P.R. (1988). *The team handbook: How to use teams to improve quality*. Madison: Joiner Associates, Inc.

Shainin, P.D. (1990). The tools of quality. Part III: Control charts. *Quality Progress, 23(8)*, 79–82.

Shewhart, W.A. (1931). *The economic control of manufactured product*. New York: Van Nostrand.

Shewhart, W.A. (1939). *Statistical method from the viewpoint of quality control*. Washington, DC: Department of Agriculture.

Walton, M. (1986). *The Deming management method*. New York: Dodd, Mead.

Appendix A

Developing an Affinity Diagram

Step 1. *Select team members.* As with all quality improvement processes, it is important to assemble the appropriate team—probably no more than five or six people—for developing the Affinity Diagram. A team with members who have experience working together and that includes people with the knowledge that will be helpful to the process will have the greatest success. If appropriate, bring special "resource" people into the ongoing quality improvement team to assist in completing the Affinity Diagram if their special expertise would be useful to the final product.

Step 2. *Develop the question.* Agree on a vaguely worded, neutral question as the focus of the diagram. For example, "What are the issues involved in planning a staff orientation program?", or, "What are the issues involved in addressing parental concerns about losing Social Security benefits?" Write the question at the top of a sheet of newsprint on a flipchart or on a chalkboard.

Step 3. *List ideas.* Following the guidelines presented for brainstorming, solicit ideas from the group. Record each idea onto the newsprint or chalkboard, while simultaneously having someone copy it onto a small card (3" × 3" or 3" × 5" Post-it Notes or index cards), with one idea per card. (You might choose to record ideas onto the cards only, rather than double-recording, but you would then lose the advantages of allowing the group to be able to see the entire list.) Keep idea statements brief, but clear (5–7 words), including both a noun and a verb, and write legibly so that the cards can be viewed from a few feet away. For example, ideas generated on the question of staff orientation might include:

- Need information on available budget.
- Need to involve existing staff.
- Need evaluation method for new program.
- Must have management approval.
- How long should the program require.
- Use both individual and small group methods.
- Need feedback on current program.
- Need to include discussion of the mission.

As with the traditional rules for brainstorming, do not allow criticism of ideas, and record them exactly as they are spoken.

Step 4. *Display the cards.* Cover a wall or large table with blank newsprint, shuffle the cards, and spread them randomly over the available space. (Use masking tape to keep index cards in place on a vertical surface.) Select a wall or table that has space for team members to move around it and reach all the cards.

Step 5. *Arrange the cards into related groups.* Use a silent process in which group members (all or a few at a time) are allowed to move the cards as they wish, without talking. Group cards together that seem to be related in some way, but do not force any card into a grouping in which it does not belong. Cards should be moved quickly and

AFFINITY DIAGRAM: IMPROVING THE STAFF RECRUITMENT SYSTEM

Mount Legion is a rehabilitation agency located in a small town in a rural area. The town is located at the point of an imaginary triangle approximately 30 miles from each of two larger cities. However, Mount Legion has always had trouble recruiting new staff employees. Part of the reason is that they found it difficult to compete for candidates with the two cities, in which many state and county jobs are located, as well as with other rehabilitation agencies. Positions that open often remain vacant for a period of time for lack of qualified candidates, or, on occasion, for lack of applicants at all.

A few years ago, Mount Legion began to changeover some of its facility-based work activity center services to community-based jobs with support. Since then employees have complained about stress and burnout in their jobs. Recently, however, Mount Legion's director became interested in using Continuous Quality Improvement to address the organization's performance and decided to try to use its methods to improve their staff recruitment. Therefore, he invited a few people to join him in investigating how they might do this. The team he pulled together included two employment training specialists, a small business owner from his board of directors, a colleague from another rehabilitation agency, a former employee, and a mid-level manager from the human resources department of a large electronics company. The steps they went through in developing an Affinity Diagram are summarized below (see Figure 10.20):

Develop the question:　What are the issues involved in improving our performance in recruiting good employees?

Brainstorm ideas:　Write ideas onto a flipchart or board, but also make a copy on Post-it Notes or cards for later use.

1. Improve salaries.
2. Make the process "friendlier" to candidates.
3. Need to identify self-interests of potential candidates.
4. Make more people aware of job openings.
5. Review/revise expectations for entry qualifications.
6. Collect and evaluate data on recruitment and hiring.
7. Need to clearly portray recent changes in our agency.
8. Reduce the time between applications and responding to candidates.
9. Expand geographic recruitment area.
10. Redefine job to reduce stress factors.
11. Identify reasons candidates should choose our jobs over those with the state, county, or other competitors.
12. Develop organization's public image as an innovator and good place to work.
13. Continuously develop potential candidates.
14. Improve titles of jobs.
15. Stop doing things that give an image that Mount Legion is a charity.
16. Improve benefits.
17. Review/revise specific recruitment process.
18. Recruit through existing staff networks.
19. Improve staff training and support to reduce initial requirements for hiring.
20. Change job parameters to make job more appealing to potential candidates.

(continued)

Organize Ideas and Write Header Cards: Silently move the cards into groups. After everyone is satisfied, develop header cards to define each group.

EXPAND AND IMPROVE RECRUITMENT PROCESS.

Expand geographic recruitment area.

Review/revise specific recruitment process.

Continuously develop potential candidates.

Develop more links between organization's members and community members.

Recruit through existing staff networks.

Make more people aware of job openings.

Get information on jobs to more places where potential candidates could be available.

USE DATA TO IMPROVE PROCESS.

Use data to improve.

Collect and evaluate data on recruitment and hiring.

Get feedback from candidates who drop out of hiring process and from those who continue through it.

IMPROVE CONTACTS WITH CANDIDATES.

Keep in touch with those who have shown interest and/or applied.

Make the process "friendlier" to candidates.

Reduce the time between applications and responding to candidates.

IDENTIFY AND USE "REASONS TO WORK FOR MOUNT LEGION."

Develop profile of organization's most successful employees, current and past.

Identify reasons candidates should choose our jobs over those with the state, county, or other competitors.

Improve recruitment materials.

Offer "a little bit of country" to city residents.

Need to identify self-interests of potential candidates.

IMPROVE THE JOB.

Improve titles of jobs.

Improve salaries.

Improve benefits.

Redefine job to reduce stress factors.

Improve staff training and support to reduce initial requirements for hiring.

Change job parameters to make job more appealing to potential candidates.

IMPROVE PUBLIC IMAGE.

Need to clearly portray recent changes in our agency.

Develop organization's public image as an innovator and good place to work.

Stop doing things that give an image that Mount Legion is a charity.

CHANGE HIRING QUALIFICATIONS.

Review/revise expectations for entry qualifications.

Look for candidates with "capacity and motivation" rather than "knowledge and skills" according to Performance Engineering Matrix.

Figure 10.20. Affinity Diagram: Improving the staff recruitment system.

240

AFFINITY DIAGRAM: IMPROVING THE STAFF RECRUITMENT SYSTEM
(continued)

21. Get information on jobs to more places where potential candidates could be available.
22. Develop profile of organization's most successful employees, current and past.
23. Improve recruitment materials.
24. Look for candidates with "capacity and motivation" rather than "knowledge and skills" according to Performance Engineering Matrix.
25. Use data to improve.
26. Offer "a little bit of country" to city residents.
27. Get feedback from candidates who drop out of hiring process and from those who continue through it.
28. Keep in touch with those who have shown interest and/or applied.
29. Develop more links between organization's members and community members.

without long deliberation. If one team member disagrees with another's placement of a card, that member should simply move it. Allow new ideas for groupings to emerge from the cards, avoiding old logic patterns and known categories, when possible. At the end of this step, cards should be positioned one-next-to-and-under-another in, most likely, four to six groupings.

Step 6. *Write header cards.* Look for the central idea of each grouping, and write it in three to five words on a card with a different color. This header should reflect both the individual content included on the cards in the grouping, as well as the "spirit" of the grouping (Brassard, 1989). Avoid jargon and clichés; look for new ways of expressing the meaning of the grouping.

Step 7. *Complete drawing the diagram.* Move any groupings that seem to be related to each other so that they are close together. Draw a box around the cards for each separate grouping. Draw a larger box around related groupings, and add a new header card at the top of this "super-grouping." To share the Affinity Diagram with others, and to obtain other input, transfer the results of the session onto another, smaller sheet of paper. Invite comments and suggestions, continuing to adjust the diagram until it best reflects the key issues or factors of the original question (adapted from Brassard, 1989).

Developing a
Relationship Diagram

Step 1. *Select team members.* Assemble a group of people to develop the diagram, including those who are closest to the problem or project, and those who have different perspectives on it. It is important that the individuals developing the Relationship Diagram have a close, working knowledge of the project or issue.

Step 2. *Develop the issue or problem statement.* Agree on a single statement as the focus of the diagram. For example, "The issues involved in planning a staff orientation program" or "The factors related to designing a program to address parental concerns about integrated employment." Write the question on a card and place it at the top of a sheet of newsprint on a flipchart or on a chalkboard.

Step 3. *Develop a set of idea cards.* To complete a Relationship Diagram, you will need a set of cards or Post-it Notes with one idea on each. These cards may be generated in any of several ways.

    a. If the Relationship Diagram is following up work on an Affinity Diagram, use the same cards.

    b. If it is following a Cause and Effect Diagram, transfer the "smallest bones"—the most basic causes—to cards.

    c. Brainstorm ideas for cards, as listed in the first steps of "Developing an Affinity Diagram."

    d. If the group has completed a Tree Diagram (or Performance Template) for the project, write the items at the lowest level of the tree on cards.

Step 4. *Display the cards.* Cover a wall or large table with blank newsprint; shuffle the cards, and spread them randomly over the available space. (Use masking tape to keep index cards in place on a vertical surface if you are not using Post-it Notes.) Select a wall or table that has space for team members to move around and reach it. Place the cards on the work surface in one of these three ways:

    a. Randomly (remove any headings from Affinity Diagram groupings)

    b. In Affinity Diagram groupings, sequentially according to cause and effect

    c. One by one—In this method, place all cards to one side of the work surface, and select one card. Then ask if any other card either causes or results from that card. Place the second card next to the first and draw an arrow between the two, from the cause to the effect. Repeat until all cards are placed.

Step 5. *Draw the arrows.* For each card ask, "Which other cards are caused or influenced by this card?" Draw an arrow from the cause card to each of the cards it affects. Be consistent in asking the question in only one direction; asking both "What does this card cause?", and "What results in this card?" only creates massive confusion.

Step 6. *Review and revise the draft.* After the group has completed its work, transfer the completed diagram to ledger paper and distribute copies to team members and others in the organization. Ask each person to review the diagram and suggest possible

RELATIONSHIP DIAGRAM: IMPROVING THE STAFF RECRUITMENT SYSTEM

Based on some preliminary data, the director of Mount Legion decided to first put some effort into the parts of the Affinity Diagram related most directly to improving the process of recruitment. Three headings from the Affinity Diagram seemed to apply:

- IMPROVE CONTACTS WITH CANDIDATES
- EXPAND AND IMPROVE RECRUITMENT PROCESS
- USE DATA TO IMPROVE PROCESS

But even within those three headings there were 12 different ideas for what needed to be done. Which should Mount Legion address first? What are the things that would affect the others the most? He chose to do a Relationship Diagram to help the group discover which few of the items needed attention first. The resulting Relationship Diagram is shown in Figure 10.21.

Counting the number of arrows that enter and leave each of the items in the diagram gave the group some help.

- Cards with the greatest number of *outgoing* arrows indicate basic activities that, if performed, would have an effect on the greatest number of other items:
  8 out—Develop more links between organization members and community members.
  7 out—Recruit through staff networks.
  7 out—Get feedback from candidates who drop out of the hiring process and from those who continue through it.
  6 out—Involve more people in the recruitment process.
  5 out—Collect and evaluate data on recruitment and hiring.
- Cards with the greatest number of *incoming* arrows indicate potential underlying issues or bottlenecks that should be considered, for they may need to be addressed as well:
  10 in—Continuously develop potential candidates.
  8 in—Improve recruitment process.
  8 in—Make more people aware of jobs available.

The team agreed that the tasks written on the three cards with the highest number of *incoming* arrows would be accomplished, in part, as a result of completion of the tasks defined on the cards with the greatest number of *outgoing* arrows. However, they decided immediately to adopt the ideas related to continuously developing potential candidates, rather than waiting for a job opening before recruiting, and to using strategies that would make more people aware when jobs actually did become available.

The real work, however, would be put into three major areas:

1. Developing more links between organization members and community members that could be used for recruiting
2. Recruiting through staff networks
3. Getting feedback from all job candidates

These three areas seemed to be possible for Mount Legion to attack initially in its efforts to improve its personnel recruitment system.

(continued)

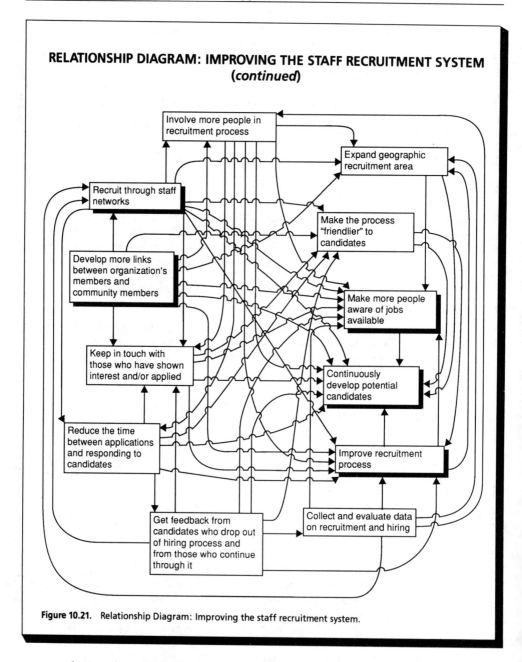

RELATIONSHIP DIAGRAM: IMPROVING THE STAFF RECRUITMENT SYSTEM
(continued)

Figure 10.21. Relationship Diagram: Improving the staff recruitment system.

changes by marking changes with a colored pen. Bring these changes to the group for discussion before revising the diagram.

Step 7. *Select key items.* During the process of drawing the diagram, patterns of relationship arrows emerge. To interpret the diagram:

    a.   Select the cards with the largest numbers of arrows either leading into or coming out of them.

    b.   The cards with *outgoing arrows* dominating are likely to be *basic causes* that, if addressed, will have effects on a large number of items.

    c.   The cards with *incoming arrows* dominating may be secondary issues or bottlenecks that are very important to address.

    d.   Review all of the other cards with fewer arrows to be sure that none of them are key items as well.

    e.   Through steps 7a–7d, reach consensus on no more than seven items for the group to pursue further.

A FEW POINTERS

1. Limit the diagram to no more than 10 or 20 cards. Fewer cards probably mean the issue is too simple for this tool; more, and the diagram will become too complex.
2. Be sure to leave sufficient space to allow for drawing lines between cards.
3. Allow only brief discussions by team members to reach consensus on the placement of cards and direction of arrows.
4. Do not allow two-way arrows. Even if it seems that two items influence each other, the group should determine which has the greater influence.
5. When one arrow must cross another, draw a curved "bridge" in the crossing arrow to make the diagram easier to read.
6. Consider the diagram that is developed as a draft that will be reviewed and revised as needed. As such, it does not have to be perfect the first time, and decisions about placements should be made quickly and easily (adapted from Brassard, 1989).

PUTTING IT ALL TOGETHER

PROCESSES TO SUPPORT CONTINUOUS IMPROVEMENT AND ORGANIZATIONAL CHANGE

The first three parts of this book presented the theoretical and historical foundation for the book; applications of quality improvement strategies to the specific issue of changeover from facility-based to integrated, community-based employment services; and a selection of the concepts, processes, and tools from quality improvement's systematic methods. In Part IV, the theoretical framework, applications, and tools are brought together through a focus on supporting staff members and recommendations for initiating and maintaining a quality improvement program.

Chapter 11 returns to strategies for empowering employees to work to achieve the mission, a principle first introduced in Chapter 2. Chapter 11 includes recommendations on hiring, orienting, training, and evaluating individual staff members, and considers these in relation to the particular demands brought on by changeover from facility-based to community-based employment services. Chapter 12 offers a blueprint for initiating quality improvement and organizational change.

The experience of one organization is presented in Chapter 13. Located in a small town in Oregon, this employment service provider, in the 1980s, made a commitment to changeover from its facility-based program to integrated employment services. They have proceeded toward this goal by implementing the methods of Continuous Quality Improvement. Chapter 13, therefore, tells their story from the first years of implementing quality improvement. It includes a number of specific examples of how staff members built the fundamental principles of Continuous Quality Improvement into the fabric of their daily operations.

Chapter 14 summarizes guidelines for supporting organizational change and quality improvement. This chapter points out pitfalls to be avoided along the way and emphasizes critical features of the process of managing for quality through change.

Chapter 11

Supporting Employees To Work To Achieve the Mission

Total changeover from facility-based to integrated community employment services requires radically different roles for all personnel in previously facility-based rehabilitation programs. Production supervisors and trainers, rather than working alongside a variety of other staff, may become job coaches, suddenly required to work on their own in a variety of far less predictable community settings. Mid-level managers, who previously could observe the performance of staff they supervised by walking around a building, find themselves, as changeover proceeds, responsible for staff working in many different locations and at varying times of the day and night.

Even organizations that change only a portion of their operations into supported employment services must grapple with these issues at least to some extent. Furthermore, these organizations are also challenged by problems resulting from operating two distinctly different types of businesses. Unfortunately, they may try to do so without recognizing those differences and clarifying the role of each program in achieving the organization's overall mission.

Clearly, providing employment services in integrated, community environments, whether or not it meets the strict definition of supported employment, is a new way of doing business. It represents a shift that calls for a new way of thinking about staff roles, as well as how organizations hire, orient, train, and support their staffs. This chapter presents some preliminary suggestions—derived from quality improvement principles as well as from lessons learned from the first years of supported employment implementation—for redefining roles, as well as for selecting, maintaining, and supporting staff.

THE NEED FOR A NEW WAY OF THINKING ABOUT EMPLOYEES

Changeover Requires New Staff Roles and Levels of Responsibility

Changeover demands that a rehabilitation organization redefine staff roles at all levels of the organization. Furthermore, the history of change in employment services for people with severe disabilities suggests that rehabilitation organizations must be prepared for an ongoing evolution of how services are delivered. This evolution will require ongoing changes in how staff roles are defined, far beyond those evident in the initial years of supported employment. Typical functional groupings of facility-based specialists—production, rehabilitation, marketing, and management functions—must be replaced with a more flexible work force. The more traditional rehabilitation roles must be replaced by roles that are more autonomous, that encompass a wider scope of potential duties, and that are constantly adjusted to the ongoing changes and improvements in how services are delivered. As a result of shifting roles, however, employees will need to possess a broader base of knowledge and skills than are currently required.

Direct Service Roles   Based on how services are now commonly offered by supported employment organizations, job coaches, also known as employment training specialists, must master a lengthy list of skills (Buckley, Albin, & Mank, 1988; Butterworth, Steere, Pancsofar, & Powell, 1990; Kregel & Sale, 1988). They need not only the basic habilitative technologies of task analysis, training, and production supervision, but also more advanced techniques of job analysis, self-management, strategies for fading support, and training for generalization and maintenance of performance. Furthermore, community-based staff must be able to analyze the social milieu of work environments and design and use strategies for increasing the acceptance and true integration of workers with severe disabilities.

With these increased demands, the settings in which community staff are working often are less forgiving of staff behavior that does not match the business culture. Co-workers and employers, unaccustomed to the support methods commonly used in sheltered settings, may object to methods that treat the employee with disabilities differently from other employees. But objections to, for example, obvious behavioral intervention techniques are far from the only issue. Studies are finding that the mere presence of a job coach from outside the company interferes with the development of social relationships between co-workers and the supported employee (e.g., Hagner, 1989; Udvari-Solner, 1990). Based on this finding, and the desire of some employers to take on a greater role with their employees with disabilities (Harper, Eder, Ramsing, & Watson, 1990; Rhodes, Sandow, Mank, Buckley, & Albin, 1991), more and more often employment specialists are training co-workers and employers to provide training and support (e.g., Mank, Rhodes, & Sandow, 1991). Therefore, rehabilitation personnel working in community settings must not only have a mastery of unobtrusive support techniques, but also be able to use nontechnical language to teach employees of the company how to use them effectively themselves.

Thus, because of the nature of the settings and constraints under which they are working, all staff members working in community settings require both greater degrees of skill in habilitative technology and greater finesse in using that technology than had been required in sheltered settings. And, individual employment training specialists working on their own in the community must rely on their own resources in large part for solving habilitative issues. They seldom have the luxury of other staff resources available to help with a particularly difficult behavioral episode or to help in deciding how to respond to another exceptional situation.

In contact with employers and the public on a daily basis, staff members in community settings must take on the roles of marketers and customer satisfaction experts as well and remain sensitive to the nature of the businesses in which they are working. In facility-based programs, staff from the production floor may seldom need to deal with anyone other than individuals receiving service and other staff persons. Community-based staff members, however, unlike their facility-based counterparts, are required to be able to talk with and support employers and co-

workers, identifying both issues and opportunities for improving employment outcomes and providing training and support to them as well as to the supported employee. Businesses want to take the lead in planning how people with disabilities
will be integrated into their work forces, and staff members working in the community must know how to support them in doing that (Rhodes et al., 1991).

Employment training specialists also must be able to perform the type of work
conducted in the business setting, whether it is operating commercial dishwashers,
assembling computer cables, or tending trees in a nursery, and to understand the
nature of the business in which they are working: What is the flow of work? When
are the regular employees under the greatest stress? What is disruptive to the setting? What are the variations in how employees behave and in how they perform
their jobs? What are the factors that signal those variations? How do factors such as
the time of day, location in the building, or presence of certain company supervisors
or customers affect how business is conducted? Thus, the staff in community settings must understand and possess skills related to the world of business, as well as
that of rehabilitation, and be able to talk knowledgeably, behave appropriately, and
analyze the changing situation on an ongoing basis.

Working in community settings, staff members must learn to do problem-solving,
use good sense, organize their time, and prioritize in a way that was not needed in
the sheltered workshop setting where managers and other support staff were
nearby. These "softer" skills are often what managers of rehabilitation organizations
find lacking in staff members when they first move into providing community-based
employment services. "Just give me people who can think on their feet" has often
been heard from managers in supported employment organizations. Clearly, the demands of working in dispersed, community locations require that "direct service"
staff possess both a broader and a more advanced set of skills and knowledge to
perform a wider variety of functions than had been necessary in sheltered settings.

Other Rehabilitation Roles   However, direct service staff are not the only
staff in rehabilitation organizations who must make a dramatic shift if changeover to
community-based employment services is to be successful. Given the costs of working in community employment settings, and the need for highly skilled and knowledgeable personnel in those settings, many organizations are finding that staff
members previously functioning as specialists (e.g., rehabilitation counselors, social
workers, placement specialists, evaluators, marketers, supervisors) must take on
greater direct service roles and broader responsibilities for changeover to occur. The
roles of these specialists, with intensive knowledge and skills in one area, often must
be "retooled" to meet the varied demands of community employment environments. And, these specialists must learn to share their special knowledge and skills
with others. For example, marketers must learn employment support strategies and
train job coaches in working with employers; rehabilitation counselors must learn
how to interact with employers and co-workers, and train others in how to assist
supported workers in dealing with job stress. The rehabilitation organization must
totally reshuffle staff members, staff responsibilities, and skill development opportunities repeatedly during the changeover process.

Management Roles   Changes necessary in direct service roles and specialist
positions notwithstanding, the demands of changeover, supporting staff working in
dispersed locations, and implementing quality improvement principles may result
in the greatest transformation occurring in the jobs of mid-level managers in rehabilitation organizations. These staff members, accustomed to supervising staff who are

working in proximity, and to operating within largely top-down organizational structures, must take on new roles in supporting staff working in difficult conditions. Generating strategies to overcome feelings of isolation of staff working alone in community settings, supervising and improving staff performance in dispersed locations, identifying the broad range of staff training and support needs, and providing the resources staff need to do their jobs well place very different requirements on managers.

Perhaps the greatest change in management roles that is required by community-based employment, however, is a change from the role of manager to one of trainer, facilitator, and supporter. Unable to be present in all employment locations at all times, managers must provide employees with the knowledge, skills, and systems they need to perform their jobs well. Managers and those in traditional specialist roles in rehabilitation can no longer afford to control pockets of knowledge and skill, acting as experts within their own defined fiefdoms. Knowledge must be "reintegrated" across functions and disciplines (Zeleny, 1989). In supported employment, their roles must include extending their special knowledge to all in the organization who might need it. If managers must understand planning, budgeting, and customer relations, at least to some extent so must secretaries, bookkeepers, job coaches, and van drivers. Furthermore, managers must take responsibility for developing and improving the processes and systems that select and support employees for their jobs.

Quality Improvement Principles
Suggest a Need for New Roles and Organizational Structures

"Empower Employees To Work To Achieve the Mission" was one of the principles of quality improvement described in Chapter 2. That chapter summarized guidelines presented by quality improvement experts for releasing the power of employees, including expanding staff roles, promoting teamwork, breaking down barriers to communication, and providing expanded decision-making authority.

The dispersion of staff into diverse community settings places an interesting requirement on rehabilitation organizations: they must rely on the decision-making ability of direct service staff to an extent that was never before needed. Agencies must rely on their employees who are working in dispersed locations—seldom seeing other staff or managers from the organization, but in continuous contact with the community—to provide highly effective services and to represent the organization well. Because of the fundamental design of the community-based employment service paradigm, the role specialization so prevalent in facility-based settings is nearly impossible to maintain. The demands of community-based services call for all employees to be highly trained, skilled across a variety of domains, well-motivated to perform well, and provided with systems that support them to do their jobs. Thus, the strategies that are recommended by Continuous Quality Improvement experts to empower employees match well with the needs of rehabilitation organizations to achieve redefinition of staff roles and new levels of performance. These strategies include changing the organization's culture and management philosophy to reflect a new level of respect for all employees, and reconsidering methods for hiring, training, and supporting employees to do their jobs. Quality improvement experts see this change largely in terms of focusing on improving the processes and systems in which staff members must work (e.g., Deming, 1986), that is, the processes and systems that hire, train, and support people to do their jobs.

An organization undergoing changeover to community-based employment services and that is also pursuing implementing the principles of quality improvement will see the need to define a new organizational structure—different from that traditionally used by many rehabilitation organizations. Instead of structures with distinct divisions for management, production, and rehabilitation, an organization needs a structure that supports the development of staff competence and involvement in managing not only their own jobs, but the work of the organization as well. Reorganization into teams that combine staff in multiple roles and with different knowledge, skills, and experience will promote the staff development, communication, and knowledge transfer needed to take advantage of a heretofore largely untapped staff resource.

With a new team-based structure (an example of which is provided in Chapter 13's description of the experience of one organization) managers' roles must shift drastically. In a team-based structure, managers' jobs must include providing for teams to assume ownership of problems and their solutions, ensuring the availability of the resources to support their desired accomplishments, and removing unnecessary bureaucratic and structural barriers to their success. Thus, existing management roles in rehabilitation organizations must be retooled as well, in skills relating to promoting participative management and staff development, as well as in community-based employment technologies.

Labor Market Trends Require New Practices

Changes in staff roles required by changeover to community-based employment services and by implementing quality improvement principles provide only some of the reasons for rehabilitation organizations to institute new staff practices. During the latter part of the 1980s, most parts of the country experienced low unemployment rates, with employers facing difficulties in finding and maintaining qualified workers, particularly to fill entry-level positions. Labor economists predict that employers will continue to face labor shortages for years to come (e.g., Fosler, 1989; Johnston & Packer, 1987). A survey of employers in Oregon found that personnel hiring, development, and retention were cited as concerns more frequently than any other category (Harper et al., 1990).

While these trends have forced employers to recognize the potential contribution of persons with severe disabilities and thus opened the doors for many of these individuals, they also have had an impact on community employment and rehabilitation organizations. Reports from the early years of supported employment efforts have indicated that support organizations are suffering from high turnover rates and difficulty in finding and maintaining qualified staff (e.g., Wehman, Kregel, & Shafer, 1989; Winking, Trach, Rusch, & Tines, 1989)—problems very similar to those found in the private sector. Inferior pay, low status, meager benefits, poor working conditions, bureaucratic red tape, and inadequate support and training are among the factors that have been cited as combining to result in high turnover rates faced by many organizations.

Yet, if rehabilitation and community-based employment organizations are to achieve their missions, they must find, develop, and maintain a cadre of staff who perform demanding jobs very well, and these organizations must accomplish this while competing for personnel in what is basically a labor-short market. Although unemployment rates move up and down based on the fluctuations of the economy, these organizations are always competing with both public and private sector employers for qualified and motivated employees. The expanded demands on staff competencies alone argue for a strategy of making long-term commitments to staff members, involving developing personnel over time to fill more and more complex roles. In service enterprises such as rehabilitation organizations, the staff is the organization's greatest resource, and the methods used for recruiting, selecting, orienting, training, and maintaining staff members must improve if rehabilitation organizations are to compete under current and future conditions.

STRATEGIES FOR REACHING NEW
LEVELS OF STAFF PERFORMANCE AND CONTRIBUTION

Tom Peters (1987) suggests, "There are no limits to the ability to contribute on the part of a properly selected, well-trained, appropriately supported, and, above all, committed person" (p. 342). Given the changes in personnel roles demanded by working in community settings, rehabilitation organizations would benefit from learning how to support their staff members to reach new heights in contributing to achieving the organization's mission. Community-based employment organizations would do well to heed the lessons that Peters and others like him offer for businesses to succeed in a chaotic, highly competitive arena. This section summarizes seven strategies for supporting employees to achieve the mission during changeover to integrated, community-based employment services.

Chapter 2 discussed some of the general strategies for the fundamental principles of quality improvement, such as moving decision-making closer to the people directly involved in an issue, breaking down barriers to communication, developing teamwork, reducing hierarchies, driving out fear, rewarding employees for uncovering problems, using methods that allow employees to assume ownership of ideas and outcomes, providing recognition to employees, respecting the knowledge of staff members who are directly involved with a process or system, and treating employees as customers. This chapter selects a few of the strategies recommended in Chapter 2 for more in-depth discussion.

Strategy #1. Improve the Organization's Culture:
Take Steps To Enhance the Dignity and Value of All Employees

A consistent message in quality improvement is that *people* are the primary source of an organization's success. Indeed, that personnel should be highly valued by organizations is such an overriding premise in Continuous Quality Improvement that it pervades nearly every book and article on the approach. The simple truth is that staff members who feel valued and who are engaged in their work perform better. That is, personnel who are actively committed to their jobs, focused on achieving desired outcomes, and closely aligned with the mission and values of the organization reach for greater levels of performance than those who view their work as merely a job, and who are not only undervalued by their employers, but are also treated as if they are obviously replaceable.

Unfortunately, rehabilitation and other human service organizations have myriad ways in which they dehumanize their staffs. The list of assaults by hierarchical structures on the dignity of the staff is remarkably long: placing direct service staff (often unnamed), who provide services most directly to the different customer groups, at the bottom of the organizational chart and compensating them with low pay and poor benefits; providing the best parking spaces to top managers only; abiding by thick personnel manuals that limit even bereavement time off; allowing little flexibility in duties and responsibilities; requiring that decisions be made by management for even the most basic issues; insisting on top-down communication from the board and executive with infrequent, if any, opportunities for the staff's thoughts to be heard; and relying on time clocks. These are among the many ways in which top managers ensure that "lower level" staff members stay in their place. Changing the way organizations view and value all personnel will require vigilant, active, and focused attention to eliminate the subtle and more obvious assaults on dignity. Taking even the simple steps needed to stop these assaults will result in amazing changes in staff commitment and performance. Start by simply treating employees as customers, and watch for the effects.

Strategy #2. Improve the Organization's Structure: Promote Teamwork and Support Self-Managing Teams

Since the 1930s, job satisfaction literature has told us that, while low pay and meager benefits may lead to job dissatisfaction, higher levels of job satisfaction result primarily from such factors as challenging work, feedback from supervisors, autonomy, importance of work, opportunity to interact with others and so forth (e.g., Herzberg, 1968; Herzberg, Mausner, & Snyderman, 1959). Participative management, job enlargement, employee involvement teams, quality circles, and markedly different organizational charts reflect the efforts of many businesses to use these lessons to tap the human potential of their organizations more effectively. Supported employment providers and rehabilitation organizations undergoing changeover to community-based employment services must heed these lessons as well.

Chapter 9 addressed the strategy of forming "quality improvement teams" for addressing specific problems in organizational processes and outcomes. This recommended strategy speaks to forming ongoing, self-managing *work teams* as the basic building blocks of an organization's structure, and taking a new perspective on the role of individual staff members in organizations. The strategy involves the following:

- *Make efforts to expand the roles of individual staff*, so that they may assume greater ownership of their contributions to the organization's outcomes.
  For example: Rather than relying on rehabilitation counselors to develop and monitor individual program plans that are then implemented largely by direct service personnel, give direct service personnel responsibility (and training) in planning individual objectives and strategies, implementing strategies, and monitoring progress.
- *Clear away barriers to communication*, such as bureaucratic hurdles, unnecessary paperwork, and jumping through hoops.
  For example: One organization used to require employment training specialists (job coaches) to go through rehabilitation specialists to communicate with an individual's home. While this rule was in effect, the employment specialists con-

SUGGESTIONS FOR ENHANCING THE DIGNITY
AND VALUE OF ALL STAFF IN THE ORGANIZATION

- If you have parking spaces reserved for top managers, eliminate them now.
- Name all staff members on the organizational chart.
- Review the organizational chart: Does the way in which you portray your structure demean any personnel?
- Take steps to improve the pay of the lowest paid staff members.
- Improve benefit packages based on the input of the staff.
- With a critical eye, review personnel manuals for policies and procedures that reduce staff dignity. Enlist the assistance of staff members in this activity.
- Maximize flexibility in duties and responsibilities.
- Give staff members authority to make the decisions needed for performing the basic functions of their jobs.
- Embed regular, formal and informal opportunities for managers and board members to listen to the input of all staff members.
- Take action on input received from the staff.
- Reduce or eliminate top-down communication in the form of memoranda from the board and executive directing action.
- Consider making all staff members salaried rather than hourly workers.
- Look for opportunities to demonstrate the organization's commitment to individual staff members.
- Provide a comfortable, pleasing place for staff to congregate informally or to hold meetings. Make sure that the room used by the staff for meetings is the same, or at least as good as, the one used by the board.
- Give staff members or teams authority to manage budgets needed to perform their jobs.
- Ask staff members to help with identifying symbols and procedures in the organization that demean staff.
- Become a housekeeping fanatic in the places managed by the organization (e.g., offices and businesses the organization owns and runs, a sheltered workshop facility if there is one).
- Occasionally, place fresh flowers where staff spend time together informally.
- Make sure that both the interior and exterior of the office look businesslike, with attractive signs, windows, walls, indoor plants, decorations, and landscaping.

stantly complained about the length of time required for resolution to simple problems. Now, when an issue arises that requires communication with home, employment specialists themselves call the home and deal with the issue directly. Eliminating the unnecessary person in the middle saves time, improves communication, and allows the employment specialists to feel more in control. Probably the most pleasant result, however, is that they now complain much less about rehabilitation specialists. And, now the rehabilitation specialists have more time to train and support employment specialists to do their jobs well.

- *Form ongoing work teams as the foundation for the organization's structure,* involving employees with different backgrounds, training, and roles to enhance integration of knowledge. Gradually expand the areas of decision-making authority in the work teams.

For example: When one rehabilitation organization (see Chapter 13) reorganized into a team structure, logistical constraints required that job coaches working in the same geographic area of the county form teams. Because this meant that teams would be made up of employees in very similar roles, the management team decided to add a job developer and someone who had once been a rehabilitation specialist to each team. This ensured that each team included members with marketing and rehabilitation skills from the start, while other team members had an opportunity to become better trained in these areas to assume new roles.

Begin by giving ongoing, structural work teams responsibility for those areas in which they are most involved, such as planning a substitute system for coverage during illness and vacation, or communicating with home providers. Gradually expand their direct authority in their jobs, so that, for example, they attend planning meetings to develop individual program plans. As team members master new skills, further expand their decision-making authority into areas traditionally reserved for management, such as hiring personnel, allocating raises, and budgeting. Be sure to provide training and support to team members to assist them in assuming new responsibilities and to follow through on the decisions made by teams. When turnover occurs, support the remaining team members in training a new colleague so that she or he can "catch up" on the skills needed to be a fully contributing member of the team.

Teams such as these will work only if team members are provided with systematic methods for making decisions and for solving work-related problems. Therefore, train all work teams in the concepts and processes related to the systematic methods of quality improvement and in a variety of tools that they can use for planning and problem-solving.

There are many potential benefits of using a team structure for an organization providing employment services in community settings. Teams provide an environment that supports employees to assume greater responsibility for the quality of their work, for their own growth, and for improving the effectiveness of their organizations. They offer a forum in which information can be communicated quickly and effectively, where training can be done informally and continuously, and individual employees can receive support and assistance in solving problems. Therefore, structured teams can help to decrease the sense of isolation of which many community-based staff in supported employment organizations complain (Butterworth et al., 1990). Teams also offer a vehicle for breaking down barriers to communication between what were formerly separate departments and for facilitating recognition of systems issues that cut across departments (Scholtes, 1987).

Employee work teams offer a way to organize a flexible structure that can expand and be shaped as environmental and organizational variables change. This is a great advantage to rehabilitation organizations undergoing changeover to community-based employment, for as the number and types of job opportunities in the community expand, and the financial and personnel commitment to the new way of working grows, staff can form new teams, or expand or restructure existing teams without reshifting the entire organization.

During the changeover process, some organizations have found it beneficial initially to establish a supported employment team that is protected from the day-to-day operations of the sheltered facility. If possible, assign staff members full-time to the new team to assist them to maintain a focus on their new activities. Protect them from the other work demands, so that time needed for team development is not used up in the daily grind. However, as soon as possible after firmly establishing integrated employment options and developing skilled personnel with community-based responsibilities, begin to integrate staff members from the sheltered facility with those in community employment. Many organizations undergoing changeover report that a division develops between the facility-based and community-based staff. Facility-based staff feel they are devalued, and that all of the organization's attention and resources are focused on moving to community-based services. The facility staff may feel defensive, jealous, and fearful of their jobs. Therefore, reintegrating community-based staff with facility staff, as well as clearly defining the role of the facility during changeover, should assist in limiting these issues. Furthermore, holding discussions with all staff to clarify the important roles in the facility-based program for supporting the changeover effort should help as well.

You might begin integrating the community-based and facility-based staffs by including one or two staff members from the facility on a supported employment team. This will help the facility personnel to understand better the nature of supporting individuals in community-based jobs and allow community employment staff members to learn from those still in the facility about the skills and interests of individuals who have yet to be placed. This interaction will also help with adjusting the organizational culture to support changeover and with recruiting other facility-based staff to assume new roles in the community: for facility staff who participate on the community team will share information with others in the facility. When the number of staff on the initial community-based employment team grows to 10–12, split the team in half before bringing in new members. In this way, employees who are experienced with team functioning, and with changeover, can assist in orienting new members to each team.

Chapters 9 and 12 present detailed information on planning for and supporting employee teams as quality improvement teams, and Chapter 13 presents the story of one organization that, in the course of changeover from facility-based to community-based employment services, overhauled its organizational structure into a set of interlocking "Work Teams" and "Project Teams."

Strategy #3.   Improve Personnel Systems:
Invest Intensely in Recruiting, Selecting, and Orienting Staff

Whether selecting from existing facility-based employees to fill new roles to support changeover to community employment services, or hiring new staff from outside the organization, it is clear that the process of selecting personnel provides the raw material from which quality and organizational transformations grow. Often, however, recruitment, selection, and orientation are treated as *pro forma* activities to be checked off the task list, rather than functions critical to the development and success of the organization.

Prepare for Interviews by Defining the Qualities Needed   Identifying new staff members should depend less on paper credentials and more on the "softer" qualities that make people work well in your organization. Consider the characteristics of your best performers, the individuals who are natural leaders and instigators of quality. List their desirable traits as well as the values that are important to doing well with the organization. Ask existing employees what is important to them in co-workers, and be sure to include these qualities in the list as well.

"All of these prescriptions have had one underlying theme: The average person will be asked to contribute much more than in the past. It doesn't follow that we need all be bionic people, but it does mean that we'd better worry about issues such as commitment from the outset."

"The task of transforming raw recruits into committed stars, able to cope with the pace of change that is becoming normal, begins with the recruiting process per se. *The best follow three tenets, unfortunately ignored by most: (1) spend time, and lots of it; (2) insist that line people dominate the process; and (3) don't waffle about the qualities you are looking for in candidates.*" (Peters, 1987, p. 379)

Consider the lessons from Tom Gilbert's Performance Engineering Matrix, presented in Chapter 6. Gilbert (1978) suggests that two personal factors be considered foremost in hiring: 1) the person's capacity for doing the job, and 2) the person's motivation for wanting the job. This recommendation is based on the relative cost and effectiveness of strategies to change these, as compared with expanding an individual employee's knowledge and skills. Indeed, in changeover, many organizations are finding it useful to hire new staff with no previous rehabilitation experience, because of the very different nature of job requirements in community-based employment services. In particular, beware of the need to overcome "bad habits" developed in previous facility-based jobs. Beyond this, however, consider an applicant's motives for working with the organization. A close match between those and the incentives available from the organization is important for developing a work force with a long-term commitment. For example, applicants motivated primarily by money, but applying for positions that pay poorly, are candidates for immediate turnover. Applicants who are motivated by strong desire to care for others may find little incentive in the organization's desire to fade direct staff support to individuals with disabilities in favor of training employers and co-workers to do so. Therefore, carefully consider the organization's incentives, values, and direction, as well, to add to the list of desired characteristics in an employee.

Based on this list, develop a set of interview questions to assist in screening for the desired characteristics. If you value creativity in employees, how do you find out if an interviewee is creative? People who are creative will have done things in the past that demonstrate creativity and should respond creatively to unusual problems posed during the interview. Ask what new ventures they helped to start, which assignments offered the greatest challenge, or what their most unusual accomplishment is. Devise questions such as this to assist you to perceive individual characteristics and motives.

Involve Staff Members at All Levels in the Recruitment and Selection Process From the start of defining the new job and the desired characteristics of the new employee, involve direct line staff along with managers and others. In a team structure, all team members should participate to some degree in recruitment and selection of new members. Traditionally, managers have held this role. However, including direct line staff, particularly individuals who will be working with the new employee, helps to build their commitment to work cooperatively with the new employee. With their involvement in the selection process, current employees become

SAMPLE LIST OF CHARACTERISTICS FOR
DEVELOPING INTERVIEW QUESTIONS FOR NEW EMPLOYEES

- Commitment to organization's missions and values
- Able to think on his or her feet
- Willing to try new ways of doing things
- Able to work in team
- Manages personal time well
- Organized
- Questions procedures that get in the way
- Adapts well to change
- Uses data to make decisions and to monitor performance
- Helps other employees with difficult assignments
- Initiates action
- Considers a variety of options
- Communicates clearly with others
- Is creative in the face of problems
- Good with people
- Likes to work independently
- Enjoys challenges

partners in the success of new employees. Furthermore, if in their roles they are closer to the position being filled, their information about the requirements for candidates will be the most useful.

Take Time for Extensive and Multiple Interviews Most interviewees can present a good image during an interview that lasts less than an hour, even when being questioned by a team of interviewers: It requires getting the interviewers to explain the job, the company, and what they are looking for, then repeating the right words in the right order when the interview team takes time to ask questions.

The selection process should include several different interviews with different employees and managers to get a clearer picture of the prospective employee's nature, motivation, capacity, and values and to determine how well they match with the needs of the company. Exhibit your organization's values openly during interviews to assist the interviewee to understand your culture, and to allow each of you to determine whether there is a fit. Be open about the drawbacks of the job, such as changing hours, isolation, and limited resources, so that the candidate is given an opportunity to understand the true picture of the job, rather than an improved version designed to lure the unsuspecting.

Many rehabilitation and human service organizations may ask, "How can we afford the time for all this?". However, given the costs associated with hiring the *wrong* person for a job, the only response is, "How can you afford not to?". An interview process involving all levels of the organization demonstrates your organization's commitment to the working team and to employee participation. Screening candidates in this way permits time for both sides to get to know each other and to determine if this is the right job for this person. Properly carried out, a strong selection process is one factor that can reduce the level of employee turnover in an organi-

Texas Instruments, Inc. carried out one of the earliest formal studies of an orientation program. During an experimental period, new employees received either a 2-hour "traditional" orientation, covering pay, benefits, parking, and so forth, or a 7-hour "socialization" program that included topics on career management and corporate politics. After 2 years, researchers compared the two groups on time required to master a new job, productivity, absenteeism, and tardiness. The employees who had attended the "socialization" program were rated significantly higher on *all* measures. Among newly hired professionals such as computer specialists and engineers who had gone through the socialization program, turnover was 40% *lower* than for those who had undergone the shorter, traditional orientation.

Corning Glass Works developed an orientation process as a strategy for solving their problem of high turnover among their professional employees. The resulting orientation process included nine 2-hour seminars spread over the first 6 months of employment, as well as self-study and work assignments that ran through the new employee's 15th or 18th month of employment. By the end of the 2nd year of testing the new system, the employees who had gone through the new orientation process had a turnover rate 69% lower than those who had not experienced the process (Zemke, 1989).

zation, simply by ensuring that new employees are well-matched both with the job and with the organizational team.

Spend Time on Orientation to the Organization's Culture, History, Mission, and Values While orientation to the organization's culture, history, mission, and values must begin during the interview and selection process, investing in orientation after hiring will also support building staff commitment to the organization. A growing body of research suggests that no orientation or a poor orientation can result in reducing the effectiveness of new employees, and contribute to dissatisfaction and turnover (Wexley & Latham, 1982; Zemke, 1989).

The outcomes achieved by some of the successful orientation programs in industry suggest several guidelines for designing an orientation process for an organization undergoing changeover:

- Provide new employees with an extensive orientation to the mission, values, philosophy, history, and culture of the organization. What are the traditions the organization treasures? How does your organization's culture differ from that of others? What does the mission mean in terms of the new employee's role? How do the organizational change activities, including changeover to community-based employment, tie into the mission?
- Treat new employees with the same care with which you want them to treat others, which will set the tone for how they will behave later. During orientation, model the behavior that will be expected of them as they interact with the customers of the organization, such as individuals with disabilities, community members, other service providers, funders, and other employees. As a part of this, consistently use language that reflects the organization's mission, and model for new (and existing) employees how they are expected to interact with others. Chapter 3, on customers and quality improvement, offered several strategies for building a customer-driven organization.

For example, at Disney parks, hotels, and resorts, people who work in the organization are never called employees. Instead, they are referred to as "cast members" who wear "costumes" instead of uniforms, and go to "rehearsals" instead of training. This use of language emphasizes Disney's mission of entertainment and underscores that everyone who works at Disney is "on-stage" whenever they are with the public (Zemke, 1989).

- Give a realistic view of working in the organization. Do not try to portray a job as glamorous when it is really a lot of hard work. Explain not only what the new employees are likely to enjoy about their new jobs, but what they are not likely to enjoy, as well. This honesty will reduce the amount of turnover that occurs because new employees' expectations were not in line with the reality of the job.

- Incorporate staff members from all parts of the organization, as well as customers, if possible, in the orientation process. Include staff members ranging from the executive director to demonstrate the new employees' importance to the organization, through direct line staff in order to give a broad, overall view of the organization. Using a variety of personnel will help new employees learn the ropes and understand better how they fit.

- Keep the orientation informal and comfortable to help new employees overcome the typical anxiety about starting a new job. Extend the orientation period to include activities that occur periodically and stretch over several months in order to give new employees a chance to settle into their jobs, become less anxious, and become better able to reflect on the information presented.

- Set expectations for your orientation program and monitor its effectiveness. The objective of an orientation program should be, for example, to improve an employee's relationship with the organization, reduce job turnover, or improve performance. Obtain feedback from staff regarding the orientation they received, and incorporate recommended changes into the process. Treat the orientation process just like any other process in the organization: Make it subject to continuous improvement.

Strategy #4.   Improve Dissemination of Knowledge: Eliminate Internal Information Filters and Isolated Experts

Organizations often use "information filters" that place barriers between staff members and between the staff and the community, including the organization's external customers. For example, an organization relying on information filters might insist that all contacts with residential providers or case managers be limited to rehabilitation specialists; all presentations on the organization to community groups and businesses be limited to managers and marketers; or all customer satisfaction surveys be conducted by managers. However, if all employees are to work for the mission, they must have access to information from those outside of the organization, as well as from managers and others in the organization. Job coaches who speak directly with residential providers, who use their personal contacts to develop additional jobs, and who survey employers are able to work more effectively for the organization than are job coaches whose interactions are filtered by managers or others.

Staff members who are viewed as experts, because of their knowledge and skills in areas that are valued by the organization, must learn to teach their knowledge and skills to others. It makes little sense for organizations to rely on only a few individuals as experts when decisions must be made. Instead, the role of the experts should

CHANGING FROM ISOLATED EXPERTS TO KNOWLEDGE DISPERSION

THE OLD WAY

Rehabilitation Specialists at ABCD Rehabilitation are highly trained in techniques such as counseling and providing behavioral support. The specialists meet with production staff or job trainers when a problem becomes big enough for those staff persons to complain about it.

THE NEW WAY

Some Rehabilitation Specialists have become lead production staff or job trainers. Those who remained as Rehabilitation Specialists now view the most important function of their role as passing along their special knowledge and skills in counseling and behavioral support to the other production staff and job trainers. The Rehabilitation Specialists try to move the knowledge through the organization at all times, particularly when things are going well. By passing along their knowledge and skills, they try to keep problems from arising.

THE OLD WAY

The Case Workers at ABCD Rehabilitation have two very important responsibilities: 1) maintaining communication with the residential providers and family members involved with individuals receiving services from ABCD, and 2) developing and tracking all individual rehabilitation plans for anyone receiving rehabilitation services from ABCD. The job is difficult. Job Trainers are constantly complaining about one thing or another that the home providers did or did not do. In fact, it is hard for the Case Worker to follow up on everything the Job Trainers want. But then, the Case Workers also are angry with the Job Trainers because the Trainers seldom carry out the individual plans as written. And getting data from the Trainers to support the plans—Forget it!

THE NEW WAY

Most Case Workers have become Job Trainers, reducing the average number of individuals receiving support assigned to Trainers. As they prepared to make this shift, Case Workers introduced Job Trainers to the family members and residential providers of the individuals they were supporting and helped them talk about how best to support the individuals. Case Workers also talked with Job Trainers about how best to deal with residential providers when a question or problem arises. They practiced a few possible scenarios and were available when the Job Trainers made their first calls to the home. Beyond this, however, Case Workers also trained Job Trainers on how to develop and track individual rehabilitation plans. The Case Workers who have become Job Trainers are still willing to help another Job Trainer when a question or issue arises. But that seldom happens. The individual plans, because they are now developed by the Job Trainers directly, have more meaning to the Trainers, and maintaining data to support the plans is no longer the issue it once was.

be to disperse their knowledge throughout the organization, particularly to those who could use that knowledge on a daily basis. Most rehabilitation organizations are replete with examples of supporting individual experts rather than dispersing knowledge to all staff members who could use it. The slogan "Knowledge Is Power" reflects the reason why knowledge should be shared with staff, rather than held by an elite few.

Strategy #5. Improve Staff Training and Feedback Systems: Provide Ongoing, Just-in-Time, Context-Based, Training, Retraining, and Performance Feedback

Quality improvement experts recommend instituting an ongoing education program for all employees as one strategy for continuously improving the performance of an organization and of the individuals in it (e.g., Deming, 1986). This training for personnel has two basic purposes: 1) improving performance in current roles, and 2) preparing employees to assume new or expanded roles in the future. Because the personnel in a rehabilitation organization undergoing changeover to community-based employment bring different sets of training, experience, knowledge, and skills to their positions, no single training program is likely to work. Therefore, an organization must continuously shape a training process for its staff that addresses a wide range of changing needs.

However, it is important to recognize that staff training is not a complete cure for specific performance problems. While training may be a good answer when employees are having difficulty, there are several other possible reasons for performance deficits, most of which lie in the systems in which those staff members must work. A variety of strategies are available for addressing specific performance issues, such as establishing clear guidelines for performance, using self-recording, and providing supervisory feedback (e.g., Bennett, 1988). Chapter 6 presented the Performance Engineering Matrix, a tool useful for analyzing performance problems and designing appropriate approaches for helping staff members to achieve desired outcomes. Use the Performance Engineering Matrix (or the other systematic methods presented in Chapters 5, 8, 9, and 10), therefore, when seeking an answer for a specific performance problem. This section of the current chapter, however, addresses training from the perspective of overall performance improvement or job changes, rather than as a remediation strategy.

Most organizations use a combination of in-house training which is provided by their own staff, and in-service training, which is provided by other organizations. Whether designing staff training sessions or selecting from those available elsewhere, several guidelines may assist in improving the effectiveness of personnel training (see Table 11.1).

Beyond training, however, it is important that managers provide frequent feedback to staff members. Use feedback to encourage and recognize efforts, accomplishments, and process improvements, as well as to support improved performance. Give attention to staff who are using the kinds of behaviors that demonstrate both a commitment to changeover to integrated employment and application of quality improvement methods. Provide feedback frequently, in a nonthreatening way. Give thank you notes to employees, and constantly let them know that they are valued by the organization.

Strategy #6. Improve Personnel
Systems: Eliminate Annual Performance Evaluations

One of the time-honored traditions in management is the annual performance appraisal of employees. Managers in rehabilitation agencies and other private and

SUGGESTIONS FOR IMPROVING STAFF TRAINING

- Use a competency-based, performance-oriented approach to specific job training (see, e.g., Buckley, Albin, & Mank, 1988; Kregel & Sale, 1988).
- Match the training formats used and training participants with desired outcomes (e.g., Buckley et al., 1988). For example, attending a presentation may give a job developer *awareness* or basic knowledge of a new technique. However, that job developer will require practice across different settings if she is to master the skill and be able to implement it across a variety of conditions.
- To get the most from sending staff to an externally sponsored seminar:
  - Send more than one staff person, if possible, so that they can support each other to implement new knowledge and skills when they return.
  - Include a manager, if possible, to assist with transferring new skills to his or her work setting, and to help with removing any barriers that may interfere with implementing the new methods.
  - Provide follow-up for staff members who have attended seminars to ensure that the awareness, knowledge, or skills desired are actually applied in the regular work setting.
  - Extend the impact of an external seminar by asking the staff members who attended to present what they learned to others.
- Develop in-house trainers and training resources. Take advantage of every opportunity to gather training videos, modules, and other materials. Invest in helping a few staff members to become skilled in providing training to others.
- Help "isolated experts" to change their jobs to focus on moving their knowledge throughout the organization, rather than offering expert advice only on request.
- Involve staff members in training that is designed to bring together personnel from different roles and types of organizations. Changeover to integrated employment services is truly a *community* issue, requiring the effective interaction of a variety of participants, such as schools, parents, businesses, other community service providers, case managers, and vocational rehabilitation counselors. Participation in joint training events will help break down the barrier to communication that may exist between staff members and these other stakeholder groups (Albin, 1989; Fraegon, 1982; Golin & Ducanis, 1981; Helge, 1981).
- Recognize the needs of adult learners when planning and carrying out training. Adult learners come to training with a wealth of experience and learning styles that set them apart from more traditional students. Opportunities to discuss content, to control the direction and focus of their learning, to use prior experiences in learning, to apply principles to their daily lives, and to practice newly acquired skills are important to their satisfaction and to the outcomes achieved by seminars (e.g., Knowles, 1980; Peterson, 1988).
- Find a way to incorporate discussion of the organization's mission and values in any group training event carried out by the organization.
- Treat the staff training program as a process that is subject to continuous improvement using systematic methods: analyze training needs and design training process (Plan), implement training (Do), evaluate its effectiveness (Check), and adjust the process based on evaluation information (Act).

Table 11.1. Appropriate formats for achieving desired training outcomes

Desired outcomes of training	Appropriate training formats
Increased *AWARENESS* of a particular philosophy, value, approach, method, model program, and so forth	Presentations Written materials Videotapes
Increased *KNOWLEDGE* of a particular philosophy, value, approach, method, model program, and so forth	Demonstration and discussion Written assignment with feedback Lecture with discussion Interactive software
Increased *IMMEDIATE SKILLS* related to a specific approach or method	Practice with feedback
Development of an *ENDURING SKILL* that will maintain long after the training session ends	Practice with feedback delivered over time in a natural setting
Development of a *GENERALIZED SKILL* that can be applied to a variety of environments after the end of the training session	Practice with feedback delivered over time with follow-up observation
SECOND GENERATION IMPACT, in which participants can train others to use the same skills	Special training for trainers, with practice and feedback over time in order to develop skills in giving presentations and using various training formats

public sector organizations conduct performance evaluations for a wide variety of purposes, such as giving feedback to employees, identifying training needs, determining candidates for promotion, and awarding raises and bonuses. Yet, on what basis are those evaluations made? And, what are the effects of such evaluations?

Quality experts believe that performance appraisal systems have destructive consequences in organizations (e.g., Deming, 1986; Scholtes, 1987). Rather than achieving the lofty expectations listed above, individual performance evaluation actually interferes with enhancing the contribution of employees to improving overall organization achievements. Indeed, Dr. Deming includes evaluation of performance, merit rating, or annual review as one of his seven "deadly diseases" of Western management. Both Dr. Deming (1986) and Peter Scholtes (1987) list a variety of reasons for this effect:

1. *The evaluation system itself is neither reliable nor valid.* When managers rate the performance of individual employees, their ratings are subject to their own personal and cultural biases and are very liable to be affected by the individual's "reputation" of past performance. Furthermore, different supervisors use the same rating system in different ways: For example, some are "hard" and others are "easy" in their ratings. And, the evaluation systems fail to recognize that the same job title does not mean that individuals are actually in the same job. Yet, organizations try to use such unreliable ratings as a basis for raises and promotions. The result is that employees do not trust management and are cynical about the evaluation system.

2. *Performance appraisal systems encourage "bad habits" from the perspective of quality improvement.* Individual employee evaluation systems lead to employees who fear "rocking the boat," who hide problems, who focus on individual outcomes rather than work group performance, and who dread disagreeing with their supervisors. Rather than working to improve processes and systems to improve

overall organizational performance, employees are forced to think about their own personal evaluations. Because they also must separate the performance of one employee from that of a work group, individual evaluations also discourage collaboration and teamwork.

3. *Most appraisal systems use a timeline that is ineffective for providing any useful performance feedback.* If performance evaluations are carried out with the purpose of giving employees feedback on their performance, it is a system that is too little too late. For feedback to be effective, it should occur at the time of the behavior and not be reserved for an annual or semiannual meeting. If feedback has been provided at the time of the event (whether it was feedback on a job well-done or suggestions for improvement), what purpose is served by repeating it at an annual review?

4. *Individual evaluations ignore the effects of the systems in which people work.* This is the most important reason for eliminating individual appraisal systems. The performance of each employee in an organization is the result of many different factors. The most significant of these are the systems in which they work: the performance "upstream" in the processes in which they work (i.e., the work done by others in a previous step of the process); the quality of the materials, machines, and other resources available to them for doing their jobs; and so forth. Indeed, Scholtes (1987) believes that systems are so much at fault that if a person is incapable of doing his or her job, it is the fault of the personnel hiring system for having hired the person to do it, not the fault of the individual inappropriately placed in the job. Unfortunately, most organizations fail to recognize that individual performance is largely the result of the systems in which they work. Thus, variations in performance of individual job coaches may be the result of variations in the demands of different job sites or employers or a multitude of other factors and have little if anything to do with the individual performers.

Dr. Deming makes these assertions based on statistical methods: using control charts (introduced in Chapter 10) to determine common and special causes of performance variation. If formulas used to develop the control chart result in all performers falling within the chart's "control limits," despite apparently wide individual variations, then it is the "common causes" (i.e., the causes that are within the system itself) that are the root cause of the performance variation. Thus, there is no basis for evaluating performance of individuals, since the systems are the reasons for the variations (Deming, 1986).

> "(A performance rating system) is unfair, as it ascribes to the people in a group differences that may be caused totally by the system that they work in." (Deming, 1986, p. 102)

If individual performance appraisal systems are not only ineffective for what they are designed to accomplish but also counterproductive, then what should an organization do in their place? First of all, do not assume that an organization *needs* a system for evaluating individual performance. Scholtes (1987) recommends determining the purposes you are trying to fulfill with the existing system, and then "unbundling" them: treating each purpose separately, and building a separate process or system for each. Then, it is possible to work on improving each of those processes to improve its performance. Therefore, recognize that people need feedback, not evaluation, and build systems that provide feedback

---

REPLACING THE ANNUAL PERFORMANCE RATING

W. Edwards Deming (1986) suggests replacing the annual performance rating with "modern principles of leadership" (p. 116):

- Provide education in leadership; use methods to improve outcomes rather than to rate people.
- Do more careful selection of people for positions.
- Provide better training for employees once they are in their jobs.
- Act as a leader and colleague rather than as a judge.
- Provide merit pay to groups involved in processes and systems, rather than to individuals.
- Recognize that employees need feedback and two-way communication, but not a top-down evaluation.
- Use numerical measures of performance as the basis for improving processes and systems, rather than for evaluating individual performance.

---

well. Help employees to get feedback from their "customers" and "suppliers" (see Chapter 3), as well as other team members. Provide recognition and rewards for uncovering problems and contributing to team efforts. Use special projects, lateral moves, and project teams as a basis for determining promotions. (Better yet, move to a flattened hierarchy so that promotions up the hierarchy are not the way in which employees measure their contribution to the organization.) At the very least, believe that employees *want* to do a good job, and help them to improve the processes in which they work so that they can do so.

Strategy #7.   Improve Employee Commitment and Contribution: Actively Work To Drive Fear Out of the Organization

> "No one can put in his best performance unless he feels secure." (Deming, 1986, p. 59)

Fears are natural emotions that are caused by anticipating danger, discomfort, or loss. However, fear, when it is prevalent in an organization, can be devastating. Employee fears rob an organization of its full potential by limiting the potential contribution of the staff and thus reducing the overall capability of the organization, including its long-term growth and viability (Lowe & McBean, 1989). Lowe and McBean (1989) describe six "monsters of fear": 1) fear of reprisal, 2) fear of failure, 3) fear of not knowing, 4) fear of providing information, 5) fear of giving up control, and 6) fear of change. These fears interfere with teamwork, fill relationships between managers and employees with distrust, and suppress the contribution of ideas. When employees work in an environment of fear, they do not openly question existing methods or the direction of supervisors, and they avoid taking risks and accepting responsibility for their actions. They try to cover up problems and errors, rather than revealing them. This desire to hide problems even leads to purposeful inaccuracy in data and re-

THE MONSTERS OF FEAR, DEFINED

Fear of Reprisal: Fear of being disciplined or fired, of receiving a poor performance evaluation, of being transferred to a less desirable job, of being humiliated, of being outcast by others, of being blamed for problems

Fear of Failure: Fear of being wrong, of making a mistake, either of which could lead to reprisal

Fear of Providing Information: Fear of pointing out problems, of being blamed for the problem the information reveals

Fear of Not Knowing: Fear of not having the information that you are expected to have

Fear of Giving Up Control: Fear of losing the balance of power, fear of losing control of people, fear of losing authority

Fear of Change: Fear of losing power, of new things, of the unknown (Deming, 1986; Lowe & McBean, 1989).

ports. As Dr. Deming (1986) states ". . . where there is fear, there will be wrong figures" (p. 266).

To reduce the negative effects of fear, managers must take action to reduce the sources of fear throughout the organization. This strategy is so important that "Drive Out Fear" is one of Dr. Deming's 14 points for the transformation of Western management (Deming, 1986). However, fear is built into the fabric of most organizations, and, even when it is not, people come into organizations with a history of fear developed through experience and stories from others. Therefore, driving out fear will require diligent and ongoing attention to eliminate both the large and small generators of fear.

INCREASING EMPLOYEE COMMITMENT AND CONTRIBUTION

According to the theories of behaviorists, employees continue to work for an organization because the rewards they receive for doing so are sufficient to outweigh the cost of the behavior that they must use to continue working. Maslowe would say it is because the job is fulfilling some aspect of that individual's hierarchy of needs. From the perspective of quality improvement, employee motivation, commitment, and contribution largely are outcomes of the systems, environment, and culture in which they work. Therefore, the strategies discussed in this chapter and throughout this book related to enhancing the dignity and value of all employees, promoting teamwork and self-managing teams, improving personnel systems including staff training and feedback, eliminating annual performance evaluations, driving out fear, and implementing systematic methods for improving organizational performance are all

SUGGESTIONS FOR DRIVING OUT FEAR

- Eliminate individual performance appraisals (see Strategy #6).
- Try to put an end to gossip that spreads negative stories about "what will happen to you if . . . ."
- Stop blaming employees for the problems of the system.
- Follow through on the suggestions made by employees.
- Reward employees for questioning the status quo, revealing problems, and offering suggestions for improving processes and systems.
- Build awareness throughout the organization of the need for change (e.g., for change to integrated employment services, for change to incorporate methods of Continuous Quality Improvement, for change to eliminate a culture of fear).
- Help all employees understand the nature of all planned changes.
- Create a shared vision in the organization so that all employees are working toward the same ends.
- Implement systematic methods of quality improvement to demonstrate that the organization looks for the sources of problems in systems and processes, rather than seeking to blame individual people.
- Train all employees in using systematic methods for problem-solving and decision-making.
- Involve employees throughout the organization in planning and carrying out change efforts.
- Assume a management philosophy that is based on trusting that employees want to do a good job and contribute to achieving the mission of the organization.
- Treat all problems as opportunities for improvement.
- Reinforce *everyone* (not just managers) for thinking and creativity.
- Address the problems in management systems and processes early in the change effort.
- Promote collaboration, cooperation, and teamwork.
- Find and eliminate the barriers that keep employees from doing things right the first time.
- Encourage open discussions in meetings that include participants from different levels and parts of the organization.
- Deal with facts without emotion.
- Be personally willing to speak up and share problems and concerns.
- Stop second-guessing the decisions made by employees.
- Find what is working well, including processes and people, and ask how they can be improved further.

important. Each of these strategies has the potential to support improvements in employee motivation, commitment, and contribution; therefore, each has the potential for making a significant difference in how successful an organization is in achieving its mission.

REFERENCES

Albin, J.M. (1989). *Inservice training for supported employment specialists: Results of competency validation surveys.* (Available from: Specialized Training Program, University of Oregon, Eugene, OR 97403-1235.)

Bennett, R.D. (1988). Improving performance without training: A three step approach. *Performance & Instruction, 1*(1), 58–68.

Buckley, J., Albin, J.M., & Mank, D. (1988). Competency-based staff training for supported employment. In G.T. Bellamy, L.E. Rhodes, D.M. Mank, & J.M. Albin, *Supported employment: A community implementation guide* (pp. 229–245). Baltimore: Paul H. Brookes Publishing Co.

Butterworth, J., Steere, D.E., Pancsofar, E.L., & Powell, T.H. (1990). The search for superman or wonderwoman: Job design and organizational supports for the supported employment professional. *Journal of Rehabilitation Administration, May,* 37–42.

Deming, W.E. (1986). *Out of the crisis.* Cambridge: Massachusetts Institute of Technology, Center for Advanced Study in Engineering.

Fosler, R.S. (1989). Demographics of the 90s: The issues and implications for public policy. *Vital Speeches of the Day, 55*(18), 572–576.

Fraegon, S. (1982). A commentary response. In B. Campbell & V. Baldwin (Eds.), *Severely handicapped/hearing impaired students* (pp. 33–45). Baltimore: Paul H. Brookes Publishing Co.

Gilbert, T.F. (1978). *Human competence: Engineering worthy performance.* New York: McGraw-Hill.

Golin, A.K., & Ducanis, A.J. (1981). Preparation for teamwork: A model for interdisciplinary education. *Teacher Education and Special Education, 4*(1), 25–30.

Hagner, D. (1989). *The social integration of supported employment employees: A qualitative study.* Syracuse, NY: Syracuse University, Center on Human Policy.

Harper, J.D., Eder, T., Ramsing, K., & Watson, D. (1990). *Oregon supported employment: A growing labor resource for business and industry.* Eugene: The Task Force on Business Participation in Supported Employment.

Helge, D. (1981). Multidisciplinary personnel preparation: A successful model of preservice team training for service delivery. *Teacher Education and Special Education, 4*(1), 13–17.

Herzberg, F. (1968). One more time: How do you motivate employees? *Harvard Business Review, 46,* 53–62.

Herzberg, F., Mausner, B., & Snyderman, B.B. (1959). *The motivation of work.* New York: John Wiley & Sons.

Johnston, W.B., & Packer, A.H. (1987). *Workforce 2000: Work and workers for the 21st century.* Indianapolis: Hudson Institute.

Knowles, M. (1980). *Modern practice of adult education.* Chicago: Follett.

Kregel, J., & Sale, P. (1988). Preservice preparation of supported employment professionals. In P. Wehman & M.S. Moon (Eds.), *Vocational rehabilitation and supported employment* (pp. 129–143). Baltimore: Paul H. Brookes Publishing Co.

Lowe, T.A., & McBean, G.M. (1989). Honesty without fear. *Quality Progress, 22*(11), 30–34.

Mank, D., Rhodes, L., & Sandow, D. (1991). *Training co-workers to teach job tasks to employees with mental disabilities.* Unpublished manuscript, Specialized Training Program, University of Oregon, Eugene.

Peters, T. (1987). *Thriving on chaos: Handbook for a management revolution.* New York: Harper & Row.

Peterson, L.J. (1988). 13 powerful principles for training success. *Performance & Instruction, 27*(2), 47–55.

Rhodes, L., Sandow, D., Mank, D., Buckley, J., & Albin, J. (1991). Expanding the role of employers in supported employment. *Journal of The Association for Persons with Severe Handicaps, 16*(4), 213–217.

Scholtes, P. (1987). *An elaboration on Deming's teachings on performance appraisal.* Madison, WI: Joiner Associates, Inc.

Udvari-Solner, A. (1990, December). *Variables associated with the integration of individuals with intellectual disabilities in supported employment settings.* Presentation made at the 17th Annual TASH Conference, Chicago.

Wehman, P., Kregel, J., & Shafer, M.S. (1989). *Emerging trends in the national supported employment initiative: A preliminary analysis of twenty-seven states.* Richmond: Virginia Commonwealth University, Rehabilitation Research and Training Center.

Wexley, K.N., & Latham, G.P. (1982). *Developing and training human resources in organizations.* Glenview, IL: Scott, Foresman.

Winking, D.L., Trach, J.S., Rusch, F.R., & Tines, J. (1989). Profile of Illinois supported employment specialists: An analysis of educational background, experience, and related employment variables. *Journal of The Association for Persons with Severe Handicaps, 14*(4), 278–282.

Zeleny, M. (1989). Quality management systems: Subject to continuous improvement? *Human Systems Management, 8*(1), 1–3.

Zemke, R. (1989). Employee orientation: A process, not a program. *Training, 26*(8), 33–38.

Chapter 12

A Blueprint for Managing the Quality Transformation

The preceding chapters have introduced quality improvement principles, strategies, and tools as a method of improving organizational and individual performance in integrated employment settings, rehabilitation, and other human services. However, many questions may remain. Where does an organization begin its quality transformation process? What first steps should management take to introduce new methods? How should an organization plan for change? What resources are required to get started? The transformation into an organization infused with the philosophy and approaches of Continuous Quality Improvement may take years to accomplish. Organizations attempting to changeover from facility-based to community-integrated employment services, while adopting quality improvement methods, have a difficult and lengthy process in front of them. The purpose of this chapter is to offer some recommendations to help organizations implement the previously presented principles and strategies in their efforts to pursue organization-wide quality transformation.

The suggestions offered in this chapter, however, provide only an approximate outline for an organizational change strategy. Each organization must define—and continuously redefine—its own plan to guide its change effort. The principles of quality improvement pertain to planning and managing the process of the quality transformation, just as they apply to the other organizational processes such as job development, job analysis, staff orientation, or office management practices. Therefore, the continuous Shewhart Cycle of Plan-Do-Check-Act must be applied to organizational change efforts, as well.

Quality improvement involves expanding the decision-making authority of all personnel in an agency. Thus, the management sequence presented here relies on the formation of project or quality improvement teams both to manage typical organizational functions and to carry out the new quality improvement efforts (see Chapter 9). This chapter assumes that the impetus for organizational change has come from within, from the top management of the organization. Whether or not this is the case, the activities for pursuing top management support would simply become an integral part of an organization's blueprint for change. This chapter provides a few recommendations for managing the overall transformation. Use this chapter in conjunction with the *Self-Assessment Guide for Changeover to Supported Employment* that was presented in Chapter 7 to pursue the dual objectives of changeover and quality transformation.

MANAGING THE QUALITY TRANSFORMATION

Secure a Quality Advisor.   **Plan**
    Select a Quality Advisor.
    Define the role of the Quality Advisor.
Establish a Guidance Team
    Select participants.
    Define the purpose of the Guidance Team.
    Educate the Guidance Team.
Develop a preliminary blueprint for change.
Implement ongoing organization-wide training.   **Do**
Activate one team.
    Select pilot project.
    Select initial team members.
    Define purpose of team.
    Provide training.
    Implement project.

Evaluate pilot project.   **Check**

Revise blueprint.   **Act-Plan**

Implement revised blueprint.   **Do**

Evaluate.   **Check**

Plan for continuous improvement.   **Act-Plan**

RECOMMENDATION #1: SECURE A QUALITY ADVISOR

As early as possible in the effort to pursue Total Quality Management, an organization should identify a individual—preferably someone from outside of the organization—who can serve as a *Quality Advisor*. A Quality Advisor is a mentor who
assists an organization or a specific quality improvement team to most effectively
achieve its quality objectives (Scholtes, 1988). The Quality Advisor plays a pivotal
role in keeping the organization moving forward in its change process, whether that
change is solely implementing quality methods or also incorporating changeover to
supported employment.

A Quality Advisor is very much like a coach, teaching, guiding, and supporting
the quality transformation effort. The Advisor's job is to help keep the organization
or specific project teams on track through the quality improvement process. This
may be done through observing team functioning, working with team leaders to
plan and evaluate team activities, and facilitating team building and conflict resolution. Quality Advisors, as needed, provide training in scientific methods or other
tools to promote effective team functioning, and provide support to staff members
in implementing those tools in real settings. With changeover to supported employment, Quality Advisors also may monitor changeover efforts and provide training
and feedback to staff members who are assuming new community roles. However,

ROLE OF A QUALITY ADVISOR

- Observe team meetings.
- Work with the team leader to help in preparing for, structuring, and evaluating team meetings.
- Assist individuals and teams in selecting data collection and display methods.
- Provide instruction to teams and to individual staff members on principles and methods of quality improvement.
- Help facilitate group process, team-building, and conflict resolution.
- Coach teams and individual staff members in applying needed skills and tools.
- Advise the management team responsible for planning and overseeing the change process on strategies for making the change process more effective.

to be most effective, Quality Advisors must remain removed from the day-to-day detail of operating the program.

Select a Quality Advisor

A Quality Advisor is a person who has training and experience in the principles of Continuous Quality Improvement, scientific approaches, and working with groups. For organizations undergoing changeover to supported employment, it is useful for the Quality Advisor to have knowledge and skills in rehabilitation services in general, as well as experience with integrated employment and the changeover process. However, such a person, with expertise in both fields, may be difficult to find.

Several possible resources may exist in any community, however. For example, some communities have developed local "Quality Councils," made up of individuals from both the private and public sectors. Quality Council members have an interest in promoting the principles of quality management throughout their communities (Lusk, Tribus, Schwinn, & Schwinn, 1989). A member of such a council might be willing to serve as a Quality Advisor. In addition, technical assistance consultants, managers of other employment service organizations that have undergone a quality transformation, college or university faculty, staff from state or county funding agencies, or management-level volunteers or consultants from business or the public sector may appropriately fill the role of Quality Advisor if they possess the requisite knowledge and skills, as well as the time and commitment needed to support the organization's change process. As supported employment continues to develop, more and more states are developing personnel who can assist with quality improvement efforts. For example as of 1992, Oregon, Georgia, Wisconsin, Virginia, and California, among others, had projects that offered training and support for Continuous Quality Improvement in supported employment or rehabilitation.

Unfortunately at this time, because the application of Continuous Quality Improvement methodology to community employment and rehabilitation services is so new, many organizations may find that *selecting* a Quality Advisor probably will be less of an issue than *finding* one with the requisite knowledge, skills, and commitment to assist in transformation efforts. Do not give up hope, however. An individual who is committed to helping the organization, has good communication skills, is knowledgeable about integrated employment services, is interested in *learning* the principles and methods of quality improvement, and is willing to put in the effort required to stay one or two steps ahead of the organization's transformation needs may be a valuable resource as well. An organization comes to understand Continuous Quality Improvement best by doing it; having a would-be Quality Advisor work with an organization through its transformation and change process may be the best answer for both parties. Applying the principles and practices of quality improvement to rehabilitation and community-based employment will require a struggle; finding someone to support the organization through that struggle, even if you are learning side-by-side, should help.

As an organization matures through its quality transformation, it should assist a few of its staff members to become skilled as Quality Advisors, able to offer support to teams in which they are not members. An organization with several project teams may find it useful to develop a cadre of internal Quality Advisors to support the efforts of internal teams, and to exchange with other organizations. Developing internal Quality Advisors requires that the chosen individuals learn the basic tools of the scientific approach and the skills related to project planning, as well as the basics of team development, managing meetings, and group facilitation. Internal Quality Advisors, however, should not be considered team members nor team leaders, for they must maintain an objective view of team functioning and needs to fulfill their role effectively.

Define the Role of the Quality Advisor

For whoever fills the "position" of Quality Advisor, clearly define that individual's particular role in the organization's transformation, and, on a regular basis, review that definition, the Advisor's performance, and the relationship between the Advisor and the team overseeing the change process. The ACORNS Test and Performance Template strategies presented in Chapter 8 may be useful in completing this step.

RECOMMENDATION #2: ESTABLISH A GUIDANCE TEAM

A Guidance Team is a group assembled to lead the organization in its quality transformation process (Scholtes, 1988; Scholtes & Hacquebord, 1987). The team and its members must have the responsibility and authority needed to manage the change, including selecting projects, allocating resources, removing barriers to change, and implementing strategies for continuing improvement.

The Guidance Team, with the support of the Quality Advisor, is the internal group responsible for managing the quality transformation of the organization or for overseeing the work of specific quality improvement teams. An organization undergoing changeover from facility-based to integrated community employment services should use the same Guidance Team to plan and monitor changeover efforts and to lead the quality transformation. The Guidance Team may, as a group, select the Quality Advisor, quality improvement projects and objectives, team leaders, and team members. However, one of its most important roles is to provide leadership for the organization's change: planning objectives and change strategies, implementing

"The guidance team is a group of managers and other key leaders who oversee and support the activities of one or more project teams. Typically, these are the same managers who chose the projects and appointed the teams in the first place, but other people may be involved. . . . Guidance team members do not conduct the actual project; they guide the efforts of the project team. They appoint the project team leader, and together with that leader determine the project's boundaries and select the other team members. (The project team leader is therefore the "internal customer" of the guidance team.) They make certain the project team has whatever resources it needs to be successful." (Scholtes, 1988, ch. 3, p. 7)

plans, checking their effectiveness in achieving objectives, and acting to revise plans or to execute their broad implementation in the organization. These "blueprints" (Scholtes & Hacquebord, 1987) for change are described more fully below.

Guidance Team members also promote the transformation and instruct others in its methods. Their position and influence as individuals should be used to encourage cooperation and support throughout the organization for the changeover and transformation processes. The quality transformation will not be achieved through 2-hour meetings held once a week. It is achieved through members of the organization embracing a new way of working together to achieve a common purpose, and living this new way in every activity. To achieve this, first the Guidance Team members must demonstrate the change: by listening and problem-solving instead of placing blame, by using scientific methods to make decisions rather than using guesswork, by viewing other personnel as their personal customers rather than as their employees, by discussing quality methods in casual conversations, by eliminating the symbols of the old hierarchical way of doing business, and by finding ways to build bridges between customers and staff and among various departments of the organization. Thus, Guidance Team members lead the organization's transformation both as a group, by planning and evaluating the transformation effort, and as individuals by exemplifying the new methods in everything they do.

ROLE OF THE GUIDANCE TEAM

- Plan, implement, review, and revise the organization's blueprint for change.
- Encourage cooperation and support from all parts of the organization.
- Oversee and support quality-focused activities.
- Identify project mission and goals.
- Determine needed resources.
- May select team leaders, Quality Advisor, and team members.
- Clear away barriers for the project teams, providing authority and implementing changes for the teams.

Select Guidance Team Members

In a typical rehabilitation organization the Guidance Team might be composed of individuals filling positions such as executive director and/or associate director, rehabilitation services director, marketing director, community employment manager, facility manager, and office manager. Indeed, the core of the Guidance Team may comprise the already-existing management team of an organization. To avoid possible later issues in communication, the Guidance Team also should include one or two representatives of direct service staff and a member of the board of directors. While the executive director need not be a full member of the group, the executive's complete support and at least partial participation are required to facilitate Guidance Team effectiveness in the organization. But, in most rehabilitation organizations undergoing changeover to community employment in addition to the quality transformation, the executive's full participation probably is imperative.

In addition to management and direct service personnel from the organization, consider carefully whether or not including the representatives of external customer groups (e.g., a funder, a consumer of services, or a business person) might be significant. For example, it might be important for some organizations to include a funder as an ongoing member of the Guidance Team, not only for that person's expertise and influence in the community service system, but also for the opportunity to educate that funder on the principles and methods of quality improvement or on the process of changeover to integrated employment services. Alternatively, some members by design may participate on a part-time basis or only for particular topics. For example, a few consumers may be invited to participate in those meetings in which the Guidance Team will address issues that most affect consumers or in which the Guidance Team needs to obtain consumer input to define or evaluate quality. Seek a

---

SAMPLE GUIDANCE TEAM MEMBERSHIP

Quality Advisor:	Consultant from university-based supported employment technical assistance project
Team leader:	Executive director
Team members:	Rehabilitation services manager
	Production manager
	Office manager
	2 Coordinators (who each provide support to 4–6 staff members who work at individual and clustered job sites)
	1 Job coach
Ad hoc members (Invited to participate in specific meetings):	Employment training specialist (job developer and job coach functions)
	Director of county developmental disabilities services program (funder)
Total full-time members:	7 + Quality Advisor

team of no more than three to eight members, striking a careful balance between adequate representation and unwieldly size. Select a team whose members include those in authority, as well as individuals who are viewed as opinion leaders and doers in the organization.

Define the Purpose of the Guidance Team

After selecting Guidance Team members, define the purpose of the team so that all members clearly understand their individual and collective roles in the change process. The ACORNS Test and Performance Templates (presented in Chapter 8) are particularly useful strategies that may be applied by the Quality Advisor or Guidance Team leader to help the Guidance Team complete this step. For an organization whose managers are new to the principles and methods of quality improvement, using these tools early in the transformation process offers an opportunity for managers to experience the power of quality improvement methods from the very beginning of the transformation process. The basic template developed by the Guidance Team for the quality transformation process at the organization described in Chapter 13 is presented here as an example. This template is only an example, however, for the process of developing their own performance template will assist Guidance Team members to achieve both clarity and consensus on their roles in their own organization's transformation.

Educate the Guidance Team

For a quality transformation to be successful, top managers and other Guidance Team members must "learn to become leaders, exemplars, and teachers of quality" (Scholtes & Hacquebord, 1987, p. 15). Fulfilling these roles requires that they continuously seek education on quality principles and methods so that they are able to integrate the quality effort into all aspects of the organization, encouraging cooperation and involvement at all levels.

SAMPLE GUIDANCE TEAM PERFORMANCE TEMPLATE

Guidance Team Purpose:

- Improve organizational performance on mission.

Major accomplishments/responsibilities of the Guidance Team:

- Define and organize quality improvement teams.
- Coach problem-solving processes and use of quality improvement tools.
- Troubleshoot organizational performance against the mission, and adjust organizational structure and resources to improve performance.
- Ensure continuous and just-in-time education and training that has a functional emphasis; that is, it is tied to daily activities with "on-site" feedback.
- Maintain communication across teams; share quality improvement methods developed or discussed by each team.

The Guidance Team members may obtain education on quality principles and methods through a variety of sources, such as:

- Attending presentations provided by the Quality Advisor or other team members
- Reading books and articles on quality improvement
- Taking a college course on statistical methods
- Attending a workshop on group facilitation methods or participative management systems
- Taking a course on human resource management, manufacturing process controls, or decision sciences from a university's college of business
- Participating in training on quality principles and methods offered at a local business for its own personnel
- Joining a local community Quality Council
- Applying and analyzing the effectiveness of quality principles and methods in all activities they perform in the organization
- Finding a course on quality improvement methods presented by a local community college or university

Whatever the methods used to acquire greater knowledge and skills related to quality transformation, it is critical that Guidance Team members actively, immediately, and continually seek additional education and resources on quality improvement.

RECOMMENDATION #3: DEVELOP A PRELIMINARY BLUEPRINT FOR CHANGE

One of the most important roles filled by the Guidance Team is planning and evaluating the transformation effort. Referred to as "blueprints" by Peter Scholtes and Heero Hacquebord (1987), quality transformation plans developed by top management encourage long-term commitment to change, specifying targeted areas and strategies for change while discouraging uncoordinated, haphazard, or "shotgun" efforts. Without a blueprint, top managers might be tempted to delegate change responsibilities, to manage the process through "playing it by ear," or to try to implement the transformation in too many areas at one time. Quality transformation and organizational changeover from facility-based to community-based employment services require careful planning and targeted efforts to succeed. It is the responsibility of the Guidance Team to ensure that plans are developed, evaluated, and adjusted to best meet the organization's changing needs. Develop a blueprint that covers a 6-month to 2-year period, with greater detail in the initial 6-month plan. Every 3–6 months, review and adjust the plan, adding detail for the next 6-month period.

"The more profound, comprehensive and widespread the proposed change, the more absolute is the need for deep understanding and active leadership by the top managers. The transformation to a quality organization is such a change." (Scholtes & Hacquebord, 1987, p. 14)

Questions for Developing a Blueprint

The development of a blueprint requires that the Guidance Team ask and answer a number of questions about how the transformation will proceed. Sample questions to assist in that effort are provided in the Appendix at the end of this chapter. When the quality transformation is coupled with changeover from facility-based to integrated employment services, the *Self-Assessment Guide for Changeover to Supported Employment*, provided in Chapter 7, offers an excellent tool for prioritizing change efforts. Follow the instructions in Chapter 7 for using the *Guide* each time the Guidance Team considers developing or revising the blueprint for change, or needs to target the next priority.

Implement Ongoing Organization-Wide Training

To ensure success, part of the blueprint for change must address how members of the organization will provide information on quality principles, methods, and current efforts. As discussed in Chapter 4, success in changeover to integrated employment services requires a supportive organizational culture. The ongoing organization-wide training that is made available during the change process is a critical factor in developing that culture. However, Continuous Quality Improvement is much more than a culture; staff members also must become adept at applying the concepts and systematic methods to everyday issues in their jobs.

Include in training the fundamental quality principles; quality methods, including concepts of a systematic approach and specific problem-solving tools; and techniques for facilitating group process. Also include training more specifically geared to community-based employment services: discussions of values along with more specific knowledge or skill-oriented training. Most important, however, treat training sessions as a regular part of every week, rather than as larger-scale special events that occur only once or twice a year. If possible, videotape training sessions to allow staff members who are dispersed in community employment locations an opportunity to view them as well. Chapter 11 includes additional guidelines for developing a staff training program.

Select a Pilot Project

For organizations embarking on a transformation process, it is important that the Guidance Team select an initial pilot project for testing the transformation efforts. Attempting initially to implement a quality transformation across all parts of the organization at the same time is likely to result in failure, as the Guidance Team will be unable to monitor and support change on so many fronts. In addition, the pilot project can offer a demonstration of the change to other members of the organization, helping to build a culture to support eventual full transformation. A pilot project offers the Guidance Team an opportunity to test strategies for effectiveness and to make needed adjustments prior to full implementation. Probably one of the most important reasons to use a pilot project, however, is that for most organizations the Guidance Team members are just learning about quality principles and methods as well. A pilot project gives them an opportunity to try their new knowledge and skills in a real setting, but does not force them to stretch too far. However, the *Point—Counterpoint* shown presents an alternative view on pilot projects.

Selecting the first project is very important for it is likely that the whole organization will be watching for its success or failure. See Chapter 9 for a list of general criteria for project selection, and an explanation of errors commonly made in project selection. For the first project, however, also try to choose a project that:

- Will have a direct impact on the organization's internal or external customers.
- Involves a process that occurs on at least a daily basis somewhere in the organization.
- Is relatively simple, with clear start and end points.
- Is important to carry out.
- Is highly visible.
- Can rely on the cooperation of key players.

POINT–COUNTERPOINT: SHOULD SEVERAL QUALITY IMPROVEMENT TEAMS BE ESTABLISHED FROM THE ONSET OF THE TRANSFORMATION?

Some organizations will find that taking a "pilot project" approach to introducing quality improvement methods leads to cultural problems. Staff members not involved with the pilot group may distrust its efforts. They may feel that the group is successful only because it is "stacked" with exceptional resources. Some personnel may be jealous of the attention the members of the pilot project team receive from the organization's managers and Quality Advisor; they may even work to undermine its effectiveness.

Part of the role of the Guidance Team must be to consider whether using a pilot project approach will be successful, or if it will create too many problems. If the Guidance Team believes a broad, organization-wide effort is required, then, consider the following recommendations:

1. *Solicit volunteers.* Do not force personnel—whether they are direct service staff, mid-level supervisory staff, or managers—to participate in the effort. Some people will want to see how it works before stepping into the process or will need to be convinced of the effectiveness of the methods by the outcomes achieved by others. Allow personnel to choose to participate in a team, or to get support for trying out some of the methods individually.

2. *Implement organization-wide training before establishing a large number of projects.* Staff members will do best when they have some understanding of the fundamental principles and the basic concepts of systematic methods. Although they need not learn the terminology or academic aspects of Continuous Quality Improvement or Total Quality Management, a good foundation in the concepts will help individuals and teams move forward in their projects.

3. *Do not just talk quality.* People in organizations have grown accustomed to management fads—fads that reflect a lot of words but not much action. When organization-wide implementation is necessary, do not just train. Consider establishing a single project in which all members of the organization can participate in some way, using that as a way of introducing concepts and principles. The "Staff Are Customers, Too" project described in Chapter 13 was a strategy for involving all staff members in an initial effort to embed quality principles and methods in one organization.

RECOMMENDATION #4: IMPLEMENT AN INITIAL PROJECT AND TEAM

Implementing the pilot project presents a challenge to the Guidance Team to introduce organizational change in a way that offers the greatest chance of success. Although this section discusses the project from the viewpoint of the first quality improvement project carried out by the organization, the Guidance Team will use similar steps in implementing later projects throughout the life of the organization. See Chapter 9 for a general discussion of project teams and the quality improvement process.

Select Initial Team Members

Selecting team members to carry out the first quality improvement project also must be done thoughtfully. If team members are not supportive, they can sabotage the effort. If only the highest qualified staff members are included, the project may not give an accurate picture of future performance. If only favorite staff members are selected, staff jealousies and distrust may grow.

Therefore, in selecting members for the first team, weigh a variety of considerations. Are staff members in general resistant to the change efforts? Should the staff be allowed to elect members for the first team? Should volunteers be solicited? Should the Guidance Team select the staff members who are most supportive of the change? Should they select staff members who represent different departments and areas of expertise? Whoever is selected, include at least one member who is viewed informally by other staff members as an opinion leader, and try to include a majority of members who are supportive of the change. Include one member of the Guidance Team as a member—but not as the team leader—to provide a strong link between the Guidance Team and the first project team.

Define Purpose of Initial Team

Once a team is assembled, it is important to clearly define the purpose of the team. This may be done jointly by the Guidance Team and the members of the quality improvement team, or it may be determined by the Guidance Team alone. In addition, it is possible to permit the quality improvement team itself to select its own project. However, because project selection is so critical, particularly early in the

---

STEPS FOR IMPLEMENTING THE PILOT PROJECT

- Select pilot project.
- Select initial team members.
- Define purpose of initial team.
- Provide training.
- Implement pilot project.
- Evaluate pilot project.

transformation process, beware. At the start of the transformation, staff members who are members of the first team probably have received little training and have even less experience with the principles and methods of quality improvement. They could become bogged down in an onerous process of project selection, losing motivation for the project before it even begins. Or, they may choose a project that is far too complex for early efforts. Therefore, it is recommended that the Guidance Team select the initial projects to be undertaken, or, at the very least, actively participate with the first team in the project selection process.

Assuming that the Guidance Team is selecting the project, they should identify their general goals for the project and the expected results. Avoid setting numerical objectives, however, because they should not be used to evaluate the team's performance. It is most helpful for the Guidance Team to prepare a mission statement for the project, setting boundaries as well as starting and ending points. In addition, indicate the resources available to the team, including time, money, and equipment. Clearly define any special authority that is being given to the team to help them fulfill their mission, such as calling in outside resources, or implementing changes to the targeted process. Finally, indicate how the Guidance Team will interact with the quality improvement team. Will they meet together, and, if so, how often? What sort of records or reports are required? The ultimate success of the team may hinge on the care taken in this initial planning and definition step.

Provide Training

In addition to the ongoing, organization-wide training program described above and in Chapter 11, the Guidance Team should make sure that members of the initial team receive the special training needed to attack the problem at hand effectively. Because they are forming the first team, their training in quality principles and methods will likely need to be accelerated over that of the larger organization. Provide training on methods just before the team is likely to need them, so that team members can practice them in the course of carrying out the quality improvement project.

Implement Project

Before this step, each part of the quality improvement transformation described in this chapter is to be performed by, or in cooperation with, the Guidance Team. The steps for implementing the project itself, however, should be undertaken by the quality improvement team alone. The team should implement steps such as those suggested in Chapter 9 to address the defined problem: analyze possible causes, collect data to identify a root cause, select and implement improvement strategies, analyze data, and plan for continuous improvement. Throughout this process, members of the Guidance Team, or the Quality Advisor, should work closely with the quality improvement team, offering "just-in-time" training and support on needed concepts and tools. Learning about systematic methods in the course of a real project is a good way of making those methods come to life for staff members. Track the progress of the team (and of subsequent teams) using a chart posted on the wall, such as the Team Status Chart presented in Figure 12.1.

Process Step	Pilot Project Team	Project Team Q	Project Team J
Step 1: Define the problem	Begun: 1/15 Completed: 2/25	Begun: 5/1 Completed: 6/1	Completed 6/1
Step 2: Analyze possible causes	Begun: 2/25 Completed: 3/17	Begun: 6/1 Completed: 6/8	
Step 3: Collect data to identify a basic cause	Begun: 3/18 Completed: 4/2	Begun: 6/9 Completed: 6/30	
Step 4: Select strategies for improvement	Completed: 4/23		
Step 5: Implement improvement strategies	Begun: 5/1 Checked: 5/20 Checked: 6/5		
Step 6: Complete data analysis	Checked: 5/21 Completed: 6/6		
Step 7: Plan for continuous improvement	Plan presented to Guidance Team, with report of project on 6/20		
Status	Completed	In-process	Forming team

Figure 12.1.   Sample Team Status Chart.

Evaluate Pilot Project

Throughout the work of the initial, or subsequent, quality improvement teams, the Guidance Team continues to play an important role in monitoring team performance, removing barriers to success, and providing needed resources to assist the team to reach desired goals. Therefore, it is important that the Guidance Team maintain close communication with the first (and subsequent) teams so that they can adjust strategies—or the organization's blueprint for change—based on current information and performance. The experience of the pilot project for quality improvement is likely to give the Guidance Team the best information about how the quality transformation in the organization is apt to proceed. Issues of faculty team selection, insufficient training, inadequate resources, improper project choice, and poor team motivation are but a few problems that may surface during the first project. Careful monitoring and evaluation of the project will help the Guidance Team address issues before broader implementation of the transformation begins.

Treat the pilot project just as any other quality improvement project, identifying possible factors to support its success, collecting and analyzing process and results data, and adjusting strategies based on those data. In all this, the Guidance Team's project is, "What are the factors required to support a successful project team?", rather than the specific content of the initial team's project.

RECOMMENDATION #5: IMPLEMENT THE SHEWHART CYCLE

This recommendation reflects the ongoing nature of quality improvement efforts that are embedded in the Shewhart Cycle of Plan-Do-Check-Act. Based on the experience with the pilot project, the Guidance Team should have sufficient information to determine whether to continue using the previously defined blueprint or to make adjustments to improve the chances for success in the change process. Evaluating and revising the blueprint for change is an ongoing process but should be done formally at least every 3–6 months. The blueprint represents the organization's plan for substantial change and requires close attention if it is to be successful. Although changes should be made when needed, the plan also must be respected so that managers are not tempted to ignore it, expand efforts too rapidly, or delegate their leadership responsibilities. As in every aspect of Total Quality Management, the blueprint is a document that should always be treated as a draft that is subject to continuous review and improvement. Implement the Shewhart Cycle for adjusting the blueprint, as a strategy for supporting the growth of the continuously upward spiral of quality improvement. Implementing Continuous Quality Improvement requires a never-ending commitment and watchfulness based on the Shewhart Cycle.

THE QUALITY TRILOGY

Joseph Juran (1986) has identified the "non-uniformities" that exist in any company as some of the powerful forces that resist a new, cohesive approach to managing for quality. These non-uniformities, translated into the field of human services, include:

- *The multiple functions of an organization,* such as in-house production, rehabilitation functions, training and support functions, office operations, management, and so forth. The personnel involved in each of the functions view their roles as unique and special to the organization.
- *The multiple levels in the organizational hierarchy,* from board members and executive director to hourly office or front-line workers. These positions vary in terms of, for example, background training and experience requirements, responsibilities and duties, and/or working conditions.
- *The multiple services and products of the organization,* such as sheltered employment services, community-based employment support services, individualized case management services, or manufactured products. Each of these differs, for example, in customers, technology, resources, and constraints.

Juran insists that these uniquenesses "constitute a serious obstacle to a unity of direction" and suggests that this obstacle can be overcome with the application of "a universal way of thinking about quality" which will fit all functions, levels, and services of the organization (Juran, 1986, p. 20). He calls his solution "The Quality Trilogy."

The Quality Trilogy (also sometimes referred to as the Juran Trilogy) recognizes that managing for quality requires implementing three basic processes: quality plan-

JURAN'S QUALITY TRILOGY

Quality planning: This is the process used for creating an operational process that will be able to meet established goals and do so under operating conditions.

Quality control: This is the process used for meeting quality goals during operations, and ensuring that operations are conducted in accordance with the quality plan. In this context, the term "control" refers to measuring and adjusting the process to achieve performance goals.

Quality improvement: This is the process for breaking through to new levels of performance, distinctly higher than those originally planned (adapted from Juran, 1986, pp. 20–21).

ning, quality control, and quality improvement. While elsewhere in this book the term "quality improvement" has been used to include all three processes, their distinction here is useful, particularly in view of this chapter's focus on planning for quality transformation. Juran's definitions of these processes are important to understand.

Quality Planning

Juran (1986) refers to *quality planning* as the process used for creating an operational process "that will be able to meet established goals and do so under operating conditions" (p. 20). Quality planning, therefore, includes identifying customers and their needs, defining features of the service to meet customer needs, establishing quality goals related to those needs, planning processes that will yield the defined features, and testing those processes to ensure that they are capable of meeting the goals under operating conditions. Thus, developing an organizational blueprint to guide transformation or planning a new community job placement are examples of processes that could benefit from the steps involved in quality planning.

Quality Control

Quality control is the process used for meeting quality goals during operations, ensuring that operations are conducted in accordance with the quality plan. In this context, "control" encompasses identifying the critical variables related to process performance and identifying standards for those variables, measuring those variables to assess actual performance, identifying any differences between actual and planned performance, and taking action on those differences. In this sense, the term "control" does not reflect the common usage of the term—that is, having power over someone or something; rather, it is a process of measuring and adjusting the process to achieve performance goals.

Quality Improvement

Quality improvement refers to "the process for breaking through to unprecedented levels of performance" (p. 21), distinctly higher than those originally planned. Quality improvement, then, includes the series of problem-solving steps introduced in Chapter 9: define the problem, analyze possible causes, collect data to identify a root cause, select strategies for improvement, implement improvement strategies, complete data analysis to prove that the strategies were effective under operating conditions, and plan for continuous improvement to maintain the gains.

Implementing the Quality Trilogy

The Quality Trilogy provides an outline for training courses in quality management that can be useful for direct line staff members, top managers, or secretarial staff. And it provides a road map for continuing to embed quality throughout the organization.

·REFERENCES

Juran, J.M. (1986). A universal approach to managing for quality: The quality trilogy. *Quality Progress, 19*(8), 19–24.

Lusk, K., Tribus, M., Schwinn, C., & Schwinn, D. (1989, April). *Creating community quality councils: Applying quality management principles in a political environment.* Paper presented at the William G. Hunter Conference, Madison.

Scholtes, P.R. (1988). *The team handbook: How to use teams to improve quality.* Madison, WI: Joiner Associates, Inc.

Scholtes, P.R., & Hacquebord, H. (1987). *A practical approach to quality.* Madison: Joiner Associates, Inc.

ADDITIONAL READINGS

QIP, Inc. (1986). *The transformation of American industry.* Miamisburg, OH: Author.

Tomasek, H. (1989). The process of inverting the organizational pyramid. *Human Systems Management, 8,* 105–112.

Some Questions for Developing a Blueprint for Change

IDENTIFY TOP PRIORITIES

- Where will we begin the change effort?
- Is the mission guiding the organization toward community-based services, a customer focus, and ongoing quality improvement?
- Is the organizational structure getting in the way of doing good things? Do stakeholders believe that integrated employment will work and support the organizational change?
- Are staff members, consumers, funders, or business customers dissatisfied with the organization and its performance? What is their biggest issue?
- What is the greatest challenge facing the organization today, in the next 6 months, in the next 2 years?
- What strategic issues or criteria should be considered in selecting the initial change project?

DEFINE INITIAL CHANGE PROJECTS

- Do we need to establish a pilot project related to the quality transformation or community-based employment, or should we take a more global, organization-wide approach?
- In which part of the organization should a pilot project be done? Which personnel should be involved?
- What are the important criteria for selecting a project? Should we choose a high-visibility project, a project that will surely result in the greatest gains, or one that addresses a critical need?

SELECT STRATEGIES

- What criteria should we use in selecting strategies?
- How will we go about implementing the targeted change?
- Who will be involved in implementing the change?
- What roles must managers fill to ensure success?
- What resources will be required? What are the timelines?
- What new roles will staff members be asked to take on? How will we support them in these roles?
- Where are the potential barriers to success? Are they people, resources, systems? How should we go about breaking down these barriers?

SELECT A COORDINATOR AND ADVISORS

- Who will coordinate implementation of the change?
- How will we prepare that person to assume coordination responsibilities?
- What sort of ongoing support and training will that person receive?

- Who will act as technical advisors for community-based employment and quality improvement? How will we prepare them for their roles? For how much time will they be available, and to whom?

DEVISE TRAINING PROGRAM

- How will we prepare managers, staff, and other key people for their roles in leading and implementing the change effort? What sort of ongoing support and training will they receive?
- How will we communicate change efforts, values, and quality principles throughout the organization to develop a culture that supports change?

PLAN EVALUATION STRATEGY

- How will we monitor the change effort? When? How often? Who will be responsible?
- How will we know if the change effort is going well or poorly? What measures will we use to monitor the effort?
- How often will the blueprint for change be reviewed and adjusted? Who will be responsible?
- How will we evaluate the actions that are taken to improve performance?

TARGET NEXT EFFORTS

- What are we likely to target as the next part of the change effort?
- What can we do now to help prepare for those next efforts? (Adapted from Scholtes & Hacquebord, 1987, pp. 18–19.)

Chapter 13

A Case Study in Quality Improvement and Organizational Change to Community-Based Employment

In 1985, an organization known as P.E. provided rehabilitation services to 46 individuals with developmental disabilities in its facility. Five additional people received support for jobs in community settings. Coming from that experience, in 1987 the organization embarked upon a course to change over all of its operations from facility-based to community-based employment. That job is far from being finished.

As of 1990, 41 people were working with support in community jobs (see Figure 13.1). During this time, the organization addressed many changes in addition to significantly expanding community employment: changes in personnel due both to an average turnover rate of 50% per year and to a 100% increase in the number of staff positions; a 58% increase in the number of people receiving services; changes in the levels and types of disabilities of the people served; and changes in the demands of the state's funding and monitoring system; to name a few. Through these changes, the board and management have maintained a consistent focus on improving the lives of the people they support. Their decision to change from providing facility-based services was based on this basic value, and not on pressures from state or county funders. P.E. is proceeding through changeover to integrated employment because the organization believes it is the right thing to do.

To help achieve the dramatic organizational changes required to shift from facility-based to fully integrated services, P.E. embraced the philosophy and methods of Continuous Quality Improvement. This work is not finished either. The organizational transformation continues. This chapter presents their experiences to date in using Continuous Quality Improvement as a strategy to support changeover to community-based services. A chronological summary of the major milestones in this transformation is presented in the Appendix at the end of this chapter.

The material in this chapter reflects work performed with P.E. during the period of May 1989 to January 1991. The author would like to thank Karen Ross, Executive Director during that time, for reviewing and contributing information for this chapter, and for her ongoing support.

P.E. ORGANIZATIONAL PROFILE

Established in 1972, P.E. is located in a primarily rural county with 47,000 residents in 745 square miles. The county's major industries include agriculture, timber, and higher education.

	1985	1990
Services:	Work activity center, supported employment	Work activity center, supported employment, community integration
Staff employees:	8.7 F.T.E.	20.5 F.T.E.
Individuals receiving services:	51	78
Community jobs:	5	41
Number in facility:	46	37
Individual placements:	2	15
Types of work:	In facility: Packaging instruction manuals and computer diskettes In community: Janitorial crew Bakery Restaurant	In facility: Simulated work and community integration activities In community: Janitorial crew Groundskeeping crew Department store Lift truck manufacturer Motel Grocery store courtesy clerks Bark mulch company State office
Work locations:	3 + facility	22 + facility
Average wages per person per month:	$36	$96

Figure 13.1.   Case study profile. (F.T.E. = full-time employees.)

INITIAL STEPS FOR CHANGE

P.E.'s transformation began where it should have, with a review of its values, mission statement, and organizational structure. The initial revision of the mission statement, which required 4 months, included repeated input from consumers, the staff, board members, consultants, and colleagues but was a necessary step for achieving consensus on the new organizational direction. Later, consistent with the developing interest in principles of Continuous Quality Improvement, management staff shortened the mission statement to three words: *Integration through Employment*. The mission is posted in offices and work spaces in the facility, as a constant reminder of the purpose for all members of the organization.

At the start of the changeover process, P.E. was organized in a manner that is familiar to many rehabilitation agencies. As changeover began, and new supported employment components were developed, that structure changed somewhat to provide stronger support to the new positions. At that time, the structure consisted of an executive director and board at the top, a manager of rehabilitation services supervising rehabilitation specialists, a manager of vocational services supervising co-

A CHANGING MISSION

THE MISSION IN 1987:

P.E. is a nonprofit corporation and operates in accordance with the 501(c)3 regulations of the Internal Revenue Service. The Corporation is registered with the State of Oregon as a Charitable Corporation.

The Corporation provides rehabilitation services to adults with mental retardation/developmental disabilities, addressing the following areas: vocational skills, social behaviors, community awareness, interpersonal skills, and recreation/leisure skills.

Each client of the Center is involved in the development of an individual plan, consisting of written goals and objectives, which are reviewed and updated semi-annually.

The goal of the organization is to allow adults with MR/DD to recognize their greatest level of independent functioning in the community. We strive to meet this goal by providing data-based training and formal and informal training in accordance with accepted methods of learning theory and behavior modification.

REVISED IN 1988:

P.E.'s goal is to provide the support services needed to maintain employment in integrated settings in our county for adults with developmental disabilities. Assessment, placement, training, and continuous follow-along services are provided to assist individuals to achieve their potential and to promote individual choice, social and economic independence, and integration in community settings. Employment services are provided in existing community businesses whenever possible. The corporation may also operate small businesses to meet individual employment needs when such businesses best support the objectives of choice, independence, and integration.

SHORTENED IN 1989:

Integration Through Employment

ordinators of various vocational components below that, and finally, direct service workshop floor and community crew supervisors (see Figure 13.2). With the organization's adoption of Continuous Quality Improvement, however, this structure was to undergo a dramatic change.

THE "STAR" STRUCTURE: INTRODUCING A NEW WAY OF BEING

The group charged with planning P.E.'s transformation consisted of the managers and coordinators of each component, along with an outside consultant, or "Quality Advisor." As time passed, this group took the name "Guidance Team" to reflect their shift in roles from "managers" and "decision-makers" to "coaches" in the change process.

For several months, P.E.'s "managers" had been tackling the question of how to define an organizational structure that would assist in empowering staff toward

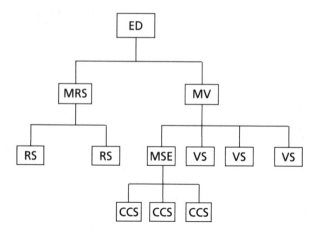

Figure 13.2. Organizational structure in 1988. (ED = executive director, MRS = manager of rehabilitation services, MVS = manager of vocational services, RS = rehabilitation specialist, MSE = manager of supported employment, VS = vocational supervisor, CCS = community crew supervisors.)

achieving the organizational mission, as well as assist in achieving continuous innovation and quality improvement. They had formed a test group, "Alpha Star," as a first effort to build a quality improvement team to help them figure out how best to transform the organization. From this group, the Guidance Team members learned many things (described later in this chapter under "The Alpha Star Experience") that led them to select the organizational design shown in Figure 13.3.

The design is based on creating four *Work Teams*, each composed of three to five program or crew supervisors, one employment specialist, one coordinator (from those formerly known as managers), and the employees with disabilities whom they support. These teams are the "points" of the star (see Figure 13.3) and are responsible for ensuring that each individual team member is placed and maintained in a satisfying job that meets P.E.'s quality guidelines. Each Work Team, therefore, is responsible for identifying individual interests and job support needs, developing general case skills, developing jobs that match individual interests, providing training and support to improve work performance and integration on specific jobs, and supporting career advancement.

In addition to Work Teams, the Star includes a few *Project Teams*, which may be formed at any time to address an identified organizational issue. Project Teams typically consist of individuals from different Work Teams. Represented as circles in the organizational design shown in Figure 13.3, the first of these Project Teams are the Guidance Team, with responsibility for reviewing and adjusting the organizational transformation; the Transportation Team, with responsibility for coordinating a transportation system that meets the needs of each of the Work Teams; and the Employment Specialist Team, with responsibility for coordinating job development activities across teams. Since the initial shift, additional temporary quality improvement Project Teams have been formed, completed their work, and disbanded. Several individuals are positioned as resources or technical consultants for teams and thus are "located" in the center of the Star, able to provide support to any of the Work Teams or Project Teams as needed.

P.E.'s transformation was much more than a shift in how managers drew the organizational structure. The purpose of the shift was to change the way staff mem-

INTRODUCING A NEW STAR

Presenting the new organizational structure—the Star—to staff members for the first time, the Guidance Team shared the values that drove the change:

> Transformation . . . involves a sort of adolescence: a period of inelegance when we shift from one way of being to a new way of being (Scholtes & Hacquebord, 1987, p. 1).
>
> Recognizing that our success is achieved through the efforts of individual employees and consumers, the organization is committed to . . .
>
> *Empowering all staff and consumers to release their hidden capacities*
>
> We believe that this can best be accomplished by treating both staff and consumers as "customers." Because quality begins with delighting the customer, a customer-focused organization listens to its customers, responds to their needs, and helps to lead them into the future. Thus, supporting both personal and professional growth of individuals and offering enjoyable, meaningful jobs that promote long-term commitment to the organization will help us to achieve quality. We also believe that the best decisions are made by those most directly involved. Therefore, we need an organizational structure that will assist us to do these things.
>
> *Continuous innovation and quality improvement*
>
> We believe that in order to support continuous innovation and quality improvement in our organization, we must be committed to continuous self-assessment, troubleshooting, and performance improvement, basing our decisions on data whenever possible. This means that we expect to always be adapting and changing, using yesterday's improvements as the first step in achieving today's. We also believe that improving communication in our organization will help to achieve quality. Therefore, we want to break down the formal barriers among us, and between us and our "external" customers. We need an organizational structure that will assist us to do these things as well.

bers viewed their jobs, the importance of their positions in the organization, and their roles in accomplishing the organization's mission. Using a creative structural design that threw away old conceptions of relationships and hierarchies was just one way of achieving these purposes. In addition, the Guidance Team felt that teams needed some tools to help them understand and implement the new way of being. Foremost among these were tools to help staff members remain focused on their team's purpose and key accomplishment areas. Therefore, part of redesigning the organizational structure included drafting key performance templates for Work Teams and for the Project Teams established at that time.

The purpose of the Work Teams was developed to support accomplishment of the organization's mission (see Figure 13.4), and that of the Project Teams to support accomplishment of the Work Teams' purpose (see Figure 13.5). The relationships among these purposes emphasized that teams functioned as customers to each other, and that working cooperatively and effectively to meet the needs of these internal customers would move the organization more rapidly toward achieving its mission.

Believing that visual symbols are effective in reminding staff members of their roles, the Guidance Team members made a key performance template (see Chapter 8 for a description of performance templates) poster for each type of team, listing the team's purpose and mission accomplishment areas. They posted copies throughout their building, in team work or meeting spaces. In addition, they developed an

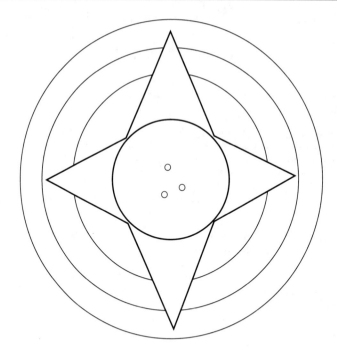

Figure 13.3. The "Star": A new organizational design to reflect a new philosophy.

agenda format for weekly team meetings based on each team's key performance template. To keep team meetings focused, all items raised must fit into one of the accomplishment areas; if not, the team questions why they need to discuss it. The Guidance Team also drafted a reporting format to be used by teams, with an emphasis
on graphs and charts to make outcomes and problem-solving highly visual. The key
performance templates for teams, meeting guidelines, sample agenda, sample team
meeting records, and a sample report are provided in the Appendix at the end of this
chapter.

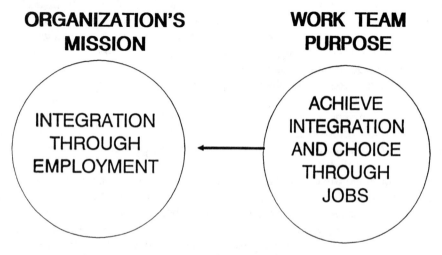

Figure 13.4. The Work Teams' purpose supports the organization.

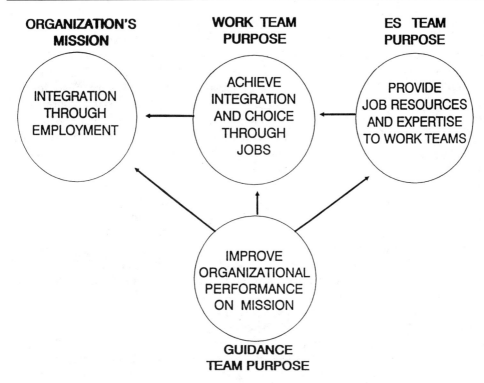

ORGANIZATION'S MISSION

INTEGRATION THROUGH EMPLOYMENT

WORK TEAM PURPOSE

ACHIEVE INTEGRATION AND CHOICE THROUGH JOBS

ES TEAM PURPOSE

PROVIDE JOB RESOURCES AND EXPERTISE TO WORK TEAMS

IMPROVE ORGANIZATIONAL PERFORMANCE ON MISSION

GUIDANCE TEAM PURPOSE

Figure 13.5. Project Team's purposes support Work Teams and P.E.'s mission. (ES = employment specialist.)

SHIFTING DECISION-MAKING AUTHORITY

The organization's long-term goal (based on the belief that decisions should be made by those most directly involved in an issue) is that teams become "self-managing work groups," operating within P.E.'s mission, values, and guidelines. Self-managing work groups would not only manage the direct service functions of the team, but also, for example, be responsible for personnel selection, evaluation, and dismissal; raises and bonuses; budget planning and control; and quality assurance. Clearly, in its previous organizational structure, they were far from achieving this goal: Management staff still held decision-making authority in many areas, direct service staff had not received the training and support needed to carry out most self-management functions, and communication was often confused and overlapping. Furthermore, prior to the organizational transformation, direct service personnel felt powerless at the bottom of the hierarchical structure, often distrusted the actions of managers, and had low morale. During 1 year prior to the shift, 67% of the staff had left their jobs.

With this background, the shift to the self-managed team concept had to occur in a series of phases, with training and support provided as staff members assumed new roles, and as a few new functions at a time shifted from management-level control to team-based control. During the initial phase of the transformation, P.E.'s objective was to assist each team to assume decision-making authority in direct service functions. That included, for example, scheduling staff coverage (including substitutes and vacation time), individual support planning, and service coordination. Specific planning for succeeding phases of the transformation is based on experience from implementing earlier phases. The original plan for achieving P.E.'s organizational transformation is described in the Implementation Blueprint presented in the Appendix at the end of this chapter. This plan was developed a few months after the initiation of the quality transformation process and offers an example of a blueprint for organizational change (Scholtes & Hacquebord, 1987).

During each phase, the Guidance Team expected to uncover problem areas and from these problems devise solutions that would be useful to the other teams. For example, one team, in addressing the issue of the appearance of team members at work, determined that Transition Meetings did not consistently occur as individuals moved into new jobs, that individual support plans and training programs did not consistently address appearance issues when they existed, and that crew and program supervisors did not have clear guidelines on what they could do if a team member arrived at work dirty or disheveled. Uncovering these problems with the appropriate processes was the first step to figuring out how to solve them. Clearly, solutions that the test group devised for these issues would be useful throughout the organization.

Although, when they developed it, the Guidance Team was convinced that the Star was the best structure to help them achieve the values and objectives listed earlier in this chapter, they were equally convinced that, as they implemented it, they would find ways to improve it. Indeed, incorporating input from other staff persons, the Guidance Team soon made minor adjustments to the design, as well as to performance templates, meeting agenda formats, meeting record formats, reporting formats, and other tools developed at the time of the shift to the Star structure. That is the method of Continuous Quality Improvement. That is the method that will lead them into the future.

LESSONS LEARNED DURING THE TRANSFORMATION

The Alpha Star Experience

P.E. tested the new Star structure by establishing one Work Team prior to full implementation. The purpose was to check the effectiveness of the proposed team structure, practice implementing quality improvement approaches with staff members, and develop a communication link among direct service personnel regarding the organizational transformation as a strategy to overcome mounting distrust. Alpha Star was the Guidance Team's first attempt at coaching a quality improvement team. Their hope was that this team would help to define the new operating guidelines that would be needed when the full structural shift took place. Each decision made by the Guidance Team related to Alpha Star included trade-offs between competing possibilities and values.

While Alpha Star was only partially successful in achieving its several purposes, it was very successful in teaching the Guidance Team lessons about how to implement quality improvement teams.

- *Selection of Team Members* The Guidance Team allowed the staff to caucus to select volunteers from within their ranks for membership in Alpha Star. This had the benefit of identifying those motivated to participate. However, more direct intervention by the Guidance Team might have resulted in recruiting members who were more supportive of the transformation, who were more committed to data-based decision-making, or who traditionally were most effective in leading staff opinions. At the time, the Guidance Team was struggling with a great deal of dissatisfaction in the ranks of direct service personnel, so the managers were willing to trade off greater control over Alpha Star's membership to demonstrate their commitment to empowering all personnel.

- *Project Selection*   The Guidance Team also allowed Alpha Star to select its first quality improvement project, rather than assigning a project. Again, this had benefit: developing group consensus on the selected project. However, the team had not yet been trained in applying systematic methods to problem identification and resolution, so those skills had to be taught concurrently. Alpha Star ended up selecting a difficult issue over which they had little control for change. Work on selecting and then pursuing that issue seemed to drag. Eventually, Alpha Star members felt frustrated by the project and felt that they had not been given the opportunity to address issues of organizational structure and operating guidelines that each had hoped to be able to pursue.

The experience of Alpha Star was invaluable in preparing for the full organizational shift. In testing Alpha Star, P.E. was applying the Shewhart Cycle to perform a pilot study to check its plan prior to full implementation of the Star structure. From this test, the Guidance Team made several adjustments, the most significant of which was in the composition of Work Teams. In an effort to expand communication across types of staff positions, Alpha Star had represented each of the different types of staff within the organization: a grocery store crew supervisor, a landscaping crew supervisor, a supervisor from the facility, a rehabilitation specialist, an employment specialist (i.e., job developer), and a Guidance Team member. As a result, Alpha Star members did not know each other, had little in common, and had difficulty finding a convenient time to meet. In the revised structure, Work Teams were organized geographically, including one Guidance Team member, one employment specialist, and all of the job coaches or supervisors working in a particular part of the county. A few Work Teams were structured to cut across these geographical lines but were established as Project Teams to address a particular issue (e.g., transportation or job development). The three rehabilitation specialist positions were eliminated. Of the three team members who had held these positions, one became a team coordinator, one left and was replaced with a direct service team member, and the third became a resource consultant for teams.

Team Notebooks

The Guidance Team quickly saw the importance of maintaining records of the decisions made by the Guidance Team and by Alpha Star. Therefore, the Guidance Team asked Alpha Star to keep meeting minutes. However, because there was no standard format, the specificity and utility of the records kept varied greatly. Because of this experience, in preparing for the shift into the Star structure, the Guidance Team developed a Team Notebook for each Work Team and Project Team.

Designed to serve as a resource manual for team members, the Team Notebooks included information on the new organizational design, quality improvement, recommended formats, and operating guidelines. The Guidance Team presented the Team Notebooks as gifts to each team during the "Kick-off Celebration" marking the

---

CONTENTS OF TEAM NOTEBOOKS

- Mission
- Quality transformation memo to staff
- Operating guidelines
- Team purpose: Work Teams
                  Guidance Team
                  Employment Specialist Team
- Star structure
- Question and answer paper discussing the changes, responding to questions raised by staff at the time of the initial shift to the Star
- Guidelines for decisions about staff coverage, service coordination, and so forth
- Role of the coordinator
- Team meeting guidelines
- Sample meeting agenda form
- Sample meeting records form
- List of team members

---

official shift to the Star structure. The Notebooks were designed to be used by each team to store meeting records and data and to serve as an orientation tool for new team members.

The Importance of Celebrating

Most of the changes P.E. has experienced over the past few years have been gradual. Celebrating small steps as well as large ones helped the staff members to see more clearly how far they had come. They held a celebration the day they shifted to the Star structure, burning their job descriptions as a visual symbol of the shift. Each month afterward they have held a mini-anniversary celebration to mark changes and improvements, reminding the staff that "things are different now." These celebrations give the organization an opportunity to recognize success and publicly reward staff accomplishments.

Celebrations have included a variety of techniques to mark changes. One month, celebration planners drew and cut out outlines of feet, asking each staff person to take one and write on it one small step they had made since the last celebration. At the 1-year celebration, staff members commented on the changes in how they perceived working at P.E. since the structural shift. As time has passed, the responsibility for planning and hosting the monthly celebrations has shifted from the Guidance Team and now rotates among the various Work Teams and Project Teams. This change has allowed increased staff ownership of and involvement in the celebrations.

Make All Great Ideas, Best Practices, and
Improvements Subject to Continuous Improvement

At the time of initiating Alpha Star, the Guidance Team was convinced that it had designed a structure that not only would be workable, but that would help dissolve the barriers to communication inherent in hierarchical structures. Switching to geo-graphically structured rather than representational teams after the Alpha Star experiment proved the Guidance Team's commitment to making decisions based on data and experience. This flexibility and responsiveness has characterized the organization throughout its transformation.

P.E.'s leader demonstrated repeatedly that all staff members should bring in new ideas to replace the old, constantly questioning the status quo. The Guidance Team encouraged risk-taking, helping staff members to learn from any mistakes they had made, rather than punishing for mistakes. Most of all, they wanted to create an environment that would allow continuous improvement of systems and processes to remove internal barriers impeding the performance of staff. The central theme of Continuous Quality Improvement—building on previous improvements to create even higher quality—requires that organizations constantly be willing to let go of previous ways of being.

Maintaining Quality Improvements

As the initial honeymoon period with Continuous Quality Improvement fades, the staff members and managers at P.E. are finding that *maintaining* structural and process improvements is at least as difficult as achieving the initial improvement. Feedback loops that continually assess and adjust processes and systems are needed, as well as individual discipline and fortitude to "stay the course" (Mosgaller, 1990).

EFFECTS OF THE QUALITY TRANSFORMATION

Staff Morale

Before P.E. adopted Continuous Quality Improvement and the new organizational structure, staff morale was low. Managers and direct service staff alike felt that there always were too many things to do, not enough time in which to do them, and too much stress along the way. Indeed, at the time of the introduction of Continuous Quality Improvement into the organization, each of the managers of the organization, including the executive director, had discussed leaving. A few had applications out for other jobs. A year later, after the development of the Star organizational structure, all managers remained at P.E. with renewed commitment to the organization. Although in the first few months after the shift to the Star structure, nine staff members left (six of whom left due to job dissatisfaction), 6 months were then completed without turnover. In the labor market of 1990, and with the abysmal salaries available for direct service personnel in Oregon, this is a remarkable feat. Despite the exodus that occurred at the beginning of the year, P.E.'s staff turnover rate dropped to 41% in 1990, from an average of 50% since 1985.

But the shift to Continuous Quality Improvement was not an instant cure for issues with staff commitment, morale, and trust. Because the design for the shift had been developed by the managers of the organization, some direct service staff members initially distrusted the change. The staff believed it was "one more gimmick" and "another way that managers are trying to get us to do more for the same money." They wondered, "If we're going to be doing their jobs for them, what will they do?" On a weekly basis the members of the Guidance Team shared their thoughts and decisions as well as solicited input from other members of the organization regarding the organizational changes. However, doubts continued in some staff members until well after the new structure and quality improvement approaches had been embedded in the organization. The Guidance Team was never able to convince some of the most severe skeptics; for the most part, these are the individuals who left within the first few months after the shift to the new structure. This experience is similar to that of other organizations involved with the quality movement—many resisters will come around, but others will have to be replaced (Holpp, 1989).

Use of Data for Decision-Making

Staff members throughout the organization more and more frequently began to bring up quality improvement ideas and seek data to use for making decisions about those ideas. This transformation in staff behavior is startling. At the beginning of their investigation into principles and methods of Continuous Quality Improvement, many staff members were disgruntled; they complained frequently that the managers did little to help them in doing the real work of the organization, and few collected or used data other than narrative case notes. They based their statements of dissatisfaction on feelings and opinions, rather than on data.

Needing a positive way to address these complaints and to introduce scientific methods to the staff, the Guidance Team began a campaign entitled "Staff Are Customers, Too." Staff members were asked to log complaints (and instances in which they were pleased) about managers. The logged complaints were then categorized as problems with timeliness of responses, lack of response to requests, inaccurate responses, and so forth. Together with the staff, the Guidance Team developed weekly Pareto Analyses (see Chapter 10) to identify the most frequently occurring issue (see Figure 13.6). The Pareto Analyses indicated that timeliness, by far, was the focus of the greatest majority of staff complaints. This information helped both staff and Guidance Team members to identify strategies to improve timeliness of responses to requests, thereby improving staff satisfaction. At the same time, staff members had the opportunity to practice a simple method of data analysis on an issue that was meaningful to them.

Since that time, the Guidance Team has provided additional training on quality improvement tools, as well as leadership in asking for data prior to decision-making. About a year into the transformation, P.E. held a staff retreat in which the staff defined two quality improvement projects, collected and analyzed data, and made recommendations for an improvement plan based on the data analysis. Since this practice, staff members have been bringing small quality improvement project ideas to weekly staff meetings, collecting and analyzing data on the spot, and using the results to make decisions or to develop plans. Staff have begun to discover the power of data to support making good decisions.

Role of Customers

Another outcome of the move to incorporate principles of Continuous Quality Improvement in daily operations has been expanded involvement with the organiza-

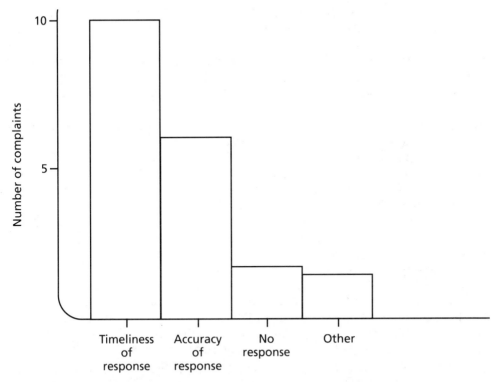

Figure 13.6. Pareto Analysis of staff complaints.

tion's customers. P.E. has defined five customer groups: individuals with disabilities, business and public sector employers, staff, residential providers, and funders. With the quality transformation, the staff began to solicit input from these groups and to use the input received to improve processes and accomplishments.

Viewing funders as customers has assisted staff members to find a new approach for working on what previously had been an adversarial relationship with one funder, taking steps toward more positive and open communication. In addition, early in the transformation process, the staff held a group interview with the director of the county's developmental disabilities services office to learn more about his interests and definitions of quality. Similarly, P.E. has worked on improving communication with residential providers, including forming a joint quality improvement team with one provider to address the most significant problems between them. P.E. has developed formats for soliciting feedback from consumers, employers, and others. Each team includes Pareto Analyses of complaints received from any of the customer groups as a standard part of its monthly report to the Guidance Team. Staff members also have begun inviting customers to participate in *ad hoc* quality improvement teams, to be a part of planning and developing new or better systems to improve performance.

Customer feedback has been used even to improve meetings held. Participants evaluate all team and organizational meetings, using feedback for improving future meetings. The staff reports that meetings are now better organized and more efficient.

THE QUALITY TRANSFORMATION AND
CHANGEOVER TO SUPPORTED EMPLOYMENT

Through all of the changes—in organizational structure, personnel roles, systems, and so forth—the organization also has continued to pursue changeover to community-based employment. As the quality transformation continued, the outcomes experienced by individuals receiving services continued to improve as well. As of the end of 1990, over 40 people were placed in supported community jobs. In addition, according to various quality dimensions, the community jobs were improving. For example, jobs developed have greater opportunities for integration than those developed a few years ago, and staff persons train co-workers to provide support, instead of keeping a "professional" between the community and the worker with disabilities.

At P.E. the impact of embracing Continuous Quality Improvement is both dramatic and subtle. Staff members have become more comfortable in revealing mistakes and more willing to take risks; they sometimes describe how the tools they are learning at work have helped them to deal with issues at home, as well. Staff members are willingly taking on additional responsibilities and authority. Indeed, they resist the temptation to fall back into former "manager" roles. Through discussions and by example, the staff are coming to understand that the Guidance Team believes that most problems are truly systems problems rather than due to the mistakes of individual employees. Although the period of time represented here is only 2 years, staff members have begun to embrace the change in both large and small ways. Problems continue to arise, and staff continue to question their course of action, but their struggle to improve goes on. The exciting part is that the transformation will never be finished. Through embracing continuous quality principles, the organization has come to understand that quality is the outcome of a process of never-ending improvement.

REFERENCES

Holpp, L. (1989). 10 reasons why total quality is less than total. *Training, 26*(10), 93–103.

Mosgaller, T. (1990, November). *Total quality management.* Presentation to the Region X Conference, Gleneden, Oregon.

Scholtes, P.R., & Hacquebord, H. (1987). *A practical approach to quality.* Madison: Joiner Associates, Inc.

Appendix

Sample Materials

Item #1. Chronology of the Start of a Quality Transformation
Item #2. Original Implementation Blueprint
Item #3. Operating Principles
Item #4. Materials Related to Work Teams
    A. Key Performance Template
    B. Meeting Agenda
    C. Meeting Records Format
    D. Monthly Performance Report Instructions
    E. Monthly Performance Report Worksheet
    F. Monthly Performance Report
Item #5. Materials Related to the Employment Specialist Team (a Project Team)
    A. Key Performance Template
    B. Meeting Agenda
    C. Monthly Report
    D. Employer Satisfaction Interview Format
Item #6. Materials Related to the Guidance Team
    A. Quality Control Plan (including Key Performance Template)
    B. Meeting Agenda
    C. Role of the Team Coordinators

ITEM #1. CHRONOLOGY OF THE START OF A QUALITY TRANSFORMATION

Year 1

January	Completed values clarification with staff: "Changeover is the only choice!"
January–April	Revised mission statement.
May	Completed training on making decisions based on mission and how each person's job related to the mission.

Year 2

February–March	Identified current issues and needs.
April	Requested assistance of a Quality Advisor in changing organizational structure and improving staff morale.
May	Shortened mission statement; defined 5-year vision and valued accomplishments.
	Developed concept and initial plan for revised organizational structure.
June	Introduced scientific methods for decision-making to support decisions being made by those most closely involved with an issue.
	Provided initial staff training in the philosophy of Continuous Quality Improvement.
July–October	Implemented trial Work Team ("Alpha Star").
September	Adjusted planned structure based on experience of Alpha Star Team.
	Less than 50% of individuals served receiving services in community rather than facility.
October	Developed guidelines for quality transformation, Team Notebooks, including operating guidelines for teams.
	Formed Guidance Team for ongoing review and adjustment of the organizational transformation.
November	Implemented full organizational shift to Star structure, identified additional staff training needs, and adjusted lines of authority for individual staff members.
	Adjusted current job support follow-up assignments for Employment Specialists and others.
December	Developed Quality Control Plan for Guidance Team.

Year 3

February	Held Guidance Team retreat:

- To draft key performance templates and reporting formats for teams
- To draft guidelines for new functions to be assumed by teams (individual support planning, scheduling coverage for staff, service coordination with home providers, obtaining customer feedback)
- To establish Team Status Chart to track the development of quality improvement methods and self-management in each team
- To implement use of monthly reports to give teams a format for organizing data to help them see how well they are doing in their jobs

	Trained team coordinators and members for new functions; implemented scheduling and coverage decision-making authority of teams.
March	Implemented shift of individual support planning and service coordination responsibility from Rehabilitation Specialists to Work Teams.
June	Held full staff retreat to practice application of quality improvement tools to currrent issues.
July	Revised substitute manuals based on customer feedback and data collected.
August	Project Team completed recommendations on how to serve people when they are unemployed.

September   Completed customer interviews with major funding sources.

October   Initiated internal customer interviews within and across teams.

                   Changed weekly training session planning committee to include a cross-section of employees.

November   Celebrated completion of 1 year since the shift to the Star structure.

Ongoing   Reviewed status of organizational transformation and guidelines for quality transformation; adjusted plan for organizational transformation based on experience.

ITEM #2.   ORIGINAL IMPLEMENTATION BLUEPRINT

May	Review and shorten mission statement.
	Define 5-year vision and valued accomplishments.
	Develop concept and initial plan for revised organizational structure.
June	Provide weekly 1-hour initial staff training on Continuous Quality Improvement principles.
July–October	Implement trial Work Team to test new organizational structure.
September	Adjust plan based on experience of trial Work Team.
October	Develop guidelines for quality transformation and Team Notebooks, including operating guidelines for teams.
November	Shift to new Star structure.
December	Develop quality control plan.

ITEM #3. OPERATING PRINCIPLES

When potential new projects are available or other significant issues are raised, the following questions will be considered:

- How will it benefit our organization?
- How does it fit our values?
- How will it benefit the people we serve?
- How will it help us to achieve our mission and 5-year vision?
- Does it fit in with what we can and cannot do?
- How does it empower everyone?
- Who are the people most involved and are they making the decision?
- How will this support the personal and professional growth of personnel?
- How will this lead to enjoyable, meaningful jobs and long-term commitment to the organization?
- How does this represent or offer opportunities for innovation, adaptation, and change?
- How will we know when this has been done well?
- How will we build in self-assessment, troubleshooting, and performance improvement?

ITEM #4A.   WORK TEAMS: KEY PERFORMANCE TEMPLATE

Purpose: Achieve Integration and Choice Through Jobs

Major Responsibilities:

- Identify job preferences and skills; encourage choice.
- Find and maintain jobs.
- Develop integration.
- Provide training and support.
- Complete service coordination with others.
- Manage team and team development.

ITEM #4B.   WORK TEAM MEETING AGENDA

Date: _____   Present: _____   _____
                                     _____   _____
                                     _____   _____
                                     _____   _____

____ Check in
____ Review minutes
____ Team building
____ Coverage issues
____ Employment Specialist update

Build Agenda Based on Accomplishments:

Identify job preferences	Find and maintain jobs	Develop integration
1.	1.	1.
2.	2.	2.
3.	3.	3.
4.	4.	4.
5.	5.	5.

Provide training and support	Service coordination	Manage team
1.	1.	1.
2.	2.	2.
3.	3.	3.
4.	4.	4.
5.	5.	5.

Meeting evaluation:

(+)   (−)   Recommendations

Items not addressed on agenda:

Next meeting: Date _____   Time _____

ITEM #4C.   WORK TEAM MEETING RECORDS FORMAT

Date_____

Topic	Main Points	Decisions	Next Step	Person Responsible

ITEM #4D.   WORK TEAM MONTHLY PERFORMANCE REPORT INSTRUCTIONS

General instructions:
- Complete the report the first week of the month for the previous month.
- Base the report on the last day of the month of the reporting period.
- Report on team members only, except for the question that asks you to list the people served from other teams.
- The monthly wage graph is completed over time. Therefore, it may be easier to complete the graph first, make a copy of the report page, and utilize the copy for the rest of the report. This will eliminate the need to redo the graph each month.

Specific instructions:

1. **Number of Team Members**   Team members, in this report, are people with disabilities who are a part of your team. Do not include people for whom your team is temporarily providing services.
2. **Number Unemployed**   The number of team members unemployed on the last day of the reporting period.
3. **Duration**   This applies to the length of time people have been unemployed. Data can be graphed on a dot plot. Each team may put the appropriate time periods on the graph depending on the length of time people have been unemployed in your team. Facility team should start counting unemployment as of 1/1/90.
4. **Number Served from Other Teams**   List the names and the number of people your team is temporarily serving for another team.
5. **Number Employed**   This number would include all people in your team employed as of the last day of the month. Include people who are working temporarily. Volunteer work is not included.
6. **Number of Individual Placements**   Total number of people in the team who are placed in individual jobs.
7. **Monthly Wage**   Add the gross wages of all team members and figure the average wage. Plot the low wage, the average wage, and the high wage for the reporting period.
8. **Blank Graph**   The team may choose to track other measures of special interest to them (e.g., number of hours of paid work). This space can be utilized to track team issues.
9. **Support**   Complete this portion for employed team members only. Use your best judgement and the following questions to help determine the appropriate category: 1) is the employee meeting work requirements with the current level of support; 2) would he or she still meet work requirements with less support?
10. **Improvement Project and Status**   Give a brief description of the data-based project your team is working on. Include the status of the project, decisions, and changes you have made based on the data.
11. **Customer Satisfaction**   List all issues by customer type (e.g., business, consumer, funders) and the number of times that issue was addressed by people in that customer category. Describe the actions taken to improve services based on the customer feedback. **Note**   One Work Team will be tracking their support issues as an improvement project. Other teams may want to do the same.
12. **Number of Incident/Accident Reports**   Total the number of health and safety related incident and accident reports for the reporting period. Include incident and accident reports for employees as well as staff team members in the count.
13. **Number to Doctor**   The total number of people on the team (staff and employees) who saw the doctor because of a work related incident or accident.
14. **Number for First Aid**   The total number of people on the team (staff and employees) who received first aid because of a work related incident or accident.
15. **Number of Days Absent**   List the total number of days absent due to illness, vacation, and other for both staff and employees.

16. **Percentage on Health and Safety Checklist**   Total the number of positive responses and the number of total responses. Figure the percentage of positive responses and list on the report.
17. **Job Advancements or Enhancements**   List any person who received a new job or enhanced duties or benefits. Include the new job/duties.
18. **ISP Information**   List all people for whom individual support plans (ISP) were held during the reporting period. Figure and report the percentage of benefits from the Benefits Checklist. List the timeliness of the ISP by month (e.g., if Chuck's ISP occurred in February, but should have been held in December, it was 2 months late; enter a 2 under timely; if it occurred in the correct month, enter a 0).

ITEM #4E.   WORK TEAM MONTHLY PERFORMANCE REPORT WORKSHEET

In the list of names below, place an asterisk(*) next to the name of anyone who is unemployed.

Name	Job	Individual job	Start date	End date	Reason	Gross wages

Total $_____

ITEM 4F. WORK TEAM MONTHLY PERFORMANCE REPORT

Team ____________ Date ____________ Covering the month ____________

# of Team members/Employees ___ # Served from other teams ___ # Unemployed ___

Average duration of unemployment _____

(List of unemployed) ____

Employed ___ # Supported by employer ___ # of individual placements ___

Second graph to be decided by team (e.g., hours of paid work)

Wage

Month

Too much support		Correct support		Too little support	

Improvement Project + Status:

Customer Satisfaction Paretos

What are the actions taken in improvements made this month based on customer feedback?

Business

times addressed

Consumer

times addressed

Advocate, funder

times addressed

Health and Safety

- # Incident reports ___
- # To doctor ___
- # For first aid ___
- # Days absent
  - staff ___
  - employees ___
- % on Health and Safety Checklist ___

Job advancements or enhancements:	Individual Plan meetings held Name % Benefits Timely?

ITEM #5A.   EMPLOYMENT SPECIALIST TEAM: KEY PERFORMANCE TEMPLATE

Purpose: Provide Job Resources and Expertise to Teams

Accomplishments:
1. Meet job development needs.
   - Identify team needs.
   - Coordinate job development efforts.
   - Establish/maintain systems.
   - Develop job development tools.
   - Make employer contacts.
2. Ensure quality job matches.
3. Ensure job analysis, initial training, individual placement follow-up.
   - Identify team needs.
   - Coordinate resources.
   - Provide technical assistance and training to employers and co-workers.
   - Establish systems.
4. Monitor/improve quality indicators and job enhancements.
   - Provide technical assistance, information, and training to teams.
   - Develop information system for finding jobs.
5. Ensure preplacement responsibilities.
   - Hold transition meeting.
   - Develop preemployment logistics checklist.
   - Complete follow-up for transition meeting.

ITEM #5B.   EMPLOYMENT SPECIALIST TEAM: MEETING AGENDA

Date: _____   Present: _____   _____
                                         _____   _____
                                         _____   _____
                                         _____   _____

____ Check in
____ Review minutes
____ Team building
____ Coverage issues
____ Team updates

Build Agenda Based on Accomplishments:

Meet job development needs	Quality job matches	Job analysis, training, follow-up
1.	1.	1.
2.	2.	2.
3.	3.	3.
4.	4.	4.
5.	5.	5.

Monitor quality	Preplacement tasks
1.	1.
2.	2.
3.	3.
4.	4.
5.	5.

Meeting evaluation: Recommendations:
(+)   (−)

Items not addressed on agenda:

Next meeting: Date _____   Time _____

ITEM #5C.   EMPLOYMENT SPECIALIST TEAM: MONTHLY REPORT

	1st day	Last day	Jobs lost	Reason
# Unemployed			1.	
# Want replacement			2.	
			3.	

Jobs developed (agreement reached) this month ____

Type of Jobs   Second graph to be
                                                        decided by team

   # |‾‾‾‾‾‾‾‾‾‾‾‾‾‾‾‾‾‾ |‾‾‾‾‾‾‾‾
        Categories

Job Status Summary
At end of month: # Individual placements ____
                   # Group sites ____   # Workers in groups ____

	Individual jobs		Group sites
# in negotiation	____	Negotiation	____
Job analysis	____	Job analysis	____
Initial training	____	Start-up	____
Fading	____		
Follow-up	____		

What actions/improvements made this month:

Troubleshooting/problem-solving issues and status:

In the list of names below, place an asterisk (*) next to the name of anyone who is unemployed.

Name	Job	(✔) Individual placement	Start date	Hours/ week	Hourly wage	Monthly wage	(✔) Job change	Reason

Employed ____   # Unemployed ____

Customer complaints

Date	From	Concerning	Action

ITEM #5D. EMPLOYER SATISFACTION: INTERVIEW FORMAT

Company _____ Coordinator _____

Date of interview _____ Work team _____

Person interviewed _____ Employment Specialist _____

A. Review issues from previous month:

Issue	Action taken	Results/comments	Still a problem?
1.			
2.			
3.			
4.			

B. Review performance on customer-defined requirements:
1.
2.
3.
4.

C. Review performance on defined requirements:
1. Staff performance
2. Transportation
3. Staff accessibility
4.

D. Future development discussions (e.g., contract renegotiations, co-worker support, hiring supervisor, shift from contract to direct hire, redesign job or task)

E. Next steps

What	By whom	By when	Last month Pareto Analysis	This month Pareto Analysis	To do

ITEM #6A.   GUIDANCE TEAM: QUALITY CONTROL PLAN

GUIDANCE TEAM PURPOSE:
IMPROVE ORGANIZATIONAL PERFORMANCE ON MISSION

Mission: Integration Through Employment

Definition of Quality	Measures
Customer satisfaction	Customer survey responses; Pareto Analyses of complaints
Integration	# individual placements: # supported by employer
Fiscal Stability	Reports requested by board
Employment	# employed, unemployed, duration; judgment of support matching need
Health and Safety	# & severity of incident reports; # days absent (staff and employees)

Mission Accomplishments/Responsibilities of the Guidance Team

1. Set with all teams their missions, primary accomplishments, measures, targets, limits, structure, and operating guidelines.
   Question: Are the teams organized to support performance? Are systems in place and being used?
   Indicators: Team Status Charts
       a.   Organization and quality improvement tools
       b.   Operational issues
       Reports from team coordinators

2. Coach problem-solving process and use of quality improvement tools.
   Question: Are the teams making good decisions?
   Indicators: Problem Resolution Reports
       Team meeting minutes/Coordinator Reports
       Monthly Performance Reports from teams

3. Troubleshoot organizational performance against mission, and adjust organizational structure and resources to improve performance.
   Question: Is performance on the mission improving?
   Indicators: Monthly Performance Reports from teams
       Guidance Team Problem Resolution Reports

4. Ensure continuous and just-in-time education and training that has a functional emphasis, that is, it is tied to daily activities with "on-site" feedback ("on-site" could mean in the team meetings).
   Question: Do staff have the knowledge and skills to improve performance?
   Indicators: Issues derived from analysis of Team Monthly Performance Reports and Problem Resolution Reports
       Requests from teams
       Staff Training Log

5. Maintain communication across teams; share quality improvement methods developed or discussed by each team.
   Question: Do teams use the "issues and outcomes" addressed by other teams?
   Indicators: Comparison of Problem Resolution Reports—Do they address similar issues and use results of other teams?

ITEM #6B.   GUIDANCE TEAM MEETING AGENDA

Date: _____   Present: _____ _____   Meeting #:_____

_____ _____

_____ _____

_____ _____

____ Check in
____ Review minutes and assignments

Build Agenda on Accomplishments:

Set missions, measures, targets	Coach problem-solving	Troubleshoot performance	Staff training	Maintain communication
1.	1.	1.	1.	1.
2.	2.	2.	2.	2.
3.	3.	3.	3.	3.
4.	4.	4.	4.	4.
5.	5.	5.	5.	5.

Meeting evaluation: Recommendations:
(+)   (−)

Items not addressed on agenda

Next meeting: Date _____ Time _____

ITEM #6C. ROLE OF THE TEAM COORDINATORS

Most Guidance Team members are also coordinators of a Work Team or Project Team. The role of the team coordinators will be changing as we develop into our self-managed teams. Initially, coordinators will:

- Ensure that decisions and daily operations are value driven and based on our mission.
- Be available to other members of the Work Team, listen to issues, help problem-find and problem-solve.
- Guide people to appropriate resources.
- Gather information for team members.
- Help team members meet necessary deadlines and paperwork requirements (e.g., the individual service planning system, monthly supported work reports, time sheets, vocational outcomes, wage and hour requirements, 1:1 training time, Employment Specialist time logs).
- Provide direct service.
- Determine training needs of team members and obtain resources.
- Maintain the coordination system with the team.
- Maintain customer relations with businesses.
- Review team member time sheets and travel reimbursements.
- Arrange for individual training for people the team serves.
- Coordinate transportation for team members.
- Help develop the team membership of self-managed teams.
- Represent the team at meetings of the Guidance Team.

Chapter 14

Perspectives on Change

Parting Words on Implementing Continuous Quality Improvement in Human Services

Continuous Quality Improvement offers a powerful methodology for achieving the vision suggested by Lowe and McBean (1989). However, the road to embracing that methodology is full of potholes and confusing intersections. Staying on the road of Continuous Quality Improvement requires vigilance, persistence, stamina, and discipline. It requires everyone to listen and respond positively to what at times may be very difficult feedback. It requires everyone to question how the organization performs its day-to-day operations and to use systematic methods to improve its processes and outcomes. It requires everyone to share a unified understanding of the wants and needs of customers, and of both collective and individual roles in meeting those wants and needs. The purpose of this chapter is to post warnings about some of the detours commonly encountered by companies that have tried to implement Continuous Quality Improvement, including the particular difficulties likely to be faced by human services organizations. This chapter concludes by discussing individual roles in supporting organizational change to quality management methods.

A ROAD MAP FOR FAILURE

Detour #1:   Failing To Link the Vision and Mission with Visible Actions

Establishing an organization-wide focus on improving quality requires more than new rhetoric. Leaders cannot simply add the language of quality to the words they speak. Rather, managers must act in new ways that support the new vision, and that demonstrate the changes in how the organization does business. If managers continue to blame people for problems, rather than searching for issues in processes and systems, or fail to use the tools and data-based methods for supporting decision-making, the other personnel will do the same. Do not treat quality improvement as just another management program largely consisting of slogans. Instead, translate quality improvement into actions that are incorporated in *everyone's* job everyday.

IMAGINE

"Let's imagine a place to work where fear is replaced by hope, trust, and honesty . . . Where we control processes not people . . . Where we view problems as opportunities and we address them by learning what is wrong not who is wrong. Where we measure systems instead of people and define procedures instead of authority. Where we ask 'how can I help?' rather than say 'It is not my job.'

Imagine a company where we work together as a team to be the very best. Where we remove barriers instead of saying 'just obey our orders.' Where we seek an answer for every problem rather than see a problem in every answer. Where we always have an idea rather than an excuse. . .

Imagine a company where a fear of knowledge is replaced by continuous learning. Where continuous improvement replaces the status quo. Where people say 'it might be difficult but it's possible' rather than 'it might be possible, but it's too difficult.' Where the only mistake is to repeat a mistake and the only true failure is a failure to try.

Imagine a company where the managers are teachers, helpers, and coaches instead of just bosses . . . Where management works on the system to help employees work better within the system. Where we have discipline in our processes instead of disciplining our people. . .

Imagine a company where fear of honesty has been replaced by an environment of honesty without fear. Imagine." (Lowe & McBean, 1989, pp. 34)

Detour #2: Not Supporting the Effort and Costs of Carrying Through the Change

Implementing an ongoing program of quality improvement in any organization is an uphill battle. Despite Philip Crosby's popular assertion that "Quality Is Free" (Crosby, 1979), adopting a quality improvement program requires significant initial and ongoing investment. Doing the work of an organization through flawless, efficient processes resulting in customer-pleasing products and services clearly costs less than the inefficiencies of poor planning, bad services, and customer complaints. But, getting there is another story.

Change of any sort requires effort. The old ways of being are familiar and comfortable, while taking on the new ways requires focused attention, training, and commitment. The "CET Model" (Change equals Effort over Time) presents a four-phase model of the level of effort required for successful change (Carr, 1989). Phase 1, in which the vision of change is introduced, is characterized by excitement, hope, and high expectations. Because the change has not actually occurred, but is only being talked about, the level of effort that must be put forth is low. The promise of the change supports interest and excitement during this phase because the real work of the change has yet to begin. That work starts in the second phase. In Phase 2, as the fun of the initial training and promises wanes, employees must begin the fight against existing habits, culture, and patterns in order to replace them with new ones. This battle is waged both within each individual in the organization, as they struggle within themselves to master the new ways, and between individuals (see the detour related to empire-builders and foot-draggers, below). As these battles continue, morale may sag and commitment to carrying out the change may waver.

In Phase 3, according to Carr, the change starts to turn the corner and becomes easier to carry out. During this phase, the new ways start to become more familiar, and it is tempting to begin to relax. However, the changes still require extra effort, and employees are at risk of falling back into the old, familiar ways if leaders and others are not diligent in supporting the new ways of performing. Finally, during Phase 4, the change is "institutionalized," and employees use the new methods naturally, everyday. The change has taken hold when "it takes no more effort to do things the new way than it did the old way" (Carr, 1989, p. 40). Many change efforts fail because leaders overemphasize Phase 1 and underestimate the effort required to go through Phases 2 and 3 of change.

Detour #3:   Allowing Empire-Builders and Foot-Draggers To Block the Change Process

Change can be very frightening. Moving from the safety of facility-based services to the uncertainties inherent in community-based services can be scary. But moving from an organization of small and large fiefdoms, run largely by power brokers, to one in which all personnel share in the organization's performance and success also can be very threatening. Staff members who see the changes as a threat to their perceived position and power in the organization may stifle organizational change efforts (Carr, 1989; Holpp, 1989). Do not allow that to happen. Demonstrate through top management action that the changes are here to stay. Help those employees adjust their jobs to support the quality improvement efforts, including providing them with support in measuring quality indicators and applying problem-solving processes. Give them a decent chance to come around. However, be prepared to replace those who do not. For these employees, the best strategy may be to offer career counseling and help for finding a new job.

Detour #4:   Leaving Quality Improvement Teams and Mid-Managers To Wander Around in Poorly Defined Projects

Taking on a new culture and way of doing business is an uphill battle. When you add to that the hard work required just to learn to implement quality improvement methods, then the difficulty of accomplishing an organizational transformation to quality improvement is clear. But if top managers leave quality teams and mid-managers to flounder around in ill-defined "improvement projects," the energy and commitment tied to the new methods will quickly wane. Particularly during early efforts to take on quality improvement, personnel may choose projects that are vague or too large. Projects such as, "Improve job satisfaction of all employees," may be overwhelming and leave teams spinning wheels but getting nowhere. Top managers must help others in the organization to define improvement targets that are reasonably within the grasp of team members, and provide guidance to help them to implement the tools and problem-solving processes in effective ways. Selecting improvement projects that are related to day-to-day problems faced by team members and that help them to perform their jobs more effectively should help. Completing such projects and seeing their results can be a powerful incentive to continue to work to transform the organization.

SPECIAL CHALLENGES IN IMPLEMENTING
QUALITY IMPROVEMENT IN REHABILITATION,
COMMUNITY-BASED EMPLOYMENT, AND OTHER HUMAN SERVICES

Implementing Continuous Quality Improvement in any organization requires hard work and diligence. However, rehabilitation, community-based employment, and other human services programs face some particular challenges that must be addressed if the transformation effort is to succeed. A few of these challenges are described briefly below.

The Challenge of Service Organizations

In service organizations, the "product" is often both "produced" and "delivered" during contact with the customer (Holpp, 1990). This basic difference between service settings and manufacturing environments may make the task of implementing quality improvement methods more challenging. Service personnel in many industries are not accustomed to viewing their work as a sequence of separate but related process steps (Kacker, 1988). If processes are not visible, it is more difficult to apply quality planning and improvement methods. Therefore, the first challenge faced by service providers is to identify and describe the processes required to deliver services. Once processes have been identified, service organizations can proceed to determine the customers of the "products" of those processes and seek information from them that will be useful in planning for improvement. Beyond this, however, service providers must use customer feedback to help identify those processes that have been continued out of tradition rather than because they satisfy a customer need or expectation.

The Challenge of Conflicting Values and Visions

The basis for a shift to Continuous Quality Improvement must be rooted in a strong and mutually held vision of the future. Simply achieving consensus on that vision *within* an organization can be difficult. However, the organization will be most successful if its vision of the future is nearly matched by the visions held by its various customer and supplier groups. Unfortunately, in many communities, employment service providers, residential providers, case managers, funders, families, individuals with disabilities, and employers do not share the same vision of integrated employment in natural settings. A service provider with a vision of building natural relationships in community settings to support individual needs and interests can expect to meet others who do not share the same values and vision. Some employers have been well-trained by the service system to expect someone to fill a specified role of "job coach." Some parents fear the dangers lurking in the community and struggle to keep their children in more segregated, and thus, presumably safer settings. Some residential providers value simplicity in staff schedules over adjusting to individual preferences of residents. Some funders care more about the amount of authority they can exhibit over service providers than the ways in which they could adjust their methods in order to support service improvements. On every front, staff members of an employment service provider may meet customers whose values and vision do not match their own.

Continuous Quality Improvement suggests that one role of a quality organization, beyond obtaining customer input, is to lead its customers into the future. Accepting that role offers one answer to conflicting values and visions. However, organizations providing services to individuals with severe disabilities have many sticky ethical issues related to leading customers into the future. How do they listen to their customer with severe disabilities, particularly when one of that customer's greatest challenges may be communication? How do they balance what they think that individual wants with conflicting demands from families or funders? How do they chart a course that satisfies customer needs while moving them into the future? Questions such as these cannot be taken lightly. However, the organization implementing quality improvement will pursue the discussions needed to find answers and will continually question the answers it finds.

The Challenge of Natural Environments

Organizations that are changing their services from segregated to integrated, community-based employment services face the challenges of trying to implement a cultural and methodological change to quality improvement with staff members who are dispersed and in constantly changing roles. As our collective wisdom about natural environments grows, we are learning more and more about how service systems get in the way of building natural relationships. Supported employment, as it was initially conceived, regulated, and implemented, has little in common with some of the more recent approaches to supporting people with disabilities in integrated work settings. As Chapter 1 discusses, the nature of employment services appears to be based on change. Now that many employment services are being delivered in natural environments, and we are learning so much more about how to work in those environments, the roles of organizations and their staff members will change continuously. Keeping pace with the changes that are demanded by natural environments will be a constant challenge as organizations try to implement quality improvement.

The Challenge of Assuring versus Improving Quality

From the early years of providing public support for services to individuals with disabilities, one part of the government's role has been to assure the quality of the services provided. This role has been based on a responsibility to safeguard the investment of public tax dollars, as well as to protect the individuals receiving services from harm. Although developed with an intention of improving services, many of the practices actually used by governmental agencies to monitor service quality have tended to place barriers in the path of ongoing program enhancement. One reason for this is that governmental methods for quality assurance have seldom kept pace with service developments. The rapid expansion of community-based employment, with its national shift from facility-based services to services provided in natural community settings, has presented just one example. All over the country, states are grappling with developing methods of assuring quality in the diverse and widely dispersed employment settings collectively referred to as "supported employment."

Because the population of individuals served are at risk for being harmed, states and service providers alike must take proactive steps to ensure the health, safety, and rights of service recipients with severe disabilities. Beyond this, however, in state after state externally based quality assurance and inspection systems have failed as a method of improving overall program quality. Continuous Quality Improvement offers a viable alternative. It incorporates a management strategy that is embedded within service provider organizations and is focused on defining and pursuing ongoing service improvement.

Continous Quality Improvement offers benefits that go beyond its direct effects on improving service quality, however. In addition, quality improvement offers a mechanism for state and local funders to participate as members of a team focused on fulfilling the same vision as the service provider. In this way, the adversarial relationships that often exist between service providers and the governmental agencies responsible for purchasing and monitoring their services can be replaced with relationships distinguished by teamwork and cooperation. When quality improvement characterizes relationships, then service providers, rather than hiding problems in order to pass the next on-site review of their programs, can expose problems for joint exploration to identify the most effective solutions (Rhodes, Mank, Sandow, Buckley, & Albin, 1990). Moving from these adversarial relationships to relationships based on mutual trust and support presents a significant challenge to service providers implementing quality improvement methods.

INDIVIDUAL ROLES IN QUALITY IMPROVEMENT

This book has largely focused on leadership roles in organizations providing employment services for individuals with severe disabilities. However, every organization is made up of many individuals, each of whom has the potential to lead the organization to or through change. Local networks of such individuals can support each other to move mountains. My effort in writing this book has been the result of a belief that one person *can* make a difference: As an author, I can influence readers who will embrace the principles and methods I am presenting here and use them to improve the quality of life available to our friends, neighbors, and relatives who have severe disabilities. You too, alone can make a difference. Whether you are an executive director, board president, or job coach in a rehabilitation agency or community-based employment organization, case manager, consultant, or county services coordinator, you too can make a difference. You can live the philosophy and methods of Continuous Quality Improvement in your own role, and thereby demonstrate a new way of working together. It is not useful to be a prophet of quality improvement if you do not live it. But, by living it, even one person can make a significant difference in how organizations do business.

> Hope sways on an edge so delicate that it is possible that the choices any one of us makes could tip the balance. If these words at moments seem to have power for you, take it as a measure of the power you have if you reach for it, if you draw it up from the dark, if you will risk it. And perhaps it is you, your reaching, your voice, your work, your joy, your love, that will make the difference. Perhaps it is up to you to reclaim the world. (Starhawk, 1982, p. 182)

REFERENCES

Carr, C. (1989). Following through on change. *Training, 26*(1), 39–43.
Crosby, P. (1979). *Quality is free: The art of making quality certain.* New York: McGraw-Hill.

Holpp, L. (1989). 10 reasons why total quality is less than total. *Training, 26*(10), 93–103.

Holpp, L. (1990). Ten steps to total service quality. *Journal of Quality and Participation, March*, 92–96.

Kacker, R.N. (1988). Quality planning for service industries. *Quality Progress, 21*(8), 39–42.

Lowe, T.A., & McBean, G.M. (1989). Honesty without fear. *Quality Progress, 22*(11), 30–34.

Rhodes, L.E., Mank, D., Sandow, D., Buckley, J., & Albin, J. (1990). Supported employment implementation: Shifting from program monitoring to quality improvement. *Journal of Disability Policy Studies, 1*(2), 1–18.

Starhawk (1982). *Dreaming the dark: Magic, sex, and politics.* Boston: Beacon Press.

INDEX

Page numbers followed by "t" or "f" indicate tables or figures, respectively.